Directory of Gradu in Applied Sport Psychology

8th Edition

Directory of Graduate Programs in Applied Sport Psychology
8th Edition

Editors

Michael L. Sachs, PhD
Temple University

Kevin L. Burke, PhD
East Tennessee State University

Elizabeth A. Loughren, MS
Temple University

Fitness Information Technology
A Division of the International Center for Performance Excellence
262 Coliseum, WVU-PE
PO Box 6116
Morgantown, WV 26506-6116

Copyright ©2007, by the Association for the Advancement of Applied Sport Psychology

All rights reserved.

Reproduction or use of any portion of this publication by any mechanical, electronic, or other means is prohibited without written permission of the publisher.

Library of Congress Card Catalog Number: 2006929320
ISBN: 1885693702

Production Editor: Corey Madsen
Cover design: 40 West Studios
Copyeditor: Katherine Kline
Proofreader: Matt Brann
Typesetter: Jamie Merlavage
Printed by Data Reproductions
Printed in the United States of America

10 9 8 7 6 5 4 3 2 1

Fitness Information Technology
A Division of the International Center for Performance Excellence
262 Coliseum, WVU-PE
PO Box 6116
Morgantown, WV 26506-6116
800.477.4348
304.293.6888 (phone)
304.293.6658 (fax)
Email: icpe@mail.wvu.edu
Website: www.fitinfotech.com

Contents

Introduction v

New Features vii

Psychologist, Psychology, and Psychological ix

Internships/Practica xi

Background Reading in Sport Psychology xiii

Careers in Sport Psychology xv

Licensure/Certification/Proficiency xvii

Comments, Questions, and Feedback xxi

Taking the Next Step: What to Ask as You Review the Directory xxiii

How to Use This Directory xxxiii

Graduate Programs in Applied Sport Psychology

Argosy University/Phoenix 1
Arizona State University 5
Ball State University 7
Barry University 9
Boise State University 11
Boston University 13
Bowling Green State University 15
California State University, East Bay 17
California State University, Fresno 19
California State University, Fullerton 23

California State University, Long Beach 25
California State University, Sacramento 29
Cleveland State University 31
DeMontfort University, Bedford 33
East Carolina University 35
East Tennessee State University 37
Florida State University 39
Georgia Southern University 41
Humboldt State University 45
Illinois State University 47
Indiana University 49
Iowa State University 51
Ithaca College 53
John F. Kennedy University 55
Kansas State University 59
La Salle University 61
Lakehead University 63
Leeds Metropolitan University 65
Manchester Metropolitan University 67
McGill University 69
Miami University 71
Michigan State University 73
Nanyang Technological University 75
Northern Illinois University 77
Optimal Performance Institute and University 79
Oregon State University 81
Pennsylvania State University 83
Purdue University 87
Queen's University 89
Rutgers University 91
San Diego State University 93
San Diego University for Integrative Studies 95
San Jose State University 99
Southeastern Louisiana University 101
Southern Connecticut State University 103
Southern Illinois University, Carbondale 107
Southern Illinois University, Edwardsville 109
Spalding University 111

Springfield College, Psychology Department 113
Springfield College, School of Graduate Studies 115
Staffordshire University 117
Stellenbosch University 119
Temple University 121
Texas Christian University 125
Texas Tech University 127
Universite de Montreal 129
Universite de Sherbrooke 131
Universite du Quebec à Trois-Rivieres 133
University College, Chichester 135
University of Alberta 137
University of Arizona 141
University of California, Los Angeles 143
University of Canberra 145
University of Edinburgh 147
University of Exeter 149
University of Florida 151
University of Georgia 153
University of Houston 155
University of Idaho 157
University of Illinois 161
University of Iowa 163
University of Kansas 165
University of Manitoba, Department of Physical Education 167
University of Manitoba, Department of Psychology 169
University of Maryland, College Park 171
University of Memphis 173
University of Minnesota 175
University of Missouri, Columbia 179
University of New Hampshire 181
University of New Mexico 183
University of North Carolina, Greensboro 185
University of North Dakota 189
University of North Texas, Department of Kinesiology, Health Promotion, and Recreation 191
University of North Texas, Department of Psychology 193
University of Northern Colorado 197
University of Northern Iowa 199

University of Ottawa 201
University of Queensland 205
University of Tennessee, Knoxville 207
University of Texas at Austin 211
University of Utah 213
University of Virginia 215
University of Waterloo 217
University of Western Australia 219
University of Western Ontario 221
University of Windsor 223
University of Wisconsin, Milwaukee 225
Utah State University 229
Victoria University 231
Virginia Commonwealth University 235
Wayne State University 237
West Virginia University 239
Western Illinois University 243

Guide to Appendices 247

Appendix A: Additions and Deletions to Directory Entries 249
Appendix B: A Word About Internships 251
Appendix C: Supervision of Applied Sport Psychology in Graduate School 257
Appendix D: Doctoral Programs in Clinical and Counseling Psychology 265
Appendix E: Graduate Training and Career Possibilities 267
Appendix F: Ethical Principles and Standards of the Association for the
  Advancement of Applied Sport Psychology 275
Appendix G: Texts in Applied Sport Psychology 283
Appendix H: References in Applied Sport Psychology: Professional and Ethical Issues 285
Appendix I: Reading List in Applied Sport Psychology: Psychological Skills Training 289
Appendix J: Reference List of Mental Training/Sport Psychology Videos 307
Appendix K: Geographical List of Graduate Programs 319
Appendix L: Contact Persons 323
Appendix M: Surfing the Net: Using the Internet for Success 327
Appendix N: Websites for Programs 351
Appendix O: Locations of Graduate Programs: Physical Education and Psychology,
  Master's and Doctoral Level 355
Appendix P: Quick Chart of Program Information: Degrees Offered, Program-Emphasis Rating,
  and Internship Possibility 359
Editor Biographies 369

Introduction

This publication is a directory of graduate programs in applied sport psychology. The directory has been developed by the Association for the Advancement of Applied Sport Psychology (AAASP) to assist students, faculty, and other interested persons who seek basic information regarding sport psychology programs. The directory contains information about each program, including the following: program address; contact persons; telephone and fax numbers; email addresses; faculty substantively involved in the program and their research/applied areas of interest; degrees offered; student information (number of students in the program, acceptance rates, admission requirements, financial assistance available); internship information; and special comments concerning the program. The directory is intended to provide a beginning point for students who are searching for a graduate program, as well as serve as a reference work for others.

A number of disclaimers/caveats must be offered. First, aspects of programs change over time. It is important to contact programs in which you (in the directory, the word "you" refers to the prospective student) might have interest and confirm the current status of the program (i.e., faculty present, degrees offered, financial assistance available, etc.). Second, no attempt has been made to define what constitutes a "program." A program may be a separate area of specialization within a department, or it may simply be a track within an existing program. The numbers, the types, and the quality of courses and internship offerings differ across programs. Varying levels of preparation for work in applied sport psychology are available. It is critical that you check with the contact persons for programs that interest you and determine whether your goals can be met adequately within the context of the program.

This directory is composed of self-reported information from the colleges and universities represented. AAASP does not endorse any of the programs per se and has not undertaken an evaluation of any of the programs. It is assumed that students interested in particular programs will evaluate them carefully. The section called "Taking the Next Step: What to Ask as You Review the Directory," written by Patricia Latham Bach, may be helpful to you as you check out the programs that interest you.

New Features

This is the eighth edition of the directory. The first edition was published in November 1986, the second in September 1989, the third in September 1992, the fourth in September 1995, the fifth in September 1998, the sixth in September 2001, and the seventh in September 2004. All information for the current "bound edition" has been updated as of May 15, 2006, to make it as current as possible. The online version of the directory is continually updated as changes are submitted.

A listing of a number of doctoral programs in clinical/counseling psychology that have indicated they offer opportunities for work in sport psychology by taking courses in the exercise/sport sciences and enroll in practica has been provided (see Appendix D). This listing derives from the fact that in recent years many students interested in applied sport psychology have expressed a desire to obtain a doctoral degree in psychology with an emphasis in applied sport psychology. The relatively small number of psychology programs that offer emphases in applied sport psychology necessitates consideration of programs that do not have concentrations in exercise/sport but do allow students the opportunity to do partial study in this area.

In the attempt to identify programs appropriate for the listing, some may have been overlooked. If you are interested in the exercise/sport area and are planning to pursue a doctoral degree in clinical/counseling psychology, you should check with the programs that interest you to ensure that the program is amenable to providing opportunities in applied sport psychology. Keep in mind that not all clinical/counseling programs consider applied sport psychology (or even exercise and sport) a "worthwhile" area of study or practice. Broach the subject carefully to avoid diminishing your chances of acceptance to the program (assuming you would still want to enroll in a program that devalues applied sport psychology).

Programs listed in the previous edition of the directory that have been deleted from this current edition and new programs that have been added can be found in Appendix A.

Psychologist, Psychology, and Psychological

The primary use of the term applied sport psychology in this directory focuses on training in educational sport psychology. Educational sport psychology emphasizes the teaching of psychological skills (i.e., PST—psychological skills training) such as goal setting, arousal control, concentration, imagery, and positive self-talk.

Some programs offer training in clinical sport psychology as well, but programs in which expertise can be developed in this area are considerably fewer. Clinical sport psychology encompasses psychological problems that demand expertise in clinical/counseling psychology. These problems, which affect both sport participants and non-sport participants, include depression, anxiety, eating disorders, substance abuse, etc. There is a continuing debate within the field about the nature of applied sport psychology, and work with exercise and sport participants often includes both educational and clinical components. The use of the term applied herein has been left sufficiently flexible to encompass programs with a variety of emphases, to provide this flexibility of opportunities for potential students in the field.

A smaller number of programs included in the directory have a primarily academic or research focus in the field. These programs may appeal to those interested in minimizing exposure to applications in the field and maximizing exposure to the academic or research side of sport psychology.

We have attempted to address questions about the emphases of various programs by including a scale that has been used successfully by Sayette, Mayne, and Norcross in their excellent book, *Insider's Guide to Graduate Programs in Clinical and Counseling Psychology* (New York: The Guilford Press, 2004/2005 edition). (For a broader discussion of this book, see Appendix D.) We asked program respondents to select one of the seven numbers on the following Likert Scale. Sayette et al. used this scale (with established validity) to allow programs to rate themselves along a clinically oriented to research-oriented continuum. We thought that this might be an effective way (as modified) to address this for our field as well. Program respondents were asked to circle the number that best reflects the emphasis/orientation of their program:

Program Rating

1 - 2 - 3	4 - 5	6 - 7
Applied Orientation	Equal Emphasis	Research Orientation

❏ Please check here if your program offers opportunities to pursue an applied orientation OR a research orientation (as opposed to an equal emphasis on both).

The following note was provided: "At the risk of starting a controversy over definitions, please note that research can be basic and/or applied, but simply indicates a focus upon research during one's program. An applied orientation means that the focus is upon applied/consulting work (which could emphasize education/performance enhancement AND/OR clinical/counseling), with a requirement/encouragement to do such work in one or more settings. Some programs will have an equal emphasis on both, and are encouraged to note this, but many programs are clearly oriented towards one side or the other, and it will be helpful for students to know this."

Most programs provided the information requested. Your feedback on whether this information is helpful (and accurate!) would be appreciated. The programs contained in this directory offer graduate degrees primarily in physical education/kinesiology/exercise and sport sciences or psychology. You should note that use of the terms psychologist, psychology, and psychological is restricted by laws in each state and province. For more information concerning this issue, contact your state's (or province's) psychology licensing board or talk with faculty members in the programs that interest you. There is an extensive set of literature on professional and ethical issues in applied sport psychology. In the appendices reference lists of books, videos, and articles are provided that you may find useful in your investigation of this area.

Internships/Practica

The directory provides information on internships available in various programs. It should be emphasized that there are internships and there are "internships." More clearly, the term internship has different connotations for different programs. When used with an APA-approved clinical/counseling program, the term refers to a program requirement and is likely to mean a full year's work that may entail 2,000 hours of supervised work in an applied clinical/counseling setting. This setting may or may not (it usually does not) involve any sport psychology work. It should be noted that internships are not affiliated with clinical/counseling programs per se. However, internships must be approved by the programs and usually, but not always, by the APA. Internship sites are often separate from the university and are generally quite competitive.

The term internship, when used with many of the physical education/kinesiology programs listed, is likely to refer to a supervised, applied experience ranging from 30 hours or so to several hundred hours of work. This type of experience is often called a practicum, rather than an internship. In any case, we use the term internship quite liberally in this directory, and it encompasses both traditional internships and practica, with a focus on applied experiences in exercise and sport. You should be sure to investigate specifically what internship/practicum opportunities are available in the programs that interest you. A few thoughts on internships are offered in Appendix B.

Background Reading in Sport Psychology

Questions are often posed about general background reading in sport psychology that examines theory, research, and practice (application). The appendices of this directory provide a listing of texts in sport psychology and exercise psychology, as well as several general references. The following list contains journals specific to sport psychology, in addition to several related journals in the sport sciences with frequent articles relevant to the field:

Specific:

International Journal of Sport Psychology
International Journal of Sport and Exercise Psychology
Journal of Applied Sport Psychology
Journal of Sport and Exercise Psychology
The Sport Psychologist

Related:

International Sports Journal
Journal of Applied Psychology
Journal of Interdisciplinary Research in Physical Education
Journal of Sport Behavior
Perceptual and Motor Skills
Research Quarterly for Exercise and Sport

Individuals particularly interested in applied sport psychology often search for useful books, both professional and trade publications. To help locate some of these volumes, included in the appendices is an updated version of an article entitled "Reading List in Applied Sport Psychology: Psychological Skills Training," which originally appeared in *The Sport Psychologist* (Vol. 5, pp. 88-91) in 1991.

Fitness Information Technology (FIT) is the publisher of this edition of the directory. FIT's address is 262 Coliseum, WVU-PE, PO Box 6116, Morgantown, WV 26506-6116 (phone: 1.800.477.4348 or 304.293.6888; fax: 304.293.6658; email: icpe@mail.wvu.edu; website: www.fitinfotech.com). FIT offers a number of other publications in exercise and sport psychology; be sure to get on their mailing list. Another publisher of note is Human Kinetics. Human Kinetics is a major sport sciences publisher, and you can obtain a catalogue of their publications by calling 1.800.747.4457 or by writing them at Box 5076, Champaign, IL 61820. Their email address is orders@hkusa.com and their website is www.humankinetics.com. There are other publishers in this area, but these two are the most specialized in exercise and sport psychology (and other areas within the sport sciences).

Careers in Sport Psychology

One of the most frequently asked questions about sport psychology concerns what one can do with a degree in the field. Division 47 (Exercise and Sport Psychology) of the American Psychological Association (APA), in joint sponsorship with AAASP and NASPSPA (North American Society for the Psychology of Sport and Physical Activity) has published a helpful brochure, *Graduate Training & Career Possibilities in Exercise & Sport Psychology*. We have reproduced this brochure in the appendices.

The Division 47 Education Committee is also the author of an excellent brochure entitled *How Can a Psychologist Become a Sport Psychologist?* This brochure can be found on Division 47's website (http://www.psyc.unt.edu/apadiv47/index.html).

Licensure/Certification/Proficiency

Licensure/Certification

Licensure as a psychologist is governed by state or provincial law (for the United States and Canada). Use of the terms psychologist, psychology, and psychological is restricted by these laws. For more information concerning this issue, you should contact your state's (or province's) psychology licensing board or talk with faculty members at the programs that interest you.

Certification, however, differs from licensure in that requirements are not based upon laws per se but are generally established by academic or professional organizations. These organizations attempt to identify the academic/practical background and sets of competencies that an "experienced professional" in the field should have. Certification programs are available in various areas of specialization within psychology, including sport psychology. Specifically, AAASP has a program that provides for certification as a "Certified Consultant, Association for the Advancement of Applied Sport Psychology" (CC, AAASP).

Important Note! In 2002, AAASP passed a proposal for "master's level certification." This means that individuals with master's degrees, who have completed all requirements for certification except for criterion number one (completion of a doctoral degree), of course, may be eligible for what is called "provisional certification." Provisional certification then allows for a student at the master's level to get an additional 300 supervised hours (beyond the 400 hours required in criterion number 8) and then become fully certified as a CC, AAASP (no provisional at that point). This important step recognizes that there are skilled consultants with master's degrees who should be eligible for Certified Consultant status, and provides a route for these individuals to do so.

The criteria for certification are the following:

AAASP Certification Criteria

Necessary levels of preparation in the substantive content areas generally require successful completion of at least three graduate semester hours or their equivalent (e.g., passing suitable exams offered by an accredited doctoral program). However, up to four upper-level undergraduate courses may be substituted for this requirement (unless specifically designated as requiring graduate credit only). It is not always necessary to take one course to satisfy each requirement. However, one course or experience cannot be used to satisfy more than one criterion, except for number 2.

1. Completion of a doctoral degree.
2. Knowledge of scientific and professional ethics and standards (can meet requirement by taking one course on these topics or by taking several courses in which these topics comprise parts of the courses or by completing other comparable experiences).
3. Knowledge of the sport psychology subdisciplines of intervention/performance enhancement, health/exercise psychology, and social psychology as evidenced by three courses or

two courses and one independent study in sport psychology (two of these courses must be taken at the graduate level).
4. Knowledge of the biomechanical and/or physiological bases of sport (e.g., kinesiology, biomechanics, exercise physiology).
5. Knowledge of the historical, philosophical, social, or motor behavior bases of sport (e.g., motor learning/control, motor development, issues in sport/physical education, sociology of sport, history and philosophy of sport/physical education).
6. Knowledge of psychopathology and its assessment (e.g., abnormal psychology, psychopathology).
7. Training designed to foster basic skills in counseling (e.g., course work on basic intervention techniques in counseling, supervised practica in counseling, clinical, or industrial/organizational psychology; graduate level only).
8. Supervised experience, with a qualified person (i.e., one who has an appropriate background in applied sport psychology), during which the individual receives training in the use of sport psychology principles and techniques (e.g., supervised practica in applied sport psychology in which the focus of the assessments and interventions are participants in physical activity, exercise, or sport; graduate level only).
9. Knowledge of skills and techniques within sport or exercise (e.g., skills and techniques classes, clinics, formal coaching experiences, organized participation in sport or exercise).
10. Knowledge and skills in research design, statistics, and psychological assessment (graduate level only).

At least two of the following four criteria must be met through educational experiences that focus on general psychological principles (rather than sport-specific ones).

11. Knowledge of the biological bases of behavior (e.g., biomechanics/kinesiology, comparative psychology, exercise physiology, neuropsychology, physiological psychology, psychopharmacology, sensation).
12. Knowledge of the cognitive-affective bases of behavior (e.g., cognition, emotion, learning, memory, motivation, motor development, motor learning/control, perception, thinking).
13. Knowledge of the social bases of behavior (e.g., cultural, ethnic, and group processes; gender roles in sport; organizational and systems theory; social psychology; sociology of sport).
14. Knowledge of individual behavior (e.g., developmental psychology, exercise behavior, health psychology, individual differences, personality theory).

Further information concerning the certification process may be obtained from the current AAASP Certification Committee chairperson, or AAASP website (www.aaasponline.org).

You may also wish to consult an excellent brochure developed by the AAASP Organization Outreach and Education Committee entitled Certified Consultant, Association for the Advancement of Applied Sport Psychology: Questions and Answers.

While most students entering graduate programs will not be eligible for certification unless they hold the master's or doctoral degree and meet the other criteria listed, this information may be of interest in planning a program of study and/or selecting a program in the first place. It should be noted that programs are not certified; individuals are certified as consultants. Certainly, your course of study should be determined by you and your advisor, and you can prepare for work in applied sport psychology in many ways. However, designing your course of study to meet (at a minimum) AAASP certification criteria, as well as state licensing criteria for training in psychology (at least the course work/areas of study component), may provide additional options for you if you are interested in working in this area. The degree to which a program can prepare you for these goals may be an important consideration in your selection of a graduate program in applied sport psychology.

Proficiency

In February, 2003, the American Psychological Association (APA) approved the designation of a particular area of expertise within psychology, a "Proficiency in Sport Psychology." The creation of this proficiency makes the field more visible to psychologists and sets an expectation of standards for psychologists practicing within this area. The proficiency thus also serves to protect and inform the general public with regard to appropriate services and skills of psychologists who describe themselves as "sport psychologists."

The recognition of this proficiency, however, has meaning only as a descriptor of a particular subarea of psychology. A committee within APA's Division of Exercise & Sport Psychology (Division 47) is actively concerned with the development of the next steps: (a) a description of what types of competence psychologists with this proficiency would have, and (b) a method of indicating competence at an individual level. The four specific areas of expertise that should be expected of psychologists with competence in sport psychology include: (1) enhancing performance and satisfaction through the systematic development of psychological skills; (2) optimizing the psychological well-being of athletes; (3) dealing with organizational and systemic issues in sports settings; and (4) understanding the developmental and social issues related to sport participation.

Information about the further development of these measures is available at http://www.apadiv47.org

(Note: The editors would like to express their sincere appreciation to Dr. Kate Hays, Past-President of Division 47 in the APA, for providing the information on the sport psychology proficiency.)

Comments, Questions, and Feedback

We welcome your comments, questions, feedback, etc. on this directory, particularly concerning ways in which we may enhance its usefulness. Your senior editors are Michael L. Sachs, in the Department of Kinesiology at Temple University (and a past president of AAASP) and Kevin L. Burke, in the Department of Kinesiology, Leisure and Sport Sciences at East Tennessee State University (and a former secretary-treasurer of AAASP). Please feel free to contact us:

Michael L. Sachs, PhD
Department of Kinesiology—048-00
Temple University
Philadelphia, PA 19122
215.204.8718 (office)
215.204.4414 (fax)
msachs@temple.edu

Dr. Kevin L. Burke, Professor and Chair,
Department of Kinesiology, Leisure and Sport Sciences,
Box 70654
East Tennessee State University
Johnson City, TN 37614-1701
423.439.4362 (office)
burkek@etsu.edu

Taking the Next Step: What to Ask as You Review the Directory

Patricia Latham Bach, RN, MS

The process of becoming a sport psychologist is, in many ways, quite similar to that undertaken by an athlete who desires high-level achievement and excellence in a given sport. The attainment of this vision requires commitment, goal setting, attentional focus, positive self-talk, resiliency, and motivation, as well as the support of significant others, friends, and faculty. As you review this directory, realize that you have embarked upon one of the first of many steps that, taken together, constitute the process of becoming a professional.

Your review of the material will help in narrowing the number of schools and types of programs that warrant further investigation and contact. Your decision is generally based upon a variety of factors but should be most strongly influenced by the vision that you hold for yourself in the future.

Sport psychology, as a discipline, is the offspring of two strong parents: psychology and sport/exercise. As part of the maturation process, sport psychology has experienced some of the "growing pains" inherent in the development of a profession and has struggled to develop a precise definition of itself, one that can be uniformly agreed upon.

As an example, to date, no universally accepted operational definition of the designation sport psychologist exists. The same holds true for a) the lack of specific and consistent educational requirements (other than those mandated for AAASP certification), b) varying degrees of emphasis placed on research versus practical application in different programs, and c) ultimately, the nature and scope of practice itself. Though there is agreement in principle, the discipline exists with a degree of "professional ambiguity" in that the roles and responsibilities of individuals in the field vary based on the chosen educational path and type of degree. Therefore, the term sport psychologist should be considered a generic title.

Basically, sport psychologists function in three different roles. Because these roles are not mutually exclusive, a degree of overlap may exist for a given individual and within a given position. Cox (2007) identified the three specialized roles as a) the research sport psychologist, b) the educational sport psychologist, and c) the clinical/counseling sport psychologist.

Cox describes the researcher as an individual who is a "scientist and scholar" (p. 10). This person may conduct theoretical and/or applied research, and may teach both undergraduate and graduate courses in sport psychology and related areas. These individuals are generally found in positions at the university level and generally require a PhD.

An educational sport psychologist is described as one who "use[s] the medium of education to teach correct principles of sport and exercise psychology to athletes and coaches ... develop[s] psychological skills for performance enhancement [and] help[s] athletes, young and old, to enjoy sport and use it as a vehicle for improving their quality of life" (Cox, 2007, p. 10). This person enjoys a broad spectrum of opportunities in that the use of performance enhancement techniques is not unique to athletes and can be applied to a variety of nonathletic consultation settings (e.g., business and industry, music and other performing arts). This person is also sometimes called a performance enhancement consultant or a sport consultant or something similar. Training for this position is generally at the master's or doctoral level.

Clinical/counseling sport psychologists are "prepared to deal with emotional and personality disorder problems that affect some athletes" (Cox, 2007, p. 10). This role requires completion of a doctoral degree in clinical or counseling psychology and may lead to licensure as a psychologist. Some individuals with preparation as clinical social workers may have some applicable background in this area. Based on training, these individuals may conduct research and work in educational and/or clinical environments, and may be eligible to receive third-party reimbursement.

Superficially, the distinctions among the three roles may seem an issue of semantics. There is a tremendous amount of educational diversity among sport psychologists. However, the differences are critical to you as an interested student in that they may strongly affect both your educational focus and training and, eventually, your ability to function within certain environments. There are a myriad of opportunities that may be found if you are willing to invest time and energy exploring the realm of professional possibilities. As a profession, sport psychology is moving to a point in its development wherein sport psychologists, by virtue of their educational choices, may choose more clearly defined career paths based on interests that may be focused on one or more of the three areas of academics, performance enhancement, and clinical practice.

As a parallel, consider the model of contemporary medical education. Students apply to either allopathic (MD) or osteopathic (DO) medical schools. In general, their standardized medical education consists of 2 years in basic sciences and 2 years in clinical rotations. Following graduation, they may enter research-oriented or clinical specialty programs, which culminate in expertise within a particular area of research, education, or practice. The educational process and requirements are well established and ultimately lead to a well-articulated terminal goal.

Unlike traditional medical education, sport psychology has not yet matured to the point wherein a uniform curriculum provides a standard foundation and subsequent systematized practice opportunities. Furthermore, the precise outcome goals of the educational process are also less clearly distinguished. Choice of a program, especially at the doctoral level, may seriously affect a student's opportunities to work with athletes and to develop expertise in an applied practice setting. Traditionally, the nonclinical PhD has been a research degree; therefore, the emphasis of most educational PhD programs in sport psychology remains one of research, not of practice. Students interested in a more applied focus should bear this in mind when making program choices for graduate education in sport psychology.

The "Process-Product" Equation

As a general strategy for evaluation, Daniel Gould (personal communication, May 1, 1995) uses a very simple, yet effective, "process-product" equation that may help guide you in your decisions relative to graduate school and, later, through your educational program. An easy way to conceptualize this equation is to ask the following question: "Is the process congruent with the product (and vice versa)?"

In virtually any situation, the product is the anticipated goal or desired outcome. In this case, the product is an identified role as a sport psychologist in education, research, or practice, or some combination thereof.

The process constitutes the means by which the outcome is obtained or achieved. In this case, a master's or doctoral program is the educational process by which one is prepared to become a sport psychologist.

The process-product equation is especially helpful in two important ways: (a) it will assist you in clearly defining your professional objectives (by asking yourself "What do I hope to achieve as a sport psychology professional?"), and (b) it will assist you in selecting programs that are congruent with your goals by helping you determine the type of process necessary for your chosen career path.

For example, a student who hopes to work exclusively in the area of sport psychology research would probably be happiest in a nonclinical PhD program with a strong research focus. Alternatively, a student who desires intensive contact with athletes in developing performance enhancement techniques may be best suited to a master's or doctoral program that provides numerous opportunities for actual practice in a supervised environment. In these examples, the tone and focus of the programs are congruent with, and supportive of, the professional goals established by the student.

Training in sport psychology can be completed at the master's and doctoral levels. Because of this, it is important that prior to embarking on your educational journey, you determine which (or both) of the two degrees will best prepare you to meet your projected goals. In some cases, a terminal master's degree (i.e., one that prepares you for a career requiring no further formal education) may prove more useful than further education at the doctoral level, based on your personal career choices.

The Graduate Training and Career Possibilities booklet (see Appendix E) states that "[m]ost of the professional employment opportunities in sport psychology require doctoral degrees from accredited colleges and universities . . . [Individuals] with master's degrees . . . compete at a distinct disadvantage for the limited number of full-time positions available in exercise and sport psychology." This statement holds true when "professional employment opportunities" incorporate more traditional university-related, academic, or research positions, and/or individual clinical practice opportunities requiring licensure. However, given the true paucity of traditional sport psychology positions, even doctoral preparation provides no guarantee of gainful employment. It merely strengthens the chances for a position in higher education or satisfies licensure requirements for practice as a psychologist. In this profession, more (i.e., doctoral vs. master's preparation) is not necessarily better but merely provides a different focus.

It is also important to note that given national trends, decreased funding is available to support educational programs in general. Given this trend, in addition to changes in the economic environment for mental health care (which may affect clinical sport psychologists), the complexion of those positions for which doctoral level preparation is required may be significantly altered. Furthermore, performance enhancement is seldom, if ever, reimbursed by third-party payers.

Students interested in graduate education in sport psychology should be aware that lucrative and exciting positions in research and practice are very difficult to find. Many positions may be exciting, but few, if any, are lucrative. However, the field is dynamic and growing, and there is hope for the future. There is a great need for those whose vision recognizes the importance of current work as a bridge to the almost limitless possibilities for this future. Therefore, master's and doctoral programs that promote high standards of academic achievement coupled with creativity, entrepreneurial skills, and flexibility should be considered to best prepare neophyte professionals for this field.

Sport Psychology Program Focus

One difficulty for aspiring students exists in learning to "read between the lines." Universities do not provide materials that intentionally foster misrepresentations. However, perceptions of program orientation may be skewed, or good intentions not made clear, due to a lack of clarity in the use of particular terms. For example, some schools allude to "applied" work. This may be interpreted as "direct contact" with athletes. However, the intention of that word may be far different in that it may be meant to imply research that has an "applied" focus. This disparity in perceptions represents quite a significant variation in actual work, and students should be clear about program focus to ensure a mutual understanding that is in everyone's best interest. It is always sad to hear about students who go to programs expecting one focus and find that that focus is not really available, making for unhappy students and faculty.

A critical difference among sport psychology programs rests in the specific program focus; that is, some programs provide greater concentration in the area of research (whether theoretical or applied), while others are oriented more towards a practice model (often considered an "applied" emphasis). To represent it graphically, one could envision a model with four quadrants, wherein emphasis on both research and practice can be evaluated. In this case, a modified Likert scale is incorporated to facilitate the process (Low = 1, High = 5):

Research and Practice Sport Psychology Program Focus Model

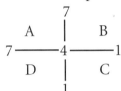

```
              Research Emphasis
                      7
              A       |      B
Applied   7 ——————4——————1
Practice      D       |      C
Emphasis              1
```

Quadrants:
A — High Research/High Practice
B — High Research/Low Practice
C — Low Research/Low Practice
D — Low Research/High Practice

It is critical to determine exactly where your interests lie in this model and to identify a compatibly matched program and advisor. For those more interested in academic research (and less so in applied/practice work), a program in Quadrant B would be most appropriate. Students who desire greater emphasis on consultation and first-hand experiences with athletes in performance enhancement, but less emphasis on research, would probably be most comfortable with a program in Quadrant D. Those who wish a mix of the two would find themselves most comfortable with a program in Quadrant A. Those most comfortable with a program in Quadrant C may be in the wrong field.

This model can be used to conduct a threefold evaluation. First, use it to identify your own interests relative to research and practice. This can be accomplished by reexamining your outcome goals or projected professional product (refer to the "Process-Product Equation" section). By determining what you would like to do, you will be able to identify where you most appropriately fit in the model. This will help you determine the type of program that will best meet your needs.

Second, the model can be beneficial in evaluating prospective programs. As you read materials and assimilate information, use the research/practice scales to rate your program choices. During your conversations with faculty and students, ask them to rate their program. Compare their evaluation with your own, based on your reading and your information gathering. Importantly, determine the degree to which these are congruent; if they are not congruent, why aren't they?

Finally, ask your potential advisor to rate his or her research versus practice focus, because an individual professor may have a somewhat different approach towards these variables than does the program as a whole. If this rating varies from your desired rating (i.e., your program preference), consider the difference carefully. A good match between student, program, and advisor is one in which there is a strong degree of congruence relative to both the educational process and the projected product. If your interests are in contrast with the interests of either the program or your advisor, the likelihood exists that no one will be happy. It is best to enter a graduate program that facilitates the possibility of a "win-win" situation, wherein a common purpose and a mutually satisfactory approach have been established. By using the model and thinking through the process-product equation, you will have a much stronger chance of completing your program in an effective and satisfying manner.

Developing Awareness

One of the best ways to prepare for entry into the field is to develop an understanding of and familiarity with the issues that challenge our development as a profession. In this way you will be better prepared to ask the questions that will lead to a clear distinction between the programs that ideally represent your interests and those that do not.

The directory, aside from simply listing programs and institutions, offers valuable information for those willing to invest a few hours in reviewing it carefully. Although this requires some time and energy now, it will save a great deal of effort in the future.

Appendix H provides an excellent overview of references that will prove helpful in developing a perspective relative to the field. These will contribute significantly to your global fund of knowledge about sport psychology. However, a number of articles and books on selected topics will prove particularly helpful to you:

Appendix H provides an excellent overview of references that will prove helpful in developing a perspective relative to the field. These will contribute significantly to your global fund of knowledge about sport psychology. However, a number of articles and books on selected topics will prove particularly helpful to you:

1. Developing an Overview of Sport Psychology (Definitions, roles, history, and current issues.)
   - Feltz, D. (1992). The nature of sport psychology. In T. S. Horn (Ed.), Advances in sport psychology (pp. 13-22). Champaign, IL: Human Kinetics.
   - Williams, J. M., & Straub, W. F. (1998). Sport psychology: Past, present, future. In J. M. Williams (Ed.), Applied sport psychology: Personal growth to peak performance (3rd ed., pp. 1-12). Mountain View, CA: Mayfield Publishing Company.
2. Variations in Scope of Practice (Overview of three different roles in which sport psychologists function.)
   - Anshel, M. H. (2000). Sport psychology: From theory to practice (4th ed.). Scottsdale, AZ: Gorsuch Scarisbrick, Publishers.
3. Career and Future Directions in Applied Sport Psychology
   - Taylor, J. (1991). Career direction, development and opportunities in applied sport psychology. The Sport Psychologist, 5, 266-280.
   - Vealey, R. S. (1988). Future directions in psychological skills training. The Sport Psychologist, 2, 318-336.
4. Guidelines for Clinical Psychology Graduate Programs (Helpful hints for developing personal essays, for successful interviewing, and for program analysis and evaluation. Specific to clinical psychology programs. Provides excellent model for sport psychology program evaluation as well. Highly recommended.)
   - Sayette, M. A., Mayne, T. J., & Norcross, J. C. (2004). Insider's guide to graduate programs in clinical and counseling psychology (2004-2005 ed.). New York: The Guilford Press.

When you have completed these readings, the differences in focus, theoretical frameworks, and projected directions of the various programs will have become much more evident. However, to discern the most subtle variations, it is best to spend time in discussion with others, both students and faculty.

Becoming a Wise Consumer

As a prospective student of graduate-level training, you must learn to become a wise consumer. Given your potential investment of time (master's programs—2 years; PhD programs—3-4 years), energy (lots), and financial resources (varies, dependent upon funding, but can be substantial), it is critical to learn as much about the program and faculty as possible. Remember, once accepted and with your program initiated, you have established a working relationship that must endure the rigors of the program and the idiosyncrasies of higher education. Though certainly not cast in stone, transfer between graduate programs is much more difficult than transfer at the undergraduate level. In fact, few doctoral programs will consider transfers with advanced standing. (Most PhD students wishing to transfer must initiate the entire process again from scratch. Some credit for courses taken may be applied, but generally relatively little.) Therefore, it is especially important in this situation to thoroughly investigate all aspects of potential programs and to choose wisely.

Given all this, it is vital for students to learn to assimilate information. Primary sources of information include the following:

1. Written materials provided by the university (these usually detail particular graduate school requirements) and the specific department (may elaborate on individual program philosophies, options, requirements, electives, etc.). This directory is one place to start, but it is important to get materials from the programs themselves.
2. On-site visit to the university enables first-hand observation of faculty-student interactions,

facilities, current research projects, and interviews with students and faculty. This can be very helpful and is strongly encouraged for your top choices. Arrangements should be made to meet with several current graduate students or, at least, to be provided with names and telephone numbers for 3-4 current students (and graduates, as appropriate) with whom you can talk about the program.

3. Telephone interviews with faculty and current students (when site visits are not possible). This is very helpful in that you can develop a "flavor" for your ability to speak and interact effectively with a professor. Students are also generally very forthcoming and will share perceptions of the program, ideas, and thoughts about faculty-student interactions—a host of information not readily evident in brochures. This is often great for establishing the "bottom line."

It is strongly encouraged to contact a program, at least by telephone, before applying. Some faculty have indicated amazement at students who apply to programs yet have never contacted the faculty or students. Written materials often do not provide enough information on which to base application decisions! Even if on-site visits or meetings at conferences are not possible, you should at least talk with faculty and current students by telephone (the faculty should be happy to give you names of students with whom you can talk) to get a feeling for what the people and the program are like. This is also helpful in the admissions process: making a positive impression over the telephone can be helpful in tilting an admissions decision your way, as opposed to your being "just a name" on an application.

Remember that your decision to enter a graduate program will affect the rest of your professional life. Your ability to work with and learn from faculty and other students is dependent upon mutual educational interests and effective communication skills. First-hand knowledge and assessment of these interests and skills cannot be gleaned solely from the directory. The time and money you spend talking with faculty and other students is a worthwhile investment in your future.

4. Conference meetings may be your first exposure to particular faculty or students from identified schools. Take advantage of these opportunities; introductions often anchor positive memories of individuals and may serve you well in the future. These meetings are especially helpful if you have many programs in which you are interested, and you want to get some information and develop impressions before narrowing your list to a more manageable number.

5. Networking with other students in the field is a tremendously valuable resource. Most students enrolled in a sport psychology graduate program have spent a great deal of effort investigating the realm of program possibilities and may be able to steer you in the right direction, saving you time, energy, and money. In many cases, department secretaries (if not the faculty) will be happy to pass your telephone number or address (including email address) along to current students, who understand the importance of making a well-informed choice of a graduate program.

6. Literature searches conducted through several of the available databases (e.g., SPORTDISCUS, PSYCH-LIT) can help you to determine the types of publications and work completed by prospective faculty. This information may serve as a springboard to further questions about your potential advisor, and demonstrates the type of preparation and motivation that faculty value in prospective students.

Above all, it is important to ask questions to clarify specific issues, concerns, and thoughts that may arise relative to a program. The following list provides a sample of the types of questions that may facilitate the process necessary to make your vision a reality and incorporates those that appeared previously in previous Directories. Use these questions to develop a profile for each program. As you rule out certain options and narrow your list, the answers to these questions may become more critical in helping you make your final decision.

An effective method of initiating this process is to develop an understanding of your needs and goals relative to your education and future career aspirations. Self-knowledge and self-awareness are central to our work as sport psychologists. It is especially important, therefore, to take some time for introspection and reflection, to help you establish baseline criteria for your search.

Questions for Introspection/Reflection

1. What aspects of the educational process are most important to me?
2. What do I wish to accomplish through my educational experience?
3. Where do I see myself professionally in 5, 10, 15 years?
4. What are my professional goals for teaching, research, and service to the profession and community?
5. What salary range would be acceptable upon graduation?
6. What type of academic/nonacademic environment would best suit my needs?
7. What resources (other than money) will I need to help me through my education? Are these accessible? If not, how will I develop these?

Note: It would be helpful to identify a faculty member who can walk you through this process. Ideally, this should be someone who has an excellent grasp of the field and who can advise you accordingly.

General Questions

1. What is the size of the institution?
2. Does the institution operate on a semester or a quarter system?
3. What type of grading system is used (e.g., letter grades, pass/fail)?
4. What is the cost per credit hour (for in-state and for out-of-state students)?
5. Where is the institution located (e.g., urban, suburban, or rural setting)?
6. What type of housing is available?
7. Are out-of-state tuition waivers available? If so, are they this available for the duration of the program, or for one year only?
8. What types and amount of financial aid are available?

The Program

1. What are the entrance requirements for the university and for the program?
2. How long has the program been in existence? Do the faculty anticipate any major changes in the program in the foreseeable future?
3. What is the usual length of the program for both master's and doctoral work?
4. Is a thesis optional for completion of master's programs? What other options, if any, are available?
5. How flexible is the program (i.e., are many electives available)? What is the relationship of the program with others on the university campus? Are students welcome to join other departments for course work and/or research or applied practice experiences?
6. Is some form of comprehensive exams required for completion of the degree programs? Are these exams written, oral, or both?
7. What are the strengths and weaknesses of the program? (This question should be asked of both faculty and students.)
8. What is the core curriculum? How is it structured? Are the courses taken in sequence available every year so that the sequence can be followed without interruption? Are these outlined on a semester-by-semester basis? Are these courses taught by graduate students or by faculty?
9. What textbooks are used, and in which courses? (This is where your familiarity with books and readings will be quite useful. See Appendix G for a helpful list.) For example, the Jean Williams text, Applied Sport Psychology: Personal Growth to Peak Performance, is a very "applied" text. If the school indicates a strong preference for applied work but fails to consider this book (or others like it) in any course, you may need to keep this in the back of your mind; it may serve as a "red flag." Do the text selections represent a broad spectrum of sport science knowledge that embraces both the research and the practice areas?
10. What is the prevailing "theoretical framework" of the department? How open-minded is the department to more creative, less scientific, and

less traditional thinking? Would this be welcomed or discouraged?
11. If the department is in psychology or counseling, is the program APA approved? If it is in these departments, does the program still provide good exposure to sport-related course work and actual practice? The same question can be posed in the opposite direction for those programs housed in departments of physical education, kinesiology, or exercise and sport sciences.
12. Describe the department's operational definition of applied work as it is provided for students at both the master's and the doctoral levels. Rate the program on the Research and Practice Sport Psychology Program Focus Model shown previously.
13. What is the ratio of applied experience to research experience at both the master's and the doctoral levels?
14. What opportunities exist for structured, consistent, supervised hands-on applied experiences? What types of relationships has the department developed with the athletic department, the community, and others to facilitate your exposure to real-world situations within the learning environment?
15. Do opportunities exist for multicultural and cross-cultural experiences and training? Is there a process or approach taught to develop sensitivity to and awareness of the cultures inherent in different types of sport and exercise populations?
16. What courses address the following topics, and in how much depth: ethics, clinical and counseling issues (if not a clinical/counseling program), communication, professional development, business practices, use of technology, leadership skills, and creative approaches to entrepreneurship.
17. What time of the day or evening are classes generally scheduled?

Practica/Internships
1. Are internships required to complete the program? If so, what are the requirements, and how are these arranged and supervised? Are these readily available, or must they be developed by students? Are they paid positions? If not required, what opportunities exist for student internships? When does this contact begin in the program sequence? Who arranges these experiences, how are they supervised, and how often is supervision available? What other opportunities have been designed to facilitate professional development activities?
2. Is academic credit available for independently arranged internships?
3. Have collaborative relationships been developed within the community to facilitate abroad spectrum of practicum experiences?

Faculty
1. What research areas are being pursued by faculty and students?
2. How are students involved in the research process? Do all students have the opportunity to engage in research, or only those who have received assistantships?
3. In what journals do the faculty publish? What books have they written? On what topics do the faculty focus?
4. What conferences do the faculty attend, and where is their work presented?
5. Regarding authorship, who is the first author on research projects, papers, book chapters, etc.? Is this a consistent practice, or one that is negotiated upfront, prior to the initiation of research or writing? How often do students appear as coauthors on papers presented at conferences and published in journals—either as first author or as second, third, etc., author?
6. What are the faculty's terminal goals for their students? How would they describe the students' marketable skills upon completion of the program?
7. Does the program allow and encourage independent research (other than that done for thesis or dissertation purposes)? Are faculty available on a consistent basis to provide feedback and guidance?
8. What is the faculty's travel schedule? How easily can students make appointments? Do other commitments (committees, etc.) play a major role in the expenditure of faculty time?

9. What types of jobs have the program's recent graduates (at both the master's and doctoral levels) obtained?

Students

1. In general, how do students like the program?
2. What attracted the students to the school and the program?
3. What do the students see as the strengths and the weaknesses of the program?
4. How flexible do the students feel the program to be regarding independent and creative thinking, individual and non-mainstream academic efforts, entrepreneurial pursuits, or membership on a student's thesis or dissertation committee?
5. What types of hands-on learning experiences are available?
6. Are funds available for student research and travel to conferences?
7. How much independent-study work is realistically allowed?
8. What type of relationship exists between students and faculty?
9. What type of relationship exists between students—competitive, cooperative, collaborative?
10. What types of work do student assistants perform?
11. Would the students choose the program again, given their present knowledge and experience?

Some Global Considerations

While no one can prescribe a means to measure the pulse of the profession, there are a few tips, easily applied, which may help create a picture of the field, the players, and the situation as it exists today.

1. Consider that best is a relative term: Good educational experiences result when the seeds of excellence are sown within a supportive environment. The best program for one student may be another's nightmare, despite the program's reputation. A best fit occurs when there is congruency in philosophy, focus, and direction between the educational team members, consistent for faculty and students. Be guided by well-informed decisions, not popular opinion.
2. Maximize your educational investment: Make program choices that will provide the greatest potential return on your educational investment. The time, energy, and effort committed to graduate programs in sport psychology should prepare you as a professional with marketable skills applicable to a variety of settings, whether your focus is research or practice. Consider programs that aspire to the Biggest Bang for the Buck Theory.
3. Maximize cross-training opportunities: Many current students and recent graduates have emphasized the importance of using elective opportunities to become well rounded, with exposure to a multidiscipline-enriched fund of knowledge. Recommendations, at a minimum, include course work in counseling, psychopathology, eating disorders, and alcohol and chemical substance abuse. These are especially important for students in nonclinical sport psychology programs. Other excellent recommendations include organizational development, entrepreneurship, and computer technology courses. The demands of the workforce are changing much more quickly than the traditional system of education. To be successful, you must be proactive, future focused, and willing to take risks.
4. Learn to create your own opportunities: One of the most important tasks in this emerging profession is gaining access to athletes. There are many ways to create opportunities for working with athletes of all ages. Consider programs in the community, with Little League, park and recreation sessions, and amateur athletic events. Skill development necessary for excellence as both a researcher and practitioner can be enhanced in this way, while you increase your visibility and presence in the athletic community.
5. Become a multimedia and multifaceted consumer: Much valuable information for sport psychologists comes from academically nontraditional sources. A tremendous amount of research and information on teamwork and competitive performance comes from business sources. Anecdotal information gleaned from newspapers, TV news and sport broadcasts, pop-

ular sport magazines, and a variety of other sources provide both real life examples and validation of our mission as sport psychologists. An increased awareness of our world and of the potential application of our knowledge and experience can only enhance the growth of the profession.

6. Become a sponge and browse the Net: The Internet provides one of the most fertile resources for information gathering. The sport psychology listserv (SPORTPSY), run by Dr. Michael Sachs at Temple University, is a bulletin board that provides a bird's-eye view of the salient issues in the field. This and several other interesting website addresses can be found in Appendix O. They will provide food for thought for prospective students and professionals alike.

Putting It All Together

The list provided above is lengthy but is intended to develop your thinking relative to important issues in sport psychology graduate education. You need not ask each question, of course, nor pose the questions exactly as phrased above. However, to get the big picture, these questions address many concerns that have arisen in the experiences of those who have gone before you.

As a sport psychologist in any of the specialized roles, the use of intuitive skills and tacit knowledge is very important. Developing these skills and learning to trust yourself in using them is a sequential process. This can be accomplished through a firmly established fund of knowledge coupled with a heightened, multisensory awareness of people, places, and dynamic situations.

As you investigate potential programs, begin to practice these intuitive skills and incorporate them into your decision-making process. Learn to assimilate information from several of the sources previously discussed (see the section on "Becoming a Wise Consumer"). Look for patterns of consistency in attitudes and responses among faculty and students, and for congruency between verbal responses and printed materials. The important message is often not what is said, but what remains unsaid. Learn to trust your gut-level feeling relative to the program, the students, and the faculty.

Despite all your efforts to know a program, this cannot truly happen until you have become a part of it. You must live the reality to know the program in its entirety. Your goal is to make the best possible choice, considering all the information available. Recognize that every program has benefits and drawbacks. The important issue is to decide which program will work best for you!

In Summary

The purpose of this chapter has been to present issues and to provide questions for students who are considering graduate education in the field of sport psychology. This chapter has attempted to represent the many issues you should consider as you enter this dynamic and exciting field. However, there will always be other, perhaps more personal, issues that may concern you, and your introspection will help you become aware of and sensitive to these needs as you explore the various graduate programs. Remember, like that of an athlete, your journey to success is determined by your energy and effort in preparation. Best wishes in making your vision become your reality!

Reference

Cox, R. H. (2007). *Sport psychology: Concepts and applications* (6th ed.). Boston, MA: McGraw-Hill.

Endnote

The author would like to express her thanks to the editors, and especially to Michael Sachs, for their assistance and valuable suggestions in preparing this chapter.

How to Use This Directory

This directory is designed to provide a starting point for students seeking a graduate program in applied sport psychology, or for faculty or other individuals interested in a reference work of graduate programs in the field. The basic information provided can guide the individual toward programs in specific geographic areas, with particular faculty involved, with internships available, and with particular degrees offered.

The information requested from programs was, of necessity, brief and is not intended to provide a basis upon which to make a final selection or rejection of a graduate program. Rather, the directory provides some basic information for a preliminary screening of programs and for contacting the appropriate person for further information. The section, "Taking the Next Step: What to Ask as You Review the Directory," will be helpful in directing your search to obtain the additional information necessary to select a graduate program in applied sport psychology.

Please note a number of important points concerning this directory:

1. The information requested for each program in this directory included the following: address, contact person, telephone and fax numbers, electronic mail address, World Wide Website, faculty substantively involved in the graduate program and their research/applied areas of interest, degrees offered, program information (students in the program, acceptance rates, admissions requirements, financial assistance available), internship information, and special comments concerning the program. However, not all programs provided all the information requested (in some cases the information may not have been available).

    Additionally, more specific information about available financial assistance has been included. Programs were asked for information about the percentages of current students in the program receiving the following forms of assistance:

    - Fellowships
    - Research assistantships
    - Teaching assistantships
    - Tuition waivers
    - Other forms of financial aid

    While most programs provided this information, the data should be used with caution. For example, while fellowships may be available at some schools, current students may have not received one. The information in the directory entry can, therefore, give you a feeling for what students are currently receiving, but it also helps to know what is available and to find out about all your options.

    Also note that some students receive more than one form of funding at any one point in their programs. Thus, percentages reported may exceed 100.

2. Faculty members substantively involved in each graduate program are listed alphabetically.

3. The degree(s) held by the faculty, such as PhD or other degrees, are not indicated. Since this information was not always available, it was thought best to omit it from the listing. However, most of the faculty listed hold a doctoral degree in physical education, psychology, or a related field.
4. Most of the programs listed focus on applied sport psychology. Some, however, are oriented towards research, with little, if any, applied component. In trying to improve our directory, we reviewed some other publications, including the excellent *Insider's Guide to Graduate Programs in Clinical and Counseling Psychology* (2004/2005 edition), by Michael Sayette, Tracy Mayne, and John Norcross (New York: The Guilford Press, 2004). In response to a request from many students for a better way to evaluate programs on their focus on research, applied work, or both, we asked programs to select one of the seven numbers on the following Likert Scale. Sayette et al. used this scale (with established validity) to have programs self-rate themselves along a clinically oriented to a research-oriented continuum. We thought that this might be an effective way to address this for our field as well. We asked program respondents to circle the number that best reflects the emphasis/orientation of their program:

Applied Orientation Emphasis
Research Orientation
❑ Please check here if your program offers opportunities to pursue an applied orientation OR a research orientation (as opposed to an equal emphasis on both).

We also included the following:

Note: At the risk of starting a controversy over definitions, please note that research can be basic and/or applied, but simply indicates a focus upon research during one's program. An applied orientation means that the focus is upon applied/consulting work (which could be focused upon education/performance enhancement AND/OR clinical/counseling), with a requirement/encouragement to do such work in one or more settings. Some programs will have an equal emphasis on both, and are encouraged to note this, but many programs are clearly oriented towards one side or the other, and it will be helpful for students to know this.

Please let your editors know if this information is helpful to you. It can be revised for the next edition to make it as useful to you as possible. Some programs did not respond to this question, and so no self-rating is indicated. In addition, we caution you again to check programs carefully. A program may self-rate as a "1" (very strong applied orientation) when they still do or require a considerable amount of research. The information is useful as a guide, not as a definitive rating.

Please also note that some programs in psychology are not applied sport psychology programs per se, but do have faculty interested in the area. This is indicated where appropriate.

5. In some cases, the number of students in the program may not seem to be consistent with the number of students that appear to be admitted each year. Some programs have provided information on the number of students in the overall department (or number admitted to the overall department) as opposed to the number of students in (or admitted to) the sport psychology area specifically. This is a good example of a program feature you would be wise to check when considering a particular program.
6. The information provided is current as of May, 2006. You should still check all information when considering a given program. New features of a program may be added: new financial resources may become available, faculty may change, etc.

Key to Abbreviations:
APA American Psychological Association
APS Australian Psychological Society
EDS Education Specialist
GPA Grade Point Average
GRE Graduate Record Examination
MAT Miller Analogies Test
PST Psychological Skills Training

Degrees Offered:

CAS	Certificate of Advanced Study
EdD	Doctor of Education
MA	Master of Arts
MAP	Master of Applied Psychology
MAS	Master of Applied Science
MEd	Master of Education

Argosy University/Phoenix

2223 West Dunlap Avenue
Phoenix, AZ 85021

Contact: Robert Harmison
Title:
Phone: 602.216.2600
Fax: 602.216.2601
Email: rharmison@argosyu.edu
Website: www.argosyu.edu
Area of Interest: Performance enhancement; sport psychology consulting with elite, collegiate, and high school athletes, coaches, and teams; counseling with athletes; consultation-seeking behavior; attitudes toward sport psychology; mental toughness

Contact: Sheryl Harrison
Title: Associate Professor
Phone: 602.216.2600
Fax: 602.216.2601
Email: sharrison@argosyu.edu
Website: www.argosyu.edu
Area of Interest: Sport psychology; individual sports; equestrians, horse/rider relationships; stress management; anxiety disorders; biofeedback; performance enhancement; health psychology

Contact: Bart Lerner
Title: Associate Professor
Phone: 602.216.2600
Fax: 602.216.2601
Email: blerner@argosyu.edu
Website: www.argosyu.edu
Area of Interest: Performance enhancement (goal setting, imagery, self-confidence), counseling, substance abuse, graduate training, injury rehabilitation

---

PROGRAM RATING

1   **2**   3   4   5   6   7

1 to 3 Applied Orientation, 3 to 6 Equal Emphasis, 6 to 7 Research Orientation

---

DEGREE OFFERED:
PsyD in clinical psychology (concentration in sport-exercise psychology), MA in sport-exercise psychology, MA in sport-exercise psychology / MA in professional counseling

NUMBER OF STUDENTS IN PROGRAM:
40-45

NUMBER OF STUDENTS IN EACH DEGREE PROGRAM:
50% MA / 50% PsyD

NUMBER OF STUDENTS WHO APPLY/ARE ACCEPTED ANNUALLY:
20-25 apply/ 12-15 accepted (MA); 20-25 apply/ 7-10 accepted (PsyD)

ADMISSION REQUIREMENTS:
GRE not required; GPA 3.0 (MA), 3.25 (PsyD.)

AVAILABLE FOR QUALIFIED STUDENTS:
Scholarships
Work study
Teaching assistantships
Other forms of financial aid

ASSISTANTSHIPS:
2% Scholarships
5% Work Study
10% Teaching Assistantships
80% Other forms of financial aid

INTERNSHIP POSSIBILITY:
Yes

INTERNSHIP REQUIRED:
Yes

NUMBER OF HOURS REQUIRED:
MA: 6 credit hours; 400 total hours. PsyD: 18 credit hours; 1000 total hours (clinical), 400 total hours (sport)

CORE GRADUATE CLASSES:
Sport Psychology Coursework:
Applied Sport Psychology I: Theory and Research; Applied Sport Psychology II: Professional Practice; Team Dynamics and Group Behavior; Psychological Aspects of Athletic Injury; Athletic Counseling; Exercise and Health Psychology; Seminar in Sport Psychology Consulting I, II, and III; Sport Practicum I and II

Sport Sciences Coursework:
Motor Learning and Development; Exercise Physiology

Psychology Coursework:
Courses such as Lifespan Development, Psychopathology; Professional and Ethical Issues; Assessment and Treatment of Diverse Populations; Person-Centered Theory and Therapy; for a more complete description, go to www.argosy.edu and link to the programs page of the Phoenix campus.

DESCRIPTION OF TYPICAL INTERNSHIP EXPERIENCE:
The sport psychology practicum experience is designed to meet AAASP certification criteria and involves working directly with athletes, coaches, and teams. Every effort is made to match practicum placements to students' career goals and interests. Past and current practicum sites include college athletic departments, athletic clubs, sport psychology private practices, sports medicine facilities, youth sport, high schools, YMCAs, and professional teams. Students also may choose to gain additional applied experiences by providing performance enhancement and consultation services to athletic populations in the Phoenix

and surrounding area through the Argosy University/Phoenix Center for Excellence in Sport (ACES). Through their involvement with ACES, students will have the opportunity to participate in individual and group projects related to the planning, development, marketing, and provision of sport psychology services to targeted populations.

COMMENTS:

PsyD in Clinical Psychology

The PsyD program in Clinical Psychology is accredited by the American Psychological Association and is designed to educate and train students to function effectively as professional psychologists. The Clinical Psychology program emphasizes the development of attitudes, knowledge, and skills essential to the training of clinical psychologists who are committed to ethically providing quality services, assuming leadership positions, and contributing to the evolving body of knowledge and practice methods. Special attention is given to issues of diversity and helping students to acquire appreciation of and skill in providing services to diverse populations.

The Sport-Exercise Psychology concentration provides students with a knowledge base in applied sport psychology, including theory, research, and professional practice. Students study the issues and problems for which sport psychology services are typically utilized and develop skills to effectively intervene in sport settings. In addition, students learn how to function as sport psychologists who are capable of providing performance enhancement and psychological services in sport settings. Graduates of the PsyD Clinical Psychology program with a concentration in Sport-Exercise Psychology are eligible to apply for licensure as psychologists and for AAASP certification.

MA in Sport-Exercise Psychology

The MA program in Sport-Exercise Psychology is designed to educate and train students to function as capable and ethical performance enhancement specialists. The two-year degree is intended to meet the needs of students seeking employment in a variety of settings, including private practice, athletic departments, coaching, exercise/health, and education, or those who will ultimately pursue their doctorate. The curriculum provides students with a foundation in applied sport psychology, an understanding of normal and abnormal psychological functioning, and a knowledge base in the physiological, motor, and psychosocial aspects of sport behavior. Graduates of the MA program in Sport-Exercise Psychology are eligible to apply for "provisional status—AAASP certification.

Students who wish to pursue certification/licensure as a professional counselor may follow a curriculum plan that allows them to fulfill the requirements for the MA program in Sport-Exercise Psychology in two years and the MA program in Professional Counseling in one additional year of study. Application to the Professional Counselinprogram is made in the second year of enrollment in the Sport-Exercise Psychology program. Graduates of the MA program in Professional Counseling are eligible to apply for licensure as a professional counselor in the state of Arizona and certification/licensure in most other states.

After completion of the MA program in Sport-Exercise Psychology, students who wish to pursue a doctoral degree may apply to the PsyD program in Clinical Psychology. MA graduates who are accepted into the PsyD program are then eligible for transfer of some credits earned in their MA program, to be determined on a case-by-case basis.

Arizona State University

Department of Kinesiology

PEBW 218
Arizona State University
Tempe, AZ 85287-0701

Contact: Jennifer Etnier
Title: Assistant Professor
Phone: 480.965.7042
Fax: 480.965.2569
Email: Jennifer.Etnier@asu.edu
Website: www.public.asu.edu/~etnierjl/
Area of Interest: Benefits of performance enhancement techniques; age, physical activity, and mental health

Contact: Debra Crews
Title: Assistant Research Professor
Phone: 480.965.4928
Fax: 480.965.2569
Email: dcrews@asu.edu
Website: www.public.asu.edu/~crewsd/
Area of Interest: Psychological benefits of exercise for special populations

Contact: Daniel M. Landers
Title: Regents' Professor
Phone: 480.965.7664
Fax: 480.965.8108
Email: landers@asu.edu
Website: www.public.asu.edu/~atdml/
Area of Interest: Arousal/anxiety/attention and performance

Contact: Darwyn E. Linder
Title: Professor
Phone: 480.965.6516
Fax: 480.965.8544
Email: Darwyn.Linder@asu.edu
Website: psych.la.asu.edu/people/faculty/dlinder.html
Area of Interest: Social perception of athletes, pain and performance

Contact: Darren C. Treasure
Title: Associate Professor
Phone: 480.965.8489, 480.965.-3913
Fax: 480.965.8108
Email: Darren.Treasure@asu.edu
Website: www.public.asu.edu/~dtreasu/
Area of Interest: Motivational aspects of physical activity

PROGRAM RATING

1   2   3   4   **5**   6   7

1 to 3 Applied Orientation, 3 to 6 Equal Emphasis, 6 to 7 Research Orientation: 5

DEGREE OFFERED:
222

NUMBER OF STUDENTS IN PROGRAM:
15

NUMBER OF STUDENTS IN EACH DEGREE PROGRAM:
75% MS/25% PhD

NUMBER OF STUDENTS WHO APPLY/ARE ACCEPTED ANNUALLY:
20 apply/6-7 accepted

ADMISSION REQUIREMENTS:
Minimum of 3.00 Jr./Sr/ GPA. Minimum of 50th percentile GRE (verbal + quantitative). Prefer sport or exercise psychology courses. Letter of intent indicating goals that are consistent with program. Mentor willing to work with student. Major research experience (undergraduate honor's thesis or master's thesis) required of PHD applicants

AVAILABLE FOR QUALIFIED STUDENTS:
Research assistantships, teaching assistantships, other forms of financial aid (including out-of-state tuition waivers)

ASSISTANTSHIPS:
0% fellowships, 50% graduate assistantships, 50% teaching assistantships, 100% tuition waivers (out of state), 20% other forms of financial aid (in-state fee waivers)

INTERNSHIP POSSIBILITY:
Yes

INTERNSHIP REQUIRED:
No

NUMBER OF HOURS REQUIRED:
10 hours per week for 15 weeks or 20 hours per week for 15 weeks

CORE GRADUATE CLASSES:
Graduate students who are enrolled in programs in exercise science psychology or related fields and who are being mentored by one of the listed faculty members may gain experience in applied sport psychology by assisting in the provision of psychological skills training to intercollegiate athletes or to other subject populations. Most often these programs are part of a research effort designed to test the efficacy of interventions or to explore psychological processes that mediate the effectiveness of applied sport psychology interventions. The major focus, therefore, is on the research effort rather than on the acquisition by the student of a broad range of intervention skills.

DESCRIPTION OF TYPICAL INTERNSHIP EXPERIENCE:

COMMENTS:
The program primarily prepares individuals for research in the psychology of exercise and sport. Students are expected to immerse themselves in research and to take research credits from their first semester to the conclusion of the program. Two teaching assistants teach several sections of an undergraduate course entitled Psychological Skills for Optimal Performance. This experience is open to doctoral students in exercise science who are committed to becoming sport researchers.

Ball State University
School of Physical Education, Sport, & Exercise Science

Ball State University
Muncie, IN 47306-0270

Contact: Jeffrey S. Pauline
Title: Graduate Advisor, Sport & Exercise Psychology
Phone: 765.285.3286
Fax: 765.285.3485
Email: jpauline@bsu.edu
Website: www.bsu.edu/physicaleducation/sportpsychology/
Area of Interest: Exercise psychology, performance enhancement, wellness, coaching

PROGRAM RATING

1   **2 to 3**   4   5   **6**   7

1 to 3 Applied Orientation, 3 to 6 Equal Emphasis, 6 to 7 Research Orientation
Depends on the program: 2-3 for Sport & Physical Education graduate programs;
6 for Exercise Science programs

DEGREE OFFERED:
MA, MS, & PhD in Bioenergetics

NUMBER OF STUDENTS IN PROGRAM:
15

NUMBER OF STUDENTS IN EACH DEGREE PROGRAM:
25% MA / 75% MS

NUMBER OF STUDENTS WHO APPLY/ARE ACCEPTED ANNUALLY:
25-30 / 6-8

ADMISSION REQUIREMENTS:
2.75 GPA (out of 4.00); GRE required only for students with a lower GPA

AVAILABLE FOR QUALIFIED STUDENTS:
Research assistantships, graduate assistantships, and other forms of financial aid

ASSISTANTSHIPS:
0% fellowships, 30-40% research assistantships (with tuition waivers), 50-60% graduate assistantships, 10% tuition waivers, 0% other forms of financial aid

INTERNSHIP POSSIBILITY:
Yes

INTERNSHIP REQUIRED:
No

NUMBER OF HOURS REQUIRED:
Internship: 9 hours per week for 15 weeks (1 semester/credit hour) for 3 semesters; Total Program: 33 credit hours for MA or MS

CORE GRADUATE CLASSES:
Sport and Exercise Psychology Core Requirements (21 credit hours; each course is a 3-credit hour course): Psychology of Injury Rehabilitation, Research Methods in Sport and Physical Education, Sport and Exercise Psychology, Psycho-Social Process of Sport and Physical Activity, Psychology of Exercise and Health, Sport Sociology. Research requirement (3-6 credit hours): Research paper (3 credit hours), Thesis (6 credit hours). Directed Electives (6-9 credit hours). Total: 33 credit hours. Course descriptions can be viewed at http://www.bsu.edu/physicaleducation/sportpsychology/coursedescripts/

DESCRIPTION OF TYPICAL INTERNSHIP EXPERIENCE:
The sport and exercise psychology internship is designed to provide an in-depth practical experience in the application of knowledge and skills related to students' career goals and interests. The internship is intended to assist students in meeting AAASP certification criteria. Students enrolled in the internship are supervised by an AAASP certified consultant. Internships are arranged by the program and internship supervisor and involve working directly with university athletes, coaches, teams, club teams, high school teams, and youth organizations. In addition to traditional sport psychology consultations, students also have the opportunity to participate in exercise adherence counseling with Ball State University's human performance laboratory.

COMMENTS:
The sport and exercise psychology program places equal importance on theory research and applied sport psychology skills. Students may choose a thesis or research project as a capstone experience. The program has strong connections with the university's athletic department, human performance laboratory, and counseling psychology and guidance services department which provides for diverse applied and research experiences for the students. A graduate minor in counseling has been established through the counseling psychology and guidance services department. All students are strongly encouraged to complete the graduate minor in counseling. Students are also able to pursue a dual master's degree in counseling psychology and sport and exercise psychology. Graduates of the master's degree program in counseling psychology can sit for the licensure examination to become professional counselors. The Sport Psychology Performance and Enhancement Center (SPPEC) at Ball State University was established in the fall of 2002. Since the center's conception, graduate students have provided applied sport psychology services for numerous individuals and groups located throughout Indiana. The center's combination of applied experiences and research has added a unique educational component to the Ball State University sport and exercise psychology graduate program.

Barry University
School of Human Performance and Leisure Studies

11300 Northeast Second Avenue
Miami Shores, FL 33161-6695

Contact: Bryan Anderson
Title:
Phone: 305.899.3494
Fax: 305.899.4809
Email: banderson@mail.barry.edu
Website:
Area of Interest:

Contact: Gualberto Cremades
Title: Assistant Professor
Phone: 305.899.3490
Fax:
Email: sportsciences@mail.barry.edu

Website: www.barry.edu/sportexercisepsychology/default.asp
Area of Interest:

Contact: Artur Poczwardowski
Title: Associate Professor
Phone: 305.899.3490
Fax:
Email: sportsciences@mail.barry.edu
Website: www.barry.edu/sportexercisepsychology/default.asp
Area of Interest:

PROGRAM RATING

1   2   3   **4**   5   6   7

1 to 3 Applied Orientation, 3 to 6 Equal Emphasis, 6 to 7 Research Orientation

DEGREE OFFERED:
MS offered in movement science with a specialization in sport and exercise psychology

NUMBER OF STUDENTS IN PROGRAM:

NUMBER OF STUDENTS IN EACH DEGREE PROGRAM:

NUMBER OF STUDENTS WHO APPLY/ARE ACCEPTED ANNUALLY:
30 apply/12 accepted

ADMISSION REQUIREMENTS:
Receipt of a bachelor's degree from a regionally accredited or internationally listed institution, as verified by two (2) official transcripts; acceptable cumulative undergraduate GPA; completion of undergraduate courses in anatomy, kinesiology or biomechanics, and introduction to psychology; sufficient undergraduate preparation or life experience, as determined by the graduate program coordinator and associate dean; acceptable test scores on the GRE; two (2) letters of recommendation; a short essay describing personal career goals and how a graduate degree from Barry University will help fulfill these goals; resume

AVAILABLE FOR QUALIFIED STUDENTS:
Graduate assistantships are available on a limited basis in Athletics and in other departments throughout the university; research assistantships may be available dependent upon funding; scholarships/grants of up to $5400 per year are available to all students based on the students' undergraduate GPAs.

ASSISTANTSHIPS:
30% graduate assistantships, 5% research assistantships, 65% scholarships/grants

INTERNSHIP POSSIBILITY:
Yes

INTERNSHIP REQUIRED:
Yes, if practicum route is chosen by the student

NUMBER OF HOURS REQUIRED:
A total of 6 credit hours

CORE GRADUATE CLASSES:

DESCRIPTION OF TYPICAL INTERNSHIP EXPERIENCE:
Both the practicum and internship will require fulfilling 3 different activities within the field. A minimum of two activities from the following list can be chosen: a)Implementing a Psychological Skills Training Program with College athletes and/or teams b)Implementing a Psychological Skills Training Program with High School athletes and/or teams c)Implementing a Psychological Skills Training Program in youth sports and/or community based programs (e.g., YMCA) d)Implementing a Psychological Skills Training Program with special population athletes such as disabled athletes e)Implementing a Psychological Skills Training Program in the clinical setting working with patients in cardiac rehabilitation, HIV, depression, aggression f)Implementing a Psychological Skills Training Program in the community

COMMENTS:
Students in the MS program can choose one of the two areas of emphasis: Sport Psychology or Exercise Psychology. Students can pursue either a thesis or an applied track within each emphasis area (i.e., sport or exercise). Our sport psychology program is designed to provide for accumulation of most AAASP certification criteria. Additional courses may be chosen, which include: Abnormal Psychology, Behavior Modification, Introduction to Neuropsychology, Health Psychology, Treatment of Substance Abuse, and Individual Counseling. A performance enhancement course is offered within the first year, emphasizing practical, hands-on performance enhancement and counseling skills development and experience, similar to what is expected for the practicum requirements. During the second year, the practicum includes direct supervision with faculty and weekly evaluations and discussions.

Boise State University
Department of Health, Physical Education, and Recreation

Boise State University
1910 University Drive
Boise, ID 83725

Contact:	Linda M. Petlichkoff	**Contact:**	Bill Kozar
Title:		**Title:**	
Phone:	208.426.1231	**Phone:**	
Fax:	208.426.1894	**Fax:**	
Email:	lpetlic@boisestate.edu	**Email:**	
Website:	www.boisestate.edu	**Website:**	
Area of Interest:	Competitive anxiety, participation motivation, goal orientation, coach/athlete interaction, coach education	**Area of Interest:**	Motor learning

PROGRAM RATING

1   2   3   **4**   5   6   7

1 to 3 Applied Orientation, 3 to 6 Equal Emphasis, 6 to 7 Research Orientation: 4

DEGREE OFFERED:
MS

NUMBER OF STUDENTS IN PROGRAM:
2 to 4

NUMBER OF STUDENTS IN EACH DEGREE PROGRAM:
100% MS

NUMBER OF STUDENTS WHO APPLY/ARE ACCEPTED ANNUALLY:
40 apply / 8-10 are accepted into the total MS program

ADMISSION REQUIREMENTS:
Minimum 3.00 GPA with an appropriate pattern of classes to provide a foundation in physical education, but 3.00 GPA over the last two years; no GRE requirement

AVAILABLE FOR QUALIFIED STUDENTS:
Graduate assistantships, other forms of financial aid

ASSISTANTSHIPS:
0% teaching assistantships, 15-18% tuition waivers, 0% other forms of financial aid

INTERNSHIP POSSIBILITY:
Several possibilities do exist on campus.

INTERNSHIP REQUIRED:
No

NUMBER OF HOURS REQUIRED:

CORE GRADUATE CLASSES:

DESCRIPTION OF TYPICAL INTERNSHIP EXPERIENCE:
Possible practicum experiences available with several teams on campus.

COMMENTS:

Boston University

School of Education, Department of Literacy and Language, Counseling and Development and School of Medicine, Program in Mental Health & Behavioral Medicine

Boston University
2 Sherborn Street
Boston, MA 02215

App date: Feb 15th

Contact:	Leonard D. Zaichkowsky
Title:	
Phone:	617.353.3378
Fax:	617.353.2909
Email:	sport@acs.bu.edu
Website:	www.bumc.bu.edu/Dept/Content.aspx?DepartmentID=391&PageID=9645
Area of Interest:	Psychophysiology/self-regulation, career transition, development of expertise

Contact: Amy Baltzell
Title: Clinical Assistant Professor
Phone: 617.358.1080
Fax:
Email: Baltzell@bu.edu

Website: www.bu.edu/education/students/prospective/graduate/programs/index.html
Area of Interest: Coping with competitive pressure, character & sport, performance enhancement, eating disorders

Contact: Adam Naylor
Title: Lecturer
Phone: 617.414.6835, 617.353.0313
Fax:
Email: ahnaylor@bu.edu
Website:
Area of Interest: Performance enhancement, family & leadership issues

PROGRAM RATING

1   2   3   4   **5**   6   7

1 to 3 Applied Orientation, 3 to 6 Equal Emphasis, 6 to 7 Research Orientation

DEGREE OFFERED:
EdM and MA; EdD

NUMBER OF STUDENTS IN PROGRAM:
12-20 (EdM); 12 (EdD)

NUMBER OF STUDENTS IN EACH DEGREE PROGRAM:
75% MEd/25% EdD

NUMBER OF STUDENTS WHO APPLY/ARE ACCEPTED ANNUALLY:
25-30 apply; 12-20 are accepted annually for master's program; 50 apply; 3-4 accepted for EdD

ADMISSION REQUIREMENTS:
Undergraduate GPA of 3.00; Strong GRE or MAT scores; Strong references; Strong exercise/sport experience

AVAILABLE FOR QUALIFIED STUDENTS:
Teaching assistantships (limited), other forms of financial aid, internal School of Education scholarships for excellent students are available.

ASSISTANTSHIPS:
0% fellowships, 0% research assistantships, 10% teaching assistantships, 25% tuition waivers, 65% other forms of financial aid.

INTERNSHIP POSSIBILITY:
Yes, both for EdM degree in School of Education, MA degree in School of Medicine, and EdD degree.

INTERNSHIP REQUIRED:
Yes (both MEd and EdD degrees)

NUMBER OF HOURS REQUIRED:
20 hours per week for the master's degree, two semesters

CORE GRADUATE CLASSES:
- Adolescent development (3 cr)
- Sport and Exercise Seminar (4 cr)
- Clinical Practice I (4 cr)
- Counseling Techniques:Sports and Exercise (4 cr)
- Theories of Counseling (3 cr)
- Foundation of Sports Science (3 cr)
- Neuroscience for Mental Health Professionals (3 cr)
- Research & Evaluation (3 cr)
- Clinical Practice II (4 cr)
- Psychological Testing (4 cr)

DESCRIPTION OF TYPICAL INTERNSHIP EXPERIENCE:
Students may intern at university counseling centers, high school counseling centers, university athletic departments (counseling & academic support), Academy for Physical & Social Development, Wellness Centers, high school sports teams.

COMMENTS:
Sport & exercise psychology at the master's degree level has two tracks. The first is an intensive 1-year program offered through the School of Education (see School of Education website link above). The second track involves a second year of training in the Mental Health & Behavioral Medicine program at the B.U. School of Medicine (see School of Medicine website link above). The doctoral degree (EdD) in sport & exercise psychology is a specialization in Counseling Psychology offered by the School of Education and is based on a scientist-practitioner model. Eligibility for admission to the EdD program requires a completed master's degree in counseling or a related field.

Bowling Green State University
School of Human Movement, Sport and Leisure Studies

Bowling Green State University
Eppler Complex
Bowling Green, OH 43403-0248

Contact: Vikki Krane
Title: Professor
Phone: 419.372.7233
Fax: 419.372.0383
Email: vkrane@bgnet.bgsu.edu
Website: www.bgsu.edu
Area of Interest: Feminist sport psychology, heterosexism in sport, body image

Contact: Bonnie Berger
Title: Professor and Director
Phone: 419.372.2334
Fax: 419.372.2877
Email: bberger@bgnet.bgsu.edu
Website: www.bgsu.edu
Area of Interest: Exercise and sport psychology: (1) mood alteration associated with diverse physical activities, (2) individual and environmental factors that influence the exercise-mood relationship, (3) use of exercise for stress management, (4) factors leading to exercise enjoyment, and (5) exercise and the quality of life

Contact: David Tobar
Title: Assistant Professor
Phone: 419.372.6914
Fax: 419.372.0383
Email: dtobar@bgnet.bgsu.edu
Website:
Area of Interest: Psychological changes associated with physical activity with an emphasis on overtraining, role of personality in sport and exercise

PROGRAM RATING

1   2   3   4   **5**   6   7

1 to 3 Applied Orientation, 3 to 6 Equal Emphasis, 6 to 7 Research Orientation

DEGREE OFFERED:
MEd

NUMBER OF STUDENTS IN PROGRAM:
5 to 8 in sport and exercise psychology/30 to 40 in the School of Human Movement, Sport and Leisure Studies

NUMBER OF STUDENTS IN EACH DEGREE PROGRAM:
100% MEd

NUMBER OF STUDENTS WHO APPLY/ARE ACCEPTED ANNUALLY:
60%

ADMISSION REQUIREMENTS:
3.0 GPA; GRE scores of 500 for each section; 3 letters of recommendation; Personal statement; Résumé

AVAILABLE FOR QUALIFIED STUDENTS:
Research assistantships, teaching assistantships, other forms of financial aid

ASSISTANTSHIPS:
0% fellowships, 20% research assistantships*, 60% teaching assistantships*, 80% tuition waivers, 20% other forms of financial aid.
*Graduate assistantships account for approximately 40% of all graduate students. These assistantships often include both teaching and research possibilities

INTERNSHIP POSSIBILITY:
No

INTERNSHIP REQUIRED:
No

NUMBER OF HOURS REQUIRED:

CORE GRADUATE CLASSES:
Flexible core—Students select four of the following courses to fulfill core requirements: Psychological Aspects of Physical Activity and Sport, Sport and Society, Teaching Movement Across the Lifespan, Motor Learning and Control, Motor Development, Biomechanics, or Physiology of Exercise. Course work also includes Research Methods and one or more statistics-related courses.

DESCRIPTION OF TYPICAL INTERNSHIP EXPERIENCE:

COMMENTS:
The sport and exercise psychology emphasis in the developmental kinesiology program takes an interdisciplinary approach to exercise science. Sport and exercise psychology is one of several concentrations within the program. Course work in this emphasis includes Psychological Parameters of Sport, Applied Sport Psychology, Exercise Psychology, and seminars and independent study in sport and exercise psychology. Additionally, many students become involved in ongoing research. Other requirements include 4 of 7 classes in the flexible core. Upon completion of core requirements, the remainder of the academic experience is developed in consultation with the student's mentor/advisor. Throughout the graduate program students work closely with nationally and internationally recognized faculty on both research and applied projects. The sport and exercise psychology emphasis places equal importance on theory research and applied sport psychology skills. Students may choose a thesis or directed project as a capstone experience and often present their research at regional and national conferences.

California State University, East Bay
Department of Kinesiology and Physical Education

California State University, East Bay
25600 Carlos Bee Boulevard
Hayward, CA 94542

Contact:	Jeff Simons	**Contact:**	Penny McCullagh
Title:	Assistant Professor	**Title:**	Professor
Phone:	510.885.4247	**Phone:**	510.885.3050
Fax:		**Fax:**	510.885.2282
Email:	jeff.simons@csueastbay.edu	**Email:**	penny.mc@csueastbay.edu
Website:		**Website:**	http://www.edschool.csuhayward.edu/departments/kpe

Area of Interest: Learning and performance enhancement, participation motivation

Area of Interest: Modeling, observational learning, imagery

PROGRAM RATING

1   2   3   **4**   5   6   7

1 to 3 Applied Orientation, 3 to 6 Equal Emphasis, 6 to 7 Research Orientation

DEGREE OFFERED:
MS

NUMBER OF STUDENTS IN PROGRAM:
10

NUMBER OF STUDENTS IN EACH DEGREE PROGRAM:

NUMBER OF STUDENTS WHO APPLY/ARE ACCEPTED ANNUALLY:

ADMISSION REQUIREMENTS:
Undergraduate degree from an accredited institution, Kinesiology preferred

AVAILABLE FOR QUALIFIED STUDENTS:

ASSISTANTSHIPS:

INTERNSHIP POSSIBILITY:
Yes

INTERNSHIP REQUIRED:
No

NUMBER OF HOURS REQUIRED:

CORE GRADUATE CLASSES:
Array of courses in different areas

DESCRIPTION OF TYPICAL INTERNSHIP EXPERIENCE:

COMMENTS:
California State University, East Bay is one of 23 campuses in the CSU system. It is located in the beautiful Bay area near San Francisco. The program is individually tailored to meet students' needs.

California State University, Fresno
Department of Kinesiology

California State University, Fresno
5275 N. Campus Drive
Fresno, CA 93740-8018

Contact: Wade Gilbert
Title: Assistant Professor
Phone: 559.278.5170
Fax: 559.278.7010
Email: wgilbert@csufresno.edu
Website: www.fresnostatesportpsych.org
Area of Interest: Exercise and sport psychology, talent development, coaching science

Contact: Dawn K. Lewis
Title: Assistant Professor
Phone:
Fax:
Email:
Website:
Area of Interest: Psychology of injury and rehabilitation

Contact: Tim Hamel
Title: Lecturer
Phone: 559.278.6049
Fax: 559.278.7010
Email: thamel@csufresno.edu
Website:
Area of Interest: Performance enhancement, stress management

Contact: Jenelle N. Gilbert
Title: Assistant Professor
Phone: 559.278.8902
Fax: 559.278.8902
Email: jgilbert@csufresno.edu
Website:
Area of Interest: Exercise and sport psychology, performance enhancement, stress and coping

PROGRAM RATING

1   2   3   4   **5**   6   7

1 to 3 Applied Orientation, 3 to 6 Equal Emphasis, 6 to 7 Research Orientation

DEGREE OFFERED:
MA with an option in sport psychology

NUMBER OF STUDENTS IN PROGRAM:
15

NUMBER OF STUDENTS IN EACH DEGREE PROGRAM:

NUMBER OF STUDENTS WHO APPLY/ARE ACCEPTED ANNUALLY:

ADMISSION REQUIREMENTS:
Undergraduate degree from an accredited institution; GRE required - verbal (450 minimum) and quantitative (430) minimum; 3.00 GPA in the last 60 semester units attempted; Non-physical education majors can enter as "conditionally classified" (see www.csufresno.edu/gradstudies)

AVAILABLE FOR QUALIFIED STUDENTS:
Research assistantships, teaching assistantships, tuition waivers, other forms of financial aid

ASSISTANTSHIPS:
15% fellowships, 35% graduate assistantships, 50% teaching assistantships/coaching, 10% tuition waivers, 20% other forms of financial aid

INTERNSHIP POSSIBILITY:
Yes

INTERNSHIP REQUIRED:
No

NUMBER OF HOURS REQUIRED:
50 hours minimum for a semester

CORE GRADUATE CLASSES:
Statistical Inference in Kinesiology, Research Methods in Kinesiology, Philosophical and Ethical Inquiry in Kinesiology, Psychobiology of Sport and Exercise, Psychology of Injury and Rehabilitation, Psychology of Sport: Mental Training

DESCRIPTION OF TYPICAL INTERNSHIP EXPERIENCE:
Supervised work with youth sport, high school, or college athletes

COMMENTS:
California State University, Fresno, is one of 23 campuses in the CSU system. Current enrollment is approximately 21,000 students in a 1,400-acre campus in northeast Fresno. The university closely approximates the multi-ethnic population of 600,000 living in the San Joaquin valley. Fresno is within easy driving distance of Sequoia Kings Canyon and Yosemite National Parks. The graduate students are diverse in age, racial/cultural backgrounds, and experience (athletic trainers, coaches, and elite performers), providing an enriching experience for students and faculty. Teaching associateships are available to qualified students for full-time and part-time positions, depending on departmental needs. This graduate option is intended for students interested in careers in coaching, performance enhancement consulting, teaching, sports medicine, athletic training, or health and fitness. The sport psychology curriculum is designed to meet core competencies listed by the Association for the Advancement of Applied Sport Psychology. The curriculum also includes course offerings in psychology, counseling, and business. In addition, the program prepares students for doctoral degrees in sport psychology or related fields such as kinesiology, education, or social psychology. Our students have been accepted into numerous doctoral programs throughout the United States. A student sport psychology club was founded in 2001. The club organizes regional workshops and conferences and hosts brown-bag seminars with coaches and researchers. Students also have supervised opportunities to consult with teams in the Fresno area. Our students regularly contribute to scientific conferences and scholarly journals, and are very active in securing internal

grants such as Robert and Norma Craig Fellowships, Research Merit Awards, Associate Students Incorporated Educational Research Grants, Graduate Travel Grants, President's Graduate Scholarships, and the Jazmyn Breeze Gilbert Memorial Award for Sport Psychology students.

California State University, Fullerton

Department of Kinesiology

California State University, Fullerton
800 North State College Boulevard
Fullerton, CA 92634-6870

Contact:	Debra Rose or Lenny Wiersma
Title:	KNES Graduate Coordinator
Phone:	714.278.3432
Fax:	714.278.5317
Email:	
Website:	www.fullerton.edu
Area of Interest:	

Contact: Patricia Laguna
Title: Associate Professor
Phone: 714.278.3783
Fax: 714.278.5317
Email: plaguna@fullerton.edu
Website: www.fullerton.edu
Area of Interest: Performance enhancement, attention control, observational learning, imagery, modeling

Contact: Carol A. Weinmann
Title: Professor
Phone: 714.278.3140
Fax: 714.278.5317
Email: cweinmann@fullerton.edu
Website: www.fullerton.edu
Area of Interest: Performance enhancement in sport and exercise, self-control, self-regulation

Contact: Kenneth Ravizza
Title: Professor
Phone: 714.278.3577
Fax: 714.278.5317
Email: kravizza@fullerton.edu
Website: www.fullerton.edu

PROGRAM RATING

1 2 **3** 4 5 6 7

1 to 3 Applied Orientation, 3 to 6 Equal Emphasis, 6 to 7 Research Orientation

---

DEGREE OFFERED:
MS

NUMBER OF STUDENTS IN PROGRAM:
25 sport and exercise psychology students

NUMBER OF STUDENTS IN EACH DEGREE PROGRAM:
100% MS

NUMBER OF STUDENTS WHO APPLY/ARE ACCEPTED ANNUALLY:
40 apply/25 accepted

ADMISSION REQUIREMENTS:
GPA of 3.20 in major (2.50 in last 60 units), GRE, essay

AVAILABLE FOR QUALIFIED STUDENTS:
Graduate assistantships, teaching associateships, other forms of financial aid

ASSISTANTSHIPS:
0% fellowships, 15% graduate assistantships, 85% teaching associateships, 0% tuition waivers, 0% other forms of financial aid

INTERNSHIP POSSIBILITY:
Yes

INTERNSHIP REQUIRED:
Yes

NUMBER OF HOURS REQUIRED:
10 hours per week plus 1-hour weekly conference

CORE GRADUATE CLASSES:
KNES 508 : Statistical Methods in Kinesiology, KNES 510: Research Methods in Kinesiology, KNES 597/598 Project/ Thesis or Comprehensive Exam, KNES 580 Advanced Studies in Sport & Exercise Psychology

DESCRIPTION OF TYPICAL INTERNSHIP EXPERIENCE:
Using applied sport psychology techniques/interventions with university athletic teams

COMMENTS:
The individual involved in this area of study is grounded in the theoretical research and practical aspects of motivation and human behavior in relation to sport and exercise for all ages and ability levels. The program is designed to prepare students for (a) a doctoral program in sport psychology; (b) an effective approach to performance enhancement in a multitude of settings; (c) consultation with athletes, coaches, and group and personal clients; and (d) a more effective approach to coaching and teaching. Three faculty serve the students in this emphasis area.

California State University, Long Beach
Department of Kinesiology

California State University, Long Beach
1250 Bellflower Boulevard
Long Beach, CA 90840

Contact: T. Michelle Magyar
Title: Assistant Professor, Coordinator of Sport Psychology & Coaching Options
Phone: 562.985.4116
Fax: 562.985.8067
Email: mmagyar@csulb.edu
Website: www.csulb.edu/depts/kpe/
Area of Interest: Psychology of excellence and leadership; lifespan development through sport and physical activity; athletic injuries; motivation; youth sport

Contact: Kevin Sverduk
Title: Lecturer
Phone:
Fax:
Email:
Website:
Area of Interest: Performance enhancement; quality practice in sport; spirituality in sport; coaching enrichment

Contact: Craig Kain
Title: Lecturer, Licensed Psychologist
Phone:
Fax:
Email:
Website:
Area of Interest: Psychology of endurance athletes; ethical issues in applied sport psychology; multi-cultural issues in sport; gay and lesbian athletes and homophobia

Contact: Sharon Guthrie
Title: Professor, Co-chair & Graduate Coordinator
Phone: 562.985.7487
Fax: 562.985.8067
Email: casteln@aol.com
Website:
Area of Interest: The influence of sport and exercise on self-esteem, body image, and identity construction; gender-related and disability-related studies; eating pathology

PROGRAM RATING

1　　2　　3　　**4**　　5　　6　　7

1 to 3 Applied Orientation, 3 to 6 Equal Emphasis, 6 to 7 Research Orientation

DEGREE OFFERED:
MS in Sport and Exercise Psychology; MA in Coaching

NUMBER OF STUDENTS IN PROGRAM:
25

NUMBER OF STUDENTS IN EACH DEGREE PROGRAM:
10-15

NUMBER OF STUDENTS WHO APPLY/ARE ACCEPTED ANNUALLY:
6 apply / 8 accepted

ADMISSION REQUIREMENTS:
A baccalaureate degree from an accredited university or college with a major in Kinesiology or the equivalent (e.g., Physical Education). Non-Kinesiology majors can enter as conditional status upon the completion of the appropriate foundational coursework (please see graduate handbook for further information). A minimum overall undergraduate grade point average (GPA) of 2.50 and a minimum overall GPA of 2.75 in upper division coursework in Kinesiology. GRE and statement of career/research objectives are also required.

AVAILABLE FOR QUALIFIED STUDENTS:
Research assistantships, teaching assistantships, tuition wavers, other forms of financial aid

ASSISTANTSHIPS:
0% fellowships 15% research assistantships 15% teaching assistantships 5% tuition wavers 2% other forms of financial aid

INTERNSHIP POSSIBILITY:
Yes

INTERNSHIP REQUIRED:
Yes

NUMBER OF HOURS REQUIRED:
Will vary

CORE GRADUATE CLASSES:
Research Methods in Kinesiology, Statistical Analysis in Kinesiology, Applied Sport and Exercise Psychology, Seminar in Sport and Exercise Psychology, Psychology of Coaching, Sport in US Culture

DESCRIPTION OF TYPICAL INTERNSHIP EXPERIENCE:
Supervised internships with youth, high school, college, semi-professional, and professional athletes in the Southern California region.

COMMENTS:
With nearly 35,000 students enrolled, California State University, Long Beach is the second largest of the 23 CSU campuses and is the third largest university in California. Since 2003, U.S. News and World Report has ranked CSULB as one of the top three in academic performance and in the top five for student diversity among western U.S. master's universities. Nestled approximately three miles from the Pacific Ocean, and 30 minutes from Los Angeles and Hollywood, "The Beach" offers a variety of cultural and

recreational activities. The Department of Kinesiology is housed within the College of Health and Human Services and offers graduate training that fulfills the core sport and exercise psychology competencies recommended by the Association for the Advancement of Applied Sport Psychology. Our graduate program is ideal for students interested in coaching, performance enhancement consulting in sport and exercise settings, and preparing for doctoral training.

California State University, Sacramento

Department of Health and Physical Education

6000 J Street
Sacramento, CA 95819

Contact: Gloria B. Solomon
Title:
Phone: 916.278.7309
Fax: 916.278.7664
Email: solomong@csus.edu
Website: www.hhs.csus.edu/
Area of Interest: Psychology of coaching, expectancy effects in sport, Psychological Skills Training

PROGRAM RATING

1   2   3   **4**   5   6   7

1 to 3 Applied Orientation, 3 to 6 Equal Emphasis, 6 to 7 Research Orientation

DEGREE OFFERED:
MS

NUMBER OF STUDENTS IN PROGRAM:
10

NUMBER OF STUDENTS IN EACH DEGREE PROGRAM:

NUMBER OF STUDENTS WHO APPLY/ARE ACCEPTED ANNUALLY:
5 apply/3 accepted

ADMISSION REQUIREMENTS:
2.80 GPA overall or 3.00 in last 60 units, undergraduate physical education degree (major or minor)

AVAILABLE FOR QUALIFIED STUDENTS:
Teaching assistantships, graduate assistantships

ASSISTANTSHIPS:
0% fellowships, 0% research assistantships, 60% teaching assistantships, 0% tuition waivers, 0% other forms of financial aid

INTERNSHIP POSSIBILITY:
Yes

INTERNSHIP REQUIRED:
No

NUMBER OF HOURS REQUIRED:
3-10 hours per week. The Master of Science in kinesiology provides a concentration in sport psychology. Flexible use of electives provides specific focus opportunities.

CORE GRADUATE CLASSES:

DESCRIPTION OF TYPICAL INTERNSHIP EXPERIENCE:
Individualized mental training for California State University, Sacramento, athletes; administration of psychological skills program for a CSUS team; administration of psychological rehabilitation program for injured athletes.

COMMENTS:
The master's program is designed to provide graduate students with a background in sport psychology through three sport psychology courses, internship experiences, and other elective options. Completion of the program will prepare students to become eligible for AAASP certification.

Cleveland State University
Department of Health, Physical Education, and Recreation

Cleveland State University
Physical Education Building 223
Cleveland, OH 44115

Contact: Susan Ziegler
Title:
Phone: 216.687.4876
Fax: 216.687.5410
Email:
Website: www.csuohio.edu
Area of Interest: Performance enhancement

PROGRAM RATING

1 2 **3** 4 5 6 7

1 to 3 Applied Orientation, 3 to 6 Equal Emphasis, 6 to 7 Research Orientation

DEGREE OFFERED:
MEd

NUMBER OF STUDENTS IN PROGRAM:
30

NUMBER OF STUDENTS IN EACH DEGREE PROGRAM:

NUMBER OF STUDENTS WHO APPLY/ARE ACCEPTED ANNUALLY:
5-10 apply/7-8 accepted

ADMISSION REQUIREMENTS:
2.75 GPA

AVAILABLE FOR QUALIFIED STUDENTS:
Teaching assistantships

ASSISTANTSHIPS:
0% fellowships, 0% research assistantships, 20% teaching assistantships, 10% tuition waivers, 0% other forms of financial aid

INTERNSHIP POSSIBILITY:
No

INTERNSHIP REQUIRED:

NUMBER OF HOURS REQUIRED:

CORE GRADUATE CLASSES:

DESCRIPTION OF TYPICAL INTERNSHIP EXPERIENCE:

COMMENTS:

DeMontfort University, Bedford

School of Physical Education, Sport, & Leisure

DeMontfort University, Bedford
37 Lansdowne Road
Bedford, MK
England
40 2BZ

Contact: Howard K. Hall
Title:
Phone: 01234.793316
Fax: 01234.350833
Email: hkhall@dmu.ac.uk
Website: www.dmu.ac.uk
Area of Interest: Motivation, stress

Contact: Steve Boutcher
Title:
Phone:
Fax:
Email:
Website:
Area of Interest: Psychophysiology

Contact: Steve Kozub
Title:
Phone:
Fax:
Email:
Website:
Area of Interest: Team cohesion and player leadership

Contact: Ken Roberts
Title:
Phone:
Fax:

Email:
Website:
Area of Interest: Movement timing and coincident-anticipation timing in children

Contact: Daniel Weigand
Title:
Phone:
Fax:
Email:
Website:
Area of Interest: Psychosocial development via sport, mental skills training, goal setting

Contact: Alistair Kerr
Title:
Phone:
Fax:
Email:
Website:
Area of Interest: Stress

Contact: Adrian Taylor
Title:
Phone:
Fax:
Email:
Website:
Area of Interest: Exercise psychology

PROGRAM RATING

1   2   3   4   5   **6**   7

1 to 3 Applied Orientation, 3 to 6 Equal Emphasis, 6 to 7 Research Orientation

DEGREE OFFERED:
MPhil and PhD are attained through research; MS is attained through a taught course.

NUMBER OF STUDENTS IN PROGRAM:
10

NUMBER OF STUDENTS IN EACH DEGREE PROGRAM:

NUMBER OF STUDENTS WHO APPLY/ARE ACCEPTED ANNUALLY:

ADMISSION REQUIREMENTS:

AVAILABLE FOR QUALIFIED STUDENTS:
Research assistantships, teaching assistantships

ASSISTANTSHIPS:
0% fellowships, 0% research assistantships, 0% teaching assistantships, 0% tuition waivers, 0% other forms of financial aid

INTERNSHIP POSSIBILITY:
No

INTERNSHIP REQUIRED:
No

NUMBER OF HOURS REQUIRED:

CORE GRADUATE CLASSES:

DESCRIPTION OF TYPICAL INTERNSHIP EXPERIENCE:

COMMENTS:
MPhil and PhD degrees are by research only. The program currently has 10 students enrolled for MPhil and PhD degrees. We also offer a taught MS in sport studies with a specialization in sport psychology. We offer both teaching and research assistantships to support graduate students studying for MPhil, PhD, or MS degrees.

East Carolina University
Department of Exercise and Sport Science

Activity Promotion Laboratory
101 Minges Coliseum
Greenville, NC 27858

Contact: Matthew Mahar
Title: Associate Professor
Phones: 252.328.0008
Fax: 252.328.4654
Email: maharm@ecu.edu
Website: www.ecu.edu/cs-hhp/exss/apl.cfm
Area of Interest: Physical activity promotion, measurement of physical activity and fitness

Contact: Katrina DuBose
Title: Assistant Professor
Phones: 252.328.1599
Fax: 252.328.4654
Email: dubosek@ecu.edu
Website:
Area of Interest: Physical activity and metabolic syndrome, youth physical activity

Contact: Tom Raedeke
Title: Associate Professor
Phones: 252.737.1292
Fax: 252.328.4654
Email: raedeket@ecu.edu
Website: www.ecu.edu/cs-hhp/exss/raedeket.cfm
Area of Interest: Social psychology of sport and exercise participation including motivation, physical activity adherence, exercise and well-being and burnout

Contact: Nick Murray
Title: Assistant Professor
Phones: 252.737.2977
Fax: 252.328.4654
Email: murrayni@ecu.edu
Website:
Area of Interest: Anxiety and visual attention

PROGRAM RATING

1   2   3   **4**   5   6   7

1 to 3 Applied Orientation, 3 to 6 Equal Emphasis, 6 to 7 Research Orientation

DEGREE OFFERED:
MA Physical Activity Promotion

NUMBER OF STUDENTS IN PROGRAM:
5-10

NUMBER OF STUDENTS IN EACH DEGREE PROGRAM:
100% MA

NUMBER OF STUDENTS WHO APPLY/ARE ACCEPTED ANNUALLY:
5 apply; 3 to 4 accepted

ADMISSION REQUIREMENTS:
GRE or MAT scores; 3.00 GPA; Three letters of reference

AVAILABLE FOR QUALIFIED STUDENTS:
Research Assistantships; Graduate Assistantships

ASSISTANTSHIPS:
Research Assistantships; Graduate Teaching Assistantships

INTERNSHIP POSSIBILITY:
Students complete a practicum (in the fitness realm) of 10 hours per week.

INTERNSHIP REQUIRED:
Yes

NUMBER OF HOURS REQUIRED:
NA

CORE GRADUATE CLASSES:
Exercise adherence, physical activity psychology, sport psychology, motor learning, assessment of physical activity and fitness, advanced measurement and evaluation in EXSS, behavioral assessment and intervention, applied behavioral analysis

DESCRIPTION OF TYPICAL INTERNSHIP EXPERIENCE:
Students complete a practicum experience related to activity promotion.

COMMENTS:
Physical Activity Promotion students will acquire an understanding of the measurement, determinants, and outcomes of physical activity. The major focus of the program is on promotion of lifestyle physical activity in children, adults, and older adults in a variety of settings. Graduates of the program will be well-prepared to continue graduate study in epidemiology or measurement of physical activity and to work in settings where they develop and deliver policy regarding physical activity, manage physical activity facilities, or promote physically active lifestyles with non-clinical populations.

East Tennessee State University
Department of Kinesiology, Leisure and Sport Sciences

East Tennessee State University
Box 70654
Johnson City, TN 37614-1701

Contact: Dr. Kevin L. Burke
Title: Professor and Chair
Phone: 423.439.4362
Fax: 423.439.5383
Email: Burkek@etsu.edu
Website: faculty.etsu.edu/burkek/
Area of Interest: Performance enhancement, optimism & pessimism, humor, superstitious behavior, and momentum

PROGRAM RATING

1   2   **3**   4   5   6   7

1 to 3 Applied Orientation, 3 to 6 Equal Emphasis, 6 to 7 Research Orientation

DEGREE OFFERED:
Master of Arts

NUMBER OF STUDENTS IN PROGRAM:
1

NUMBER OF STUDENTS IN EACH DEGREE PROGRAM:
1

NUMBER OF STUDENTS WHO APPLY/ARE ACCEPTED ANNUALLY:
10-15 apply/ 1 accepted

ADMISSION REQUIREMENTS:
Undergraduate degree in psychology, physical education, exercise science, sport management or related field; GRE scores; 2.7 cumulative undergraduate grade point average on a 4.0 scale; Three letters of recommendation; Resume and contact information for at least three academic references; Essay explaining goals and reasons for desiring to study with the Department of PEXS and ETSU.

AVAILABLE FOR QUALIFIED STUDENTS:
Various forms of financial assistance are available through the Office of Financial Aid. More information may be found at www.etsu.edu/finaid/default.asp. In addition, Graduate Assistantships and Tuition

Scholarships are available in the Department of Physical Education, Exercise and Sport Sciences (PEXS) which includes teaching in the Active Lifestyles and Wellness Program or "Fit Kids" program (coe.etsu.edu/department/pexs/fkactivities.htm), research assistants with PEXS Faculty, and various other duties. Other opportunities may be available in campus recreation, intercollegiate athletics, student activities, and other campus areas. Application materials for Graduate Assistantship and Tuition Scholarship positions may be obtained from the Program Coordinator.

ASSISTANTSHIPS:
70% Teaching & Research Assistantships, 25% Tuition Scholarships, 5% Other Assistantships

INTERNSHIP POSSIBILITY:
Yes. Students may take "independent study" course(s) (1-3 semester hours credit each) in which students would need to acquire at least a minimum of 10, 20, or 30 hours of direct consulting contact with clients. Students are expected to have a minimum of 10 direct consulting contact hours with clients for each semester credit hour earned.

INTERNSHIP REQUIRED:
The internship is not required.

NUMBER OF HOURS REQUIRED:
The internship is not required. However, students may earn from 1-6 semester credit hours.

CORE GRADUATE CLASSES:
Core Requirements (15 hours): SALM 5250: Sport Psychology (3 hrs); SALM 5215: Sport in Society (3 hrs); SALM 5230: Legal Issues in Physical Education & Sport (3 hrs); PEXS 5430: Administration of Physical Education & Athletics (3 hrs); EDFN 5950: Methods of Research (3 hrs)

DESCRIPTION OF TYPICAL INTERNSHIP EXPERIENCE:
Students may have the opportunity to work with teams and individual athletes and exercisers under direct supervision of Dr. Burke.

COMMENTS:
Students will earn a very marketable degree in either 1) Sport Management or 2) Exercise Physiology and Performance, with the ability to take two or more sport psychology related courses and complete a related thesis. Graduates of this program will be able to pursue a jobs related to Sport Psychology, Exercise Physiology, Sport Management, Coaching, and/or other related venues. Students will also be well prepared for advanced study (i.e., doctoral program).

Florida State University
Department of Educational Research

Program in Educational Psychology, B-197
Florida State University
Tallahassee, FL 32306

July 1st deadline

Contact:	Gershon Tenenbaum	**Contact:**	Bob Eklund
Title:		**Title:**	
Phone:	850.644.8780	**Phone:**	850.645.2909
Fax:	850.644.8776	**Fax:**	
Email:		**Email:**	eklund@coe.fsu.edu
Website:		**Website:**	www.epls.fsu.edu/edpsych/sportPsych.htm

Area of Interest: Methodological and measurement perspectives and methods in sport and exercise psychology; cognition and decision making in the development of motor skills and expertise; motivation and exertion in physical tasks: a social-cognitive perspective

Area of Interest: Social psychology of sport and exercise; self presentation and physical activity participation; athlete burnout

PROGRAM RATING

1   2   3   **4**   5   6   7

1 to 3 Applied Orientation, 3 to 6 Equal Emphasis, 6 to 7 Research Orientation: 4

DEGREE OFFERED:
MS, PhD

NUMBER OF STUDENTS IN PROGRAM:
25 to 30

NUMBER OF STUDENTS IN EACH DEGREE PROGRAM:
50% MS/50% PhD

NUMBER OF STUDENTS WHO APPLY/ARE ACCEPTED ANNUALLY:
40 apply/10 accepted

ADMISSION REQUIREMENTS:
Minimum GPA of 3.00, minimum GRE score of 1000

AVAILABLE FOR QUALIFIED STUDENTS:
Teaching assistantships, other forms of financial aid

ASSISTANTSHIPS:
10% fellowships, 10% research assistantships, 10% teaching assistantships, 10% tuition waivers, 10% other forms of financial aid

INTERNSHIP POSSIBILITY:
Yes

INTERNSHIP REQUIRED:
Yes, for the PhD

NUMBER OF HOURS REQUIRED:
A minimum of 8 semester hours

CORE GRADUATE CLASSES:

DESCRIPTION OF TYPICAL INTERNSHIP EXPERIENCE:
Assignment to one of Florida State University's varsity athletic teams, assignment to one of Tallahassee's mental health or wellness clinics

COMMENTS:
Psychological processes and conditions associated with athletics and sports situations are studied in the graduate program. Although the academic side (research, theory) of sport psychology is emphasized, students are offered practical (clinical, analytical) experiences in various sport programs. Students can be prepared to teach at the university level; to conduct research; and to serve as consultants to athletes, sport organizations, and those who participate in sport.

Georgia Southern University
Jiann-Ping Hsu School of Public Health

PO Box 8076
Georgia Southern University
Statesboro, GA 30460-8076

Contact: Daniel R. Czech
Title: Assistant Professor
Phone: 912.486.7424
Fax: 912.681.0381
Email: drczech@georgiasouthern.edu
Website: www.georgiasouthern.edu/~drczech/
Area of Interest: Performance enhancement, Exercise and health behavior change, cultural studies, spirituality, optimism, humor

PROGRAM RATING

1 **2** 3 4 5 6 7

1 to 3 Applied Orientation, 3 to 6 Equal Emphasis, 6 to 7 Research Orientation

DEGREE OFFERED:
MS with a major in kinesiology, sport psychology emphasis

NUMBER OF STUDENTS IN PROGRAM:
14

NUMBER OF STUDENTS IN EACH DEGREE PROGRAM:
14

NUMBER OF STUDENTS WHO APPLY/ARE ACCEPTED ANNUALLY:
40 apply/7 accepted

ADMISSION REQUIREMENTS:
Potential students must have a 2.75 minimum undergraduate GPA and a minimum GRE verbal score of 400, and must submit the GRE quantitative and analytical writing scores. Students who do not meet these admission requirements may be granted "provisional admission" status if they have a minimum GPA of 2.50 and a minimum GRE verbal score of 350 in addition to submitting the GRE quantitative and analytical writing scores. Applicants must submit a full vitae or résumé that includes but is not limited to the following information: a) undergraduate education, b) work history, c) professional experiences, d) membership and participation in professional organizations, and e) other experiences related to sport

psychology. Applicants must complete the Emphasis Area Decision Form and submit the contact information {names, addresses, email addresses, and telephone numbers} for a minimum of three academic references. Online application is available at: https://www.gasou.edu/secure/cogs/application.html

AVAILABLE FOR QUALIFIED STUDENTS:
Teaching assistantships, research assistantships, and other assistantships are available on a variable basis.

ASSISTANTSHIPS:
10% research assistantships, 90% teaching assistantships 80% tuition waivers, 10% other forms of assistance

INTERNSHIP POSSIBILITY:
Yes. The internship is a practicum course in which students have the opportunity to work with teams and individuals for at least one semester.

INTERNSHIP REQUIRED:
Yes. The practicum course is required.

NUMBER OF HOURS REQUIRED:
Three semester hours, minimum, are required for completion of the practicum course.

CORE GRADUATE CLASSES:
Kinesiology Investigative Core (6 semester hours; each course is a 3-semester-hour course): Research Design in Kinesiology and Data Analysis in Kinesiology.

Sport Psychology Emphasis (30 semester hours; each course is a 3-semester-hour course): Psychology of Peak Performance, Team Dynamics, Current Issues in Sport Psychology, Sport Psychology Interventions, Practicum in Sport Psychology, three Guided Electives, and Thesis. Thesis = 6 total hours; Program Grand Total = 36 semester hours. The typical course sequence is as follows: Fall Semester #1—Psychology of Peak Performance, Research Design in Kinesiology, and Elective; Spring Semester #1—Team Dynamics, Data Analysis in Kinesiology, and Elective; Fall Semester #2—Sport Psychology Interventions, Elective, and Thesis; Spring Semester #2—Current Issues in Sport Psychology, Practicum in Sport Psychology, and Thesis. (Summer semester course offerings may alter this course sequence.)

DESCRIPTION OF TYPICAL INTERNSHIP EXPERIENCE:
Students enroll in a practicum course wherein, under the supervision of an AAASP-certified consultant, they have the opportunity to complete a minimum of 30 hours of intervention experiences. These experiences include but are not limited to structuring and applying intervention/performance enhancement techniques with teams and/or individual athletes/exercisers.

COMMENTS:
The MS program in kinesiology with an emphasis in sport psychology is based on the integration of science and application in performance enhancement. The sport psychology program will help prepare graduates for certification by the Association for the Advancement of Applied Sport Psychology. The educational foundation gives students the opportunity to be both well-grounded in the fundamentals of the scientific process and involved in supervised individual and group/team interventions. The program consists of 36 semester credit hours, including course work in research methods, data analysis, individual and

team interventions, team dynamics, the psychological aspects of elite performance, and current issues in sport psychology. All graduating students are required to complete both a sport psychology practicum and a research thesis. The purpose of the Georgia Southern University Sport Psychology Laboratory is to provide facilities and equipment for the teaching, research, and service roles of faculty and students interested in the antecedents and consequences of sport performance. The laboratory supports instruction in motor learning control and skill, the psychology of performance and coaching, and the psychological dynamics of exercise. The research conducted in the laboratory focuses on but is not limited to the following topics: momentum, humor, performance slumps, concentration, team dynamics, and social influences. The service activities of the laboratory focus on individual training sessions, team training workshops, and group training for athletes and coaches. The laboratory space is partitioned into three areas: the instructional area, the testing/consulting room, and the control/observation room. Equipment is available to measure fine, gross, simple, and complex motor skills, as well as cognitive-affective factors associated with sport performance and psychological responses to physical and psychological stressors. The lab is also equipped with audiovisual equipment for imagery research and training. An IBM computer station, complete with a web connection, is available for word processing, data acquisition and analysis, and laboratory-based instruction. The email address for the Sport Psychology Laboratory is sppsylab@georgiasouthern.edu

Humboldt State University
Department of Health and Physical Education

Forbes Complex—Physical Education Department
Humboldt State University
Arcata, CA 95521

Contact: Al Figone	**Contact:** Chris Hopper
Title:	**Title:**
Phone: 707.826.3557	**Phone:**
Fax: 707.826.5446	**Fax:**
Email:	**Email:**
Website:	**Website:**
Area of Interest: Coaching education	**Area of Interest:** Health psychology with families, social psychological aspects of sports for persons with disabilities

PROGRAM RATING

1   2   3   4   5   6   7

1 to 3 Applied Orientation, 3 to 6 Equal Emphasis, 6 to 7 Research Orientation: Unrated

DEGREE OFFERED:
MA

NUMBER OF STUDENTS IN PROGRAM:
40

NUMBER OF STUDENTS IN EACH DEGREE PROGRAM:

NUMBER OF STUDENTS WHO APPLY/ARE ACCEPTED ANNUALLY:
15 apply/12 accepted

ADMISSION REQUIREMENTS:
3.00 GPA

AVAILABLE FOR QUALIFIED STUDENTS:
Research assistantships, teaching assistantships, other forms of financial aid

ASSISTANTSHIPS:

INTERNSHIP POSSIBILITY:
Yes

INTERNSHIP REQUIRED:
No

NUMBER OF HOURS REQUIRED:
Nine credit hours

CORE GRADUATE CLASSES:

DESCRIPTION OF TYPICAL INTERNSHIP EXPERIENCE:
Community sport organizations; college athletic programs; the Wellness Institute (exercise psychology opportunities); and school-, family-, or community-based health psychology

COMMENTS:
The MA program has four areas of emphasis: adapted, athletic training, exercise physiology/wellness, and teaching/coaching. Students can pursue an applied exercise/sport psychology area of specialization within each emphasis area. Students are encouraged to complete their theses in exercise/sport psychology. The Humboldt campus is located on the northwest coast of California, 250 miles north of San Francisco. The quality of life is exceptional.

Illinois State University
Department of Health, Physical Education, and Recreation

Horton Fieldhouse - 5120
Illinois State University
Normal, IL 61790-5120

Contact:	Anthony J. Amorose	**Contact:**	Bill Vogler
Title:		**Title:**	Graduate Coordinator
Phone:	309.438.8590	**Phone:**	309.438.5782
Fax:	309.438.5037	**Fax:**	
Email:	ajamoro@ilstu.edu	**Email:**	
Website:	www.ilstu.edu	**Website:**	
Area of Interest:	Development of self-evaluations and motivational orientations, coaching behavior	**Area of Interest:**	

PROGRAM RATING

1   2   3   4   5   **6**   7

1 to 3 Applied Orientation, 3 to 6 Equal Emphasis, 6 to 7 Research Orientation

DEGREE OFFERED:
MS

NUMBER OF STUDENTS IN PROGRAM:
3 to 5

NUMBER OF STUDENTS IN EACH DEGREE PROGRAM:
100% MS

NUMBER OF STUDENTS WHO APPLY/ARE ACCEPTED ANNUALLY:
40 apply/3 accepted

ADMISSION REQUIREMENTS:
3.20 GPA, 1100 GRE

AVAILABLE FOR QUALIFIED STUDENTS:
Teaching assistantships, other forms of financial aid (including tuition waivers)

ASSISTANTSHIPS:
0% fellowships, 0% research assistantships, 100% teaching assistantship, variable number of tuition waivers (some available), 0% other forms of financial aid

INTERNSHIP POSSIBILITY:
Yes

INTERNSHIP REQUIRED:
No

NUMBER OF HOURS REQUIRED:
Up to 8 credit hours are possible; no more than 6 may apply toward fulfillment of degree requirements.

CORE GRADUATE CLASSES:

DESCRIPTION OF TYPICAL INTERNSHIP EXPERIENCE:
Open for students to arrange

COMMENTS:

Indiana University
Department of Kinesiology

Indiana University
HPER 112-1
Bloomington, IN 47405

Contact: John S. Raglin
Title:
Phone: 812.855.1844
Fax: 812.855.6778
Email: raglinj@indiana.edu
Website: www.indiana.edu/~kines/
Area of Interest: Anxiety and athletic performance, personality, overtraining, exercise and mental health, psychobiology of sport, exercise adherence

PROGRAM RATING

1   2   3   4   5   6   **7**

1 to 3 Applied Orientation, 3 to 6 Equal Emphasis, 6 to 7 Research Orientation

DEGREE OFFERED:
MS in applied sport science with a specialization in sport psychology

NUMBER OF STUDENTS IN PROGRAM:
1

NUMBER OF STUDENTS IN EACH DEGREE PROGRAM:

NUMBER OF STUDENTS WHO APPLY/ARE ACCEPTED ANNUALLY:
1 to 2

ADMISSION REQUIREMENTS:
GPA of 2.80 or higher; GRE minimum total of 800 for verbal and quantitative

AVAILABLE FOR QUALIFIED STUDENTS:
Teaching assistantships

ASSISTANTSHIPS:
0% fellowships, 0% research assistantships, 75% teaching assistantships, 0% tuition waivers, 0% other forms of financial aid

INTERNSHIP POSSIBILITY:
No

INTERNSHIP REQUIRED:
No

NUMBER OF HOURS REQUIRED:

CORE GRADUATE CLASSES:

DESCRIPTION OF TYPICAL INTERNSHIP EXPERIENCE:
Previous students have conducted research projects with varsity athletic teams or with participants in summer youth sport camps. There are no internships per se available.

COMMENTS:
The program is a Master of Science in human performance with a specialization in sport psychology. The degree emphasizes research in issues related to exercise and mental health, and emphasizes sport rather than application. The program is intended to serve as preparation for the student interested in pursuing a doctorate in sport psychology with a specialization in the psychobiological aspects of sport.

Iowa State University
Department of Health and Human Performance

Iowa State University
Ames, IA 50010

Contact: Rick Sharp
Title:
Phone: 515.294.8650
Fax: 515.294.8740
Email: rlsharp@iastate.edu
Website: www.iastate.edu
Area of Interest:

PROGRAM RATING

1 2 3 **4** 5 6 7

1 to 3 Applied Orientation, 3 to 6 Equal Emphasis, 6 to 7 Research Orientation

DEGREE OFFERED:
MS

NUMBER OF STUDENTS IN PROGRAM:
5 active/5 part-time

NUMBER OF STUDENTS IN EACH DEGREE PROGRAM:

NUMBER OF STUDENTS WHO APPLY/ARE ACCEPTED ANNUALLY:
5 apply/3 accepted

ADMISSION REQUIREMENTS:
3.00 GPA; GRE general test recommended

AVAILABLE FOR QUALIFIED STUDENTS:
Teaching assistantships

ASSISTANTSHIPS:
0% fellowships, 0% graduate assistantships, 10% teaching assistantships, 0% tuition waivers, 0% other forms of financial aid

INTERNSHIP POSSIBILITY:
Yes

INTERNSHIP REQUIRED:
No

NUMBER OF HOURS REQUIRED:
3-6 credit hours

CORE GRADUATE CLASSES:

DESCRIPTION OF TYPICAL INTERNSHIP EXPERIENCE:
Students may (a) audit an undergraduate sport psychology class, develop and deliver lectures, develop test questions, grade test questions; (b) observe and, where appropriate, assist in Psychological Skills Training with teams and individual athletes; (c) work individually, where appropriate, with individual athletes; or (d) do performance analysis employing interpersonal process recall (IPR).

COMMENTS:

Ithaca College
Department of Graduate Studies in Exercise and Sport Sciences

Ithaca College
Ithaca, NY 14850

Contact: Greg A. Shelley
Title: Graduate Chair and Director of Sport Psychology, Associate Professor
Phone: 607.274.1275
Fax: 607.274.7055
Email: gshelley@ithaca.edu
Website: www.ithaca.edu/grad/grad1/
Area of Interest: Applied sport psychology, counseling student-athletes, leadership, and team building

Contact: Noah Gentner
Title: Assistant Professor
Phone: 607.274.1338
Fax: 607.274.7055
Email: ngentner@ithaca.edu
Website:
Area of Interest: Applied sport psychology, quality of life, motivation, and communication

Contact: Jeff Ives
Title: Associate Professor
Phone: 607.274.1751
Fax: 607.274.7055
Email: jives@ithaca.edu
Website:
Area of Interest: Motor behavior

Contact: Gary Sforzo
Title: Professor
Phone: 607.274.3359
Fax: 607.274.7055
Email: sforzo@ithaca.edu
Website:
Area of Interest: Psychophysiology

Contact: Mary Turner DePalma
Title: Professor
Phone: 607.274.1323
Fax: 607.274.7055
Email: depalma@ithaca.edu
Website:
Area of Interest: Sport psychology

PROGRAM RATING

1   **2**   3   4   5   6   7

1 to 3 Applied Orientation, 3 to 6 Equal Emphasis, 6 to 7 Research Orientation

---

DEGREE OFFERED:
MS (concentrations in sport psychology, exercise physiology, and human performance)

NUMBER OF STUDENTS IN PROGRAM:
20-30 total (across three concentrations)

NUMBER OF STUDENTS IN EACH DEGREE PROGRAM:
100% MS

NUMBER OF STUDENTS WHO APPLY/ARE ACCEPTED ANNUALLY:
50-60 apply/8-12 accepted in each concentration

ADMISSION REQUIREMENTS:
3.00 GPA from accredited institution, successful completion of related core courses, GRE

AVAILABLE FOR QUALIFIED STUDENTS:
Teaching assistantships, coaching assistantships, research assistantships, athletic training assistantships, wellness (personal training) assistantships

ASSISTANTSHIPS:
10% research assistantships, 30% coaching assistantships, 30% teaching assistantships, 30% other forms of financial aid

INTERNSHIP POSSIBILITY:
Yes, internships are available in all three concentrations.

INTERNSHIP REQUIRED:
No

NUMBER OF HOURS REQUIRED:
Thesis (30 credit hours); nonthesis (36 credit hours)

CORE GRADUATE CLASSES:
Psychological Perspectives of Sport, Psychological Applications to Sport Performance, Counseling Student-Athletes, Effective Team Building, Motivation for Superior Performance, Leadership in Sport and Exercise, Case Studies in Applied Sport Psychology, Professional Practice Issues in Sport Psychology, Applied Exercise Psychology

DESCRIPTION OF TYPICAL INTERNSHIP EXPERIENCE:
*Applied sport psychology (performance enhancement) work with selected college sports teams; supervised counseling (in sport psychology) with selected athletes, teams, and/or groups (see Comments)

COMMENTS:
Sport psychology is a concentration, along with exercise physiology and human performance, in a 30-credit MS program with a thesis and a 36-credit MS program without a thesis. The sport psychology concentration is applied in nature, emphasizing the development and implementation of Mental Training Programs (MTPs) for individual athletes, coaches, and teams. Courses in applied sport and exercise psychology, counseling, team building, motivation, and leadership are designed to emphasize practical, hands-on sport counseling skill development and experience. Internship experiences exist for selected students who have completed the appropriate first-year courses.

John F. Kennedy University
Graduate School of Professional Psychology

John F. Kennedy University
100 Ellinwood Way
Pleasant Hill, CA 94523-4817

Contact: Gail Solt
Title: Director
Phone: 925.969.3413
Fax: 925.969.3401
Email: gsolt@jfku.edu
Website: www.jfku.edu
Area of Interest: Children and sports, optimal performance

Contact: Alison Rhodius
Title: Associate Professor, Research Coordinator
Phone: 925.969.3414
Fax: 925.969.3401
Email: arhodius@jfku.edu

Website: www.jfku.edu
Area of Interest: Performance enhancement, elite archery, qualitative research methods in sport psychology.

Contact: Karlene Sugarman
Title: Assistant Professor & Field Coordinator
Phone: 925.969.3431
Fax: 925.969.3401
Email: sugarman@jfku.edu
Website: www.jfku.edu
Area of Interest: Ethics, group dynamics, mental training skills, women in sport

PROGRAM RATING

1   **2**   3   4   5   6   7

1 to 3 Applied Orientation, 3 to 6 Equal Emphasis, 6 to 7 Research Orientation

DEGREE OFFERED:
MA (in Sport Psychology and MA in Counseling Psychology, with a specialization in Sport Psychology); MA/clinical PsyD linked program, Certificates in Exercise and Sport Performance and Sport Management.

NUMBER OF STUDENTS IN PROGRAM:
70

NUMBER OF STUDENTS IN EACH DEGREE PROGRAM:
65% MA in Sport Psychology; 20% MA/clinical PsyD linked program; 10% Exercise and Sport Performance and Sport Management Certificates; 5% MA in counseling psychology with specialization in Sport Psychology

NUMBER OF STUDENTS WHO APPLY/ARE ACCEPTED ANNUALLY:
40-50 apply/20+ accepted

ADMISSION REQUIREMENTS:
Appropriate academic background, interview and/or three letters of recommendation, strong interest in the field, statement of career goals and objectives, appropriate prerequisites, work experience (if applicable)

AVAILABLE FOR QUALIFIED STUDENTS:
Forms of financial aid

ASSISTANTSHIPS:
0% fellowships, 0% research assistantships, 0% teaching assistantships, 10% tuition waivers, 45% other forms of financial aid

INTERNSHIP POSSIBILITY:
Yes

INTERNSHIP REQUIRED:
Yes

NUMBER OF HOURS REQUIRED:
Minimum of 560 hours (16 units) for the MA in Sport Psychology; minimum of 140 hours (6 units) for the sport psychology component of the MA/clinical PsyD; 840 hours (24 units) for all components of the MA in counseling psychology with a specialization in Sport Psychology.

CORE GRADUATE CLASSES:
Sport Psychology; Sport and Society; Cross-Cultural Awareness; Optimal Sport Performance (A&B); Group Process for Consultants; Psychology of Coaching; Counseling Skills (I&II); Sport Psychology Approaches to Child, Adolescent, and Family Therapy; Theory and Practice of Sport Camp Process; Supervised Field Experience (1-4); Psychopathology Assessment; Assessment Strategies; Ethics in Sport Psychology; Performance Enhancement; Sports Medicine and The Psychology of Injury; Master's Thesis (Proposal A-C).

DESCRIPTION OF TYPICAL INTERNSHIP EXPERIENCE:
The program requires four quarters of supervised field experience. Each internship is over the course of 11 weeks with a minimum hour requirement of 140 hours in total. Over the course of the four internships students will have a minimum total of 560 hours. The first two internships are part of our LEAP (Life Enhancement Through Athletic and Academic Participation) Program, the first being summer camps (sports camps and Orin Allen Youth Rehabilitation Facility Challenge Camp). These camps take place at the end of the students' first year. They provide unique settings in which children and adolescents acquire new skills in sports while enhancing their self-confidence and problem-solving abilities. The second internship takes place at one of our LEAP high school sites. These sites provide interns with the opportunity to teach sport psychology techniques as life skills and as performance enhancement on and off the playing field as well as contribute to the academic support system. The third and fourth internships can take place in a variety of sports settings with varying age and sport levels. One option is PEG (Performance Enhancement Group for Injured Athletes) which is offered at Bay Area Colleges. Here interns have the opportunity to facilitate a weekly group session for injured athletes where they can teach sport psychology techniques to help aid in the recovery and rehabilitation that surround being injured. Other approved settings have included recreational/club sports and organizations, high schools, colleges and physical and psychological health centers and organizations. While in the internships students have an individual

supervisor as well as group supervision with an AAASP (Association for the Advancement of Applied Sport Psychology) certified consultant and the students' peers. The program requires four quarters of supervised field experience. Each internship is over the course of 11 weeks with a minimum hour requirement of 140 hours in total. Over the course of the four internships students will have a minimum total of 560 hours. The first two internships are part of our LEAP (Life Enhancement Through Athletic and Academic Participation) Program. The first being summer camps (Elementary sports camps and Orin Allen Youth Rehabilitation Facility Challenge Camp). These camps take place at the end of the students first year. They provide unique settings in which children and adolescents acquire new skills in sports while enhancing their self-confidence and problem-solving abilities. The second internship takes place at one of our LEAp high school sites. These sites provide interns with the opportunity to teach sport psychology techniques as life skills on and off the playing field as well as contribute to the academic support system. The third and fourth internships can take place in a variety of sports settings with varying age and sport levels. One option is PEG (Performance Enhancement Group for Injured Athletes) which is offered at Bay Area Colleges. Here interns interns have the opportunity to facilitate a weekly group session for injured athletes where they can teach sport psychology techniques to help aid in the recovery and rehabilitation that surround being injured. Other approved settings have included recreational/club sports and organizations high schools colleges and physical and psychological health centers and organizations. While in the internships students have an individual supervisor as well as group supervision with an instructor and their peers.

COMMENTS:

Offering three degree options for the students interested in sport psychology allows for flexibility in terms of the choices they can make whilst at John F. Kennedy University. One of the three options is a relatively new addition to the existing opportunities. To stay at the forefront of curriculum growth JFKU has developed a course that links two programs: the MA in Sport Psychology and the clinical Doctor of Psychology (PsyD) program. The missions of the two programs are similar, providing a strong foundation in basic counseling skills and training students to serve multicultural and diverse populations. The full-time student starts in the sport psychology department for the first year and then moves into the clinical PsyD program for the following four years. The MA in Sport Psychology would normally be conferred after year three and the doctoral degree after year five of the full-time program. Successful completion of this linked program will enable students to practice under the auspices of sport psychology, apply for AAASP certification and be eligible to take the psychology licensing exam for the state of California. This new and innovative program is an excellent opportunity for advancement in the fields of both applied sport psychology and clinical psychology. Students may also choose to pursue the MA in counseling psychology with a specialization in sport psychology. This course means they may qualify for the Marriage and Family Therapy (MFT) in California and also work with athletes and coaches through their sport psychology training. In addition to the degree courses, we offer graduate-level certificates in Exercise and Sport Performance and Sport Management. These certificates can be taken independently of degree work at JFKU or concurrently with the programs. The certificate in Exercise and Sport Performance focuses more on the physiological aspects of sport and would be an ideal program for someone looking to be eligible for AAASP certification (either in conjunction with their MA in Sport Psychology or in addition to clinical or counseling psychology training). The certificate in Sport Management would suit someone who was interested in pursuing careers in organizations such as sport event planning, professional sports and university athletic programs.

Kansas State University
Department of Kinesiology

Natatorium 8
Kansas State University
Manhattan, KS 66506

Contact:	David Dzewaltowski	**Contact:**	Stewart Trost
Title:	Assistant Professor	**Title:**	Associate Professor
Phone:	785.532.7750	**Phone:**	785.532.6765
Fax:	785.532.7733	**Fax:**	
Email:	dadx@ksu.edu	**Email:**	strost@ksu.edu
Website:	www.kstatechi.org	**Website:**	

Area of Interest (Dzewaltowski): Individual and Environmental Influences on Physical Activity, Physical Activity Behavior Change Theory, Translation of Research to Evidence-Based Practice Out-of-School Time Physical Activity Interventions for Children and Youth

Area of Interest (Trost): Psychosocial and environmental determinants of physical activity behavior, Assessment of physical activity in children and adolescents, Prevention and treatment of childhood obesity, Relationship between physical activity and other health behaviors.

Contact:	Mary McElroy	**Contact:**	Melissa Bopp
Title:	Professor	**Title:**	Assistant Professor
Phone:	785.532.6765	**Phone:**	785.532.6765
Fax:		**Fax:**	
Email:	mmcelro@ksu.edu	**Email:**	mbopp@ksu.edu
Website:		**Website:**	

Area of Interest (McElroy): Social environmental influences on physical activity, Balancing work and family roles, Cultural competencies in kinesiology, Historical aspects of public health physical activity

Area of Interest (Bopp): Promoting and understanding physical activity, Physical activity participation in underserved populations, Behavioral interventions, Reducing health disparaties, Faith-based interventions

PROGRAM RATING

1   2   3   4   **5**   6   7

1 to 3 Applied Orientation, 3 to 6 Equal Emphasis, 6 to 7 Research Orientation: Unrated

DEGREE OFFERED:
MS in Kinesiology with emphasis in exercise psychology; Master in Public Health with emphasis in physical activity; PhD in Public Health Nutrition and Physical Activity

NUMBER OF STUDENTS IN PROGRAM:
5 to 10

NUMBER OF STUDENTS IN EACH DEGREE PROGRAM:

NUMBER OF STUDENTS WHO APPLY/ARE ACCEPTED ANNUALLY:
variable apply/variable accepted

ADMISSION REQUIREMENTS:
GRE scores, 3.00 GPA, three letters of reference

AVAILABLE FOR QUALIFIED STUDENTS:
Research assistantships, teaching assistantships

ASSISTANTSHIPS:

INTERNSHIP POSSIBILITY:
Yes (MPH)

INTERNSHIP REQUIRED:
Required for MPH

NUMBER OF HOURS REQUIRED:

CORE GRADUATE CLASSES:

DESCRIPTION OF TYPICAL INTERNSHIP EXPERIENCE:

COMMENTS:
The Department of Kinesiology, located in the College of Arts and Sciences, offers graduate preparation at the master's and at the doctoral level (with Human Nutrition) with emphases in exercise psychology and public health. Students interested in applying exercise psychology to promote physical activity are encouraged to seek an MS degree and seek ACSM certification or an MPH degree. Students interested in careers as scientists are well grounded in exercise psychology and are trained as public health physical activity scientists (MS, MPH, and/or PhD).

La Salle University
Doctor of Psychology Program, Box 842

La Salle University
Philadelphia, PA 19141

Contact: Frank Gardner, PhD, ABPP
Title: Director
Phone: 215.951.1350
Fax: 215.951.5140
Email: gardner@lasalle.edu
Website: www.lasalle.edu/academ/grad/doc_psych/docpsych.htm
Area of Interest: Clinical sport psychology, mindfulness and acceptance-based performance intervention, evidence-based practice of sport psychology

PROGRAM RATING

1   2   **3** - **4**   5   6   7

1 to 3 Applied Orientation, 3 to 6 Equal Emphasis, 6 to 7 Research Orientation

DEGREE OFFERED:
PsyD

NUMBER OF STUDENTS IN PROGRAM:
100 total students

NUMBER OF STUDENTS IN EACH DEGREE PROGRAM:
2-3 students per year in sport-performance psychology concentration (6 total at present)

NUMBER OF STUDENTS WHO APPLY/ARE ACCEPTED ANNUALLY:
175-120 apply (15-20 for sport-performance psychology concentration); 20-25 are accepted (2-3 in sport-performance psychology concentration).

ADMISSION REQUIREMENTS:
15 credits in psychology; minimum GPA of 3.00; minimum GRE score of 50th percentile in Verbal, Quantitative, Writing, & Psychology

AVAILABLE FOR QUALIFIED STUDENTS:
Work-study and some tuition-remission funding are available.

ASSISTANTSHIPS:
Teaching assistantships and undergraduate teaching opportunities are available.

INTERNSHIP POSSIBILITY:
Yes. All students must complete 1200 hours of clinical externship and 2000 hours of clinical internship. Students in sport-performance psychology concentration complete 600 of 1200 required externship hours in sport psychology externship.

INTERNSHIP REQUIRED:
Yes (as per above)

NUMBER OF HOURS REQUIRED:
1200 externship, 2000 internship

CORE GRADUATE CLASSES:
Theory and Research in Applied Sport Psychology, Principles and Practices of Applied Sport Psychology, Motor Learning and Development, Foundations of Exercise and Sport Science. Also, one of the following three is required: Counseling and Consulting in Applied Sport Psychology, Hypnosis and Self-Regulation, or Executive Coaching and Organizational Consulting.

DESCRIPTION OF TYPICAL INTERNSHIP EXPERIENCE:
Each student in the sport-performance psychology concentration completes 600 of his or her required 1200 total externship hours in our Division I Athletic Department, fully integrated into the department. Students work with teams and individuals for performance enhancement; provide clinical-counseling services; integrate with sport medicine in injury rehabilitation activities and concussion-related, neuropsychological assessment; and are involved in student-athlete leadership training, life skills training, and drug/alcohol interventions.

COMMENTS:

Lakehead University
School of Kinesiology

955 Oliver Road
Lakehead University
Thunder Bay, ON
Canada
P7B 5E1

Contact:	Jane Crossman	**Contact:**	Joey Farrell
Title:	Professor & Graduate Coordinator	**Title:**	Associate Professor & Undergraduate Coordinator
Phone:	807.343.8642	**Phone:**	807.346.7754
Fax:	807.343.8944	**Fax:**	807.343.8944
Email:	Jane.Crossman@lakeheadu.ca	**Email:**	
Website:	bolt.lakeheadu.ca/~kinesiology/wp/?pg=47	**Website:**	www.lakeheadu.ca/
Area of Interest:	Psychological rehabilitation from athletic injury, mental training	**Area of Interest:**	Motivation and goal setting

PROGRAM RATING

1   2   3   **4**   5   6   7

1 to 3 Applied Orientation, 3 to 6 Equal Emphasis, 6 to 7 Research Orientation

DEGREE OFFERED:
MSc

NUMBER OF STUDENTS IN PROGRAM:
14-16

NUMBER OF STUDENTS IN EACH DEGREE PROGRAM:
12-15

NUMBER OF STUDENTS WHO APPLY/ARE ACCEPTED ANNUALLY:
6-7

ADMISSION REQUIREMENTS:
Honors degree, minimum 70% standing. If degree is not in physical education, a qualifying year may be necessary.

AVAILABLE FOR QUALIFIED STUDENTS:
Graduate assistantships, entrance scholarships, bursaries

ASSISTANTSHIPS:
100% Graduate assistantship in 2005/06 valued at $7747 (Canadian)

INTERNSHIP POSSIBILITY:
Yes

INTERNSHIP REQUIRED:
No

NUMBER OF HOURS REQUIRED:
10 - 20 hours per week

CORE GRADUATE CLASSES:
Kine. 5010 - Research Methods and Design (1/2 credit) Kine. 5011 - Design and Analysis in Kinesiology (1/2 credit) Thesis (Kinesiology 5901) (2.5 credits)

DESCRIPTION OF TYPICAL INTERNSHIP EXPERIENCE:
Students may assist in the teaching of undergraduate courses including laboratory sessions. Please visit our website bolt.lakeheadu.ca/~kinesiology/ for an overview of both our graduate and undergraduate course offerings.
Students may assist in the teaching of undergraduate courses or may teach activity courses. Other possible tasks include assisting in research or supervising the microcomputer laboratory.

COMMENTS:
Lakehead University provides the opportunity for qualified students to study for a M.Sc. degree in Kinesiology. The degree program focuses on the study of human performance from a scientific perspective. The program of study centres around seven areas of content:
1. adapted physical activity
2. biomechanics
3. biostatistics
4. clinical exercise physiology
5. epidemiology
6. motor control and learning
7. sport and exercise psychology

Leeds Metropolitan University
Carnegie School of Leisure and Sport Studies

Leeds Metropolitan University
Beckett Park Campus
Leeds,
England
LS6 3QS

Contact:	Mark Nesti	**Email:**	
Title:		**Website:**	
Phone:	0113 2837566	**Area of Interest:**	Motivation, self-determination theory
Fax:			
Email:	M.Nesti@lmu.ac.uk		
Website:		**Contact:**	Remco Polman
Area of Interest:	Existential psychology, anxiety and sport	**Title:**	
		Phone:	
		Fax:	
Contact:	Nikos Ntoumanis	**Email:**	
Title:		**Website:**	
Phone:		**Area of Interest:**	Motor control and learning
Fax:			

PROGRAM RATING\

1   2   3   **4**   5   6   7

1 to 3 Applied Orientation, 3 to 6 Equal Emphasis, 6 to 7 Research Orientation

DEGREE OFFERED:
MSc (sport and exercise psychology), MPhil/PhD (sport and exercise psychology)

NUMBER OF STUDENTS IN PROGRAM:
30

NUMBER OF STUDENTS IN EACH DEGREE PROGRAM:
25 MSc; 5 MPhil/PhD

NUMBER OF STUDENTS WHO APPLY/ARE ACCEPTED ANNUALLY:
30 apply/20 accepted

ADMISSION REQUIREMENTS:
Good undergraduate degree in related area (2:1 honors)

AVAILABLE FOR QUALIFIED STUDENTS:
None listed

ASSISTANTSHIPS:
no financial assistance listed

INTERNSHIP POSSIBILITY:
No

INTERNSHIP REQUIRED:

NUMBER OF HOURS REQUIRED:

CORE GRADUATE CLASSES:

DESCRIPTION OF TYPICAL INTERNSHIP EXPERIENCE:

COMMENTS:
The program at Leeds Metropolitan University builds on the long-established and internationally respected work of Carnegie College in the area of PE sport and leisure over the past 65 years. From such a solid foundation, the highly successful current course, which has been offered since 1993, has recently been redeveloped and improved to meet the changing needs of students and employers in sport and exercise as we enter the new millennium. This is reflected in a dynamic and flexible course structure that allows the student to pursue disciplined basic knowledge but does not overlook the need to provide opportunities to acquire vocationally relevant skills and professional competencies. The core modules include Biomechanics: Theory and Measurement, Essentials of Exercise Physiology, Psychology and Sport, Research Methods, and Dissertation. The core module in Psychology and Sport will examine a broad range of sport psychology literature and research and will evaluate the contributions of mainstream psychology to the study of sport, as well as the contributions of sport to an understanding of psychology.

Manchester Metropolitan University
MMU Chesire

Hassall Road
Alsager, England
ST 7 2HL

Contact:	Nick Smith	**Contact:**	Paul Holmes
Title:		**Title:**	
Phone:	44.161.247.5455	**Phone:**	
Fax:	44.161.247.6375	**Fax:**	
Email:	n.c.smith@mmu.ac.uk	**Email:**	
Website:	www.mmu.ac.uk	**Website:**	

Area of Interest: Psychophysiology, stress and coping, anxiety and cognition

Area of Interest: Psychophysiology, imagery and modeling

PROGRAM RATING

1   2   3   **4**   5   6   7

1 to 3 Applied Orientation, 3 to 6 Equal Emphasis, 6 to 7 Research Orientation

DEGREE OFFERED:
MSc, Mphil, PhD

NUMBER OF STUDENTS IN PROGRAM:
35

NUMBER OF STUDENTS IN EACH DEGREE PROGRAM:
5% MSc/70% MPhil (with upgrade to PhD possible)/25% PhD

NUMBER OF STUDENTS WHO APPLY/ARE ACCEPTED ANNUALLY:
80 Msc apply/25 Msc accepted; 30 PhD apply/10 PhD accepted

ADMISSION REQUIREMENTS:
Write for specifics. Decisions are based on profiles.

AVAILABLE FOR QUALIFIED STUDENTS:
Teaching assistantships

ASSISTANTSHIPS:
10% fellowships, 20% research assistantships, 10% teaching assistantships, 5% tuition waivers, 55% other forms of financial aid

INTERNSHIP POSSIBILITY:
No

INTERNSHIP REQUIRED:

NUMBER OF HOURS REQUIRED:

CORE GRADUATE CLASSES:

DESCRIPTION OF TYPICAL INTERNSHIP EXPERIENCE:

COMMENTS:
The programme is a traditional British university model, with substantial emphasis on research, but placed within a vibrant and rapidly developing department that achieved a 5* rating (the highest grade awarded) for its research in 2001. In addition, the department runs a full-time/part-time taught master's degree (much closer to the usual U.S. programme) in applied sport and exercise psychology. The department currently hosts over 25% of the government-funded sport science support programmes with elite athletes. Major projects in stress/performance, coach education, and match analysis are also features of the department's research portfolio.

McGill University
Department of Kinesiology & Physical Education

McGill University
475 Pine Avenue West
Montreal, PQ
Canada
H2W 1S4

Contact:	Gordon Bloom	**Contact:**	Todd Loughead
Title:		**Title:**	
Phone:	514.398.4184, ext. 0516	**Phone:**	514.398.4184, ext. 0528
Fax:		**Fax:**	
Email:	gordon.bloom@mcgill.ca	**Email:**	todd.loughead@mcgill.ca
Website:	www.education.mcgill.ca/phys_ed/default.htm	**Website:**	

Area of Interest: Coaching, Team Building, Concussion Injuries

Area of Interest: Group Cohesion, Psychology of Physical Activity, Hockey Aggression

PROGRAM RATING

1   2   3   4   **5**   6   7

1 to 3 Applied Orientation, 3 to 6 Equal Emphasis, 6 to 7 Research Orientation

DEGREE OFFERED:
MA with thesis (please read "comments")

NUMBER OF STUDENTS IN PROGRAM:
10-12

NUMBER OF STUDENTS IN EACH DEGREE PROGRAM:
6-7 MA; 2-3 PhD

NUMBER OF STUDENTS WHO APPLY/ARE ACCEPTED ANNUALLY:
15 apply/5 accepted

ADMISSION REQUIREMENTS:
Cumulative GPA above 3.00 on a 4.00 scale – average of accepted students approximately 3.5, Undergraduate degree in kinesiology preferable; undergraduate degree in psychology or other closely-related discipline is accepted if combined with sport science courses and/or experiences.

AVAILABLE FOR QUALIFIED STUDENTS:
Fellowships, research assistantships, part-time work in Athletics

ASSISTANTSHIPS:
10% fellowships, 10% research assistantships, 80% teaching assistantships, 80% part-time work in PE or Athletics

INTERNSHIP POSSIBILITY:
Yes

INTERNSHIP REQUIRED:
No

NUMBER OF HOURS REQUIRED:
N/A

CORE GRADUATE CLASSES:
Statistics, Research Methods, Sport Psychology, Exercise Psychology, Motor Learning

DESCRIPTION OF TYPICAL INTERNSHIP EXPERIENCE:

COMMENTS:
The Department of Kinesiology and Physical Education does not offer a formal PhD program. However it is possible for exceptionally well qualified students to be admitted to an Ad Hoc doctoral program within our department. Strong students interested in pursuing an Ad Hoc PhD program may work in concert with a McGill faculty member to complete the admission application. The student is expected to present a detailed dissertation proposal and identify course work to be followed. In addition, the student must justify that McGill is the appropriate place of study and that it has sufficient physical, financial, and human resources to support the student's program. Thus, in order to complete the application requirements, a student must first obtain the support of a faculty member and thesis committee who will facilitate the process. Contact should be made directly with the faculty member.

Miami University
Department of Physical Education, Health, and Sport Studies

Phillips Hall
Miami University
Oxford, OH 45056

Contact: Robert Weinberg
Title:
Phone: 513.529.2728 513.529.2700
Fax: 513.529.5006
Email: weinber@muohio.edu
Website: www.units.muohio.edu/eap/phs/index.html
Area of Interest: Cognitive strategies, goal setting, anxiety, mental training

Contact: Ben Sibley
Title:
Phone: 513.529.2700
Fax: 513.529.5006
Email:
Website:
Area of Interest: Mental Health and Physical Activity; Children's Affective Responses to Physical Activity

Contact: Thelma S. Horn
Title:
Phone: 513.529.2700
Fax: 513.529.5006
Email:
Website:
Area of Interest: Children's perceived competence, coaching behavior, stress reactivity

Contact: Robin S. Vealey
Title:
Phone: 513.529.2700
Fax: 513.529.5006
Email:
Website:
Area of Interest: Anxiety, self-confidence, psychological skills training, coaching behavior

Contact: Jay Kimiecik
Title:
Phone: 513.529.2700
Fax: 513.529.5006
Email:
Website:
Area of Interest: Exercise psychology, motivation, peak experience

PROGRAM RATING

1   2   3   **4**   5   6   7

1 to 3 Applied Orientation, 3 to 6 Equal Emphasis, 6 to 7 Research Orientation

DEGREE OFFERED:
MS

NUMBER OF STUDENTS IN PROGRAM:
15

NUMBER OF STUDENTS IN EACH DEGREE PROGRAM:

NUMBER OF STUDENTS WHO APPLY/ARE ACCEPTED ANNUALLY:
30 apply/8 accepted

ADMISSION REQUIREMENTS:
3.00 minimum undergraduate GPA, three letters of recommendation, GRE

AVAILABLE FOR QUALIFIED STUDENTS:
Teaching assistantships

ASSISTANTSHIPS:
0% fellowships, 10% research assistantships, 50% teaching assistantships, 0% tuition waivers, 20% other forms of financial aid

INTERNSHIP POSSIBILITY:
Yes

INTERNSHIP REQUIRED:
No

NUMBER OF HOURS REQUIRED:
36

CORE GRADUATE CLASSES:
Psychological Foundations in Sport Social Psychology in Sport and Exercise Psychological Interventions in Sport

DESCRIPTION OF TYPICAL INTERNSHIP EXPERIENCE:
Psychological skills intervention with university teams and individual athletes; collegiate, high school, and/or youth sport coaching; acting as an editorial assistant for sport psychology journals; academic counseling for university student-athletes; coaching education

COMMENTS:
Students may select either the thesis (36 total credits required) or the nonthesis (36 total credits required) option. Nonthesis students may complete their degrees in one calendar year. Thesis students should plan on two years to complete the degree. A comprehensive oral exit examination is required of all students. The curriculum is based on a cross-disciplinary perspective with required course work in psychological, sociocultural, motoric, and physiological foundations of sport and/or exercise. Electives may include courses in counseling and psychology, as well as independent study and research with faculty in the area. An ongoing sport and exercise psychology seminar is attended by students and faculty in which professional and research issues are discussed and group research projects are coordinated. The program emphasizes knowledge of theory, research, and practice in sport psychology. Opportunities for collaborative research with faculty and psychological intervention with athletes are available for students, and every attempt is made to match student interests with faculty expertise. Selected faculty research interests include goal setting, confidence, coaching behaviors, imagery, motivation, exercise motivation, and optimal experience. Both quantitative and qualitative methodologies are encouraged. The program has been successful in placing students in sport/exercise psychology doctoral programs as well as in coaching, academic counseling, and corporate fitness positions.

Michigan State University
Department of Kinesiology

201 IM Sports Circle
Michigan State University
East Lansing, MI 48824

Contact: Dan Gould	**Email:**
Title:	**Website:** www.educ.msu.edu/
Phone:	**Area of Interest:** Achievement motivation, anxiety, youth in sports, goal setting
Fax:	
Email:	
Website:	**Contact:** Deborah Feltz
Area of Interest: Stress and burnout, talent development, parental influences	**Title:**
	Phone:
	Fax:
Contact: Martha Ewing	**Email:**
Title:	**Website:**
Phone: 517.353.4652	**Area of Interest:** Self-efficacy, collective efficacy
Fax: 517.353.2944	

PROGRAM RATING

1   2   3   4   **5**   6   7

1 to 3 Applied Orientation, 3 to 6 Equal Emphasis, 6 to 7 Research Orientation

DEGREE OFFERED:
MS, PhD

NUMBER OF STUDENTS IN PROGRAM:
30

NUMBER OF STUDENTS IN EACH DEGREE PROGRAM:
60% MS/40% PhD

NUMBER OF STUDENTS WHO APPLY/ARE ACCEPTED ANNUALLY:
10-15 apply/2-3 accepted

ADMISSION REQUIREMENTS:
Minimum score of 1000 on GRE (verbal + quantitative or verbal + analytic or quantitative + analytic), major or minor in physical education, thesis in master's program

AVAILABLE FOR QUALIFIED STUDENTS:
Fellowships, research assistantships, teaching assistantships, other forms of financial aid (Dean's Scholars, Dissertation Grants, etc.)

ASSISTANTSHIPS:
20% fellowships, 5% research assistantships, 40% teaching assistantships, 45% tuition waivers, 5% other forms of financial aid

INTERNSHIP POSSIBILITY:
Yes

INTERNSHIP REQUIRED:
No

NUMBER OF HOURS REQUIRED:
None required.

CORE GRADUATE CLASSES:

DESCRIPTION OF TYPICAL INTERNSHIP EXPERIENCE:
Each doctoral student receives the opportunity to do applied work with a college, high school, or club sport team in a supervised experience.

COMMENTS:
An interdepartmental master's degree with urban studies is also available for interested students. Qualified students may complete a master's degree in counseling psychology.

Nanyang Technological University
School of Physical Education

Nanyang Technological University
National Institute of Education
469 Bukit Timah Road
Singapore, 259756

Contact: Daniel Smith
Title:
Phone: 65.460.5368
Fax: 65.468.7506
Email: desmith@nie.edu.sg
Website:
Area of Interest: Psychological skills training for performance enhancement with elite athletes, use of psychological variables in predicting future success, crosscultural comparisons in elite athletes

Contact: Harry Tan
Title:
Phone: 65.460.5358
Fax: 65.468.7506
Email: ekhtan@nie.edu.sg

Website:
Area of Interest: Psychological issues related to intervention programs for special populations, such as obese adolescents and children; socialization of new physical education college students

Contact: Nick Aplin
Title:
Phone: 65.460.5364
Fax: 65.468.7506
Email: ngaplin@nie.edu.sg
Website:
Area of Interest: Values and pursuit of sports excellence in Singapore, with particular reference to the status of women during the post-war period and the period of national independence

PROGRAM RATING

1   2   3   **4**   5   6   7

1 to 3 Applied Orientation, 3 to 6 Equal Emphasis, 6 to 7 Research Orientation

DEGREE OFFERED:
MA by course work (7 courses and a thesis), MA by research (2 courses and a thesis), PhD by research (4 courses and a thesis)

NUMBER OF STUDENTS IN PROGRAM:

NUMBER OF STUDENTS IN EACH DEGREE PROGRAM:
10 in the sport psychology graduate program, 50 in the School of PE graduate program

NUMBER OF STUDENTS WHO APPLY/ARE ACCEPTED ANNUALLY:

ADMISSION REQUIREMENTS:
Admission to the graduate programs requires application to NIE on prescribed forms available from the Student Affairs Division. The following items must be submitted prior to final acceptance: Application for Admission as a Higher Degree Candidate; recent TOEFL and GRE scores (This applies to foreign students. Additionally, an English Proficiency Test is administered by NIE during the first semester in attendance for students whose first language is not English. Some students may receive English tests in their home countries prior to acceptance at NTU.); official transcripts of all undergraduate and graduate work taken at institutions other than NTU; and two Academic Reference Reports. Admission also requires a written proposal of the student's research topic and an interview with the dean, the potential supervisor, and the graduate studies officer.

AVAILABLE FOR QUALIFIED STUDENTS:
A $1,400 ($800 USD)-per-month scholarship is awarded to full-time, master's-by-research students. A $1,500 ($900 USD)-per-month scholarship is awarded to all full-time, PhD-by-research students.

ASSISTANTSHIPS:

INTERNSHIP POSSIBILITY:
Internships are available to implement psychological skills training programs with sports teams at a local high school. A few students in the past have also secured internships with the Singapore Sports Council, where they implemented psychological skills training programs with national team athletes and teams.

INTERNSHIP REQUIRED:

NUMBER OF HOURS REQUIRED:

CORE GRADUATE CLASSES:

DESCRIPTION OF TYPICAL INTERNSHIP EXPERIENCE:

COMMENTS:

Northern Illinois University
Department of Kinesiology and Physical Education

Northern Illinois University
Anderson Hall
DeKalb, IL 60115-2854

Contact: Laurice Zittel
Title: Graduate Program Director
Phone: 815.753.1425
Fax: 815.753.1413
Email: lzape@niu.edu
Website: www3.niu.edu/knpe/
Area of Interest:

Contact: Moira E. Stuart
Title: Assistant Professor
Phone: 815.753.0137
Fax: 815.753.1413
Email: mestuart@niu.edu
Website:
Area of Interest: Leadership effectiveness, moral development

Contact: Paul Carpenter
Title: Department Chair
Phone:
Fax:
Email:
Website:
Area of Interest:

PROGRAM RATING

1   2   3   **4**   5   6   7

1 to 3 Applied Orientation, 3 to 6 Equal Emphasis, 6 to 7 Research Orientation

DEGREE OFFERED:
MSEd

NUMBER OF STUDENTS IN PROGRAM:
75 (entire graduate program)

NUMBER OF STUDENTS IN EACH DEGREE PROGRAM:

NUMBER OF STUDENTS WHO APPLY/ARE ACCEPTED ANNUALLY:
75 apply / 25 accepted

ADMISSION REQUIREMENTS:
GPA of 2.75 (4.00 scale); GRE of 400 minimum each area (quantitative, verbal); transcripts; two letters of recommendation; goal statement

AVAILABLE FOR QUALIFIED STUDENTS:
Fellowships, research assistantships, teaching assistantships, other forms of financial aid

ASSISTANTSHIPS:
0% fellowships, 5% research assistantships, 35% teaching assistantships, 5% tuition waivers, unknown percentage of other forms of financial aid

INTERNSHIP POSSIBILITY:
No

INTERNSHIP REQUIRED:
No

NUMBER OF HOURS REQUIRED:
33 credit hours

CORE GRADUATE CLASSES:
Psychology of Sport and Exercise; Psychology of Coaching; Sport and Society; Orientation to Counseling

DESCRIPTION OF TYPICAL INTERNSHIP EXPERIENCE:

COMMENTS:
The MSEd degree program offers a specialization in sport and exercise psychology with opportunities to gain hands-on experience in applied sport settings. Students who wish to do so may be involved in ongoing research projects.

Optimal Performance Institute and University

1030 E. El Camino Real, #322
Sunnyvale, CA 94087

Contact: John J. Farley
Title: President
Phone: 408.200.7426
Fax:
Email: johnfarley@opi.edu
Website: www.opi.edu
Area of Interest:

PROGRAM RATING

1   2   **3**   4   5   6   7

1 to 3 Applied Orientation, 3 to 6 Equal Emphasis, 6 to 7 Research Orientation

DEGREE OFFERED:
MA

NUMBER OF STUDENTS IN PROGRAM:
20-30

NUMBER OF STUDENTS IN EACH DEGREE PROGRAM:
10

NUMBER OF STUDENTS WHO APPLY/ARE ACCEPTED ANNUALLY:
10-20

ADMISSION REQUIREMENTS:
Bachelor's and/or master's degree in related field or bachelor's/master's in another field if student has experience in coaching or athletics

AVAILABLE FOR QUALIFIED STUDENTS:

ASSISTANTSHIPS:

INTERNSHIP POSSIBILITY:
Yes. Internships/practica (300 hours) are one possibility for a final project.

INTERNSHIP REQUIRED:

NUMBER OF HOURS REQUIRED:

CORE GRADUATE CLASSES:

DESCRIPTION OF TYPICAL INTERNSHIP EXPERIENCE:

COMMENTS:
Our program focuses on hypnosis, neurolinguistic programming, and actual counseling of athletes for performance enhancement. It also focuses on utilizing effective communication skills and techniques to improve performance while understanding the underlying psychological, emotional, and energetic interactions taking place in the athletic environment.

Oregon State University
Exercise and Sport Science Department

Oregon State University
Langton Hall
Corvallis, OR 97331

Contact: Vicki Ebbeck	**Contact:** Bradley J. Cardinal
Title: Associate Professor	**Title:** Professor
Phone: 541.737.6800 (office)	**Phone:** 541.737.6800 (office)
Fax: 541.737.2788	**Fax:** 541.737.2788
Email: vicki.ebbeck@oregonstate.edu	**Email:** brad.cardinal@oregonstate.edu
Website: www.hhs.oregonstate.edu/exss/graduate/index.html	**Website:** www.hhs.oregonstate.edu/exss/graduate/index.html
Area of Interest: Lifespan social psychology, motivation, self-concept development	**Area of Interest:** Exercise psychology, exercise behavior change, professional issues

PROGRAM RATING

1 2 3 4 5 **6** 7

1 to 3 Applied Orientation, 3 to 6 Equal Emphasis, 6 to 7 Research Orientation

DEGREE OFFERED:
MS, PhD

NUMBER OF STUDENTS IN PROGRAM:
12

NUMBER OF STUDENTS IN EACH DEGREE PROGRAM:
50% MS/50% PhD

NUMBER OF STUDENTS WHO APPLY/ARE ACCEPTED ANNUALLY:
20 apply/2 PhD and 2 master's thesis are accepted. An open number of master's comprehensive-exam applicants are accepted.

ADMISSION REQUIREMENTS:
Letters of recommendation, GRE scores, satisfactory GPA, transcripts, letter of intent

AVAILABLE FOR QUALIFIED STUDENTS:
Teaching assistantships, other forms of financial aid

ASSISTANTSHIPS:
0% fellowships, 0% research assistantships, 75% teaching assistantships (including a tuition waiver), 0% tuition waivers (via teaching assistantships), 0% other forms of financial aid

INTERNSHIP POSSIBILITY:
No

INTERNSHIP REQUIRED:
No

NUMBER OF HOURS REQUIRED:
N/A

CORE GRADUATE CLASSES:
Motivation in Physical Activity, Psychosocial Factors in Physical Activity, Lifespan Sport & Exercise Psychology

DESCRIPTION OF TYPICAL INTERNSHIP EXPERIENCE:
N/A

COMMENTS:
The sport and exercise psychology program at Oregon State University is research oriented, with an emphasis in social psychology of physical activity. Recent research projects conducted in the department have investigated the role of physical activity in how survivors of domestic violence feel and view themselves, and a team-building intervention designed to enhance the self-concepts of physical education students, as well as theoretical and applied strategies for enhancing physical activity behavior among diverse populations. The Sport and Exercise Psychology Lab is central to every phase of the research projects conducted by faculty and students. The lab is equipped with Macintosh and PC computers and printers, a scanner, transcribers, television monitors, and video/DVD equipment. In addition, an interview room adjoins the lab and allows for one-on-one data collections. In recent years, funding for research and related projects conducted through the Sport and Exercise Psychology Lab has been obtained from several sources, including the Association for the Advancement of Applied Sport Psychology, the John C. Erkkila Endowment for Health and Human Performance, and the National Institute on Disability and Rehabilitative Research of the U.S. Department of Education. Comprehensive exam and thesis options are available for master's students. Both master's students completing theses and doctoral students are trained to conduct independent research, and doctoral students are exposed to additional experiences, such as teaching sport and exercise psychology classes, publishing research articles, preparing grant proposals, and presenting at conferences. The three graduate sport and exercise psychology courses adopt a theory-to-practice approach that enables current research and theory to be applied to practical situations. Course work is supplemented with small-group or individual reading sessions designed to examine sport and exercise psychology topics in greater detail. All students benefit from informal as well as formal interactions with fellow students and program faculty. In addition, each academic program is carefully tailored to meet the professional needs and interests of the student. The overriding goal is to mentor students in their intellectual and professional development. More specifically, graduates of the program are able to enhance their existing careers or transition into new careers—be they in administration, coaching, the health-fitness industry, teaching, recreation services, or research—through their advanced study in sport and exercise psychology. While master's degree candidates are more broadly educated, doctoral candidates are specifically prepared for positions in higher education or government agencies or for postdoctoral fellowships.

Pennsylvania State University
Department of Kinesiology

Pennsylvania State University, 266 Recreational Building
University Park, PA 16802

Contact: David E. Conroy
Title: Assistant Professor of Kinesiology
Phone: 814.863.3451
Fax: 814.865.1275
Email: David-Conroy@psu.edu
Website: www.personal.psu.edu/dec9
Area of Interest: Achievement motivation (especially avoidance aspects such as fear of failure); Nonconscious motivation underlying self-criticism; Interpersonal processes and perceptions; Youth sport interventions to promote social development (for more information, see www.personal.psu.edu/dec9/lab).

Contact: Danielle Symons Downs
Title: Assistant Professor of Kinesiology
Phone: 814.863.0456
Fax: 814.865.1275
Email: dsd11@psu.edu
Website: www.personal.psu.edu/dsd11
Area of Interest: Psychosocial determinants of exercise among pregnant and postpartum women and children; application of theoretical models to exercise (theory of planned behavior, transtheoretical model); exercise dependence; body image. Dr. Downs is the director of the Exercise Psychology Laboratory at Penn State (for more information, see www.personal.psu.edu/dsd11)

Contact: Sam Slobounov
Title: Associate Professor of Kinesiology
Phone: 814.865.3146
Fax: 814.865.1275
Email: sms18@psu.edu
Website: www.personal.psu.edu/sms18
Area of Interest: Cognitive and affective aspects of motor skill acquisition; psychological causes and consequences of sport injury; psychological effects of exercise; EEG and voluntary movements; computer graphic visualization of movement dynamics (for more information, see www.personal.psu.edu/sms18)

Contact: Steriani Elavsky
Title: Assistant Professor of Kinesiology
Phone: TBA – see website TBA – see website
Fax: TBA – see website
Email: TBA – see website
Website: www.hhdev.psu.edu/kines/faculty
Area of Interest: Exercise and health psychology; Social cognitive determinants and consequences of physical activity with the emphasis on the aging process; Physical activity effects on menopause management; Physical activity interventions to promote health; psychological well-being and quality of life in middle-aged and older adults; Other research interests include exercise adherence, exercise effects on self-esteem, emotion, symptom reporting, and quality of life.

Contact: David Yukelson
Title: Affiliate Associate Professor of Kinesiology
Phone: 814.865.0407
Fax: 814.863.1539
Email: v39@psu.edu
Website: www.mascsa.psu.edu/psychology.html
Area of Interest: Mental skills training and the psychology of performance excellence; Group cohesion and team dynamics; Interpersonal communication and leadership effectiveness; Self-regulation techniques for controlling anxiety and managing stress effectively; Developmental issues that impact student-athlete welfare. Dr. Yukelson is an applied sport psychologist who works with athletic teams at Penn State. He is also an affiliate associate professor in the Department of Kinesiology. Although Dr. Yukelson has graduate faculty status and can serve on graduate students' supervisory committees, he is not in a position to admit graduate students due to his full-time responsibilities with the Athletic Department. Students need to seek admission with Drs. Conroy, Downs, Elavsky, or Slobounov

PROGRAM RATING

1   2   3   4   5   **6**   7

1 to 3 Applied Orientation, 3 to 6 Equal Emphasis, 6 to 7 Research Orientation

DEGREE OFFERED:
MS, PhD

NUMBER OF STUDENTS IN PROGRAM:
5

NUMBER OF STUDENTS IN EACH DEGREE PROGRAM:

NUMBER OF STUDENTS WHO APPLY/ARE ACCEPTED ANNUALLY:
Varies

ADMISSION REQUIREMENTS:
Departmental policy requires as an absolute minimum a 3.00 GPA and a combined GRE (verbal + quantitative) score of 1000. Admission is competitive and admitted students typically have scores substantially above the stated minimums.

AVAILABLE FOR QUALIFIED STUDENTS:
Fellowships, research assistantships, teaching assistantships, other forms of financial aid

ASSISTANTSHIPS:
18% fellowships, 70% graduate assistantships, 94% tuition waivers, 12% other forms of financial aid (grants)

INTERNSHIP POSSIBILITY:
Yes

INTERNSHIP REQUIRED:
No

NUMBER OF HOURS REQUIRED:
The structure of each student's program of study is determined by his or her advisor and supervisory committee. Students are required to take two courses (see below), but the rest of their program of study is completely flexible.

CORE GRADUATE CLASSES:
PhD candidates are expected to take six credits of Kinesiology graduate level courses and KINES 590 (Colloquium). MS students are required to take KINES 530 (Experimental Design & Research Methods), as well as six credits of Kinesiology graduate level courses and two semesters of KINES 590 (Colloquium).

DESCRIPTION OF TYPICAL INTERNSHIP EXPERIENCE:

Dr. Slobounov offers opportunities for students interested in head injuries to work under his direct supervision in the football concussion laboratory. Advanced graduate students also may have an opportunity to work with Dr. Yukelson within the Morgan Academic Support Center for Student-Athletes and the Penn State Athletic Department (e.g., help with mental training class, write articles for student-athlete newsletter, participate in supervised counseling team interactions). Interested students should contact their prospective mentors and Dr. Yukelson to determine whether this experience would be available to and appropriate for them.

COMMENTS:

The graduate program in the Department of Kinesiology is nationally and internationally prominent in several research areas in the broad field of Kinesiology. This prominence is due to individual faculty excellence, the production and dissemination of quality research, and the mentoring and graduation of excellent graduate students. The program emphasizes research and scholarly activity in the chosen area of emphasis, typically interdisciplinary in nature. Graduate study in kinesiology at Penn State is mentor-based. Prospective students are strongly encouraged to identify and make contact with potential faculty mentors prior to the application process. Faculty do not necessarily accept students every year, so students should check with potential mentors before applying.

Purdue University
Department of Health, Kinesiology, and Leisure Studies

Purdue University
Lambert 113
West Lafayette, IN 47907

Contact: Alan Smith
Title:
Phone: 765.494.3178 or 765.496.6002
Fax:
Email: alsmith@cla.purdue.edu
Website: www.cla.purdue.edu/sportpsych
Area of Interest: Exercise and sport psychology

PROGRAM RATING

1   2   3   4   5   **6**   7

1 to 3 Applied Orientation, 3 to 6 Equal Emphasis, 6 to 7 Research Orientation

DEGREE OFFERED:
MS, PhD

NUMBER OF STUDENTS IN PROGRAM:
8

NUMBER OF STUDENTS IN EACH DEGREE PROGRAM:
40% MS/60% PhD

NUMBER OF STUDENTS WHO APPLY/ARE ACCEPTED ANNUALLY:
30 apply/1-2 accepted

ADMISSION REQUIREMENTS:

AVAILABLE FOR QUALIFIED STUDENTS:
Research assistantships, teaching assistantships, other forms of financial aid

ASSISTANTSHIPS:

INTERNSHIP POSSIBILITY:
While the program has a strong research emphasis, applied experiences are available to students. Three appointments (quarter time) exist for doctoral students with the Boilermaker Sport and Performance Psychology Services, which provides sport psychology services to Purdue intercollegiate student-athletes,

teams, and coaches. Assistantships and internships are also available with the A. H. Ismail Center for Health, Exercise, and Nutrition.

INTERNSHIP REQUIRED:

NUMBER OF HOURS REQUIRED:

CORE GRADUATE CLASSES:

DESCRIPTION OF TYPICAL INTERNSHIP EXPERIENCE:

COMMENTS:

The graduate program at Purdue University has a strong research emphasis and focuses on the social psychology of sport and exercise. Faculty research targets motivational processes in sport and other physical activity settings, as well as psychosocial/developmental aspects of the youth sport experience. Primary interests of the faculty include (a) why people strive to belong and achieve in physical activity contexts, (b) how social relationships (especially among peers) are associated with sport and physical activity motivation, and (c) how to best measure psychosocial constructs of relevance to the physical domain. Graduate course work is available in social psychology of sport, exercise psychology, and applied sport psychology. Special topics courses are regularly offered that address current student and faculty interests.

Queen's University
School of Physical and Health Education

Queen's University
Kingston, ON
Canada
K7L 3N6

Contact: Jean Cote
Title: Associate Professor
Phone: 613.533.3054
Fax: 613.533.2009
Email: jc46@post.queensu.ca
Website: www.phe.queensu.ca/employees/faculty/faculty_detail.php?show=cote
Area of Interest: Children in sport, expert performance, coaching, parental influence

Contact: Lucie Levesque
Title: Assistant Professor
Phone: 613.533.6000 x 78164
Fax: 613.533.2009
Email: levesqul@post.queensu.ca
Website: www.phe.queensu.ca/employees/faculty/faculty_detail.php?show=levesque
Area of Interest: Physical activity/exercise involvement and health promotion

Contact: Janice Deakin
Title: Director and Associate Professor
Phone: 613.533.6601
Fax: 613.533.2009
Email: deakinj@post.queensu.ca
Website: www.phe.queensu.ca/employees/faculty/faculty_detail.php?show=deakin
Area of Interest: Expert performance, coaching

PROGRAM RATING

1   2   3   4   5   **6**   7

1 to 3 Applied Orientation, 3 to 6 Equal Emphasis, 6 to 7 Research Orientation

DEGREE OFFERED:
MA, PhD

NUMBER OF STUDENTS IN PROGRAM:
12

NUMBER OF STUDENTS IN EACH DEGREE PROGRAM:
8 MA/ 4 PhD

NUMBER OF STUDENTS WHO APPLY/ARE ACCEPTED ANNUALLY:
15 apply/4-5 accepted

ADMISSION REQUIREMENTS:

Minimum of a high-B average from a four-year degree in physical education/kinesiology, etc., or in psychology with a background in sport involvement; TOEFL of 600 for students with English as a second language

AVAILABLE FOR QUALIFIED STUDENTS:

Fellowships, research assistantships, teaching assistantships

ASSISTANTSHIPS:

Yes

INTERNSHIP POSSIBILITY:

Yes

INTERNSHIP REQUIRED:

No

NUMBER OF HOURS REQUIRED:

CORE GRADUATE CLASSES:

DESCRIPTION OF TYPICAL INTERNSHIP EXPERIENCE:

Students may do a supervised internship/practicum with intercollegiate athletes (the university has 46 varsity teams) or in exercise counseling. Community-based physical activity promotion opportunities are also available.

COMMENTS:

Students are expected to take a course in a cognate department, normally Psychology, Business (Organizational Behavior), or Education. The program offers the opportunity to focus on applied sport and exercise psychology. Normally, all students accepted receive funding.

Rutgers University
Graduate School of Applied and Professional Psychology

152 Frelinghuysen Road
Piscataway, NJ 08854

Contact: Dr. Charlie Maher
Title: Professor
Phone: 732.445.2000, x103
Fax: 732.445.4888
Email: camaher@rci.rutgers.edu
Website: gsappweb.rutgers.edu/SportPsychology/SportPsych.htm

Area of Interest: Assessment and intervention in sport psychology; performance enhancement with athletes and performing artists; personal development of athletes; organizational development of athletic departments; evaluation of sport psychology programs and services; coach consultation; professional practice of sport psychology.

PROGRAM RATING

1   2   3   4   **5**   6   7

1 to 3 Applied Orientation, 3 to 6 Equal Emphasis, 6 to 7 Research Orientation

DEGREE OFFERED:
PsyD, PhD degree students; This "program"—that is, the Sport Psychology Concentration of the Graduate School of Applied and Professional Psychology—is open to doctoral students in all areas of psychology who have been admitted to one of the psychology programs at Rutgers University and who want to concentrate part of their study in sport psychology. In addition, post doctoral students in psychology and sports medicine as well as students at the master's level may be able to participate in the concentration based on an interview with Dr. Maher

NUMBER OF STUDENTS IN PROGRAM:
22

NUMBER OF STUDENTS IN EACH DEGREE PROGRAM:
85 % doctoral level and 15% post doctoral

NUMBER OF STUDENTS WHO APPLY/ARE ACCEPTED ANNUALLY:
8-10 annually are offered enrollment

ADMISSION REQUIREMENTS:
Students can choose to participate in the Sport Psychology Concentration if they have been admitted to a doctoral program in psychology at Rutgers University. In order to become eligible to participate, each interested student is interviewed for two to three hours by Dr. Maher in terms of the student's professional interests and needs as these relate to sport psychology.

AVAILABLE FOR QUALIFIED STUDENTS:
Paid supervised practica and related field experiences with college and high school athletic teams, including but not limited to Rutgers University teams, along with supervised experiences with soccer academies and other athletic programs serving elite athletes.

ASSISTANTSHIPS:
None at this time in terms of teaching assistantships.

INTERNSHIP POSSIBILITY:
Yes; these are customized to needs of students

INTERNSHIP REQUIRED:
Supervised field experiences are required for students in the Sport Psychology Concentration

NUMBER OF HOURS REQUIRED:
9-12 credit hours

CORE GRADUATE CLASSES:
"Theory, Research and Practice in Sport Psychology"; "Assessment and Intervention in Sport Psychology"; Business Planning for Sport Psychology Practice"; independent study options in sport psychology also are available

DESCRIPTION OF TYPICAL INTERNSHIP EXPERIENCE:
Supervised practica and internship experiences are varied and typically developed by the student in conjunction with Dr. Maher and other faculty who are associated with and contribute to the Sport Psychology Concentration. These other contributing faculty are located in the Department of Sports Medicine, Department of Exercise Sciences, and the Graduate of Applied and Professional Psychology. Students can include work with individuals or teams, ranging from youth to professional competitors in the range of sport psychology settings.

COMMENTS:
The Sport Psychology Concentration currently and primarily serves students who have been admitted to doctoral programs in psychology at Rutgers University—particularly in clinical, counseling, school, organizational psychology—and who, within that context, choose to concentrate part of their courses of study in the area of sport psychology, with a focus on professional practice. In addition, post doctoral and post professional preparation individuals in psychology, nursing, sports medicine and allied health fields also may be able to enroll in the Concentration. Upon completion of the Sport Psychology Concentration, each student, in addition to transcripts of courses taken, is provided a "Certificate of Achievement in Sport Psychology", which delineates courses taken, supervised field experiences completed, other consulting projects and assignments completed, the nature and scope of the dissertation if it is focused on sport psychology, and all other relevant accomplishments. Student also receive supervised experience and feedback in portfolio development and management as well as in all other aspects of professional practice including assisting students with marketing themselves for consulting opportunities, jobs, and other assignments. For more information about the parameters of the Sport Psychology Concentration, the potentially interested individual can contact Dr. Charlie Maher.

San Diego State University
Department of Exercise and Nutritional Sciences

San Diego State University
San Diego, CA 92182-7251

online app.

Contact: Simon Marshall
Title: Assistant Professor
Phone: 619.594.7272
Fax: 619.594.6553
Email: slevy@mail.sdsu.edu
Website: www-rohan.sdsu.edu/dept/ens/ens_web/faculty/levy.htm
Area of Interest: Exercise psychology, exercise behavior change, determinants and measurement of physical activity and sedentary behavior

Contact: Thomas L. McKenzie
Title: Professor Emeritus
Phone: 619.594.5672
Fax: 619.594.6553
Email: tmckenzie@sdau.edu
Website: www-rohan.sdsu.edu/dept/ens/ens_web/faculty/mckenzie.htm
Area of Interest: Applied behavior analysis, performance enhancement

Contact: Robert Mechikoff
Title: Professor
Phone: 619.594.1925
Fax: 619.594.6553
Email: rmechiko@mail.sdsu.edu
Website: www-rohan.sdsu.edu/dept/ens/ens_web/faculty/mechikoff.htm
Area of Interest: Psychology of coaching, social psychology, historical and philosophical development of sport and physical education/exercise science

Contact: Susan Levy
Title: Assistant Professor
Phone: 619.594.5672
Fax: 619.594.6553
Email: slevy@mail.sdsu.edu
Website: www-rohan.sdsu.edu/dept/ens/ens_web/faculty/levy.htm
Area of Interest: Exercise motivation; influence of self-perceptions on exercise behaviors; measurement and evaluation in sport and exercise

PROGRAM RATING

1   2   3   4   **5**   6   7

1 to 3 Applied Orientation, 3 to 6 Equal Emphasis, 6 to 7 Research Orientation

DEGREE OFFERED:
MA in Kinesiology, specialization in Exercise & Sport Psychology

NUMBER OF STUDENTS IN PROGRAM:
10 in E & SP specialization

NUMBER OF STUDENTS IN EACH DEGREE PROGRAM:
20 in MA program

NUMBER OF STUDENTS WHO APPLY/ARE ACCEPTED ANNUALLY:
15-20 apply/10 accepted

ADMISSION REQUIREMENTS:
950 GRE, 3.00 GPA last 60 units

AVAILABLE FOR QUALIFIED STUDENTS:
Research assistantships, teaching assistantships, other forms of financial aid

ASSISTANTSHIPS:
0% fellowships, 20% research assistantships, 30% teaching assistantships, 5% tuition waivers, 0% other forms of financial aid

INTERNSHIP POSSIBILITY:
Yes

INTERNSHIP REQUIRED:
Yes

NUMBER OF HOURS REQUIRED:
144

CORE GRADUATE CLASSES:
ENS 671 (Seminar in Advanced Sport & Exercise Psychology), ENS 688 (Applied Psychology of Effective Coaching), ENS 689 (Applied Psychology for Superior Performance), ENS 793 (Exercise/Sport Psychology Internship). A new course, currently an elective (ENS 696, Psychological Aspects of Exercise and Physical Activity Behavior), has also been added.

DESCRIPTION OF TYPICAL INTERNSHIP EXPERIENCE:
Students may opt to pursue internship opportunities in research, applied exercise psychology, or applied sport psychology. Research internships typically require involvement in contract research projects. Experiences involve study design, data collection, data analysis, and report writing for publication in peer-reviewed journals. Applied exercise psychology experiences typically involve behavioral counseling for adoption and maintenance of physical activity in different settings (e.g., worksite, community, etc.). Applied sport psychology internships follow an educational model of service delivery, which often includes the development of mental skills training programs for collegiate and local athletes. Interns may also serve in local business and sport organizations.

COMMENTS:
Students are able to select their courses of study to reflect their own interests and backgrounds. A core of courses is required of all students so that they become exposed to the breadth of topics in the discipline. Further courses are elected to meet each student's specific interests. The main strength of the specialization is that it allows students to become exposed to the spectrum of opportunities in both exercise and sport psychology. It is designed to reflect the extensive resources in physical activity, exercise and sport that are available in the San Diego region. Additional programs of interest in which students can take electives include the Public Health program in the Graduate School of Public Health at SDSU, and the joint doctoral program in Clinical Psychology between the department of psychology at SDSU and the department of Psychiatry at the University of California at San Diego.

San Diego University for Integrative Studies

5703 Oberlin Drive
Suite 208
San Diego, CA 92121

Contact: Cristina Bortoni Versari
Title:
Phone: 858.638.1999
Fax: 858.638.1990
Email: cversari@sduis.edu
Website: www.sduis.edu
Area of Interest: Career transition and athletic retirement, athletes and personality type, business principles of sport psychology, performance enhancement, distance learning education, NBA players

Contact: Peter Lambrou
Title:
Phone: 858.638.1999
Fax: 858.638.1990
Email: sduis@sduis.edu
Website: www.sduis.edu
Area of Interest: Nutrition and Lifestyle Management, Clinical Hypnosis, Energy Psychology

Contact: Jim Bauman
Title:
Phone: 858.638.1999
Fax: 858.638.1990
Email: sduis@sduis.edu
Website: www.sduis.edu
Area of Interest: Performance Enhancement, Intervention Techniques, Psychology of Coaching, Olympic athletes

Contact: Ray Trybus
Title:
Phone: 858.638.1999
Fax: 858.638.1990
Email: sduis@sduis.edu
Website: www.sduis.edu
Area of Interest: Director of Research, Clinical Psychology

Contact: Ray DiCicio
Title:
Phone: 858.638.1999
Fax: 858.638.1990
Email: sduis@sduis.edu
Website: www.sduis.edu
Area of Interest: Addictions and their effect on the team and family, Post Traumatic Stress Disorder (PTSD), meditation methods, clinical skills

Contact: Robert Nideffer
Title:
Phone: 858.638.1999
Fax: 858.638.1990
Email: sduis@sduis.edu
Website: www.sduis.edu
Area of Interest: TAIS, Assessment, performance enhancement

Contact: Todd Fenner
Title:
Phone: 858.638.1999
Fax: 858.638.1990
Email: sduis@sduis.edu
Website: www.sduis.edu
Area of Interest: Meditation Techniques, Tibetan Buddhist Psychology, Transpersonal Psychology

Contact: Hilse Barbosa
Title:
Phone: 858.638.1999
Fax: 858.638.1990
Email: sduis@sduis.edu
Website: www.sduis.edu
Area of Interest: Personal and career development, personality type, Myers Briggs Type Indicator, team building

Contact: David Lavalle
Title:
Phone: 858.638.1999
Fax: 858.638.1990
Email: sduis@sduis.edu
Website: www.sduis.edu
Area of Interest: Career Transition and Athletic Retirement, Performance Enhancement

Contact: Robin Pratt
Title:
Phone: 858.638.1999
Fax: 858.638.1990
Email: sduis@sduis.edu
Website: www.sduis.edu
Area of Interest: Cognition, information processing, attention and learning, and sport performance enhancement

Contact: Maureen Moss
Title:
Phone: 858.638.1999
Fax: 858.638.1990
Email: sduis@sduis.edu
Website: www.sduis.edu
Area of Interest: Depth Psychology, Group Therapy, Clinical Skills Training, Legal and Ethical Issues

Contact: Roy Nasby
Title:
Phone: 858.638.1999
Fax: 858.638.1990
Email: sduis@sduis.edu
Website: www.sduis.edu
Area of Interest: Nutrition and lifestyle management, acupuncture, acupressure, and other alternative approaches to treating injured athletes

Contact: Jerry Livesay
Title:
Phone: 858.638.1999
Fax: 858.638.1990
Email: jlivesay@sduis.edu
Website: www.sduis.edu
Area of Interest: Clinical and sport psychology research, psychopharmacology, assessment and evaluation

PROGRAM RATING

1 2 3 4 5 6 7

1 to 3 Applied Orientation, 3 to 6 Equal Emphasis, 6 to 7 Research Orientation

DEGREE OFFERED:
PhD in Psychology with specialization in Sport Psychology, MA in Sport Counseling, Certificate in Sport Psychology, Doctor of Psychology, Marriage and Family Therapy, Transpersonal Psychology, Expressive Arts Therapy

NUMBER OF STUDENTS IN PROGRAM:
80

NUMBER OF STUDENTS IN EACH DEGREE PROGRAM:
40 MA/30 PhD/10 certificate

NUMBER OF STUDENTS WHO APPLY/ARE ACCEPTED ANNUALLY:
25 (Students who meet admission requirements are accepted.)

ADMISSION REQUIREMENTS:

MA in sport counseling—Undergraduate degree, PhD in sport psychology—master's degree and 35 units of graduate level psychology courses and 25 unites of sport counseling courses, Certificate in sport psychology – Undergraduate degree

AVAILABLE FOR QUALIFIED STUDENTS:

ASSISTANTSHIPS:

INTERNSHIP POSSIBILITY:

Yes. The San Diego University for Integrative Studies is the home of Pro Sport Counseling, Inc., a counseling center for athletes. Internship opportunities are available to qualified SDUIS students.

INTERNSHIP REQUIRED:

Yes, for PhD

NUMBER OF HOURS REQUIRED:

250

CORE GRADUATE CLASSES:

Career Transition and Athletic Retirement, Performance Enhancement, Counseling Skills Training, Group Therapy, Sport Psychology Business Principles, Nutrition and Lifestyle Management, Psychopathology, Assessment and Evaluation in Sport Psychology, Advanced Intervention Techniques in Sport Psychology.

DESCRIPTION OF TYPICAL INTERNSHIP EXPERIENCE:

COMMENTS:

The sport psychology program at the San Diego University for Integrative Studies consists of an 18-month degree in sports counseling and a 36-48-month PhD program in sport psychology. Both programs are designed to meet the needs of professionals dedicated to helping athletes and preparing them to be more effective in sports and in their personal lives during and after their athletic careers. A unique humanistic approach considering individual dimensions of mind, body, and spirit in their social, cultural, and environmental contexts is combined with personal development, technical, and professional skills. Graduates in sport psychology consult with individual athletes, teams, athletic organizations, committees, and national and international governing bodies. Graduates are also able to effectively teach, coach, and develop programs tailored for this unique population. Through intensive training and internships, graduates enhance their competence and professional skills to better serve others. Individuals who wish to pursue licensing as an MFT or psychologist will have the opportunity to add courses that are required for the State of California licensing exam. The faculty of the sport psychology program consists of experienced professionals who have proven results in applying psychology to such areas as performance enhancement, substance abuse, athletic career transition, retirement, testing and evaluation, individual and family counseling, crisis intervention, group techniques, communication and relationship skills, and gender issues. Leaders in the field of sport psychology enhance the quality of the program as guest lecturers; they guarantee the diversity of approaches in working with clients in the field of sports. Courses are offered on a quarter system. All three programs are also available through a distance learning program. MA in Sport Counseling: this program provides students with the theoretical and practical training needed to help athletes become more effective in sport and in their practical lives. Emphasis is on practical counseling skills and innovative techniques for working with athletes and sport professionals to promote wellness and effectiveness in their endeavors. PhD in Sport Psychology: The needs of athletes, coaches, fitness specialist, psychologist, and other professionals who specialize in sports have changed increasingly over the years. The challenges of understanding the dynamics of psychological changes and their relationships to athletic performance have become the focus of attention for professionals in sports. Students are trained in a variety of sport psychology approaches and techniques that prepare them to consult with athletes, teams, and athletic organizations. Students can also add courses that are required to become a licensed psychologist or MFT. Certificate Programs in Sport Counseling: This program is designed for the working professional who wishes to expand her/his skills and abilities in the areas of performance enhancement, sport counseling, and effective methods of working with athletes, coaches, and others in the expanding sports industry.

San Jose State University

Department of Kinesiology

One Washington Square
San Jose State University
San Jose, CA 95192-0054

Contact: David M. Furst
Title:
Phone: 408.924.3039
Fax: 408.924.3053
Email: furstd@kin.sjsu.edu
Website: www.sjsu.edu/sportpsych
Area of Interest: Endurance athletes, disabled athletes, association/dissociation

Contact: Ted Butryn
Title:
Phone: 408.924.3068
Fax:
Email: tbutryn1@kin.sjsu.edu
Website:

Area of Interest: Intersections between sport psychology, sport sociology, and cultural studies, cognitions and mood states of endurance athletes, Psychosocial impact of "cyborg sport," and "whiteness studies" and sport

Contact: Matt Masucci
Title:
Phone: 408.924.3021
Fax:
Email: mmasucci@kin.sjsu.edu
Website:
Area of Interest: Qualitative analyses of sport, Sport and narratives, Subculture of Mixed Martial Arts, Subculture of bicycle racing

PROGRAM RATING

1   2   3   4   5   **6**   7

1 to 3 Applied Orientation, 3 to 6 Equal Emphasis, 6 to 7 Research Orientation

DEGREE OFFERED:
MA

NUMBER OF STUDENTS IN PROGRAM:
15

NUMBER OF STUDENTS IN EACH DEGREE PROGRAM:

NUMBER OF STUDENTS WHO APPLY/ARE ACCEPTED ANNUALLY:
5 apply/5 accepted

ADMISSION REQUIREMENTS:
BA with a major or minor in physical education, minimum GPA of 3.00 in last 60 semester units (or minimum of 2.75 and on probation), no undergraduate course deficiencies. Students are encouraged but not required to submit GRE scores. Non-PE majors can enter as "conditionally classified."

AVAILABLE FOR QUALIFIED STUDENTS:
Teaching assistantships, other forms of financial aid

ASSISTANTSHIPS:
0% fellowships, 0% research assistantships, 20% teaching assistantships, 0% tuition waivers, 30% other forms of financial aid, 50% no financial Aid; Students have an opportunity to assist with new and ongoing research projects run through the newly established Qualitative Research Lab. The lab is equipped with the latest analog and digital recording devices, as well as QSR N7 qualitative software

INTERNSHIP POSSIBILITY:
Yes

INTERNSHIP REQUIRED:
No

NUMBER OF HOURS REQUIRED:

CORE GRADUATE CLASSES:

DESCRIPTION OF TYPICAL INTERNSHIP EXPERIENCE:
Depending on the clinical/applied work being done with the various teams and athletic departments, the student will work with these teams under the direction of one of the clinical sport psychologists.

COMMENTS:
Professors at San Jose State University have been involved with sport psychology as long or longer than those at any other university in the United States. Former professors, including and Dorothy Hazeltine Yates, Thomas Tutko, and the late Bruce Ogilvie have achieved national and international recognition for their applied work with athletes on every level, from Olympic to professional to youth sport. Currently housed within the Department of Kinesiology, the sport psychology program is integrative and interdisciplinary in nature, and students may combine their studies with sport sociology, motor learning, athletic training, and other kinesiology sub-disciplines. Further, the program features faculty with an expertise in various forms of qualitative research. Courses available to students are Undergraduate and Graduate Sport Psychology, Psychology of Coaching, Exercise and Mental Health, Diversity, Stress, and Health, Motivation, Cognition, Personality, Nutrition and Sport, and others.

Southeastern Louisiana University
Department of Kinesiology and Health Studies

Southeastern Louisiana University
Hammond, LA 70402

Contact: Dan Hollander	**Email:**
Title:	**Website:**
Phone: 504.549.3870	**Area of Interest:** Self-talk, videotape feedback, imagery
Fax: 504.549.5119	
Email: dhollander@selu.edu	
Website: www.selu.edu	**Contact:** Marcus Kilpatrick
Area of Interest: Exercise and sport psychology	**Title:**
	Phone:
	Fax:
Contact: Eddie Hebert	**Email:**
Title:	**Website:**
Phone:	**Area of Interest:** Exercise psychology
Fax:	

PROGRAM RATING

1   2   3   4   5   **6**   7

1 to 3 Applied Orientation, 3 to 6 Equal Emphasis, 6 to 7 Research Orientation

DEGREE OFFERED:
MA

NUMBER OF STUDENTS IN PROGRAM:
2 in sport psychology /42 in overall program

NUMBER OF STUDENTS IN EACH DEGREE PROGRAM:

NUMBER OF STUDENTS WHO APPLY/ARE ACCEPTED ANNUALLY:
1 applies/1 accepted in sport psychology program; 15 apply/13 accepted in overall program

ADMISSION REQUIREMENTS:
Undergraduate GPA of 2.5 (or 3.0 in last 2 years), GRE of 800

AVAILABLE FOR QUALIFIED STUDENTS:

ASSISTANTSHIPS:
50% fellowships (5% in overall program), 50% research assistantships (10% in overall program), 0% teaching assistantships (5% in overall program), 100% tuition waivers (25% in overall program), 0% other forms of financial aid

INTERNSHIP POSSIBILITY:
Yes

INTERNSHIP REQUIRED:
No

NUMBER OF HOURS REQUIRED:
Students concentrating in counseling have a greater opportunity to participate in internship experiences than do those concentrating in exercise science.

CORE GRADUATE CLASSES:

DESCRIPTION OF TYPICAL INTERNSHIP EXPERIENCE:
Educational sport psychology with individual- or team-sport athletes, various opportunities in the athletic training room with injured athletes

COMMENTS:

Southern Connecticut State University
Human Performance Laboratory

Southern Connecticut State University
Moore Fieldhouse
501 Crescent Street
New Haven, CT 6515

Contact: David S. Kemler
Title:
Phone: 203.392.6040
Fax: 203.392.6020
Email: Kemlerd1@southernct.edu
Website: www.southernct.edu
Area of Interest: Sport psychology, exercise psychology

Contact: Robert S. Axtell
Title: Graduate Coordinator
Phone:
Fax:
Email:
Website:
Area of Interest: Exercise physiology

Contact: David W. Martens
Title:
Phone:
Fax:
Email:
Website:
Area of Interest: Biomechanics

Contact: Sharon Misasi
Title:
Phone:
Fax:
Email:
Website:
Area of Interest: Sport psychology, social psychology

Contact: Karl F. Rinehardt
Title:
Phone:
Fax:
Email:
Website:
Area of Interest: Exercise physiology

Contact: Joan A. Finn
Title:
Phone:
Fax:
Email:
Website:
Area of Interest: Psychophysiology

Contact: Jin Jin Yang
Title:
Phone:
Fax:
Email:
Website:
Area of Interest: Motor learning

PROGRAM RATING

1   2   3   **4**   5   6   7

1 to 3 Applied Orientation, 3 to 6 Equal Emphasis, 6 to 7 Research Orientation

DEGREE OFFERED:
MS in Exercise Science

NUMBER OF STUDENTS IN PROGRAM:
100

NUMBER OF STUDENTS IN EACH DEGREE PROGRAM:
85 HP; 15 Sport Psychology

NUMBER OF STUDENTS WHO APPLY/ARE ACCEPTED ANNUALLY:
20 apply/10 accepted

ADMISSION REQUIREMENTS:
2.50 GPA

AVAILABLE FOR QUALIFIED STUDENTS:
Graduate assistantships, other forms of financial aid

ASSISTANTSHIPS:
Possible to apply for Research Fellowship (10 Fellowships per year @ $5,000 for full time students); Graduate School Graduate Assistantship (10 per year @ $ 10,000)

INTERNSHIP POSSIBILITY:
Yes

INTERNSHIP REQUIRED:
No

NUMBER OF HOURS REQUIRED:
150 hours

CORE GRADUATE CLASSES:

DESCRIPTION OF TYPICAL INTERNSHIP EXPERIENCE:
See Comments.

COMMENTS:
The sport psychology concentration is designed to offer the student in-depth study in the areas of health, psychology, performance enhancement, social psychology, and intervention. This interdisciplinary approach presents 33 credits of course work from a variety of disciplines. Our program is an interdisciplinary program geared toward helping students to achieve their goals as they pursue fulfilling careers. The benefits of our program are twofold: First, we offer flexibility throughout the program, allowing students to select a wide range of options, including emphases in performance enhancement, health, psychology, and social psychology. Students are encouraged to take courses in psychology, public health, counseling and school psychology, and business, as well as marriage and family therapy. Second, because we are a rather small school (as compared with others in this field), we can offer students greater opportunities to

integrate theory and application as they hone their skills in a supervised environment with athletic teams. Participating teams include the University of Connecticut and Yale University as well as Southern Connecticut State University athletic departments. This background prepares students for advanced study, hospital wellness programs, corporate and commercial fitness centers, community agencies, coaching enhancement, or other related fields of study. Graduate assistantships are available for qualified applicants. Further information related to curriculum and research assistantships may be obtained by contacting Dr. David S. Kemler.

Southern Illinois University, Carbondale

Department of Physical Education

Southern Illinois University, Carbondale
Carbondale, IL 62901-4310

Contact: Julie Partridge
Title: Assistant Professor
Phone: 618.453.3324
Fax: 618.453.3329
Email: jpartrid@siu.edu
Website: www.siu.edu/departments/coe/physed
Area of Interest: Emotional coping (shame), social influence, youth sports

Contact: Elaine Blinde
Title:
Phone: 618.453.3119
Fax: 618.453.3329
Email: Blinde@siu.edu
Website: www.siu.edu/departments/coe/physed/
Area of Interest: Gender dynamics in sport, sport retirement, disability dynamics, empowerment, homophobia

Contact: Sarah McCallister
Title:
Phone:
Fax:
Email:
Website:
Area of Interest: Youth sports, teaching and coaching effectiveness, gender dynamics, disability issues, baseball

PROGRAM RATING

1   2   3   **4**   5   6   7

1 to 3 Applied Orientation, 3 to 6 Equal Emphasis, 6 to 7 Research Orientation

DEGREE OFFERED:
MS

NUMBER OF STUDENTS IN PROGRAM:
12 (social psychology of sport)

NUMBER OF STUDENTS IN EACH DEGREE PROGRAM:

NUMBER OF STUDENTS WHO APPLY/ARE ACCEPTED ANNUALLY:
12 apply/6 accepted

ADMISSION REQUIREMENTS:
GRE, three current letters of recommendation or evaluation forms, undergraduate and graduate transcripts

AVAILABLE FOR QUALIFIED STUDENTS:
Fellowships, research assistantships, teaching assistantships, other forms of financial aid

ASSISTANTSHIPS:
0% fellowships, 10% research assistantships, 40% teaching assistantships, 80% tuition waivers, 50% other forms of financial aid

INTERNSHIP POSSIBILITY:
Yes, a full internship is available. Practicum experiences in applied sport psychology working directly with athletes and/or exercisers are available.

INTERNSHIP REQUIRED:
No

NUMBER OF HOURS REQUIRED:
36 total

CORE GRADUATE CLASSES:

DESCRIPTION OF TYPICAL INTERNSHIP EXPERIENCE:
Individual and team consultation experiences, independent-study practica, practical experience through applied sport psychology graduate courses

COMMENTS:
A wide range of teaching and research opportunities is available to graduate students through departmental assistantships and faculty grants. Students are provided opportunities to engage in both quantitative and qualitative research projects. In addition to the many courses offered by the Department of Kinesiology in the social psychological domain, students are encouraged to take courses in counseling psychology and sociology. Excellent relationships have been established with related departments on campus. A sport psychology laboratory provides students with computers, office space, a seminar room, and facilities and equipment for consultation and interviewing.

Southern Illinois University, Edwardsville

Department of Kinesiology and Health Education

Southern Illinois University Edwardsville
Box 1126
Vadalabene Center
Edwardsville, IL 62026-1126

Contact:	Curt L. Lox	**Contact:**	Kim Hurley
Title:	Professor & Associate Dean	**Title:**	Assistant Professor
Phone:	618.650.5961	**Phone:**	618.650.2306
Fax:	618.650.3359	**Fax:**	618.650.3719
Email:	clox@siue.edu	**Email:**	khurley@siue.edu
Website:	www.siue.edu/EDUCATION/kinesiology/index.html	**Website:**	

Area of Interest: Exercise and sport psychology, behavioral medicine, coaching

Area of Interest: Physical self-perceptions and well-being, social influences on PA behavior

PROGRAM RATING

1   2   3   4   **5**   6   7

1 to 3 Applied Orientation, 3 to 6 Equal Emphasis, 6 to 7 Research Orientation

DEGREE OFFERED:
MSEd

NUMBER OF STUDENTS IN PROGRAM:
15

NUMBER OF STUDENTS IN EACH DEGREE PROGRAM:

NUMBER OF STUDENTS WHO APPLY/ARE ACCEPTED ANNUALLY:
15 apply/10 accepted

ADMISSION REQUIREMENTS:
Undergraduate GPA of 2.75 or a graduate transfer GPA of 3.0; autobiographical statement of purpose. No standardized tests are required for either U.S. or international students.

AVAILABLE FOR QUALIFIED STUDENTS:

ASSISTANTSHIPS:
5% fellowships, 5% research assistantships, 5% teaching assistantships, 10% tuition waivers, 25% other forms of financial aid

INTERNSHIP POSSIBILITY:
Yes

INTERNSHIP REQUIRED:
No

NUMBER OF HOURS REQUIRED:
3 credit hours

CORE GRADUATE CLASSES:

DESCRIPTION OF TYPICAL INTERNSHIP EXPERIENCE:
Working with university athletic teams. Opportunities also exist for internships in exercise rehabilitation and wellness settings.

COMMENTS:
The emphasis of the graduate sport and exercise psychology program is on research and academic sport and exercise psychology. Applied sport psychology issues are included, however, and opportunities exist for an individual to gain experience developing and implementing educational psychological skill programs. Opportunities also exist in exercise psychology settings for those individuals interested in corporate fitness, wellness, and rehabilitation. The specific research interests of Curt Lox are exercise and special populations (e.g., AIDS, elderly) and motivational and affective aspects of exercise and mental health. Kim Hurley examines physical self-perceptions and well-being, social influences on PA behavior.

Spalding University
Department of Psychology

Spalding University
851 S. Fourth
Louisville, KY 40203

Contact: Thomas Titus	**Contact:** John James
Title: Chairman	**Title:**
Phone: 502.585.9911	**Phone:**
Fax: 502.585.7159	**Fax:**
Email:	**Email:**
Website: www.spalding.edu	**Website:**
Area of Interest: Learning, addictions	**Area of Interest:** Systems theory
Contact: Barbara Williams	**Contact:** David Morgan
Title:	**Title:**
Phone:	**Phone:**
Fax:	**Fax:**
Email:	**Email:**
Website:	**Website:**
Area of Interest: Supervision issues	**Area of Interest:** Learning
Contact: John Kalafat	**Contact:** Thomas Bergandi
Title:	**Title:**
Phone:	**Phone:**
Fax:	**Fax:**
Email:	**Email:**
Website:	**Website:**
Area of Interest: Crisis intervention, consultation	**Area of Interest:** Sport psychology

PROGRAM RATING

1 2 3 4 5 6 7

1 to 3 Applied Orientation, 3 to 6 Equal Emphasis, 6 to 7 Research Orientation

DEGREE OFFERED:
MA /PsyD

NUMBER OF STUDENTS IN PROGRAM:
120

NUMBER OF STUDENTS IN EACH DEGREE PROGRAM:
20% MA/80% PsyD

NUMBER OF STUDENTS WHO APPLY/ARE ACCEPTED ANNUALLY:
30 MA apply/5 MA accepted; 400 PsyD apply/25 PsyD accepted

ADMISSION REQUIREMENTS:
GRE minimum for three tests: 1500 (MA) 1600 (PsyD), three letters of recommendation, autobiography, professional/academic writing sample, personal interview for PsyD program

AVAILABLE FOR QUALIFIED STUDENTS:
Research assistantships, other forms of financial aid

ASSISTANTSHIPS:
0% fellowships, 28% research assistantships, 0% teaching assistantships, 5% tuition waivers (scholarships), 100% other forms of financial aid (student loans)

INTERNSHIP POSSIBILITY:
Yes (may not be in applied sport psychology per se)

INTERNSHIP REQUIRED:
Yes

NUMBER OF HOURS REQUIRED:
650 hours (MA), 2000 hours (PsyD)

CORE GRADUATE CLASSES:

DESCRIPTION OF TYPICAL INTERNSHIP EXPERIENCE:
Numerous experiences are available for clinical training (e.g., hospitals, outpatient agencies, drug and alcohol agencies, correctional facilities, community mental health centers).

COMMENTS:

Springfield College
Psychology Department

Springfield College
Springfield, MA 1109

online app.

Contact: Judy L. Van Raalte
Title: Professor of Psychology
Phone: 413.748.3388
Fax: 413.748.3854
Email: jvanraal@spfldcol.edu
Website: www.spfldcol.edu
Area of Interest: Social psychology of sport and exercise (attributions, self-talk)

Contact: Britton W. Brewer
Title:
Phone:
Fax:
Email:
Website:
Area of Interest: Pain and injury in sport and exercise

Contact: Allen Cornelius
Title:
Phone:
Fax:
Email:
Website:
Area of Interest: Research, statistics, humor
Contact: Burt Giges

Title:
Phone:
Fax:
Email:
Website:
Area of Interest: Intervention skills, self-awareness

Contact: Al Petitpas
Title:
Phone: 413.748.3325
Fax: 413.748.3854
Email:
Website: www.spfldcol.edu
Area of Interest: Personal and career development of athletes, youth development through sport

Contact: Delight Champagne
Title:
Phone:
Fax:
Email:
Website:
Area of Interest: Career development of athletes

PROGRAM RATING

1   2   3   **4**   5   6   7

1 to 3 Applied Orientation, 3 to 6 Equal Emphasis, 6 to 7 Research Orientation

---

DEGREE OFFERED:
MEd /MS/CAS

NUMBER OF STUDENTS IN PROGRAM:
24

NUMBER OF STUDENTS IN EACH DEGREE PROGRAM:
80% MS/20% MEd

NUMBER OF STUDENTS WHO APPLY/ARE ACCEPTED ANNUALLY:
45 apply/12 accepted

ADMISSION REQUIREMENTS:
Psychology or physical education majors preferred; applied experience helpful. Completed application, five letters of support, and personal statement required.

AVAILABLE FOR QUALIFIED STUDENTS:
Fellowships, research assistantships, teaching assistantships, other forms of financial aid

ASSISTANTSHIPS:
15% fellowships, 15% research assistantships, 30% teaching assistantships, 15% tuition waivers, 0% other forms of financial aid

INTERNSHIP POSSIBILITY:
Yes

INTERNSHIP REQUIRED:
Yes, for all degrees

NUMBER OF HOURS REQUIRED:
Minimum of 300 hours required.

CORE GRADUATE CLASSES:

DESCRIPTION OF TYPICAL INTERNSHIP EXPERIENCE:
Academic/athletic counseling at colleges and universities, sports counseling in sport medicine clinics, career and personal development with athletes in sport agencies, work with college athletic teams Academic/athletic counseling at colleges and universities, sports counseling in sport medicine clinics, career and personal development with athletes in sport agencies, work with college athletic teams

COMMENTS:
The athletic counseling program offers course work in psychology, physical education, and counseling. The primary job market for graduates has been academic athletic counseling positions at major universities. Approximately 25% of graduates go directly into counseling psychology doctoral programs to gain the credentials necessary to develop independent practices in counseling with emphases in sport psychology.

Springfield College
School of Graduate Studies

Springfield College
Springfield, MA 1109

Contact:	Betty L. Mann	Email:	
Title:		Website:	
Phone:	413.748.3125	Area of Interest:	Measurement, research design, structural equation modeling
Fax:	413.748.3745		
Email:			
Website:	www.springfieldcollege.edu	Contact:	Mimi Murray
Area of Interest:	Research advisement	Title:	
		Phone:	
Contact:	Tracy Fogarty	Fax:	
Title:		Email:	
Phone:		Website:	
Fax:		Area of Interest:	Sport psychology

PROGRAM RATING

1   2   3   **4**   5   6   7

1 to 3 Applied Orientation, 3 to 6 Equal Emphasis, 6 to 7 Research Orientation

DEGREE OFFERED:
MS (thesis required), DPE (specialization in sport psychology)

NUMBER OF STUDENTS IN PROGRAM:
12 MS/8 DPE in sport psychology

NUMBER OF STUDENTS IN EACH DEGREE PROGRAM:
60% MS/40% DPE

NUMBER OF STUDENTS WHO APPLY/ARE ACCEPTED ANNUALLY:
15-20 MS apply/8-10 MS accepted; approximately 6 DPE apply/ 2-3 DPE accepted

ADMISSION REQUIREMENTS:
MS: GPA, references, applicant's statement of objectives; DPE: GPA, GRE, references, applicant's statement of objectives

AVAILABLE FOR QUALIFIED STUDENTS:
Associateships (fellowships), graduate assistantships, other forms of financial aid

ASSISTANTSHIPS:
20% fellowships (include all forms of research/teaching assistantships and tuition waivers), 0% research assistantships, 0% teaching assistantships, 0% tuition waivers, 0% other forms of financial aid

INTERNSHIP POSSIBILITY:
Sport psychology consulting internship experience is required for students in the doctoral program.

INTERNSHIP REQUIRED:

NUMBER OF HOURS REQUIRED:

CORE GRADUATE CLASSES:

DESCRIPTION OF TYPICAL INTERNSHIP EXPERIENCE:

COMMENTS:
The sport psychology concentration at the master's level is designed for students who have a scholarly interest in the field and wish to pursue the interest further in doctoral programs of study. The intent of the program is to provide a theoretical understanding of sport from a philosophical, sociological, psychological, and physiological perspective, particularly as this knowledge may be practically applied to helping athletes maximize sport performance. A thesis is required. The doctoral concentration in sport psychology has been designed to allow students, upon the completion of the degree, to meet requirements for certification by the AAASP. In addition to theory-based and applied sport psychology course work, a series of seminars is offered, concerning current issues and trends in the field, including model building, race, gender, and ethics. Students also complete course work in athletic counseling and psychopathology, as well as in related areas of physical education, including motor learning and control, motor development, exercise physiology, and sociology. Students in the department are working on a variety of research topics. Some of the current research includes: self-perception of children following resistance training, state anxiety and performance within objective and subjective sports, competitive orientation and goal orientation among intercollegiate athletes, effects of weekly stressors on athletic injury, sport confidence and the home advantage, imagery and injury rehabilitation, sport goal orientation differences by gender and athletic level of college students in Taiwan, use of performance enhancement techniques with visually impaired athletes, comparing leadership preferences and perceptions of intercollegiate athletes, coaches, and directors of athletics, the relationship between personality characteristics and likelihood of seeking medical attention, and continuity and retention of female coaches.

Staffordshire University
Division of Sport, Health, and Exercise

Staffordshire University
Leek Road
Stoke-on-Trent,
United Kingdom
ST4 2DF

Contact: Geoffrey Paul
Title:
Phone:
Fax: (44) 1782-747167
Email: sctbdh@cr41.staffs.ac.uk
Website: www.staffs.ac.uk/schools/health/she/shehole.htm
Area of Interest: Expertise in skilled behavior

Contact: Jayne Mitchell
Title:
Phone:
Fax:
Email:
Website:
Area of Interest: Exercise epidemiology, exercise psychology

Contact: Basil Ashford
Title:
Phone:
Fax:
Email:
Website:
Area of Interest: Sport psychology

Contact: John Erskine
Title:
Phone:
Fax:
Email:
Website:
Area of Interest: Motor learning/control

Contact: Nigel Gleeson
Title:
Phone:
Fax:
Email:
Website:
Area of Interest: Exercise physiology

Contact: Jo Doyle
Title:
Phone:
Fax:
Email:
Website:
Area of Interest: Sport psychology

Contact: Tom Mercer
Title:
Phone:
Fax:
Email:
Website:
Area of Interest: Exercise physiology

Contact: Kim Buxton
Title:
Phone:
Fax:
Email:
Website:
Area of Interest: Exercise psychology

PROGRAM RATING

1   2   3   4   **5**   6   7

1 to 3 Applied Orientation, 3 to 6 Equal Emphasis, 6 to 7 Research Orientation

DEGREE OFFERED:
MPhil/MS (sport science)/PhD

NUMBER OF STUDENTS IN PROGRAM:
10 to 20

NUMBER OF STUDENTS IN EACH DEGREE PROGRAM:
3-4 MPhil/6-10 MS/2-3 PhD

NUMBER OF STUDENTS WHO APPLY/ARE ACCEPTED ANNUALLY:
12 accepted

ADMISSION REQUIREMENTS:
Undergraduate degree, marks/grades, references

AVAILABLE FOR QUALIFIED STUDENTS:
Research assistantships, teaching assistantships

ASSISTANTSHIPS:
0% fellowships, 25% research assistantships, 0% teaching assistantships, 0% tuition waivers, 0% other forms of financial aid

INTERNSHIP POSSIBILITY:
Yes

INTERNSHIP REQUIRED:
No

NUMBER OF HOURS REQUIRED:

CORE GRADUATE CLASSES:

DESCRIPTION OF TYPICAL INTERNSHIP EXPERIENCE:
Work with teams; work in leisure/fitness centers; work in performance center; work with individuals

COMMENTS:

Stellenbosch University
Department of Sport Science

Stellenbosch University
Private Bag X1
Matieland, Stellenbosch
Republic of South Africa
7602

Contact:	Justus R. Potgieter	**Contact:**	Liz Bressan
Title:		**Title:**	
Phone:	(27) 21-8084915	**Phone:**	
Fax:	(27) 21-8084817	**Fax:**	
Email:	jrp@maties.sun.ac.za	**Email:**	
Website:		**Website:**	
Area of Interest:	Performance enhancement, exercise psychology	**Area of Interest:**	Motor learning

PROGRAM RATING

1   2   3   4   5   **6**   7

1 to 3 Applied Orientation, 3 to 6 Equal Emphasis, 6 to 7 Research Orientation

DEGREE OFFERED:
MHS/ PhD

NUMBER OF STUDENTS IN PROGRAM:
15 part-time students

NUMBER OF STUDENTS IN EACH DEGREE PROGRAM:
66% MHS/34% PhD

NUMBER OF STUDENTS WHO APPLY/ARE ACCEPTED ANNUALLY:
10 apply/9 accepted

ADMISSION REQUIREMENTS:
Recognized honor's degree for MA, recognized MA for PhD

AVAILABLE FOR QUALIFIED STUDENTS:
Teaching assistantships (limited)

ASSISTANTSHIPS:
0% fellowships, 0% research assistantships, 25% teaching assistantships, 0% tuition waivers, 0% other forms of financial aid

INTERNSHIP POSSIBILITY:
No

INTERNSHIP REQUIRED:

NUMBER OF HOURS REQUIRED:

CORE GRADUATE CLASSES:

DESCRIPTION OF TYPICAL INTERNSHIP EXPERIENCE:

COMMENTS:
Each student develops his or her own program of study. Emphasis is placed on the research dissertation.

Temple University
Department of Kinesiology

(048-00)
Philadelphia, PA 19122

Contact:	Melissa Napolitano	**Contact:**	Michael L. Sachs
Title:	Associate Professor	**Title:**	Professor
Phone:	215.204.1947	**Phone:**	215.204.8718
Fax:	215.204.4414	**Fax:**	215.204.4414
Email:	melissa.napolitano@temple.edu	**Email:**	msachs@temple.edu
Website:	www.temple.edu/chp/kinesiology/human_mov.htm	**Website:**	

Area of Interest: Exercise psychology, health behavior change, behavior change theories, technology and interventions, women's health, obesity

Area of Interest: Exercise psychology, psychology of running, exercise addiction/dependence, professional and ethical issues

PROGRAM RATING

1   2   3   4   **5**   6   7

1 to 3 Applied Orientation, 3 to 6 Equal Emphasis, 6 to 7 Research Orientation

DEGREE OFFERED:
MEd/PhD

NUMBER OF STUDENTS IN PROGRAM:
35 (majority are part-time)

NUMBER OF STUDENTS IN EACH DEGREE PROGRAM:
40% MS / 60% PhD

NUMBER OF STUDENTS WHO APPLY/ARE ACCEPTED ANNUALLY:
25 apply/10 accepted

ADMISSION REQUIREMENTS:
Undergraduate GPA of 3.00 and MAT or GRE for MA program (GRE for PhD program), but specific score not required for standardized tests. Portfolio approach emphasized wherein the totality of student's academic, work, life, and exercise/sport experiences is considered. Telephone or personal interview required. TOEFL required for students whose undergraduate degree was from an institution where the language of instruction was not English.

AVAILABLE FOR QUALIFIED STUDENTS:
Fellowships (university-wide competition), graduate assistantships, research assistantships

ASSISTANTSHIPS:
0% fellowships, 0% research assistantships, 20% teaching assistantships (include tuition waivers), 0% tuition waivers, 4% other forms of financial aid

INTERNSHIP POSSIBILITY:
Yes

INTERNSHIP REQUIRED:
Yes, for the PhD; optional for the MEd (Please see note in Comments on clinical internship/practicum option.)

NUMBER OF HOURS REQUIRED:
At least 3 credit hours; usually 6 credit hours

CORE GRADUATE CLASSES:
Psychology of Kinesiology, Sociology of Kinesiology, Psychosocial Testing in Exercise and Sport Psychology, Intro Graduate Applied Sport Psychology Class, Research Methods, Statistics

DESCRIPTION OF TYPICAL INTERNSHIP EXPERIENCE:
Quite varied and typically developed by the student—can include work with individuals or teams ranging from youth to Olympic-level competitors in exercise/wellness and sport psychology settings. Quite varied and typically developed by the student—can include work with individuals or teams ranging from youth to Olympic-level competitors in exercise/wellness and sport psychology settings.

COMMENTS:
Each student develops as personal a program of study as is possible. There are some specific course requirements (especially at the doctoral level, where a core set of courses is required). The internship is "required" for each student's program of study at the doctoral level and often is taken by students at the master's level as well. The master's program has three options: thesis, project, and clinical internship/practicum. The clinical internship/practicum is a 300-hour, supervised internship experience designed to provide the student with a quality applied experience in exercise and sport psychology. Each student assists in selecting/obtaining an internship site. Students have worked, for example, at the Velodrome in Allentown, PA; with two gymnastics schools in PA and NJ; at a local tennis center; with national-level triathletes and swimmers; with varsity teams at area colleges; and with Temple's fencing, field hockey, football, lacrosse, basketball, softball, volleyball, and tennis teams. There is also an applied sport psychology/research/discussion group—ESPATU—Exercise and Sport Psychology in Action at Temple University, part of the Exercise and Sport Psychology Division (ESPD) of the Biokinetics Research Laboratory. The group has put on programs to advance public awareness of sport psychology (such as work at Penn Relays). The group also critiques members' applied (as part of supervision) and research efforts, helping members to prepare for upcoming conference presentations and providing them a sounding board for research ideas. The Carole A. Oglesby Endowed Scholarship provides a significant level of financial support for graduate students interested in work on African American women in sport. The graduate program attempts to offer students as much flexibility as possible in meeting their goals for graduate study. The doctoral program provides an opportunity to prepare for AAASP certification, if the

student has this as one of her or his goals. The graduate students are diverse in age, racial/cultural backgrounds, and experience (athletic training, social work, counseling psychology, coaching, etc.), providing an enriching experience for students and faculty. The program has had an international flavor over the years, with students (some currently in the program) from Australia, Canada, England, India, Indonesia, Israel, Greece, and several Caribbean nations. Dr. Melissa Napolitano, a clinical psychologist who works extensively in areas of exercise promotion and health behavior change, is joining the faculty in September, 2006. Her research and applied experience, in addition to her work on grants at the foundation and national (i.e., NIH) levels, bring a strong and exciting research focus in the exercise psychology area to the program. Temple University and Philadelphia provide an exciting experience for those who choose the Temple challenge!

Texas Christian University
Department of Kinesiology

Texas Christian University
TCU Box 297730
Fort Worth, TX 76129

Contact:	Matt Johnson	**Contact:**	Debbie Rhea
Title:		**Title:**	
Phone:	817.257.6866	**Phone:**	
Fax:	817.257.7702	**Fax:**	
Email:	m.johnson@tcu.edu	**Email:**	
Website:	www.kinesiology.tcu.edu	**Website:**	

Area of Interest: Coach/athlete relationships, applied sport psychology, quality of life, youth sport, phenomenology

Area of Interest: Eating disorders, muscle dysmorphia, exercise psychology

PROGRAM RATING

1   2   3   4   5   **6**   7

1 to 3 Applied Orientation, 3 to 6 Equal Emphasis, 6 to 7 Research Orientation

DEGREE OFFERED:
MS

NUMBER OF STUDENTS IN PROGRAM:
5

NUMBER OF STUDENTS IN EACH DEGREE PROGRAM:

NUMBER OF STUDENTS WHO APPLY/ARE ACCEPTED ANNUALLY:
1-2

ADMISSION REQUIREMENTS:
Undergraduate GPA of 3.00, GRE, two letters of recommendation, purpose/goal statement

AVAILABLE FOR QUALIFIED STUDENTS:

ASSISTANTSHIPS:
0% fellowships, 20% research assistantships, 30% teaching assistantships, 100% tuition waivers, 50% other forms of financial aid (graduate coaching assistantships)

INTERNSHIP POSSIBILITY:
Yes

INTERNSHIP REQUIRED:
No

NUMBER OF HOURS REQUIRED:
3 credit hours

CORE GRADUATE CLASSES:
Advanced Motor Behavior, Exercise Physiology, Advanced Biomechanics, Graduate Statistics

DESCRIPTION OF TYPICAL INTERNSHIP EXPERIENCE:
An internship might consist of serving as a consultant with campus athletic teams, with supervision and specialized training. Other internship opportunities include teaching elementary physical education in a lab school focusing on sociomoral skill development.

COMMENTS:
This program offers a master's degree in kinesiology. It includes broad-based course work in kinesiology, with an emphasis in sport psychology. Opportunities for internships are available for second-year, master's-level students. The program of study for each student is personalized to meet professional interests and to build on academic limitations. Students coming from an exercise science background are offered more course work in psychology; students coming from a psychology background take more courses in the exercise sciences. A sport psychology lab offers opportunities to engage in ongoing research projects. The graduate students are diverse in age and background. Approximately 50% are planning to pursue doctoral-level work.

Texas Tech University
Health, Physical Education, and Recreation

Texas Tech University
PO Box 43011
Lubbock, TX 79409-3011

Contact: Lanie Dornier
Title:
Phone: 806.742.3371
Fax: 806.742.1688
Email: Lanie.Dornier@ttu.edu
Website: www.hess.ttu.edu
Area of Interest:

PROGRAM RATING

1   2   3   4   5   **6**   7

1 to 3 Applied Orientation, 3 to 6 Equal Emphasis, 6 to 7 Research Orientation: 6

DEGREE OFFERED:
MS/EdD (interdisciplinary, through the College of Education)

NUMBER OF STUDENTS IN PROGRAM:
10

NUMBER OF STUDENTS IN EACH DEGREE PROGRAM:

NUMBER OF STUDENTS WHO APPLY/ARE ACCEPTED ANNUALLY:

ADMISSION REQUIREMENTS:
Must take GRE; sliding scale is applied using GRE score and last 60 hours GPA.

AVAILABLE FOR QUALIFIED STUDENTS:
Research assistantships, teaching assistantships, other forms of financial aid

ASSISTANTSHIPS:
0% fellowships, 10% research assistantships, 50% teaching assistantships, 50% tuition waivers, 50% other forms of financial aid

INTERNSHIP POSSIBILITY:
Yes

INTERNSHIP REQUIRED:
No

NUMBER OF HOURS REQUIRED:
Three-hour course requiring 120 hours of contact on site

CORE GRADUATE CLASSES:

DESCRIPTION OF TYPICAL INTERNSHIP EXPERIENCE:
Athletes from various teams within the university routinely receive training in psychological skills. Internship possibilities are available with these athletes.

COMMENTS:
An interdisciplinary area of emphasis in applied sport psychology is available within the MS program and within the EdD program through the College of Education. It is designed on an individual basis according to the student's background and career goals. Courses in physical education, psychology, and educational and counseling psychology might typically be included in the area of emphasis.

Universite de Montreal

Departement d'Education Physique

Universite de Montreal
CP 6128 Succursale 'A'
Montreal, QB
Canada
H3C 3J7

Contact: Wayne R. Halliwell
Title:
Phone: 514.343.7008
Fax: 514.343.2181
Email:
Website:
Area of Interest: Motivation, mental preparation

Contact: Claude Alain
Title:
Phone:
Fax:
Email:
Website:
Area of Interest: Information processing, preparation to react

Contact: Luc Proteau
Title:
Phone:
Fax:
Email:
Website:
Area of Interest: Learning, movement control, individual differences

Contact: Claude Sarrazin
Title:
Phone:
Fax:
Email:
Website:
Area of Interest: Decision making, intervention

PROGRAM RATING

1　　2　　3　　4　　5　　6　　7

1 to 3 Applied Orientation, 3 to 6 Equal Emphasis, 6 to 7 Research Orientation: Unrated

DEGREE OFFERED:
MS/PhD

NUMBER OF STUDENTS IN PROGRAM:
40

NUMBER OF STUDENTS IN EACH DEGREE PROGRAM:
70% MS/30% PhD

NUMBER OF STUDENTS WHO APPLY/ARE ACCEPTED ANNUALLY:
20 apply/10 accepted

ADMISSION REQUIREMENTS:
BA, BSc, or BPE (usually in physical education or psychology)

AVAILABLE FOR QUALIFIED STUDENTS:
Research assistantships, teaching assistantships, other forms of financial aid

ASSISTANTSHIPS:

INTERNSHIP POSSIBILITY:
No

INTERNSHIP REQUIRED:

NUMBER OF HOURS REQUIRED:

CORE GRADUATE CLASSES:

DESCRIPTION OF TYPICAL INTERNSHIP EXPERIENCE:

COMMENTS:
The program is currently an academically oriented research program. However, a licensed psychologist is on staff and teaches two graduate courses in clinical psychology. Courses are given in French, but the majority of readings are in English and theses may be written in English.

Universite de Sherbrooke
Departement de Kinanthropologie

Universite de Sherbrooke
2500 Boulevard de l'Universite
Sherbrooke, QBC
Canada
JlK 2Rl

Contact: Paul Deshaies
Title:
Phone: 819.821.8000 (x3721)
Fax: 819.821.7970
Email: pdeshaies@feps.usherb.ca
Website: www.usherbrooke.ca
Area of Interest: Daily physical education for elementary schools, psychobiological analysis of performance

Contact: Georges B. Lemieux
Title:
Phone:
Fax:
Email:
Website:
Area of Interest: Learning, observation

Contact: Marc Belisle
Title:
Phone:
Fax:
Email:
Website:
Area of Interest: Motives for involvement, stress management

Contact: Pierre Demers
Title:
Phone:
Fax:
Email:
Website:
Area of Interest: Sociology of physical education

PROGRAM RATING

1   2   3   4   **5**   6   7

1 to 3 Applied Orientation, 3 to 6 Equal Emphasis, 6 to 7 Research Orientation

DEGREE OFFERED:
MS

NUMBER OF STUDENTS IN PROGRAM:
25

NUMBER OF STUDENTS IN EACH DEGREE PROGRAM:
20 apply/15 accepted

NUMBER OF STUDENTS WHO APPLY/ARE ACCEPTED ANNUALLY:

ADMISSION REQUIREMENTS:
Bachelor's degree in movement science, physical education, or equivalent

AVAILABLE FOR QUALIFIED STUDENTS:
Research assistantships, teaching assistantships, other forms of financial aid

ASSISTANTSHIPS:
10% fellowships, 10% research assistantships, 10% teaching assistantships, 0% tuition waivers, 60% other forms of financial aid

INTERNSHIP POSSIBILITY:
No

INTERNSHIP REQUIRED:

NUMBER OF HOURS REQUIRED:

CORE GRADUATE CLASSES:

DESCRIPTION OF TYPICAL INTERNSHIP EXPERIENCE:

COMMENTS:
The program is not specifically in applied sport psychology but in kinanthropology. The program emphasizes a systematic approach applied to contexts such as athletic competition, physical fitness, and adapted physical activity. Within this framework, classes are offered in areas such as sport psychology, sport sociology, and environmental factors. Research activities count for 24 of the 45 credits required and it is here that the student can concentrate on a specific area of interest.

Universite du Quebec à Trois-Rivieres

Departement des Sciences de l'Activite-Physique

Universite du Quebec à Trois-Rivieres
C.P 500 Trois-Rivieres
Quebec, Canada
G9A 5H7

Contact:	Pierre Lacoste		**Contact:**	Denis Methot
Title:			**Title:**	
Phone:	819.376.5128, poste 3780		**Phone:**	
Fax:	819.376.5092		**Fax:**	
Email:			**Email:**	
Website:			**Website:**	
Area of Interest:	Intervention strategies		**Area of Interest:**	Training and performance

PROGRAM RATING

1   2   3   4   5   6   7

1 to 3 Applied Orientation, 3 to 6 Equal Emphasis, 6 to 7 Research Orientation: Unrated

DEGREE OFFERED:
MS

NUMBER OF STUDENTS IN PROGRAM:
24

NUMBER OF STUDENTS IN EACH DEGREE PROGRAM:

NUMBER OF STUDENTS WHO APPLY/ARE ACCEPTED ANNUALLY:
23 apply/21 accepted

ADMISSION REQUIREMENTS:
Bachelor's degree, 3.2 GPA

AVAILABLE FOR QUALIFIED STUDENTS:
Research assistantships, teaching assistantships

ASSISTANTSHIPS:

INTERNSHIP POSSIBILITY:
Yes

INTERNSHIP REQUIRED:
No

NUMBER OF HOURS REQUIRED:
45 hours (3 credits)

CORE GRADUATE CLASSES:

DESCRIPTION OF TYPICAL INTERNSHIP EXPERIENCE:

COMMENTS:
The program offers two options: (a) professional and (b) research.

University College, Chichester

School of Sports Studies
College Lane, Chichester
West Sussex, England
PO19 4PE

Contact:	Jan Graydon	**Email:**	
Title:		**Website:**	
Phone:	01243 816320	**Area of Interest:**	Stress management
Fax:	01243 816080		
Email:	100443.2067@compuserve.com	**Contact:**	Terry McMorris
Website:		**Title:**	
Area of Interest:	Gender issues, motor skills	**Phone:**	
		Fax:	
Contact:	Ian Maynarrd	**Email:**	
Title:		**Website:**	
Phone:		**Area of Interest:**	Cognitive processes and fatigue
Fax:			

PROGRAM RATING

1   2   3   4   5   6   7

1 to 3 Applied Orientation, 3 to 6 Equal Emphasis, 6 to 7 Research Orientation: Unrated

DEGREE OFFERED:
Mphil/MS/PhD

NUMBER OF STUDENTS IN PROGRAM:
6

NUMBER OF STUDENTS IN EACH DEGREE PROGRAM:
Different system

NUMBER OF STUDENTS WHO APPLY/ARE ACCEPTED ANNUALLY:
6 apply/1-2 accepted

ADMISSION REQUIREMENTS:
Good standing, undergraduate degree in sport science or related area or psychology

AVAILABLE FOR QUALIFIED STUDENTS:

ASSISTANTSHIPS:

INTERNSHIP POSSIBILITY:
Consultancy experience available.

INTERNSHIP REQUIRED:

NUMBER OF HOURS REQUIRED:

CORE GRADUATE CLASSES:

DESCRIPTION OF TYPICAL INTERNSHIP EXPERIENCE:
Funding is difficult. There is sometimes the possibility of laboratory work or governing-body-funded consultancy work.

COMMENTS:
At present the master's and doctoral programs are not taught per se. Higher degree qualification is by research.

University of Alberta
Faculty of Physical Education and Recreation

University of Alberta
E488 Van Vliet Centre
Edmonton, Alberta
Canada
T6G 2H9

Contact: Anne Jordan
Title: Faculty Graduate Coordinator
Phone: 780.492.3198
Fax: 780.492.2364
Email: anne.jordan@ualberta.ca
Website: www.physedandrec.ualberta.ca
Area of Interest:

Contact: Billy Strean
Title: Associate Professor
Phone: 780.492.3890
Fax: 780.492.2364
Email: billy.strean@ualberta.ca
Website: www.per.ualberta.ca/Staff_bios/bstrean/
Area of Interest: Sport and exercise psychology, play, games, and fun; sport and physical activity instruction

Contact: Nicholas L. Holt
Title: Assistant Professor
Phone: 780.492.7386
Fax: 780.492.2364
Email: nick.holt@ualberta.ca
Website: www.physedandrec.ualberta.ca/pdfs/nickholt04.pdf
Area of Interest: Primary areas of interest include talent development, coping, youth sport and physical activity, qualitative research methodology, pedagogy.

Contact: John Dunn
Title: Associate Professor
Phone: 780.492.2831
Fax: 780.492.2364
Email: john.dunn@ualberta.ca
Website: www.per.ualberta.ca/jdunn/
Area of Interest: Sport psychology. Primary areas of interest include perfectionism, anxiety, and motivation in sport. Secondary area of interest in scale construction and psychometrics.

Contact: John C. Spence
Title: Associate Professor
Phone: 780.492.1379
Fax: 780.492.2364
Email: john.Spence@ualberta.ca
Website: www.ualberta.ca/~sedlab
Area of Interest: Exercise psychology, determinants of physical activity and sedentary behavior.

Contact: Brian Maraj
Title: Associate Professor
Phone: 780.492.5910
Fax: 780.492.1008
Email: bmaraj@ualberta.ca
Website: www.ualberta.ca/~bmaraj
Area of Interest: Perceptual motor behavior, primary area of interest is motor learning/control, most recently in persons with Down syndrome as well as other special populations. Secondary area of interest in the ecological approach to visual perception.

Contact: Ron Plotnikoff
Title: Professor
Phone: 780.492.1358
Fax: 780.492.2364
Email: ron.plotnikoff@ualberta.ca
Website: www.chps.ualberta.ca/research/ron_plotnikoff_r.htm
Area of Interest: Exercise and health behavior changes

Contact: Kerry S. Courneya
Title: Professor and Canada Research Chair in Physical Activity and Cancer
Phone: 780.492.1031 780.492.2829 (Lab)
Fax: 780.492.8003
Email: kerry.courneya@ualberta.ca
Website: www.per.ualberta.ca/kcourneya
Area of Interest: Behavioral medicine/exercise psychology

Contact: Wendy Rodgers
Title: Professor
Phone: 780.492.2677
Fax: 780.492.2364
Email: wendy.rodgers@ualberta.ca
Website: www.per.ualberta.ca/images/research/wrodgers.pdf
Area of Interest: Social psychology of exercise, health, and lifestyle behavior

PROGRAM RATING

1   2   3   4   5   **6.5**   7

1 to 3 Applied Orientation, 3 to 6 Equal Emphasis, 6 to 7 Research Orientation

DEGREE OFFERED:
MA /PhD

NUMBER OF STUDENTS IN PROGRAM:
8 to 12

NUMBER OF STUDENTS IN EACH DEGREE PROGRAM:
9 Master's/3 PhD

NUMBER OF STUDENTS WHO APPLY/ARE ACCEPTED ANNUALLY:
12-15 apply/3-4 accepted

ADMISSION REQUIREMENTS:
Four-year degree in P.E., master's in related field

AVAILABLE FOR QUALIFIED STUDENTS:
Graduate assistantships, scholarships, other forms of financial aid

ASSISTANTSHIPS:
Yes

INTERNSHIP POSSIBILITY:
Not officially

INTERNSHIP REQUIRED:

NUMBER OF HOURS REQUIRED:

CORE GRADUATE CLASSES:

PEDS 540: The Psychology of Performance in Sport and Physical Activity; PEDS 542: Social Science Perspectives in Physical Activity, Fitness, and Well-Being; PEDS 543: Seminar in the Learning and Memory of Movement; PEDS 544: Psychological Dimensions of Athletic Behaviour in the Competitive Sport Environment; PEDS 545: Exercise Oncology; PEDS 582: Psychosocial Dimensions in Sport and Physical Activity; PEDS 642: Advanced Seminar in the Psychology of Sport and Physical Activity; PERLS 541: Social Cognitive Approaches to Health-Promoting Behavior; PERLS 542: Social Science Perspectives of Physical Activity, Fitness, and Well-Being

DESCRIPTION OF TYPICAL INTERNSHIP EXPERIENCE:

COMMENTS:

University of Arizona
Department of Psychology

University of Arizona
Tucson, AZ 85721

Contact: Jean M. Williams
Title: Sport Psychology Information
Phone: 520.621.6984
Fax: 520.621.9306
Email: williams@u.arizona.edu
Website: www.arizona.edu
Area of Interest: Psychology of injury, relationship of psychological states to performance, performance enhancement, coaching behaviors, group dynamics

Contact: Jeff Stone
Title: Associate Professor of Social Psychology
Phone: 520.621.2438
Fax: 520.621.9306
Email: jeffs@u.arizona.edu
Website: www.arizona.edu/~jeffs
Area of Interest: Social psychology of sport, stereotyped perceptions of athletes, the role of stereotype threat in athletic preparation and performance, media images of athletes

Contact: Dawn Baugh
Title: Psychology Graduate Secretary
Phone: 520.621.7456
Fax:
Email: dawn@u.arizona.edu
Website: www.arizona.edu
Area of Interest:

PROGRAM RATING

1   2   3   4   **5.5**   6   7

1 to 3 Applied Orientation, 3 to 6 Equal Emphasis, 6 to 7 Research Orientation

DEGREE OFFERED:
PhD

NUMBER OF STUDENTS IN PROGRAM:

NUMBER OF STUDENTS IN EACH DEGREE PROGRAM:

NUMBER OF STUDENTS WHO APPLY/ARE ACCEPTED ANNUALLY:

ADMISSION REQUIREMENTS:
See Psychology Department website.

AVAILABLE FOR QUALIFIED STUDENTS:
Fellowships, teaching assistantships, other forms of financial aid

ASSISTANTSHIPS:

2% fellowships, 8% research assistantships, 90% teaching assistantships, 0% tuition waivers, 0% other forms of financial aid (Percentages are approximate; however, 100% of the students receive fellowships, research assistantships, or teaching assistantships for at least 4 years.)

INTERNSHIP POSSIBILITY:

Yes, up to 400 hours in sport psychology

INTERNSHIP REQUIRED:

No, except for the clinical program

NUMBER OF HOURS REQUIRED:

CORE GRADUATE CLASSES:

DESCRIPTION OF TYPICAL INTERNSHIP EXPERIENCE:

Internships are available with community athletes and university athletes for both performance enhancement and life skills development. Internships are also available at substance abuse centers, corporations, and fitness/wellness centers, primarily for stress management, general health promotion, and personal development.

COMMENTS:

There is no MS in sport psychology. The Department of Psychology offers only a PhD program with majors in the following areas: clinical psychology, social psychology, cognitive psychology, developmental psychology, psychobiology, and policy and law. Students within these major areas, in addition to fulfilling the requirements for the major, can declare a minor in sport psychology and thereby pursue course work, research, and internships specific to their sport psychology interests. We will not accept new applications for admission with an interest in sport psychology until Fall 2005. The graduate program emphasizes research training in order to equip students for both academic and applied careers. It strongly encourages interdisciplinary study for students and reflects the faculty's own interdisciplinary orientation to scholarship.

University of California, Los Angeles
Department of Psychology

University of California, Los Angeles
Attn.: UCLA PhD Program in Social Psychology
1285 Franz Hall, Box 951563
Los Angeles, CA 90095-1563

Contact: Bernie Weiner
Title: Professor of Psychology
Phone: 310.825.2750
Fax: 310.206.5895
Email: Weiner@psych.ucla.edu
Website: www.ucla.edu
Area of Interest: Cognitive approaches to motivations, applications to education, achievement motivation, and emotion

Contact: Robert Bjork
Title:
Phone:
Fax:
Email:
Website:
Area of Interest: Cognitive psychology, memory

Contact: Tara K. Scanlan
Title: Professor and Director of the International Center for Talent Development
Phone:
Fax:
Email:
Website:
Area of Interest: Motivation and emotion in athletes—youth sport through elite—as well as in performers in other talent domains (e.g., art, music, education). Interests include developmental and significant-other issues, and an integration of quantitative and qualitative research approaches. Currently developing a model of sport commitment and examining the role of enjoyment within this framework. The model is to be investigated and applied across talent domains. Also interested in effective parenting, teaching, and coaching for the gifted and talented.

PROGRAM RATING

1 2 3 4 5 **6** 7

1 to 3 Applied Orientation, 3 to 6 Equal Emphasis, 6 to 7 Research Orientation

DEGREE OFFERED:
PhD only (no MS)

NUMBER OF STUDENTS IN PROGRAM:

NUMBER OF STUDENTS IN EACH DEGREE PROGRAM:

NUMBER OF STUDENTS WHO APPLY/ARE ACCEPTED ANNUALLY:
100-120 apply/5-10 accepted

ADMISSION REQUIREMENTS:
Three letters of recommendation (preferably from research psychologists), GRE General Test, and GRE Subject Test in Psychology. All admitted students must have taken the following courses: Statistics; one course in either biology or zoology; two courses in physics or chemistry; and at least one mathematics course, preferably calculus or probability. Additionally, students should have taken two of the following: learning, physiological, or perception/information processing; and two of the following: developmental, social, or personality/abnormal psychology. Note: Although it is possible to gain admission with deficiencies in these requirements, they must be remedied within the first four quarters of graduate study.

AVAILABLE FOR QUALIFIED STUDENTS:
Postdoctoral fellowships, fellowships, research assistantships, teaching assistantships, other forms of financial aid (All students are covered by one or more of the above.)

ASSISTANTSHIPS:

INTERNSHIP POSSIBILITY:
Outreach: See comments (no traditional sport psychology internships).

INTERNSHIP REQUIRED:

NUMBER OF HOURS REQUIRED:

CORE GRADUATE CLASSES:

DESCRIPTION OF TYPICAL INTERNSHIP EXPERIENCE:

COMMENTS:
Sport psychology is offered within the Department of Psychology's social psychology area and is central to the newly founded International Center for Talent Development (ICTD). The ICTD is multidisciplinary and includes research, instruction, and outreach components. Postdoctoral fellowships and research assistantships are available. The ICTD focuses on understanding and facilitating the development of talent across a diverse range of domains (e.g., sport, music, art, education) and skill levels (e.g., youth-sport through world-class athletes). Talent development is viewed broadly to include issues such as the development of expertise; motivation and emotion; development (cognitive, motoric, and social); significant-other influences (family, coaches, teachers, peers); and the sociology involved in establishing talent domains. Center functions include research, outreach, and education.

University of Canberra

Centre for Sports Studies
PO Box 1
Belconnen, ACT
Australia
2616

Contact: John B. Gross
Title:
Phone: (06) 2012009
Fax: (06) 2015999
Email: gross@science.canberra.edu.au
Website: www.canberra.edu.au
Area of Interest: Coaching behaviors—attributions and sports performance

PROGRAM RATING

1   **2**   3   4   5   6   7

1 to 3 Applied Orientation, 3 to 6 Equal Emphasis, 6 to 7 Research Orientation

DEGREE OFFERED:
Graduate Diploma in applied psychology

NUMBER OF STUDENTS IN PROGRAM:
3

NUMBER OF STUDENTS IN EACH DEGREE PROGRAM:
100% Graduate Diploma

NUMBER OF STUDENTS WHO APPLY/ARE ACCEPTED ANNUALLY:
10 apply/3 accepted

ADMISSION REQUIREMENTS:
Graduate Diploma—three years of psychology plus a sports science major

AVAILABLE FOR QUALIFIED STUDENTS:

ASSISTANTSHIPS:
0% fellowships, 0% research assistantships, 0% teaching assistantships, 0% tuition waivers, 0% other forms of financial aid

INTERNSHIP POSSIBILITY:
Yes

INTERNSHIP REQUIRED:
No

NUMBER OF HOURS REQUIRED:
None

CORE GRADUATE CLASSES:

DESCRIPTION OF TYPICAL INTERNSHIP EXPERIENCE:
Graduate Diploma—two weeks' attendance at an academy or institute of sport

COMMENTS:
The Graduate Diploma in applied psychology involves one year of course work, including a major research project and a two-week placement at an academy or institute of sport. Fees per year for the Graduate Diploma are approximately $12,000 (Australian).

University of Edinburgh
Department of PE, Sport, & Leisure Studies

University of Edinburgh
Cramond Road North
Edinburgh, Scotland
EH4 6JD

Contact: Dave Collins
Title:
Phone: 44.131.312.6001
Fax: 44.131.312.6375
Email: d.collins@ed.ac.uk
Website:
Area of Interest: Interdisciplinary approaches to research and support in sport and exercise psychology

Contact: Richard Cox
Title:
Phone:
Fax:
Email:
Website:
Area of Interest: Mood-state profiling, behavioural aspects of sport psychology

Contact: Angela Abbott
Title:
Phone:
Fax:
Email:
Website:
Area of Interest: Talent identification and development

Contact: Helen Milne
Title:
Phone:
Fax:
Email:
Website:
Area of Interest: Imagery and MSM

Contact: Duncan Mascarenhas
Title:
Phone:
Fax:
Email:
Website:
Area of Interest: Psychology of officiating

Contact: Patrick Mortimer
Title:
Phone:
Fax:
Email:
Website:
Area of Interest: Team decision making

Contact: Gavin Loze
Title:
Phone:
Fax:
Email:
Website:
Area of Interest: Sport psychophysiology

Contact: Hugh Richards
Title:
Phone:
Fax:
Email:
Website:
Area of Interest: Coping, social identity

PROGRAM RATING

1   2   3   4   5   6   7

1 to 3 Applied Orientation, 3 to 6 Equal Emphasis, 6 to 7 Research Orientation: Unrated

DEGREE OFFERED:
MSc/MPhil/PhD

NUMBER OF STUDENTS IN PROGRAM:
25

NUMBER OF STUDENTS IN EACH DEGREE PROGRAM:
12 MSc, 13 MPhil/PhD

NUMBER OF STUDENTS WHO APPLY/ARE ACCEPTED ANNUALLY:
25 apply/8 accepted

ADMISSION REQUIREMENTS:
First (and possibly master's) degree in a cogent subject, demonstrated interest in and commitment to chosen area, telephone/personal interview (plus university admission requirements)

AVAILABLE FOR QUALIFIED STUDENTS:

ASSISTANTSHIPS:
10% fellowships, 30% research assistantships, 20% teaching assistantships

INTERNSHIP POSSIBILITY:
Yes

INTERNSHIP REQUIRED:
No

NUMBER OF HOURS REQUIRED:

CORE GRADUATE CLASSES:

DESCRIPTION OF TYPICAL INTERNSHIP EXPERIENCE:
Extremely varied and personalized. Degree of hands-on experience depends on time of year, sport season, etc.

COMMENTS:

University of Exeter
School of Health Sciences

University of Exeter
Heavitree Road
Exeter, United Kingdom
EX1 2LU

Contact:	Tim Rees	**Contact:**	Andrew Sparkes
Title:		**Title:**	
Phone:	+44 1392 262892	**Phone:**	
Fax:	+44 1392 264726	**Fax:**	
Email:	E.M.Davies@exeter.ac.uk	**Email:**	
Website:	www.ex.ac.uk/sshs	**Website:**	
Area of Interest:		**Area of Interest:**	Interpretive paradigm, body and self, innovation and change

PROGRAM RATING

1   2   3   4   5   **6**   7

1 to 3 Applied Orientation, 3 to 6 Equal Emphasis, 6 to 7 Research Orientation

DEGREE OFFERED:
MSc in Sport and Health Sciences; MPhil/PhD

NUMBER OF STUDENTS IN PROGRAM:
45

NUMBER OF STUDENTS IN EACH DEGREE PROGRAM:
25 MSc; 20

NUMBER OF STUDENTS WHO APPLY/ARE ACCEPTED ANNUALLY:
55 MSc apply, 30 accepted; 30 MPhil/PhD apply, 4-10 accepted

ADMISSION REQUIREMENTS:
Good honors degree (2.1) or B average, usually in psychology or exercise and sport sciences

AVAILABLE FOR QUALIFIED STUDENTS:

ASSISTANTSHIPS:
competitive scholarships available for £1000 to £2500

INTERNSHIP POSSIBILITY:
No

INTERNSHIP REQUIRED:
No

NUMBER OF HOURS REQUIRED:

CORE GRADUATE CLASSES:
For MSc and MPhil/PhD students follow two core quantitative and qualitative research methods modules. For MSc, students also undertake a dissertation and choose 6 modules form 8 options (pediatric exercise science; clinical exercise physiology; biomechanics; laboratory techniques; body, self, and culture; sport and social change; current issues in sport and exercise psychology; applied sport and exercise psychology.

DESCRIPTION OF TYPICAL INTERNSHIP EXPERIENCE:

COMMENTS:
In the exercise and sport psychology group at Exeter, expertise exists in the following: social psychology of sport; elite sport performance; psychometrics and instrument development; effectiveness of physical activity promotion interventions; physical activity and psychological well-being; exercise and public health; large scale public intervention programmes; relationships between intentions and volition in exercise psychology; hedonic happiness, eudemonic happiness, life aspiration and physical activity; cognitive mechanisms underlying sexual harassment in sport; data analysis using structural equation modeling, hierarchical linear modeling, and meta-analysis. Staff members in this area are Dr Nikos Chatzisarantis, Dr Tim Rees, and Dr Adrian Taylor. Qualitative data analysis is relatively new to exercise and sport psychology, and in Professor Sparkes, Exeter has the foremost authority on the topic in European exercise and sport sciences. Other staff members in this area are Dr Dave Brown and Dr Brett Smith.

University of Florida
Department of Applied Physiology and Kinesiology

College of Health and Human Performance
25 Florida Gymnasium
University of Florida
Gainesville, FL 32611

Contact: Christopher M. Janelle
Title: Associate Professor
Phone: 352.392.0584 (x 1270)
Fax: 352.392.0316
Email: cjanelle@hhp.ufl.edu
Website: www.hhp.ufl.edu/ess/FACULTY/cjanelle/cjanelle.htm
Area of Interest: Attention, visual search, emotion, expertise, body-image issues

Contact: Peter Giacobbi, Jr.
Title: Assistant Professor
Phone: 352.392.0584 (x 1324)
Fax: 352.392.5262
Email: pgiacobb@hhp.ufl.edu
Website: www.hhp.ufl.edu/ess/FACULTY/pgiacobbi/pgiacobbi.htm
Area of Interest: Arousal/anxiety regulation, coping skills, athlete coachability

Contact: Heather A. Hausenblas
Title: Assistant Professor
Phone: 352.392.0584 (x 1292)
Fax: 352.392.5262
Email: heatherh@hhp.ufl.edu
Website: www.hhp.ufl.edu/ess/FACULTY/heatherh/heatherh.htm
Area of Interest: Exercise psychology, eating disorders, exercise dependence, body image

PROGRAM RATING

1   2   3   4   5   **6**   7

1 to 3 Applied Orientation, 3 to 6 Equal Emphasis, 6 to 7 Research Orientation

DEGREE OFFERED:
MS/PhD (sport and exercise psychology specialization)

NUMBER OF STUDENTS IN PROGRAM:
30

NUMBER OF STUDENTS IN EACH DEGREE PROGRAM:
40% MS/60% PhD

NUMBER OF STUDENTS WHO APPLY/ARE ACCEPTED ANNUALLY:
40 apply/8 accepted

ADMISSION REQUIREMENTS:
1000 GRE (the higher the better), 3.00 GPA (minimum)

AVAILABLE FOR QUALIFIED STUDENTS:

Teaching assistantships, other forms of financial aid

ASSISTANTSHIPS:

5% fellowships, 5% research assistantships (including tuition waivers), 50% teaching assistantships (including tuition waivers)

INTERNSHIP POSSIBILITY:

Yes

INTERNSHIP REQUIRED:

No

NUMBER OF HOURS REQUIRED:

To be negotiated

CORE GRADUATE CLASSES:

DESCRIPTION OF TYPICAL INTERNSHIP EXPERIENCE:

Flexible

COMMENTS:

Emphasis is on the study of cognitive, psychological, and psychobiological factors contributing to learning and performance excellence, as well as on psychological factors associated with exercise and fitness performance. The orientation is toward the scholarly aspects of the specialization, with research conducted in laboratory or field settings. Students can be involved in applied settings. Students at the master's level are prepared primarily for doctoral work, and doctoral graduates are prepared primarily for university positions and secondarily for applied settings.

University of Georgia
Department of Kinesiology

University of Georgia
115 I Ramsey Center
300 River Road
Athens, GA 30602-6554

Contact: Rod K. Dishman
Title: Professor
Phone: 706.542.9840
Fax: 706.542.3148
Email: rdishman@uga.edu
Website: www.coe.uga.edu/kinesiology
Area of Interest: Exercise neuroscience, stress, determinants of exercise adherence, physical activity intervention

Contact: Patrick J. O'Connor
Title: Professor
Phone: 706.542.4382
Fax: 706.542.3148
Email: poconnor@uga.edu
Website: www.coe.uga.edu/kinesiology
Area of Interest: Feelings of energy and fatigue, acute and chronic pain, anxiety, depression, sleep

Contact: Phil Tomporowski
Title: Associate Professor
Phone: 706.542.4183
Fax: 706.542.3148
Email: ptomporo@uga.edu
Website: www.coe.uga.edu/kinesiology
Area of Interest: Effects of acute and chronic exercise on information processing and cognition, particularly in older adults

PROGRAM RATING

1   2   3   4   5   6   **7**

1 to 3 Applied Orientation, 3 to 6 Equal Emphasis, 6 to 7 Research Orientation

DEGREE OFFERED:
MS/PhD

NUMBER OF STUDENTS IN PROGRAM:
6 to 8

NUMBER OF STUDENTS IN EACH DEGREE PROGRAM:
50% MS/50% PhD

NUMBER OF STUDENTS WHO APPLY/ARE ACCEPTED ANNUALLY:
Approximately 10 apply/approximately 2-3 accepted

ADMISSION REQUIREMENTS:
1000 GRE, undergraduate GPA of 3.00 (2.60 for MA), graduate GPA of 3.50. A TOEFL score of 600 is required for foreign students. A student with a BA or BS can be admitted to the PhD program if the fol-

lowing formula is satisfied: undergraduate GPA x 1000 + GRE verbal + GRE quantitative > 4300. Preference is given to students who have strong backgrounds in biopsychology, cognitive science, and/or exercise science and who have research interests compatible with ongoing research in the program.

AVAILABLE FOR QUALIFIED STUDENTS:
Research assistantships, teaching assistantships

ASSISTANTSHIPS:
60% fellowships/laboratory assistantships, 40% teaching assistantships, 0% tuition waivers, 0% other forms of financial aid

INTERNSHIP POSSIBILITY:
No

INTERNSHIP REQUIRED:

NUMBER OF HOURS REQUIRED:

CORE GRADUATE CLASSES:
See **Website:** www.uga.edu/exs

DESCRIPTION OF TYPICAL INTERNSHIP EXPERIENCE:

COMMENTS:
The Department of Kinesiology has well-equipped Exercise Psychology and Cognition and Skill-Acquisition laboratories. The Exercise Psychology Lab is equipped for assessing psychophysiological phenomena including GSR, ECG, EMG, EEG, impedance electrocardiography, beat-to-beat blood pressures, and polysomnography under controlled and field conditions. The Cognition and Skill-Acquisition Laboratory is equipped for assessing human cognition, information processing, and learning. The Aging and Physical Performance Exercise Vascular Biology Metabolism and Body Composition Athletic Training and the Muscle Biology Laboratories of the Exercise Physiology program support interdisciplinary research. Collaboration with laboratories in pharmacology, behavioral neuroscience, foods and nutrition, and medical microbiology permit collaborative studies of psychopharmacologic, brain, molecular, neuroendocrine, and psychoimmunologic responses to exercise and behavioral stressors. The Exercise Physiology Laboratories permit cross-disciplinary research in exercise science. A Fitness Center conducts Adult Fitness and Cardiac Rehabilitation programs for university faculty/staff and the Athens Community. Currently funded NIH projects are studying interventions to increase physical activity in the community and at the workplace, the effects of exercise training during pregnancy, and the effects of exercise training on cognitive function among children.

University of Houston
Department of Health, Physical Education, and Recreation

104 Garrison Gym
University of Houston
Houston, TX 77204-6321

Contact: Dale G. Pease
Title: Professor
Phone: 713.743.9838
Fax: 713.743.9860
Email: dpease@uh.edu
Website: www.hhp.uh.edu
Area of Interest: Sport psychology, motor learning, leadership, psychophysiology

Contact: Norma Olvera
Title: Assistant Professor
Phone: 713.743.9848
Fax: 713.743.9860
Email: nolvera@uh.edu
Website: www.hhp.uh.edu
Area of Interest: Psychological factors and physical activity

Contact: Charles Layne
Title: Associate Professor and Chair
Phone: 713.743.9868
Fax: 713.743.9860
Email: Charles.Layne@mail.uh.edu
Website: www.hhp.uh.edu
Area of Interest: Motor learning, motor control

Contact: Luc Tremblay
Title: Assistant Professor
Phone: 713.743.9335
Fax: 713.743.9860
Email: Ltremblay@uh.edu
Website: www.hhp.uh.edu
Area of Interest: Motor control, motor development

PROGRAM RATING

1 2 3 4 5 **6** 7

1 to 3 Applied Orientation, 3 to 6 Equal Emphasis, 6 to 7 Research Orientation

DEGREE OFFERED:
MEd in physical education, MS in exercise science (emphasis area within motor behavior track), PhD in kinesiology (emphasis area in sport/exercise psychology)

NUMBER OF STUDENTS IN PROGRAM:
12

NUMBER OF STUDENTS IN EACH DEGREE PROGRAM:
50% MEd and MS/50% PhD

NUMBER OF STUDENTS WHO APPLY/ARE ACCEPTED ANNUALLY:
15 apply/5-6 accepted

ADMISSION REQUIREMENTS:

MEd: GRE (30% verbal + quantitative and 3.5 writing), 3.0 GPA; MS and PhD: GRE (35% verbal + quantitative and 4.0 writing), 3.25 GPA

AVAILABLE FOR QUALIFIED STUDENTS:

Research assistantships, teaching assistantships

ASSISTANTSHIPS:

0% fellowships, 10% research assistantships, 70% teaching assistantships, 100% tuition waivers (for those who qualify), 0% other forms of financial aid

INTERNSHIP POSSIBILITY:

Available, but very limited

INTERNSHIP REQUIRED:

No

NUMBER OF HOURS REQUIRED:

36 hours for MED and MS; 66 for PhD

CORE GRADUATE CLASSES:

PhD—18 hours required (Statistics, Measurement, and Research Design). 15-hour psychological core includes Theory and Application.

DESCRIPTION OF TYPICAL INTERNSHIP EXPERIENCE:

COMMENTS:

Focus of program is on education and research.

University of Idaho
Division of Health, Physical Education, Recreation, and Dance

University of Idaho
107 PEB
Moscow, ID 83844-2401

Contact: Damon Burton
Title:
Phone: 208.885.2186
Fax: 208.885.5929
Email: dburton@uidaho.edu
Website: www.uidaho.edu/ed/hperd/
Area of Interest: Motivation/goal setting, stress/anxiety, coaching education, PST program evaluation, exercise adherence, leadership

PROGRAM RATING

1 2 3 **4** 5 6 7

1 to 3 Applied Orientation, 3 to 6 Equal Emphasis, 6 to 7 Research Orientation

DEGREE OFFERED:
MS/PhD

NUMBER OF STUDENTS IN PROGRAM:
MS program: 3 to 4 full-time/1 to 2 part-time; PhD program: 3 or 4 full-time/1 to 2 part-time

NUMBER OF STUDENTS IN EACH DEGREE PROGRAM:
50% MS/50% PhD

NUMBER OF STUDENTS WHO APPLY/ARE ACCEPTED ANNUALLY:
MS program: 18-20 apply/1-2 accepted; PhD program: 12-15 apply/maximum of 1 accepted

ADMISSION REQUIREMENTS:
MS program: minimum of 3.00 GPA, 1000 GRE; PhD program: 3.00 GPA undergraduate, 3.50 GPA master's, 1050 GRE

AVAILABLE FOR QUALIFIED STUDENTS:
Teaching assistantships, one assistantship through Vandal Sport Psychology Services

ASSISTANTSHIPS:
Master's (4): 0% fellowships, 0% graduate assistantships, 75% teaching assistantships, 0% tuition waivers, 25% other forms of financial aid. PhD (2): 0% fellowships, 50% graduate assistantships, 50% teaching assistantships, 0% tuition waivers, 0% other forms of financial aid

INTERNSHIP POSSIBILITY:
Yes, MS and PhD

INTERNSHIP REQUIRED:
Yes, MS and practicum at PhD level

NUMBER OF HOURS REQUIRED:
6-9 credit hours

CORE GRADUATE CLASSES:

DESCRIPTION OF TYPICAL INTERNSHIP EXPERIENCE:
Master's internships can be conducted as part of Vandal Sport Psychology Services or, by arrangement, in the Washington State University Athletic Department. Previous students have held internships in such sports as basketball, golf, volleyball, tennis, gymnastics, and track and field—all at the university level (except for gymnastics). Normally, sport-related internships involve developing, implementing, and evaluating PST programs for individual athletes and teams. Additionally, doctoral practica can be set up in the UI Counseling Center.

COMMENTS:
Our two-year master's program is designed to develop good researchers and skilled consultants, with the program placing relatively equal emphasis on research and application. Students typically use their degrees as steppingstones into such career fields as (a) coaching/teaching; (b) sports medicine, exercise and wellness; and (c) PhD work in educational or clinical sport psychology. The program has good flexibility in both curriculum and internship possibilities, and most recent master's students have completed by graduation all course work and about 150 of the 400 hours of supervised sport psychology internship/practicum work necessary to become a certified AAASP consultant. Master's requirements call for 45 credits of course work, with 33 credits in sport psychology and sport science courses supplemented by elective course work in psychology and counseling. Washington State University is only eight miles away, in Pullman. Thus, master's internship possibilities are available in a variety of sports, either at WSU or through Vandal Sport Psychology Services (VSPS) in the Idaho Athletic Department. During their first year, master's students attain consultation experience working as mentors in our mental training courses for varsity athletes; then, during their second year, they normally begin consulting with VSPS before doing their 6-credit internships. Master's students may combine their internships and theses to test applied sport psychology questions or to evaluate the effectiveness of PST programs implemented on teams with whom they are consulting. However, many students also select traditional thesis topics in such areas as motivation, stress/coping, anxiety, goal setting, and exercise adherence. Doctoral program: Our doctoral program is designed to employ a focus similar to that of our master's program, but most elective course work is taken at WSU, in psychology and counseling psychology. Currently, students take 20-1 credits of course work in WSU's APA-approved counseling psychology program as well as 12 credits of psychology foundation courses. Doctoral students currently are doing 80% or more of the 60+ hours of service per week we currently provide to the Vandal Athletic Department through Vandal Sport Psychology Services.

The doctoral program also places relatively equal emphasis on research and application skills, and students have opportunities to gain practical experience in ongoing research projects, academic teaching, and VSPS/WSU sport psychology consultation.

University of Illinois
Department of Kinesiology

University of Illinois
336 Freer Hall
906 South Goodwin Avenue
Urbana, IL 61801

Contact: Edward McAuley
Title: Professor
Phone: 217.333.6487 (Academic Affairs Office)
Fax: 217.244.7322
Email: emcauley@uiuc.edu
Website: www.kines.uiuc.edu/expsych/
Area of Interest: Exercise and health psychology, aging, social cognitive factors and adherence

Contact: Steven Petruzzello
Title: Associate Professor
Phone: 217.244.7325
Fax: 217.244.7322
Email: petruzze@staff.uiuc.edu
Website:
Area of Interest: Psychophysiology of exercise

Contact: Charles Hillman
Title: Assistant Professor
Phone: 217.244.2663
Fax: 217.244.7322
Email: chhillma@staff.uiuc.edu
Website:
Area of Interest: Exercise psychophysiology

PROGRAM RATING

1 2 3 4 5 6 **7**

1 to 3 Applied Orientation, 3 to 6 Equal Emphasis, 6 to 7 Research Orientation

DEGREE OFFERED:
MS/PhD

NUMBER OF STUDENTS IN PROGRAM:
12

NUMBER OF STUDENTS IN EACH DEGREE PROGRAM:
50% MS/50% PhD

NUMBER OF STUDENTS WHO APPLY/ARE ACCEPTED ANNUALLY:
20 apply/4-5 accepted

ADMISSION REQUIREMENTS:
GPA of 3.00 on a 4.00 scale; GRE total score of 1500 for MS, 1800 for PhD

AVAILABLE FOR QUALIFIED STUDENTS:
Fellowships, research assistantships, teaching assistantships, tuition waivers

ASSISTANTSHIPS:
5% fellowships, 60% research assistantships, 35% teaching assistantships, 0% tuition waivers

INTERNSHIP POSSIBILITY:
No

INTERNSHIP REQUIRED:
No

NUMBER OF HOURS REQUIRED:

CORE GRADUATE CLASSES:

DESCRIPTION OF TYPICAL INTERNSHIP EXPERIENCE:

COMMENTS:
Students are encouraged to pursue interdisciplinary research interests in this program, as many such opportunities exist on campus. Faculty in the area of exercise and sport psychology engage in collaborative research with faculty from Community Health, Medicine, Psychology, and the Beckman Institute for Advanced Science and Technology, as well as with individuals in other areas of Kinesiology. Our faculty have well-equipped laboratories for conducting their own research and that of their graduate students. A new (2003) 3200-square-foot Exercise Psychology Laboratory has recently been added to our facilities. Most of the research being conducted in the area of exercise psychology is funded by the National Institutes of Health. Graduate students are offered a unique opportunity to be a part of a number of large, interdisciplinary research teams during the course of their studies. We encourage prospective students to contact faculty personally to discuss research, teaching, and educational opportunities in exercise and sport psychology at the University of Illinois. In addition, our departmental homepage is very well developed and contains considerable information about the faculty and the program.

University of Iowa
Department of Sport, Health, Leisure, and Physical Studies

University of Iowa
E102 Fieldhouse
Iowa City, IA 52242

Contact: Dawn E. Stephens
Title: Associate Professor, Sport Psychology
Phone: 319.335.9348, 319.335.9335 (main office)
Fax: 319.335.6669
Email: dawn-e-stephens@uiowa.edu
Website: www.uiowa.edu/~hss/faculty/Stephens.htm
Area of Interest: Psychosocial predictors of physical activity, motivational issues, social norms, quantitative research methods

Contact: Kerry R. McGAnnon
Title: Assistant Professor, Health Promotion
Phone: 319.335.8455
Fax: 319.335.6669
Email: Kerry-mcgannon@uiowa.edu
Website: www.uiowa.edu/~hss/faculty/Mcgannon.htm
Area of Interest: Critical interpretations of exercise and physical activity participation, social theory and its applications to exercise and physical activity, self and identity, qualitative research methods.

PROGRAM RATING

1 2 3 4 5 6 **7**

1 to 3 Applied Orientation, 3 to 6 Equal Emphasis, 6 to 7 Research Orientation

DEGREE OFFERED:
MA/PhD

NUMBER OF STUDENTS IN PROGRAM:
10

NUMBER OF STUDENTS IN EACH DEGREE PROGRAM:
60% MA/40% PhD

NUMBER OF STUDENTS WHO APPLY/ARE ACCEPTED ANNUALLY:
MA: 12 apply / 3 or 4 accepted, PhD: 5 apply, 1 accepted

ADMISSION REQUIREMENTS:
GRE: 50th percentile in Verbal and Quantitative and score of 4.5 or above for GRE writing component, 3.00 GPA, 3 letters of recommendation, transcripts

AVAILABLE FOR QUALIFIED STUDENTS:
Fellowships, research assistantships, teaching assistantships

ASSISTANTSHIPS:
(Vary) 5% Fellowships, 20% Research Assistantships, 75% Teaching assistantships.

INTERNSHIP POSSIBILITY:
No

INTERNSHIP REQUIRED:
No

NUMBER OF HOURS REQUIRED:

CORE GRADUATE CLASSES:

DESCRIPTION OF TYPICAL INTERNSHIP EXPERIENCE:

COMMENTS:
This program's emphasis is on critical theoretical perspectives and both quantitative and qualitative research methodologies to study the socio-cultural determinants of physical activity participation with an emphasis on marginalized segments of the populations (e.g., women, people of low socio-economic status).

University of Kansas
Department of Health, Sport, and Exercise Sciences

University of Kansas
161 Robinson
Lawrence, KS 66045

Contact:	David Templin	**Email:**	
Title:		**Website:**	
Phone:	913.864.0778	**Area of Interest:**	Social psychology of sport
Fax:	913.864.3343		
Email:		**Contact:**	Mark Thompson
Website:	www.ukans.edu	**Title:**	
Area of Interest:	Applied psychology of sport	**Phone:**	
		Fax:	
Contact:	Jim LaPoint	**Email:**	drt@ku.edu
Title:		**Website:**	
Phone:		**Area of Interest:**	
Fax:			

PROGRAM RATING

1   2   3   4   5   6   7

1 to 3 Applied Orientation, 3 to 6 Equal Emphasis, 6 to 7 Research Orientation

DEGREE OFFERED:
MS/EdD/PhD

NUMBER OF STUDENTS IN PROGRAM:
10 MS/10 PhD

NUMBER OF STUDENTS IN EACH DEGREE PROGRAM:
50% MS/50% PhD

NUMBER OF STUDENTS WHO APPLY/ARE ACCEPTED ANNUALLY:
30 MS apply/10-15 MS accepted; 20 PhD apply/3 PhD accepted

ADMISSION REQUIREMENTS:
MS: undergraduate degree in physical education, GPA of 3.00; PhD: undergraduate or master's degree in physical education, master's GPA of 3.50, undergraduate GPA of 3.00, GRE verbal + quantitative > or = 1000, coaching or playing background in sport

AVAILABLE FOR QUALIFIED STUDENTS:
Teaching assistantships (PhD)

ASSISTANTSHIPS:
0% fellowships, 0% research assistantships, 25% teaching assistantships, 25% tuition waivers, 50% other forms of financial aid

INTERNSHIP POSSIBILITY:
Yes (PhD)

INTERNSHIP REQUIRED:
Yes (PhD)

NUMBER OF HOURS REQUIRED:
One season or semester required; two years possible

CORE GRADUATE CLASSES:

DESCRIPTION OF TYPICAL INTERNSHIP EXPERIENCE:
Several options are available. First, the student can work as a sport psychology consultant for a high school district (with five high schools). Second, the student can spend consulting time in the University of Kansas Peak Performance Clinic, working with individual athletes and doing high school team seminars. Third, the student can work as a sport psychology consultant with one of the 16 teams at the university.

COMMENTS:
The program offers course work and opportunities that are applied in nature. Students are prepared in the doctoral program to pursue careers in higher education as applied sport psychologists or to work as applied sport psychology consultants in private practice. The program includes the Peak Performance Clinic and an internship program involving the University of Kansas Athletic Department and Kansas City High School athletic programs. Students who are accepted must have a strong sporting background (playing and/or coaching), a background in physical education or a related field, and strong interpersonal skills. An interview is suggested at the doctoral level. This program does not lead to licensure.

University of Manitoba
Department of Physical Education

University of Manitoba
Faculty of Physical Education and Recreation Studies
Frank Kennedy Building
Winnipeg, MB
Canada
R3T 2N2

Contact: Dennis Hrycaiko
Title: Physical Education
Phone: 204.474.8764
Fax: 204.474.7634
Email: hrycaik@Ms.UManitoba.ca
Website: www.UManitoba.ca/Faculties/Physed/
Area of Interest: Research and applied, various aspects of sport performance enhancement

PROGRAM RATING

1   2   3   **4**   5   6   7

1 to 3 Applied Orientation, 3 to 6 Equal Emphasis, 6 to 7 Research Orientation

DEGREE OFFERED:
MA/MSc/PhD (Note: The MA and PhD degrees are in clinical psychology, an APA-approved program. Sport psychology is a subspecialty within clinical psychology. The MSc degree in physical education has a specialization in sport psychology.)

NUMBER OF STUDENTS IN PROGRAM:
37 MSc in physical education

NUMBER OF STUDENTS IN EACH DEGREE PROGRAM:
30% MA/70% PhD in clinical psychology; 6 students in sport psychology

NUMBER OF STUDENTS WHO APPLY/ARE ACCEPTED ANNUALLY:
10 apply/1-2 accepted in clinical psychology; 10 apply/5-6 accepted in sport psychology

ADMISSION REQUIREMENTS:
Must meet Department of Psychology requirements for clinical psychology program. Check with programs for specific admissions requirements.

AVAILABLE FOR QUALIFIED STUDENTS:
Teaching assistantships

ASSISTANTSHIPS:
5% fellowships, 5% research assistantships, 10% teaching assistantships, 0% tuition waivers, 0% other forms of financial aid

INTERNSHIP POSSIBILITY:
Yes

INTERNSHIP REQUIRED:
Yes. PhD students in clinical psychology must complete an APA-approved internship in Canada or the US.

NUMBER OF HOURS REQUIRED:
The APA-accredited internship is for one academic year (September to May) and does not specify a number of hours.

CORE GRADUATE CLASSES:

DESCRIPTION OF TYPICAL INTERNSHIP EXPERIENCE:
Varies widely, but emphasis is clinical psychology.

COMMENTS:
Physical Education offers a Master of Science degree program with the opportunity to specialize in sport psychology. The program has considerable flexibility and can be tailored to meet interests of individual students. In the clinical psychology program, students apply to one of two streams, a generalist stream or a behavior modification stream. Students who select the behavior modification stream have the option of receiving specialized training in sport psychology. Training includes readings; courses in sport psychology; thesis research in sport psychology; and sport psychology practica with Dr. Martin, working with a provincial sport team. Training is very behaviorally oriented.

University of Manitoba
Department of Psychology

University of Manitoba
St. Paul's College
Winnipeg, MB
Canada
R3T 2M6

Contact: Garry Martin
Title: Psychology
Phone: 204.474.8589
Fax: 204.275.5421
Email:
Website: www.UManitoba.ca/Faculties/Physed/
Area of Interest: Research/applied performance enhancement

PROGRAM RATING

1   2   3   **4**   5   6   7

1 to 3 Applied Orientation, 3 to 6 Equal Emphasis, 6 to 7 Research Orientation

DEGREE OFFERED:
MA/MSc/PhD (Note: The MA and PhD degrees are in clinical psychology, an APA-approved program. Sport psychology is a subspecialty within clinical psychology. The MSc degree in physical education has a specialization in sport psychology.)

NUMBER OF STUDENTS IN PROGRAM:
55 in clinical psychology

NUMBER OF STUDENTS IN EACH DEGREE PROGRAM:
30% MA/70% PhD in clinical psychology; 6 students in sport psychology

NUMBER OF STUDENTS WHO APPLY/ARE ACCEPTED ANNUALLY:
10 apply/1-2 accepted in clinical psychology; 10 apply/5-6 accepted in sport psychology

ADMISSION REQUIREMENTS:
Must meet Department of Psychology requirements for clinical psychology program. Check with programs for specific admissions requirements.

AVAILABLE FOR QUALIFIED STUDENTS:
Teaching assistantships

ASSISTANTSHIPS:
5% fellowships, 5% research assistantships, 10% teaching assistantships, 0% tuition waivers, 0% other forms of financial aid

INTERNSHIP POSSIBILITY:
Yes

INTERNSHIP REQUIRED:
Yes. PhD students in clinical psychology must complete an APA-approved internship in Canada or the US.

NUMBER OF HOURS REQUIRED:
The APA-accredited internship is for one academic year (September to May) and does not specify a number of hours.

CORE GRADUATE CLASSES:

DESCRIPTION OF TYPICAL INTERNSHIP EXPERIENCE:
Varies widely, but emphasis is clinical psychology.

COMMENTS:
Physical Education offers a Master of Science degree program with the opportunity to specialize in sport psychology. The program has considerable flexibility and can be tailored to meet interests of individual students. In the clinical psychology program, students apply to one of two streams, a generalist stream or a behavior modification stream. Students who select the behavior modification stream have the option of receiving specialized training in sport psychology. Training includes readings; courses in sport psychology; thesis research in sport psychology; and sport psychology practica with Dr. Martin, working with a provincial sport team. Training is very behaviorally oriented.

University of Maryland, College Park
Department of Kinesiology

University of Maryland
HLHP Building
College Park, MD 20742

Contact:	Donald H. Steel
Title:	Coordinator
Phone:	301.405.2490
Fax:	301.314.9167
Email:	
Website:	
Area of Interest:	Anxiety

Contact:	Brad D. Hatfield
Title:	
Phone:	301.405.2490, 301.405.2450 (office)
Fax:	301.314.9167
Email:	bh5@umail.umd.edu
Website:	
Area of Interest:	

Contact:	Seppo Iso-Ahola
Title:	
Phone:	
Fax:	
Email:	
Website:	
Area of Interest:	Social psychology and mental training

Contact:	Elizabeth Y. Brown
Title:	
Phone:	
Fax:	
Email:	
Website:	
Area of Interest:	Sportvision

PROGRAM RATING

1   2   3   4   5   **6**   7

1 to 3 Applied Orientation, 3 to 6 Equal Emphasis, 6 to 7 Research Orientation

DEGREE OFFERED:
MA/PhD

NUMBER OF STUDENTS IN PROGRAM:
40

NUMBER OF STUDENTS IN EACH DEGREE PROGRAM:
50% MA/50% PhD

NUMBER OF STUDENTS WHO APPLY/ARE ACCEPTED ANNUALLY:

ADMISSION REQUIREMENTS:
3.00 GPA, GRE

AVAILABLE FOR QUALIFIED STUDENTS:
Teaching assistantships

ASSISTANTSHIPS:
10% fellowships, 0% research assistantships, 90% teaching assistantships, 0% tuition waivers, 0% other forms of financial aid

INTERNSHIP POSSIBILITY:
No

INTERNSHIP REQUIRED:

NUMBER OF HOURS REQUIRED:

CORE GRADUATE CLASSES:

DESCRIPTION OF TYPICAL INTERNSHIP EXPERIENCE:

COMMENTS:
The program is oriented towards the social psychology and the psychophysiological aspects of exercise and sport psychology. There is collaborative laboratory support with the Exercise Physiology Lab at the University of Maryland, as well as with other federal research institutions and the Naval Medical Research Institute at the Bethesda Naval Hospital. The clinical aspects of sport psychology are currently limited to academic coverage with the graduate course work.

University of Memphis
Department of Health and Sport Sciences

University of Memphis
Field House 1069
Memphis, TN 38152

Contact: Mary Fry
Title:
Phone: 901.678.4986, 901.678.4410 (department)
Fax: 901.678.3591
Email: maryfry@memphis.edu
Website: hmse.memphis.edu
Area of Interest: Motivation to participate in physical activity across the life span, developmental sport psychology, achievement motivation research, motivational climate

PROGRAM RATING

1   2   3   **4**   5   6   7

1 to 3 Applied Orientation, 3 to 6 Equal Emphasis, 6 to 7 Research Orientation

DEGREE OFFERED:
MS in exercise and sport science

NUMBER OF STUDENTS IN PROGRAM:
20 to 25

NUMBER OF STUDENTS IN EACH DEGREE PROGRAM:

NUMBER OF STUDENTS WHO APPLY/ARE ACCEPTED ANNUALLY:
20 apply/10 accepted

ADMISSION REQUIREMENTS:
GRE or MAT scores, undergraduate degree with acceptable GPA, letters of recommendation, application with written statement of goals

AVAILABLE FOR QUALIFIED STUDENTS:

ASSISTANTSHIPS:
0% fellowships, 20% research assistantships, 80% teaching Teaching, research, and administrative graduate assistantships are available

INTERNSHIP POSSIBILITY:
Yes

INTERNSHIP REQUIRED:
No

NUMBER OF HOURS REQUIRED:
36 semester hours

CORE GRADUATE CLASSES:

DESCRIPTION OF TYPICAL INTERNSHIP EXPERIENCE:

COMMENTS:

University of Minnesota
School of Kinesiology

University of Minnesota
Cooke Hall
1900 University Ave. SE
Minneapolis, MN 55455

Contact: Diane Wiese-Bjornstal
Title: Associate Professor, School of Kinesiology
Phone: 612.625.6580
Fax: 612.626.7700
Email: dwiese@umn.edu
Website: www.education.umn.edu/kin/faculty/dwiese.htm
Area of Interest: Sport psychology, psychology of sport injury, youth sport

Contact: Mary Jo Kane
Title: Professor, School of Kinesiology
Phone: 612.625.3870
Fax: 612.625.8147
Email: maryjo@umn.edu
Website: education.umn.edu/tucker/center/
Area of Interest: Sport sociology, women in sport and leisure

Contact: Nicole LaVoi
Title: Associate Director, Tucker Center for Research on Girls & Women in Sport
Phone: 612.626.6055
Fax: 612.626.7700
Email: nmlavoi@umn.edu
Website: education.umn.edu/KLS/faculty/LaVoi.html
Area of Interest: Social psychology of sport, coaching science, youth sport, sport sociology, women in sport and leisure

Contact: Aynsley Smith
Title: Affiliated U of M Graduate Faculty from Mayo Clinic, Rochester
Phone: 507.266.1783
Fax: 507.266.1803
Email: smith.aynsley@mayo.edu
Website: www.mayoclinic.org/spportsmed-center-rst/doctors.html
Area of Interest: Sport psychology, psychology of sport injury, applied sport psychology consulting, psychophysiology

PROGRAM RATING

1   2   3   4   **5**   6   7

1 to 3 Applied Orientation, 3 to 6 Equal Emphasis, 6 to 7 Research Orientation

DEGREE OFFERED:
MA and PhD in Kinesiology

NUMBER OF STUDENTS IN PROGRAM:
15

NUMBER OF STUDENTS IN EACH DEGREE PROGRAM:
7 MA/8PhD

NUMBER OF STUDENTS WHO APPLY/ARE ACCEPTED ANNUALLY:
Typically about 10 apply to the MA and about 10 apply to the PhD; about 2 MA and 2 PhD students accepted annually

ADMISSION REQUIREMENTS:
GRE or MAT scores must be submitted (preferred, but not required, minimum scores of 4.5 analytical writing, 450 verbal, 500 quantitative), TOEFL scores must be submitted if English is second language (required minimum of 213 computer version or 550 paper version needed), GPA—required minimums of 3.0 overall undergraduate, 3.5 overall graduate work needed, three letters of recommendation, sample of scholarly writing, completed application forms including statement of goals, resume

AVAILABLE FOR QUALIFIED STUDENTS:
Research assistantships, Teaching assistantships, Other forms of financial aid (doctoral dissertation grants, graduate school scholarships, block grants, tuition waivers, and minority student fellowships), all given on a competitive basis.

ASSISTANTSHIPS:
70% Teaching Assistantships, 10% Research Assistantships, 10% Partial Tuition Waivers, 10% Partial Block Grant funding

INTERNSHIP POSSIBILITY:
Yes, at the PhD level

INTERNSHIP REQUIRED:
Not required

NUMBER OF HOURS REQUIRED:
Not required, but can be arranged at the PhD level; 3-6 semester credits (approx. 45 clock hours required per academic credit)

CORE GRADUATE CLASSES:
Sample programs of study for the MA and PhD in Kinesiology with an emphasis in sport psychology can be found via education.umn.edu/kls/kinesiology/degrees.html. Core classes in sport psychology include the following: KIN 5126-Sport Psychology; KIN 5136-Psychology of Coaching; KIN 5723-Psychology of Sport Injury; KIN 8126-Seminar: Sport Psychology; KIN 8696-Internship: Applied Sport Psychology.

DESCRIPTION OF TYPICAL INTERNSHIP EXPERIENCE:
Self-directed and planned cooperatively between student, faculty, and participating unit, agency, or school. Students can earn academic credits for the supervised internship via KIN 8696-Internship: Applied Sport Psychology. All internships adopt an educational sport psychology and/or performance enhancement focus.

COMMENTS:

The academic focus of the graduate program is largely social-psychological and cognitive-behavioral in nature, with somewhat equal emphasis on (a) conducting independent applied research in sport psychology, (b) gaining teaching experience in sport psychology, and, to a lesser extent, (c) gaining educational consulting experience in applied sport psychology. Graduate students in kinesiology emphasizing sport psychology develop much of their own academic program of study by selecting courses from the science-based curriculum in kinesiology and from other disciplines throughout the university, most typically including educational psychology, child psychology, psychology, sociology, and public health. The Tucker Center for Research on Girls and Women in Sport education.umn.edu/tuckercenter/> has particular relevance for students interested in studying the psychology and sociology of sport as they relate to the participation of girls and women.

University of Missouri, Columbia

Department of Educational, School, and Counseling Psychology

University of Missouri, Columbia
16 Hill Hall
Columbia, MO 65211

Contact:	Richard H. Cox	**Email:**	beckn@missouri.edu
Title:	Professor	**Website:**	
Phone:	573.882.7602	**Area of Interest:**	Clinical sport psychology
Fax:	573.884.5989		
Email:	coxrh@missouri.edu	**Contact:**	Rick McGuire
Website:	www.missouri.edu/index.cfm	**Title:**	Head Track Coach
Area of Interest:	Counseling sport psychology	**Phone:**	573.882.0727
		Fax:	573.884.7577
Contact:	Niels Beck	**Email:**	mcguirer@missouri.edu
Title:	Professor	**Website:**	
Phone:	573.884.1829	**Area of Interest:**	Motivation and coaching
Fax:	573.884.5936		

PROGRAM RATING

1   2   3   4   **5**   6   7

1 to 3 Applied Orientation, 3 to 6 Equal Emphasis, 6 to 7 Research Orientation

DEGREE OFFERED:
MA, MEd, PhD

NUMBER OF STUDENTS IN PROGRAM:
10

NUMBER OF STUDENTS IN EACH DEGREE PROGRAM:
6 MA/4 PhD

NUMBER OF STUDENTS WHO APPLY/ARE ACCEPTED ANNUALLY:
Admission into counseling psychology program is very competitive. Approximately 1 PhD and 4 Master's students admitted annually.

ADMISSION REQUIREMENTS:
GPA (3.0 minimum), GRE (preferred minimum for verbal + quantitative of 1000 for Master's and 1200 for doctorate), letters of support, research experience, applied experience.

AVAILABLE FOR QUALIFIED STUDENTS:
Research assistantships, teaching assistantships (doctorate only)

ASSISTANTSHIPS:

Fellowships, research assistantships, teaching assistantships, tuition waivers, other forms of financial aid. Note: PhD candidates can expect some financial support in the form of an assistantship, a scholarship, and/or a fellowship, plus an academic fee waiver (in- and out-of-state).

INTERNSHIP POSSIBILITY:

Yes

INTERNSHIP REQUIRED:

Yes, for PhD (There are two kinds of internships: the APA-approved, year-long capstone experience and the 400-hour sport psychology internship.)

NUMBER OF HOURS REQUIRED:

Nine semester hours of practicum are required for Master's candidates; 400 hours of sport psychology internship and the full-time equivalent of one year of an APA-approved internship are required for PhD candidates.

CORE GRADUATE CLASSES:

Core courses are in counseling psychology, with support courses in sport psychology.

DESCRIPTION OF TYPICAL INTERNSHIP EXPERIENCE:

In the typical sport psychology internship, the student works out a cooperative arrangement with an intercollegiate or scholastic coach and program. In the the APA-approved capstone internship, students are matched with a national site.

COMMENTS:

The PhD program in counseling psychology at MU is APA-approved and is consistently ranked among the top five programs nationally. Sport psychology is a subspecialty in counseling psychology, offered through the Department of Educational, School, and Counseling Psychology. Counseling psychology students, with a strong interest in sport psychology, graduate with a degree in counseling psychology with support work in sport psychology. The doctorate in counseling psychology with a subspecialty in sport psychology is designed to qualify the recipient to become a licensed counseling psychologist as well as an AAASP-certified applied counseling sport psychologist.

University of New Hampshire
Department of Kinesiology

University of New Hampshire
209 New Hampshire Hall
Durham, NH 03824

Contact: Heather Barber
Title: Associate Professor
Phone: 603.862.2058
Fax: 603.862.0154
Email: hb@cisunix.unh.edu
Website: www.unh.edu
Area of Interest: Motivation, Coaching Education, Gender in Sport

Contact: Ron Croce
Title:
Phone:
Fax:
Email:
Website:
Area of Interest: Neuropsychology

Contact: Karen Collins
Title: Assistant Professor
Phone: 603.862.0361
Fax: 603.862.0154
Email: Karen.Collins@unh.edu
Website: www.unh.edu
Area of Interest: Coaching education, social issues in coaching

PROGRAM RATING

1   2   3   **4**   5   6   7

1 to 3 Applied Orientation, 3 to 6 Equal Emphasis, 6 to 7 Research Orientation

DEGREE OFFERED:
MS

NUMBER OF STUDENTS IN PROGRAM:
7 to 10

NUMBER OF STUDENTS IN EACH DEGREE PROGRAM:

NUMBER OF STUDENTS WHO APPLY/ARE ACCEPTED ANNUALLY:
8-10 apply / 5 accepted

ADMISSION REQUIREMENTS:
GRE (average student scores 1050), GPA (average student has 3.25 on 4.00 scale)

AVAILABLE FOR QUALIFIED STUDENTS:
Teaching assistantships, coaching assistantships, other forms of financial aid

ASSISTANTSHIPS:

0% fellowships, 0% graduate assistantships, 50% teaching assistantships/coaching assistantships, 20% tuition waivers, 10% other forms of financial aid

INTERNSHIP POSSIBILITY:

Yes

INTERNSHIP REQUIRED:

No

NUMBER OF HOURS REQUIRED:

8 credit hours

CORE GRADUATE CLASSES:

DESCRIPTION OF TYPICAL INTERNSHIP EXPERIENCE:

Experiential learning in a setting appropriate to the student's objectives. Sport psychology students can either work on campus with the University of New Hampshire athletic program or off campus in approved sport organizations.

COMMENTS:

The University of New Hampshire offers a Master of Science in Kinesiology: Sport Studies, with a concentration in sport psychology. The concentration includes an optional internship with one of the university athletic teams, as well as required courses and a thesis.

University of New Mexico
Department of Physical Performance and Development

University of New Mexico
Albuquerque, NM 87131

Contact: Joy Griffin
Title:
Phone: 505.277.3534
Fax: 505.277.6227
Email: jgriffin@unm.edu
Website: www.unm.edu/~sportad/
Area of Interest: Multicultural issues, performance enhancement

Contact: Vonda Long
Title:
Phone:
Fax:
Email:
Website:
Area of Interest: Self-concept development, experiential learning (Dr. Long is the main contact person in the counselor education program.)

Contact: Todd Seidler
Title:
Phone:
Fax:
Email:
Website:
Area of Interest: Sport administration

PROGRAM RATING

1   2   3   **4**   5   6   7

1 to 3 Applied Orientation, 3 to 6 Equal Emphasis, 6 to 7 Research Orientation

DEGREE OFFERED:
MS, PhD

NUMBER OF STUDENTS IN PROGRAM:
80

NUMBER OF STUDENTS IN EACH DEGREE PROGRAM:
75% MS/25% PhD

NUMBER OF STUDENTS WHO APPLY/ARE ACCEPTED ANNUALLY:
50-60 apply/20-25 accepted

ADMISSION REQUIREMENTS:
Bachelor's or master's degree in physical education, exercise science, health psychology, or counseling (other degrees will be evaluated by department); undergraduate GPA of 3.00 or better; three letters of recommendation; written statement of career goals and areas of interest; history of prospective student's sport background; completed application form, including transcripts and official GRE scores

AVAILABLE FOR QUALIFIED STUDENTS:
Teaching assistantships

ASSISTANTSHIPS:
Fellowships (1 official fellowship), teaching assistantships (4-6 TAs), coaching assistantships and sport administration assistance in athletics, tuition waivers (vary), other forms of financial aid (vary)

INTERNSHIP POSSIBILITY:
Yes

INTERNSHIP REQUIRED:
Yes

NUMBER OF HOURS REQUIRED:
6 credit hours

CORE GRADUATE CLASSES:

DESCRIPTION OF TYPICAL INTERNSHIP EXPERIENCE:
Internship experiences are available in work with high school, collegiate, semiprofessional, and professional teams; other possibilities are available with faculty approval.

COMMENTS:
Our sport psychology program at UNM is designed to provide all of the criteria necessary for AAASP certification. Sport administration, physical education, and counselor education programs combine to provide an interdisciplinary approach that capitalizes on the strengths of several excellent programs to meet the current needs of the sport counselor. This program is ideal for professionals who wish to teach; conduct research; and work with athletes in academic, athletic, or private organizations. A bonus of our program is that the graduate (besides having the criteria for AAASP certification) has expertise in sport administration and can be hired by an athletic department to be a sport counselor and can also multitask. The PhD graduate can teach in the sport psychology and sport administration fields. Budget constraints in academic and athletic departments may give the graduate student who is academically and experientially prepared to do many tasks an advantage in the hiring process. An applied orientation and/or a research orientation is tailored to the unique career needs and directions of each graduate student. The program is flexible, especially at the PhD level, to enable students to design their own course work (within the AAASP criteria mandates) to meet specific educational and employment objectives.

Program Mission Statement:
Our mission is to prepare graduate students for a wide range of sport-related positions within organizations that are typically educational/professional in nature and scope. We strive to provide a superior educational experience to students by supporting our teaching with research in the areas of sport psychology administration and leadership. In addition, we provide service and program visibility through community involvement and representation in regional and national organizations. In congruence with this mission, we provide educational opportunities and experiences in the following areas: (a) interscholastic and intercollegiate athletics, (b) amateur and professional sport, (c) public and private sport organizations, and (d) the academic study of sport.

University of North Carolina, Greensboro

Department of Exercise and Sport Science

University of North Carolina, Greensboro
Greensboro, NC 27402-6170

Contact: Diane L. Gill
Title: Professor
Phone: 336.334.4683, 336.334.5573 (department main office)
Fax: 336.334.3238
Email: dlgill@uncg.edu
Website: www.uncg.edu/ess/faculty/dianegill.html
Area of Interest: Social psychology of sport and exercise; Physical activity and wellness

Contact: Jennifer L. Etnier
Title: Associate Professor
Phone: 336.334.3037, 336.334.5573 (department main office)
Fax: 336.334.3238
Email: jletnier@uncg.edu
Website:
Area of Interest: Exercise psychology; Exercise/Physical activity and cognition

Contact: Renee Newcomer Appaneal
Title: Assistant Professor
Phone: 336.256.0280, 336.334.5573 (department main office)
Fax: 336.334.3238
Email: rrnewcom@uncg.edu
Website: www.uncg.edu/ess/faculty/renee-newcomer.html
Area of Interest: Applied sport and exercise psychology; Psychology of injury and rehabilitation

PROGRAM RATING

1   2   3   4   **5**   6   7

1 to 3 Applied Orientation, 3 to 6 Equal Emphasis, 6 to 7 Research Orientation

DEGREE OFFERED:
MS, PhD

NUMBER OF STUDENTS IN PROGRAM:
25

NUMBER OF STUDENTS IN EACH DEGREE PROGRAM:
60% MS/40% PhD

NUMBER OF STUDENTS WHO APPLY/ARE ACCEPTED ANNUALLY:
60 apply/8 accepted

ADMISSION REQUIREMENTS:
Admission is based on previous academic performance (GPA), GRE scores, letters of reference, a statement of career goals and objectives, past experience, and accomplishments. A visit to campus is strongly recommended for all candidates and highly recommended for PhD candidates.

AVAILABLE FOR QUALIFIED STUDENTS:
Research assistantships, teaching assistantships

ASSISTANTSHIPS:
5% fellowships, 25% research assistantships, 25% teaching assistantships, 50% of funded students also receive tuition waivers (out-of-state waiver only awarded with research and/or teaching assistantships), 0% other forms of financial aid

INTERNSHIP POSSIBILITY:
Yes

INTERNSHIP REQUIRED:
No

NUMBER OF HOURS REQUIRED:
May range from 0-12 credit hours

CORE GRADUATE CLASSES:
Sport and Exercise Psychology, Applied Sport Psychology, Practicum / Internship in Applied Sport Psychology, Psychological Aspects of Sport Injury & Rehabilitation, Exercise Psychology, Social Psychology, Advanced seminars and special topics courses typically offered alternate years

DESCRIPTION OF TYPICAL INTERNSHIP EXPERIENCE:
Applied graduate training begins first with foundation coursework then practicum/internship. Students may enroll in practicum / internship courses up to a maximum of 6 (MS practicum) or 12 (PhD practicum + internship). Students may begin training through observation or assisting current student-consultants. Sport psychology consultation includes mental skills training with area youth, adolescents, and collegiate student-athletes. Additional practicum opportunities exist in sport injury and exercise adherence settings, as well as assisting staff with NCAA CHAMPS/Life Skills programming. Supervision is provided to students by Dr Newcomer Appaneal who is a Certified Consultant – AAASP), and methods of supervision include peer consultation, group and individual meetings, as well as review of videotape.

COMMENTS:
The UNCG graduate program in sport and exercise psychology offers MS and PhD degrees and prepares students for careers as teachers, researchers, coaches, exercise leaders, or sport and exercise psychology consultants. The UNCG program is staffed by three full-time faculty with expertise in three complementary areas within the field, providing depth and breadth of knowledge in sport and exercise psychology. Extensive research training and experience are provided, with the goal of developing top-flight sport and exercise psychology scholars. In addition, students have the opportunity to develop applied sport and exercise psychology consulting competencies (based on a scientist-practitioner model). The PhD program enables students to pursue in-depth, research-oriented study in sport and exercise psychology, in a program designed to meet individual career goals and needs. Several graduate sport and exercise psychology

courses are offered on a regular basis, and special-topics courses and independent studies are often available. The department also offers graduate courses in exercise physiology, sports medicine, pedagogy, motor behavior, and sociohistorical sport studies. Many students take graduate courses offered through other departments and programs across campus, including UNCG's highly regarded psychology and counseling PhD programs. Our Sport and Exercise Psychology Laboratory is adjacent to other departmental labs (i.e., Applied Neuromechanics and Exercise Physiology), and collaborative projects are common.

University of North Dakota

Department of Kinesiology

University of North Dakota
Box 8235
Grand Forks, ND 58202

Contact:	Sandra Short (Moritz)	**Contact:**	Jim Whitehead
Title:	Associate Professor (Kinesiology) & Adjunct Professor (Psychology)	**Title:**	Associate Professor
Phone:	701.777.4325	**Phone:**	701.777.4347
Fax:	701.777.3531	**Fax:**	701.777.3531
Email:	Sandra_short@und.nodak.edu	**Email:**	james_whitehead@und.nodak.edu
Website:	www.und.edu	**Website:**	www.und.edu

Area of Interest: Sport psychology — (1) mental imagery applied to sport and exercise and (2) efficacy beliefs (self, team and coaching) in sport

Area of Interest: Exercise psychology — motivation, physical self-perceptions

PROGRAM RATING

1   2   3   **4**   5   6   7

1 to 3 Applied Orientation, 3 to 6 Equal Emphasis, 6 to 7 Research Orientation

DEGREE OFFERED:
MS, PhD (via experimental Psychology program)

NUMBER OF STUDENTS IN PROGRAM:
25

NUMBER OF STUDENTS IN EACH DEGREE PROGRAM:

NUMBER OF STUDENTS WHO APPLY/ARE ACCEPTED ANNUALLY:
20 apply/10 accepted

ADMISSION REQUIREMENTS:
GRE (scores above 900 Verbal plus Quantitative, and neither score below 400 is considered adequate), satisfactory TOEFL scores for applicants who are not native English-speakers; undergraduate GPA of 2.75 overall or 3.00 in the last 2 years, minimum of 20 credits in undergraduate physical education or equivalent (we require students to have an adequate background in Kinesiology but an applicant without satisfactory undergraduate preparation may be admitted but will be required to remove deficiencies by completing necessary undergraduate courses without receiving graduate credit for them. More specifically, we require our graduate students to have at least one course in 4 areas: exercise physiology or biomechanics; sport or exercise psychology or sport sociology; motor learning or motor development; adapted PE).

AVAILABLE FOR QUALIFIED STUDENTS:

Teaching assistantships, tuition waivers

ASSISTANTSHIPS:

5% research assistantships, 40% teaching assistantships, 25% tuition waivers, 30% graduate student assistantships with Athletics

INTERNSHIP POSSIBILITY:

Yes, on demand.

INTERNSHIP REQUIRED:

No

NUMBER OF HOURS REQUIRED:

CORE GRADUATE CLASSES:

Sport Psychology, Sport Psychology for Teams, Exercise Psychology, Sport Sociology, Research Methods, Statistics

DESCRIPTION OF TYPICAL INTERNSHIP EXPERIENCE:

Assisting with performance enhancement for athletes, teams, and coaches; Teaching undergraduate performance enhancement class, assisting in coaching minor program, supervising coaching practica, supervising fitness lab

COMMENTS:

Qualified applicants may complete a PhD in the Experimental Psychology Program with a specialization in sport psychology.

University of North Texas
Department of Kinesiology, Health Promotion, and Recreation

University of North Texas
Center for Sport Psychology and Performance Excellence, Department of Kinesiology
Box 13857
Denton, TX 76203

Contact: Christy Greenleaf
Title:
Phone: 940.565.3415
Fax: 940.565.4904
Email: cgreenleaf@coefs.coe.unt.edu
Website:
Area of Interest: Body image and disordered eating among exercisers and athletes

Contact: Karen Cogan
Title:
Phone: 940.565.2671
Fax: 940.565.4682
Email: cogan@dsa.unt.edu
Website:
Area of Interest: Gender issues in sport and performance enhancement

Contact: Scott Martin
Title:
Phone: 940.565.3418
Fax: 940.565.4904
Email: smartin@coe.unt.edu
Website: www.coe.unt.edu/martin
Area of Interest: Attitudes toward and expectations about sport psychology, coaching and leadership behaviors, and physical inactivity and obesity

Contact: Trent Petrie
Title:
Phone: 940.565.4718
Fax: 940.565.4682
Email: petriet@unt.edu
Website:
Area of Interest: Eating disorders, athletic injuries, sport psychology counseling and life skills training

PROGRAM RATING

1   2   3   4   5   6   7

1 to 3 Applied Orientation, 3 to 6 Equal Emphasis, 6 to 7 Research Orientation: Unrated

DEGREE OFFERED:
MS in kinesiology

NUMBER OF STUDENTS IN PROGRAM:
10 to 15 (master's)

NUMBER OF STUDENTS IN EACH DEGREE PROGRAM:

NUMBER OF STUDENTS WHO APPLY/ARE ACCEPTED ANNUALLY:

ADMISSION REQUIREMENTS:
Master's—800 GRE (375 minimum on verbal and quantitative); MS—2.80 GPA

AVAILABLE FOR QUALIFIED STUDENTS:
Research assistantships, teaching assistantships, other forms of financial aid

ASSISTANTSHIPS:
15% fellowships/scholarships, 15% research assistantships, 40% teaching assistantships, 15% tuition waivers (partial tuition waivers for out-of-state students), 60% other forms of financial aid

INTERNSHIP POSSIBILITY:
Yes

INTERNSHIP REQUIRED:
No

NUMBER OF HOURS REQUIRED:

CORE GRADUATE CLASSES:

DESCRIPTION OF TYPICAL INTERNSHIP EXPERIENCE:

COMMENTS:
The University of North Texas Center for Sport Psychology and Performance Excellence is a multidisciplinary center devoted to offering sport psychology interventions, research, and training. The MS is offered through the Department of Kinesiology, Health Promotion, and Recreation.

University of North Texas
Department of Psychology

University of North Texas
Center for Sport Psychology and Performance Excellence, Department of Psychology
Box 311280
Denton, TX 76203

Contact: Trent Petrie
Title: Professor, Director - Center for Sport Psychology
Phone: 940.565.4718
Fax: 940.565.4682
Email: petriet@unt.edu
Website: www.sportpsych.unt.edu
Area of Interest: Eating disorders, athletic injuries, sport psychology counseling and life skills training

Contact: Scott Martin
Title: Associate Professor
Phone: 817.565.3427
Fax: 817.565.4904
Email: smartin@coefs.coe.unt.edu
Website: www.coe.unt.edu/
Area of Interest: Sport and exercise psychology, goal attainment, attitudes and expectations about sport psychology, coaching behaviors

Contact: Karen Cogan
Title: Staff Psychologist, Counseling and Testing Center
Phone: 940.565.2671
Fax: 940.565.4682
Email: cogan@dsa.unt.edu
Website: www.sportpsych.unt.edu
Area of Interest: Gender issues in sport and performance enhancement

Contact: Christy Greenleaf
Title: Assistant Professor
Phone: 940.565.3415
Fax: 940.565.4904
Email: cgreenleaf@coefs.coe.unt.edu
Website: www.sportpsych.unt.edu
Area of Interest: Body image and disordered eating among exercisers and athletes

PROGRAM RATING

1   2   3   **4**   5   6   7

1 to 3 Applied Orientation, 3 to 6 Equal Emphasis, 6 to 7 Research Orientation

DEGREE OFFERED:

PhD in counseling psychology, with specialization in applied sport psychology

NUMBER OF STUDENTS IN PROGRAM:

Eight students are admitted annually into the doctoral program. Of these, two to four pursue the specialization in sport psychology.

NUMBER OF STUDENTS IN EACH DEGREE PROGRAM:

Eight students are admitted annually into the doctoral program. Of these, two to four pursue the specialization in sport psychology.

NUMBER OF STUDENTS WHO APPLY/ARE ACCEPTED ANNUALLY:

Under number of students who apply annually, add: 80-100 students apply each year to the counseling psychology doctoral program. Of these, approximately 30% are interested in the sport psychology specialization.

ADMISSION REQUIREMENTS:

For up to date information on admission requirements, visit the Department of Psychology's website at www.psyc.unt.edu/index.shtml

AVAILABLE FOR QUALIFIED STUDENTS:

Research assistantships, teaching assistantships, other forms of financial aid

ASSISTANTSHIPS:

15% fellowships/scholarships, 15% research assistantships, 40% teaching assistantships, 15% tuition waivers (partial tuition waivers for out-of-state students), 60% other forms of financial aid

INTERNSHIP POSSIBILITY:

Yes. Students who enter the counseling psychology program will complete 3-4 years of general practicum training prior to their predoctoral clinical internship. In addition, students specializing in sport psychology will complete 4-5 years of applied sport psychology practica through the Center for Sport Psychology and Performance Excellence.

INTERNSHIP REQUIRED:

As part of the doctoral counseling psychology requirements, all students will complete a one-year predoctoral internship at an APA-accredited site. This internship generally is completed during the student's final year of school, following completion of all coursework, comprehensive examinations, and dissertation. Former students have completed their internships at university counseling centers, medical centers, VAs, and community mental health centers.

NUMBER OF HOURS REQUIRED:

For the most current information on courses and hour requirements, visit the Department of Psychology's website at www.psyc.unt.edu/index.shtml and the Center for Sport Psychology's website at www.sportpsych.unt.edu

CORE GRADUATE CLASSES:

For the most current information on courses and hour requirements, visit the Department of Psychology's website at www.psyc.unt.edu/index.shtml and the Center for Sport Psychology's website at www.sportpsych.unt.edu

DESCRIPTION OF TYPICAL INTERNSHIP EXPERIENCE:

During students' 4-5 years of applied sport psychology practicum training, they will have opportunities to work with individual athletes, intact teams, coaches, athletic trainers, and athletic department administrators. Although most of this work will be done at the college level, students may have opportunities to work with athletes and teams at the youth sport and recreational level. In the practica, students will be embedded with a team or organization for several years and will provide comprehensive sport psychology services, including performance enhancement interventions, team building, systems analysis, coach mentoring, and individual counseling.

COMMENTS:

The University of North Texas Center for Sport Psychology and Performance Excellence is a multidisciplinary center devoted to offering sport psychology interventions, research, and training. The MS is offered through Kinesiology, Health Promotion, and Recreation; the PhD is offered through the counseling psychology program (APA-approved program).

University of Northern Colorado
Department of Kinesiology

University of Northern Colorado
Greeley, CO 80639

Contact:	Robert Brustad	**Contact:**	Megan Babkes
Title:		**Title:**	
Phone:	970-351-1737	**Phone:**	970-351-1809
Fax:	970.351.1762	**Fax:**	970-351-1762
Email:	bob.brustad@unco.edu	**Email:**	megan.babkes@unco.edu
Website:	www.unco.edu	**Website:**	

Area of Interest: Social psychology of sport, psychosocial aspects of children's sport and physical activity, exercise psychology, coaching effectiveness, motivation, physical activity promotion

Area of Interest: Social psychology of sport, psychosocial aspects of children's sport and physical activity, peer and sibling influence in sport, physical activity promotion, aging

PROGRAM RATING

1   2   3   4   5   **6**   7

1 to 3 Applied Orientation, 3 to 6 Equal Emphasis, 6 to 7 Research Orientation

DEGREE OFFERED:
MA/PhD

NUMBER OF STUDENTS IN PROGRAM:
10

NUMBER OF STUDENTS IN EACH DEGREE PROGRAM:
70% MS / 30% PhD

NUMBER OF STUDENTS WHO APPLY/ARE ACCEPTED ANNUALLY:
10 MS apply/3 MS accepted; 8 PhD apply/1 PhD accepted

ADMISSION REQUIREMENTS:
GPA and GRE scores operate on a sliding scale: minimum GPA of 3.00 for MS; minimum GPA of 3.50 and GRE of 1500 (verbal + quantitative + analytical writing) for PhD.

AVAILABLE FOR QUALIFIED STUDENTS:
Research assistantships, teaching assistantships, other forms of financial aid

ASSISTANTSHIPS:

20% fellowships, 0% research assistantships, 30% teaching assistantships, 30% tuition waivers, 10% other forms of financial aid

INTERNSHIP POSSIBILITY:

Yes

INTERNSHIP REQUIRED:

No

NUMBER OF HOURS REQUIRED:

6 credit hours

CORE GRADUATE CLASSES:

SES 624: Advanced Developmental Kinesiology/SES 635 Sport and Exercise Psychology; SES 665 Advanced Sociological Kinesiology; SES 629 Motivation; SES 625 Lab Techniques in Sport & Exercise Psychology

DESCRIPTION OF TYPICAL INTERNSHIP EXPERIENCE:

Work with university athletic teams; work in health and exercise settings, work with community sport and recreation programs. Work with university athletic teams; work in health and exercise settings.

COMMENTS:

The program focus at the University of Northern Colorado is on the social psychology of sport and physical activity. It is expected that students will develop an excellent background in social psychological theory and will apply this knowledge to the study of sport and exercise behavior. Particular areas of interest of current faculty and students include the study of motivation, exercise behavior and adherence, children's sport and physical activity involvement, and coaching effectiveness. Master's and doctoral students are expected to supplement their departmental course work with courses from the departments of psychology and sociology. There is not a major emphasis on applied sport psychology in this program. However, some course work is available in the applied (intervention) area.

University of Northern Iowa
School of Health, Physical Education, and Leisure Services

203 Wellness/ Recreation Center
Cedar Falls, IA 50614-0241

Contact: Julee Jacobson
Title:
Phone: 319.273.6475
Fax:
Email: julee.jacobson@uni.edu
Website:
Area of Interest:

PROGRAM RATING

1 2 3 4 **5** 6 7

1 to 3 Applied Orientation, 3 to 6 Equal Emphasis, 6 to 7 Research Orientation

DEGREE OFFERED:
MA in physical education with sport and exercise psychology focus

NUMBER OF STUDENTS IN PROGRAM:
3-5

NUMBER OF STUDENTS IN EACH DEGREE PROGRAM:
3-5

NUMBER OF STUDENTS WHO APPLY/ARE ACCEPTED ANNUALLY:
7 apply / 4 accepted

ADMISSION REQUIREMENTS:
Undergraduate GPA of 3.00 with two letters of recommendation. Students from countries where the native language is not English are required to score a minimum of 500 on the TOEFL.

AVAILABLE FOR QUALIFIED STUDENTS:
Fellowships (university-wide competition) graduate assistantships, research assistantships

ASSISTANTSHIPS:
10% fellowships, 0% research assistantships, 25% teaching assistantships (include tuition waivers), 0% tuition waivers, 14% other forms of financial aid

INTERNSHIP POSSIBILITY:
Yes

INTERNSHIP REQUIRED:
No

NUMBER OF HOURS REQUIRED:
Minimum of 30 semester hours is required

CORE GRADUATE CLASSES:
Research Methods for Health, Physical Education and Leisure Services, Sport Psychology, Quantitative methods, Research experiences, Computer Applications in Physical Education, Biomechanics

DESCRIPTION OF TYPICAL INTERNSHIP EXPERIENCE:

COMMENTS:
The program at the University of Northern Iowa provides a variety of experiential learning experiences for students while working one-on-one with a faculty mentor. For practicum, students have been mentored to teach undergraduate courses while other students have been guided to coach at the collegiate or high school level. Additionally, student-driven research teams are formed each semester. The research teams meet for at least a year, complete a research study, and submit a manuscript to a journal for publication. The research teams meet in the Psychomotor Behavior Laboratory, which can be used to conduct various forms of research including experimental, interviews, observation, and computer-based work. The graduate program also offers a range of seminar classes (e.g., motivational processes, communication and leadership in sport, gender and sport) that allow students to examine topics in greater depth. Finally, the program promotes and encourages interdisciplinary learning and research.

University of Ottawa
School of Human Kinetics

University of Ottawa
125 University
Ottawa, ON
Canada
KIN 6N5

Contact: Lise O'Reilly
Title:
Phone: 613.562.5800 x5752
Fax: 613.562.5149
Email: lcosa@uottawa.ca
Website: www.health.uottawa.ca/hkgrad
Area of Interest:

Contact: Michelle Fortier
Title:
Phone:
Fax:
Email:
Website:
Area of Interest: Physical activity behavior, motivation, social influences, gender

Contact: John Salmela
Title:
Phone:
Fax:
Email:
Website:
Area of Interest: Coach expertise, qualitative analysis

Contact: Diane Ste. Marie
Title:
Phone:
Fax:
Email:
Website:
Area of Interest: Cognitive processes in judging, eating behaviors in athletes

Contact: Terry Orlick
Title:
Phone:
Fax:
Email:
Website:
Area of Interest: Performance excellence, quality of life, mental training with children

Contact: Pierre Trudel
Title:
Phone:
Fax:
Email:
Website:
Area of Interest: Coaching, intervention, qualitative methodology

PROGRAM RATING

1   2   3   4   5   **6**   7

1 to 3 Applied Orientation, 3 to 6 Equal Emphasis, 6 to 7 Research Orientation
Our nonthesis option in intervention and consulting has a strong applied orientation (1), whereas our thesis option has a strong research orientation (6).

DEGREE OFFERED:
MA; PhD (possibility through the Faculties of Education and Psychology)

NUMBER OF STUDENTS IN PROGRAM:
30 (20 thesis, 10 nonthesis)

NUMBER OF STUDENTS IN EACH DEGREE PROGRAM:
85% MA/15% PhD

NUMBER OF STUDENTS WHO APPLY/ARE ACCEPTED ANNUALLY:
45 apply/25 accepted

ADMISSION REQUIREMENTS:
B+ in sport science or related area within education or psychology

AVAILABLE FOR QUALIFIED STUDENTS:
Research assistantships, teaching assistantships, other forms of financial aid

ASSISTANTSHIPS:
5% fellowships, 70% research assistantships, 100% teaching assistantships, 10% tuition waivers, 0% other forms of financial aid

INTERNSHIP POSSIBILITY:
Yes

INTERNSHIP REQUIRED:
Yes, for the nonthesis option

NUMBER OF HOURS REQUIRED:
360 hours

CORE GRADUATE CLASSES:

DESCRIPTION OF TYPICAL INTERNSHIP EXPERIENCE:
Intervention with university teams and individual athletes for performance enhancement, intervention with elementary and middle schools for student quality of life, intervention with inactive individuals to foster an active lifestyle, collaboration with other health professionals to intervene in hospital settings

COMMENTS:
The School of Human Kinetics Faculty of Health Sciences offers an MA in human kinetics with a specialization in sport/exercise psychology and performance enhancement that is unique in the world. A multidisciplinary, research-based thesis program is offered in the overlapping fields of performance and life enhancement that may continue to a doctoral level. A unique, nonthesis program in consultation and intervention directed toward performance and life enhancement is also offered, which combines applied course work with supervised internships. The school has a good assistantship program. First-year students are provided with teaching/research assistantships of a minimum of $3,500. Second-year students may

have teaching/research assistantship but will often receive support from their advisors' research grants. Students with a grade point average of 8.5 or better are eligible for an admission scholarship (tuition + $8,000). Students can benefit from a large and diverse group of experienced sport, exercise, and performance psychology staff members who are bilingual, have numerous research grants, and have expertise in qualitative and quantitative research as well as applied fieldwork.

University of Queensland
Schools of Human Movement Studies and Psychology

University of Queensland
Queensland,
Australia
4072

Contact:	Stephanie Hanrahan
Title:	Associate Professor
Phone:	(61) 7-3365-6453, (61) 7-3365-6240 (main office)
Fax:	(61) 7-3365-6877
Email:	Steph@hms.uq.edu.au
Website:	www.hms.uq.edu.au/
Area of Interest:	Mental skills training, attributions/motivation, special populations

Contact:	Bruce Abernethy
Title:	Professor
Phone:	
Fax:	(61) 7-3365-6877
Email:	
Website:	www.hms.uq.edu.au/
Area of Interest:	Expertise, perception, and production of movement patterns; skill acquisition

Contact:	Cliff Mallett
Title:	Lecturer
Phone:	(61) 7.3365.6765
Fax:	(61) 7.3365.6877
Email:	cmallett@hms.uq.edu.au
Website:	
Area of Interest:	Motivational processes of elite athletes; coaching effectiveness

PROGRAM RATING

1   2   3   **4**   5   6   7

1 to 3 Applied Orientation, 3 to 6 Equal Emphasis, 6 to 7 Research Orientation

DEGREE OFFERED:
Research Master's (MPhil); Master of Sport and Exercise Psychology (MSEP)—course work, research, and practica; PhD

NUMBER OF STUDENTS IN PROGRAM:
15 to 25

NUMBER OF STUDENTS IN EACH DEGREE PROGRAM:
5% research Master's/65% MSEP/30% PhD

NUMBER OF STUDENTS WHO APPLY/ARE ACCEPTED ANNUALLY:
MSEP: 10-15 apply; 5 are accepted. Research Master's and PhD: 5-10 apply; 2-3 are accepted.

ADMISSION REQUIREMENTS:
There are different requirements for different degrees. The MSEP requires a 4-year psychology degree.

AVAILABLE FOR QUALIFIED STUDENTS:
Research assistantships, teaching assistantships, other forms of financial aid

ASSISTANTSHIPS:
10% research assistantships, 70% teaching assistantships, 10% tuition waivers, 10% other forms of financial aid (Note: Scholarships and tuition waivers are only available for the PhD program.)

INTERNSHIP POSSIBILITY:
Yes, for the MSEP

INTERNSHIP REQUIRED:
Yes, for the MSEP

NUMBER OF HOURS REQUIRED:
1000 for the MSEP

CORE GRADUATE CLASSES:
The research master's and the PhD require no core classes; the degrees focus entirely on research. The MSEP core classes are as follows: Introduction to Applied Practice in Sport and Exercise Psychology, Counseling, Advanced Sport and Exercise Psychology, Interdisciplinary Perspectives of Human Movement Studies, Ethics and Professional Issues in Clinical Psychology, Organizational Psychology, Psychological Skills Training, Techniques in Sport, Internship, Externships, and Dissertation

DESCRIPTION OF TYPICAL INTERNSHIP EXPERIENCE:
Students may work with university sports clubs/sport associations; private practitioners; or community/high school/state/national athletes, teams, or coaches. There are often opportunities to work with sport programs within the Queensland Academy of Sport or the Australian Institute of Sport. Additionally, there is one nonsport placement (e.g., counseling, organizational, forensic, clinical).

COMMENTS:
The sport and exercise psychology programs are run jointly by the School of Human Movement Studies and the School of Psychology. Traditionally, master's and doctoral programs in Australia have been predominantly research-based. The Master of Sport and Exercise Psychology offered at the University of Queensland is a professionally oriented training program and includes course work, research, and practicum (internship) components. The academic year coincides with the calendar year, with classes beginning in February. Overseas applicants for the MSEP program must have their undergraduate credentials checked by the Australian Psychological Society (APS) to determine if they are equivalent to an APS-accredited undergraduate degree. Applications for the MSEP close in late September. Applications are accepted any time for research-only degrees.

University of Tennessee, Knoxville
Department of Exercise, Sport, and Leisure Studies

University of Tennessee, Knoxville
1914 Andy Holt Avenue
Knoxville, TN 37996-2700

Contact: Craig A. Wrisberg
Title:
Phone: 865.974.1283
Fax: 865.974.8981
Email: mwirtz@utk.edu
Website: web.utk.edu/7/Esals
Area of Interest: Performance enhancement, competition strategies, effects of augmented information on performance, sources of stress, quality of life of athletes

Contact: Joe Whitney
Title: Mental Training Director and Adjunct Professor
Phone: 865.974.3850
Fax:
Email: whitney@utk.edu
Website:
Area of Interest: Performance enhancement, confidence, mental training

Contact: Leslee Fisher
Title: Assistant Professor
Phone: 865.974.9973
Fax: 865.974.8981
Email: lfisher2@utk.edu
Website:
Area of Interest: Performance enhancement, positive psychology, health and exercise psychology, cultural studies of sport

Contact: Jeff Fairbrother
Title: Assistant Professor
Phone: 865.974.3616
Fax: 865.974.8981
Email: jfairbr1@utk.edu
Website:
Area of Interest: Motor performance and learning, practice structure, development of sport expertise

Contact: Joy De Sensi
Title: Professor and Department Head
Phone: 865.974.1282
Fax: 865.974.8981
Email: desensi@utk.edu
Website:
Area of Interest: Sociocultural aspects of gender, race, ethnicity, and multiculturalism in sport; leadership and ethics in sport management

PROGRAM RATING

1 2 3 **4** 5 6 7

1 to 3 Applied Orientation, 3 to 6 Equal Emphasis, 6 to 7 Research Orientation

DEGREE OFFERED:
MS, PhD

NUMBER OF STUDENTS IN PROGRAM:
25 to 30 MS; 9-10 PhD

NUMBER OF STUDENTS IN EACH DEGREE PROGRAM:
75% MS/25% PhD

NUMBER OF STUDENTS WHO APPLY/ARE ACCEPTED ANNUALLY:
40-50 apply/25-30 accepted (Most do not receive financial support from department); MS, PhD 20-25 apply/2-3 accepted (all receive teaching assistantships)

ADMISSION REQUIREMENTS:
MS: minimum 3.00 undergraduate GPA, PhD: minimum 3.00 undergraduate and 3.25 graduate GPA, Minimum 50th percentile on verbal component and 50th percentile on quantitative component on the GRE; minimum score of 4.5 on GRE writing sample. Both MS and PhD applications require completion of a departmental application, an additional writing sample, and three rating forms/recommendation letters.

AVAILABLE FOR QUALIFIED STUDENTS:
Graduate assistantships in athletics/sport psychology, research assistantships (when faculty obtain grant money), physical activity program teaching assistantships.

ASSISTANTSHIPS:
0% Fellowships, 0% research assistantships, 70% teaching assistantships, 20% athletics assistantships, 90% tuition waiver (comes with all assistantships), 10% other forms of financial aid

INTERNSHIP POSSIBILITY:
Yes

INTERNSHIP REQUIRED:
Sometimes. The student's committee determines the specific requirements based on the student's past and present experiences and on the student's outcome objectives.

NUMBER OF HOURS REQUIRED:
3 hours minimum; 15 hours are possible including additional independent work and/or research.

CORE GRADUATE CLASSES:
Depends on student's past and present experiences and on student's outcome objectives.

DESCRIPTION OF TYPICAL INTERNSHIP EXPERIENCE:
Working with teams and/or individual athletes.

COMMENTS:
Degree programs are individually tailored as much as possible to the career goals of students. Support for the program is also provided by faculty from programs in clinical and counseling psychology, and from personnel associated with the Department of Intercollegiate Athletics. While the primary emphasis is on performance enhancement, a strong interest in and commitment to research and scholarly activity are an expectation of all students. Faculty and students in sport psychology are also concerned about the impact of factors such as gender, race, sexual orientation, class, and power on sport participants. Students are exposed to both quantitative and qualitative research methods and are encouraged to participate in projects using each form of analysis. The focus of faculty research in recent years has included the following topics: the relationship of life stress and recovery processes to the performance of athletes; the quality of

life of intercollegiate athletes; the effect of performance reminders on subsequent sport performance; athletes' perceptions of and preferences for different coach communication styles; and the intersection of cultural studies and sport psychology.

University of Texas at Austin
Department of Kinesiology and Health Education

University of Texas at Austin
Bellmont Hall 222
Austin, TX 78712

Contact: John B. Bartholomew
Title:
Phone: 512.471.4407
Fax: 512.471.0946
Email: john.bart@mail.utexas.edu
Website:
Area of Interest: Exercise and health psychology, stress reactivity, mood effects of aerobic and resistance exercise

PROGRAM RATING

1   2   3   4   5   **6**   7

1 to 3 Applied Orientation, 3 to 6 Equal Emphasis, 6 to 7 Research Orientation

DEGREE OFFERED:
MA, Med, PhD

NUMBER OF STUDENTS IN PROGRAM:
6 to 10

NUMBER OF STUDENTS IN EACH DEGREE PROGRAM:
50% Master's/50% PhD

NUMBER OF STUDENTS WHO APPLY/ARE ACCEPTED ANNUALLY:

ADMISSION REQUIREMENTS:
Minimum GPA of 3.00 (last 2 years), GRE scores of 1000

AVAILABLE FOR QUALIFIED STUDENTS:
Fellowships, research assistantships, teaching assistantships

ASSISTANTSHIPS:
0% fellowships, 0% research assistantships, 0% teaching assistantships

INTERNSHIP POSSIBILITY:
Yes, but there is no formal placement program.

INTERNSHIP REQUIRED:
No

NUMBER OF HOURS REQUIRED:

CORE GRADUATE CLASSES:

DESCRIPTION OF TYPICAL INTERNSHIP EXPERIENCE:

COMMENTS:
The University of Texas at Austin offers an MA and an MEd in kinesiology with an area specialization in exercise and sport psychology. The PhD program is in health education with a specialization in health psychology. The program is primarily focused on research in health and exercise psychology. Students are strongly encouraged to seek out collaborative experiences both within the department (e.g., exercise physiology, health behavior, physical development and aging) and outside the department (e.g., psychology and educational psychology). As a result, students develop their own programs from psychophysiological, social-psychological, or behavior-change perspectives as best fits their research interests. There is not a major focus on applied sport psychology within the program.

University of Utah
Exercise and Sport Science Department

University of Utah
Salt Lake City, UT 84112

Contact: Keith Henschen	**Contact:** Barry Schultz
Title:	**Title:** Graduate Coordinator
Phone: 801.581.7558 (department office)	**Phone:** 801.581.4440
Fax: 801.585.3992	**Fax:**
Email: khensche@hsc.utah.edu	**Email:** bshultz@hsc.utah.edu
Website: www.health.utah.edu/ess/	**Website:**
Area of Interest: Performance enhancement	**Area of Interest:**

Contact: Maria Newton	**Contact:** Justine Reel
Title:	**Title:**
Phone: 801.581.4729	**Phone:** 801.581.3481
Fax: 801.585.3992	**Fax:**
Email: maria.newton@health.utah.edu	**Email:** justine.reel@health.utah.edu
Website: www.health.utah.edu/ess/	**Website:** www.health.utah.edu/ess/
Area of Interest: Motivation, youth, caring, climate interventions, optimizing the experience of physical activity	**Area of Interest:** Community advocacy, outreach, and education

PROGRAM RATING

1   2   3   4   **5**   6   7

1 to 3 Applied Orientation, 3 to 6 Equal Emphasis, 6 to 7 Research Orientation

DEGREE OFFERED:
MS, PhD

NUMBER OF STUDENTS IN PROGRAM:
20

NUMBER OF STUDENTS IN EACH DEGREE PROGRAM:
70% MS / 30% PhD

NUMBER OF STUDENTS WHO APPLY/ARE ACCEPTED ANNUALLY:
30 apply / 10 accepted

ADMISSION REQUIREMENTS:
The MS requires a 3.00 GPA and two letters of reference. The PhD requires a 3.30 GPA, 51 on the MAT or 1000 on the GRE, and three letters of recommendation.

AVAILABLE FOR QUALIFIED STUDENTS:
We offer traditional teaching assistantships as well as fellowship opportunities. We hold biweekly research "club" meetings to facilitate individual and collaborative research. We have established relationships with athletic teams on campus and Olympic training facilities in Park City. These are wonderful opportunities to interact with athletes in a supervised manner. We also offer two sequential courses on the pedagogy of higher education for those interested in teaching in higher education as a profession.

ASSISTANTSHIPS:

INTERNSHIP POSSIBILITY:
Yes

INTERNSHIP REQUIRED:
Yes, for PhD

NUMBER OF HOURS REQUIRED:
10 quarter hours

CORE GRADUATE CLASSES:

DESCRIPTION OF TYPICAL INTERNSHIP EXPERIENCE:

COMMENTS:

University of Virginia
Department of Human Services—Kinesiology

University of Virginia
201 Memorial Gymnasium
Charlottesville, VA 22903

Contact: Diane E. Whaley
Title: Assistant Professor
Phone: 434.924.6193
Fax:
Email: dew6d@virginia.edu
Website:
Area of Interest: Self-identity in middle and older adult exercisers, gender issues

Contact: Maureen R. Weiss
Title: Professor
Phone: 434.924.7860
Fax: 434.924.1389
Email: mrw5d@virginia.edu

Website: www.curry.edschool.virginia.edu/kinesiology/sprtpsy/
Area of Interest: Developmental issues related to self-perceptions, social influences (peers, parents, coaches), motivation, modeling, and moral development

Contact: Linda K. Bunker
Title: Professor
Phone:
Fax:
Email: lbunker@virginia.edu
Website:
Area of Interest: Motor learning, youth sport, women in sport

PROGRAM RATING

1   2   3   4   5   **6**   7

1 to 3 Applied Orientation, 3 to 6 Equal Emphasis, 6 to 7 Research Orientation
(This rating is not meaningful. Our emphasis is on applied research, not a dichotomy of research vs. application.)

DEGREE OFFERED:
MEd, PhD

NUMBER OF STUDENTS IN PROGRAM:
10-12 MEd/4 PhD

NUMBER OF STUDENTS IN EACH DEGREE PROGRAM:
75% MEd/25% PhD

NUMBER OF STUDENTS WHO APPLY/ARE ACCEPTED ANNUALLY:
30 MEd apply/6 MEd accepted; 20 PhD apply/1 PhD accepted

ADMISSION REQUIREMENTS:
Minimum 1500 on three GRE scores or 1000 on two GRE scores, 3.00 GPA, two letters of recommendation (Admissions decisions are made by April 1 for Fall. Fall admissions only.)

AVAILABLE FOR QUALIFIED STUDENTS:
Fellowships, research assistantships, teaching assistantships, other forms of financial aid

ASSISTANTSHIPS:
PhD: 100% fellowships, 100% research assistantships, 100% teaching assistantships, 100% tuition differentials, 100% other forms of financial aid; MEd: 50% fellowships, 50% research assistantships, 50% teaching assistantships, 0% tuition differentials, 100% other forms of financial aid

INTERNSHIP POSSIBILITY:
Yes

INTERNSHIP REQUIRED:
No

NUMBER OF HOURS REQUIRED:

CORE GRADUATE CLASSES:

DESCRIPTION OF TYPICAL INTERNSHIP EXPERIENCE:
Public schools, community agencies, athletics

COMMENTS:
The area of sport and exercise psychology addresses the social influences and individual factors related to participation and performance. Two major categories of questions comprise the focus of this field: (a) How does participation in sport and exercise contribute to the personal development of participants? And (b) how do psychological factors influence participation and performance in sport and exercise? The first category includes topics such as self-esteem, character development, intrinsic motivation, and the ability to cope with anxiety and stress. Topics under the second category include social support; motivation; self-confidence; and methods such as goal setting, arousal control, and mental imagery. The research program will specialize in "developmental sport and exercise psychology," an area that investigates age-related patterns in social and psychological factors related to participation in physical activity across the lifespan. Central topics will include determinants of self-esteem (i.e., perceptions of competence, social factors); motivational factors related to participation and performance (i.e., contextual and individual factors); and social influences on participation and performance (i.e., parents, peers, coaches). The applied aspect of the program entails opportunities for translating theory and practice to a variety of practical settings, such as athletics, exercise and fitness management, sport management, and youth organizations. The sport and exercise psychology program is committed to providing graduate students with the knowledge, skills, and experiences that will prepare them with the theoretical and practical background to be marketable for desired careers in athletics, health, or fitness, or for continued graduate training. Students who pursue a terminal master's degree will be prepared for positions as teachers, coaches, or professionals in fitness or athletic clubs. Students will also be well-prepared to go on to PhD programs to pursue research and teaching careers in higher education. Students in the doctoral program will be excellently prepared for careers in academe through their study of the breadth and depth of the field as well as through ample opportunities to engage in research, teaching, mentoring students, collaborating in grant writing, and participating in professional service activities.

University of Waterloo

Department of Kinesiology

University of Waterloo
Waterloo, ON
Canada
N2L 3G1

Contact: Dr. Nancy Theberge
Title: Professor and Associate Chair of Graduate Studies
Phone: 519.888.4567 x3534
Fax:
Email: theberge@healthy.uwaterloo.ca
Website:
Area of Interest:

Contact: F. Allard
Title:
Phone:
Fax:
Email:
Website:
Area of Interest: Cognitive factors in movement performance, expert/novice differences

Contact: K. DuCharme
Title: Adjunct
Phone:
Fax:
Email:
Website:
Area of Interest: Motivation; goal setting; self-efficacy; adherence in exercise, health, and sport

Contact: W. Neil Widmeyer
Title: Adjunct
Phone:
Fax:
Email:
Website:
Area of Interest: Group cohesion, group dynamics, collective efficacy, aggression in sport, team building in groups

---

PROGRAM RATING

1   2   3   **4**   5   6   7

1 to 3 Applied Orientation, 3 to 6 Equal Emphasis, 6 to 7 Research Orientation

---

DEGREE OFFERED:
MS, PhD

NUMBER OF STUDENTS IN PROGRAM:
14 full- and part-time in psychomotor behavior/social psychology (Five of these students are supervised by faculty listed above.)

NUMBER OF STUDENTS IN EACH DEGREE PROGRAM:
45% MS/55% PhD

NUMBER OF STUDENTS WHO APPLY/ARE ACCEPTED ANNUALLY:
36 MS apply/10 MS accepted; 16 PhD apply/7 PhD accepted

ADMISSION REQUIREMENTS:
Minimum B+ average in undergraduate (for MS) or graduate (for PhD) work; three letters of reference; copy of recent term paper (MS) or master's thesis (PhD); letter explaining interest in graduate program; GRE scores (verbal, quantitative, analytical)

AVAILABLE FOR QUALIFIED STUDENTS:
Research assistantships, teaching assistantships, other forms of financial aid

ASSISTANTSHIPS:
50% fellowships (from major granting agencies only), 100% research assistantships, 100% teaching assistantships, N/A tuition waivers, 75% other forms of financial aid (Note: These percentages apply only to full-time students studying social and sport psychology.)

INTERNSHIP POSSIBILITY:
Yes, for PhD only

INTERNSHIP REQUIRED:
No

NUMBER OF HOURS REQUIRED:
Dependent on internship available

CORE GRADUATE CLASSES:

DESCRIPTION OF TYPICAL INTERNSHIP EXPERIENCE:
Specific to the PhD program developed and appropriate to the needs of the PhD student

COMMENTS:
Sport psychology interests can be satisfied through the area in kinesiology called psychomotor behavior. Sport psychology is offered at the MS and PhD levels in psychomotor behavior, which is divided into three areas: (a) psychological and social psychological approaches to examining motor behavior, health, exercise, and rehabilitation; (b) motor control; and (c) motor learning and skill acquisition. Applicants with sport psychology interests apply in the first area in psychomotor behavior. Students can undertake problems incorporating interventions, but these must be examined in a research framework. For example, a problem must include a treatment and a control group to examine intervention effects. International authorities in psychology at Waterloo include Donald Meichenbaum (adjunct faculty in clinical psychology) and Mark Zanna (attitudes). The kinesiology program emphasizes a range of basic and applied research problems of human movement, including topics in sport, health, exercise, ergonomics, rehabilitation, and leisure. The student whose sport psychology interests are health-related will find close ties between the Department of Kinesiology and the Department of Health Studies and Gerontology. Dr. Brawley is a cross-appointed professor to both departments, where the faculty of applied health science is housed. Dr. Brawley is a past president of AAASP and serves on the editorial boards of the Journal of Sport and Exercise Psychology and the Journal of Applied Sport Psychology. He is currently the associate chair of graduate studies for the Department of Kinesiology. All PhD graduates of the program in the last 5 years have been placed in faculty positions in universities in Canada and the U.S.

University of Western Australia
Sport Psychology Laboratory, Department of Human Movement

Department of Human Movement
University of Western Australia
Nedlands, Western Australia
6907

Contact:	J. Robert Grove	**Contact:**	Sandy Gordon
Title:		**Title:**	
Phone:	61.8.9380.2361	**Phone:**	61.8.9380.2361
Fax:	61.8.9380.1039	**Fax:**	
Email:	Bob.Grove@uwa.edu.au	**Email:**	sgordon@cyllene.uwa.edu.au
Website:	www.general.uwa.edu.au/~hmweb/	**Website:**	

Area of Interest: Social psychology of sport, exercise and health psychology

Area of Interest: Social psychology of sport, performance enhancement

PROGRAM RATING

1   2   3   **4**   5   6   7

1 to 3 Applied Orientation, 3 to 6 Equal Emphasis, 6 to 7 Research Orientation

DEGREE OFFERED:
MS, PhD

NUMBER OF STUDENTS IN PROGRAM:
15

NUMBER OF STUDENTS IN EACH DEGREE PROGRAM:
67% master's/33% PhD

NUMBER OF STUDENTS WHO APPLY/ARE ACCEPTED ANNUALLY:
12-15 apply/4-5 accepted

ADMISSION REQUIREMENTS:
Master's: background in sport science and psychology at the undergraduate level; PhD: completion of research thesis at honours or master's level

AVAILABLE FOR QUALIFIED STUDENTS:
Fellowships, research assistantships. The financial aid is university-wide rather than specific to the department. It is competitive and based on a ranking of all the candidates being considered.

ASSISTANTSHIPS:

0% fellowships, 20% research assistantships, 10% teaching assistantships, 0% tuition waivers, 10% other forms of financial aid

INTERNSHIP POSSIBILITY:

Yes

INTERNSHIP REQUIRED:

Recommended but not required for PhD; available and selective for MS

NUMBER OF HOURS REQUIRED:

1000 hours (consistent with Australian Psychological Society guidelines for approved degree programs)

CORE GRADUATE CLASSES:

DESCRIPTION OF TYPICAL INTERNSHIP EXPERIENCE:

Course credit is available for hands-on work with sport teams and/or individual athletes. Experiences vary but usually include working with teams and/or players for a 6-to-9-month period under the supervision of a faculty member. Activities undertaken include needs assessment, intervention, and evaluation of treatment effects.

COMMENTS:

The MS includes course work in social psychology of sport, applied sport psychology, and exercise psychology. Supervised internships can be taken as electives within the MS program. The PhD is research-based, with course work required only if the student's background is considered deficient in relevant areas. PhD candidates are expected to spend 2-4 years conducting and publishing research in a specific area within exercise and sport psychology. We recommend but do not require that doctoral students take part in both a teaching internship and a field internship. PhD candidates are also encouraged to pursue external grants to support their research.

University of Western Ontario
School of Kinesiology

University of Western Ontario
Faculty of Health Sciences
London, ON
Canada
N6A 3K7

Contact:	Craig R. Hall	**Contact:**	Albert V. Carron
Title:	Professor	**Title:**	Professor
Phone:	519.661.2111 x88388	**Phone:**	519.661.2111 x 85475
Fax:	519.661.2008	**Fax:**	519.661.2008
Email:	chall@uwo.ca	**Email:**	bcarron@uwo.ca
Website:	www.uwo.ca/kinesiology/	**Website:**	www.uwo.ca/kinesiology/
Area of Interest:	Imagery, self-efficacy	**Area of Interest:**	Group dynamics, home advantage

PROGRAM RATING

1   2   3   4   5   **6**   7

1 to 3 Applied Orientation, 3 to 6 Equal Emphasis, 6 to 7 Research Orientation

DEGREE OFFERED:
MA, PhD

NUMBER OF STUDENTS IN PROGRAM:
75

NUMBER OF STUDENTS IN EACH DEGREE PROGRAM:
50% MA/50% PhD

NUMBER OF STUDENTS WHO APPLY/ARE ACCEPTED ANNUALLY:
100 apply/15-20 accepted

ADMISSION REQUIREMENTS:
Master's: honors BA or equivalent in kinesiology, mid-B average; PhD: MA/MS in kinesiology

AVAILABLE FOR QUALIFIED STUDENTS:
Research assistantships, teaching assistantships, other forms of financial aid

ASSISTANTSHIPS:
25% fellowships, 20% research assistantships, 70% teaching assistantships, 0% tuition waivers, 5% other forms of financial aid

INTERNSHIP POSSIBILITY:
Yes

INTERNSHIP REQUIRED:
No

NUMBER OF HOURS REQUIRED:

CORE GRADUATE CLASSES:

DESCRIPTION OF TYPICAL INTERNSHIP EXPERIENCE:

COMMENTS:
Developing psychological intervention programs for varsity athletes

University of Windsor
Department of Kinesiology

University of Windsor
401 Sunset Avenue
Windsor, ON
Canada
N9B 3P4

Contact:	Krista Chandler	**Contact:**	Todd Loughead
Title:	Associate Professor	**Title:**	Assistant Professor
Phones:	519.253.3000 ,ext. 2446	Phones:	519.253.3000,ext. 2450
Fax:	519.973.7056	Fax:	519.973.7056
Email:	chandler@uwindsor.ca	Email:	loughead@uwindsor.ca
Website:	www.uwindsor.ca/hk/chandler	Website:	www.uwindsor.ca/hk/loughead

Area of Interest: Imagery, Body Image (Exercise Addiction, Drive for Muscularity), Youth Sport, Performance Enhancement

Area of Interest: Group Dynamics, Cohesion, Athlete Leadership, Aggression, Youth Sport

PROGRAM RATING

1   2   3   4   **5**   6   7

1 to 3 Applied Orientation, 3 to 6 Equal Emphasis, 6 to 7 Research Orientation

DEGREE OFFERED:
Master of Human Kinetics (MHK)

NUMBER OF STUDENTS IN PROGRAM:
60

NUMBER OF STUDENTS IN EACH DEGREE PROGRAM:
N/A

NUMBER OF STUDENTS WHO APPLY/ARE ACCEPTED ANNUALLY:
15 apply/4 accepted

ADMISSION REQUIREMENTS:
The MHK requires a B average and two letters of reference.

AVAILABLE FOR QUALIFIED STUDENTS:
We offer traditional teaching assistantships as well as scholarship opportunities. We hold biweekly research "club" meetings to facilitate individual and collaborative research. We have established relationships with athletic teams. These are wonderful opportunities to work with athletes.

ASSISTANTSHIPS:
Yes

INTERNSHIP POSSIBILITY:
Yes

INTERNSHIP REQUIRED:
No

NUMBER OF HOURS REQUIRED:

CORE GRADUATE CLASSES:
Advanced Topics in Sport and Exercise Psychology, Advanced Topics in Group Dynamics

DESCRIPTION OF TYPICAL INTERNSHIP EXPERIENCE:

COMMENTS:
Our program is unique in that it offers a low student-advisor ratio, which allows students to participate in various research projects. As a result, students receive individualized mentorship.

University of Wisconsin, Milwaukee

Department of Human Movement Sciences

University of Wisconsin, Milwaukee
412 Enderis Hall
PO Box 413
Milwaukee, WI 53201

Contact: Barbara B. Meyer
Title:
Phone: 414.229.4591
Fax: 414.229.2619
Email: bbmeyer@uwm.edu
Website: www3.uwm.edu/chs/faculty/faculty.asp?facultyID=51
Area of Interest: Emotional intelligence in sport, performance enhancement & psychological skills training, social psychology, psychology of injury

Contact: J. Carson Smith
Title: Assistant Professor
Phone: 414.229.5553
Fax: 414.229.2619
Email: jcarson@uwm.edu
Website: www3.uwm.edu/chs/faculty/faculty.asp?facultyID=119
Area of Interest: Anxiety, depression, emotional reactivity, stress, psychophysiology, neuroscience, exercise adherence, public health

PROGRAM RATING

1   2   3   4   **5**   6   7

1 to 3 Applied Orientation, 3 to 6 Equal Emphasis, 6 to 7 Research Orientation

DEGREE OFFERED:
MS & PhD

NUMBER OF STUDENTS IN PROGRAM:
25-30

NUMBER OF STUDENTS IN EACH DEGREE PROGRAM:
MS = 25-30; PhD = 2-4

NUMBER OF STUDENTS WHO APPLY/ARE ACCEPTED ANNUALLY:
MS = 10/2-5

ADMISSION REQUIREMENTS:
MS degree program: (a) undergraduate GPA of 2.75 or better, (b) GRE total score (verbal + quantitative) of 1000 PhD program: (a) MS degree or equivalent, (b) GPA of 3.0 or better on all previous coursework, (c) GRE, (d) sample of written work, (e) letter outlining the applicant's academic and professional back-

ground, as well as specific interests and goals for the PhD program, (f) three letters of recommendation from from individuals familiar with the applicant's intellectual achievement and potential, (g) agreement from an eligible faculty member to serve as the applicant's major professor.

AVAILABLE FOR QUALIFIED STUDENTS:

Teaching assistantships (for core undergraduate courses such as sport & exercise psychology, exercise physiology, motor learning, etc.) Research assistantships (dependent upon extramural funding) Project assistantships & hourly work (dependent upon extramural funding) Other forms of financial aid (e.g., fellowships, travel awards)

ASSISTANTSHIPS:

20% fellowships and/or research assistantships, 30% teaching assistantships, 20% project assistantships & hourly work

INTERNSHIP POSSIBILITY:

Yes, interdisciplinary internships may be arranged in conjunction with other campus disciplines, such as psychology or counseling.

INTERNSHIP REQUIRED:

No

NUMBER OF HOURS REQUIRED:

CORE GRADUATE CLASSES:

DESCRIPTION OF TYPICAL INTERNSHIP EXPERIENCE:

Dependent upon the needs of the student and the internship "site," as well as the availability of faculty supervisors. Attempts will be made to amass the hours required for AAASP certification. Dependent on student interest and faculty availability

COMMENTS:

MS degree program: The Department of Human Movement Sciences at the University of Wisconsin-Milwaukee offers a Master of Science degree program emphasizing applied research in the human movement sciences. The program provides instruction and research opportunities for students interested in studying the biopsychosocial aspects of human movement. The thrust of the curriculum is the integration of the body of knowledge fundamental to the science of human movement through study in at least three of the five subdisciplines represented by the faculty in the program (i.e., psychology of physical activity, sociology of physical activity, motor control, exercise physiology, and biomechanics). The integrative nature of the human movement sciences degree provides an excellent foundation for continued education in the movement sciences, psychology, and other health-related disciplines (e.g., athletic training, physical therapy, medicine). The psychology of physical activity emphasis at the University of Wisconsin-Milwaukee includes two tracks (i.e., sport psychology, exercise psychology). The focus of the sport psychology track is on the symbiotic relationship between the psyche and sport participation/performance, as well as the applications emanating from these relationships. The focus of the exercise psychology track is on the study of the brain and behavior in both leisure-time physical activity and exercise settings, including the mental health effects related to the psychobiological, behavioral, and social cognitive antecedents and consequences of physical activity. Students in both tracks are encouraged to participate in collaborative and original research projects, as well as to consider applied outlets for their work. PhD program: The PhD in Health Sciences is an interdisciplinary degree program designed to accomplish three major objectives: 1) provide advanced study and research training opportunities in the human health sciences; 2) produce cohorts of scholars capable of advancing the discovery, dissemination, and application of new knowledge in the health sciences; and 3) prepare future academic leaders in the health sciences. The curriculum includes a set of core courses providing a comprehensive structure for doctoral education including: 1) philosophical foundations; 2) concepts and practices that contribute to students' development as teaching scholars; 3) research methods; and 4) a series of seminars that build students' critical thinking skills, familiarity with a range of health sciences research topics, and experience in scholarly dialogue and presentation. In addition to the core courses, the program includes concentration and cross-disciplinary courses in areas such as disability and rehabilitation, diagnostic and biomedical sciences, human movement sciences (e.g., sport & exercise psychology), population health, and health administration/policy. Independent research and the dissertation will be structured according to the choice of specialization. For additional information, see: www3.uwm.edu/chs/academics/doctoral/

Utah State University
Department of Health, Physical Education, and Recreation

Utah State University
Logan, UT 84322-7000

Contact: Richard Gordin
Title:
Phone: 435.797.1506
Fax: 435.797.3759
Email: gordin@cc.usu.edu
Website: www.usu.edu/
Area of Interest: Intervention/performance enhancement

PROGRAM RATING

1   2   **3**   4   5   6   7

1 to 3 Applied Orientation, 3 to 6 Equal Emphasis, 6 to 7 Research Orientation

DEGREE OFFERED:
MS

NUMBER OF STUDENTS IN PROGRAM:
2 to 5

NUMBER OF STUDENTS IN EACH DEGREE PROGRAM:

NUMBER OF STUDENTS WHO APPLY/ARE ACCEPTED ANNUALLY:
2-5 apply/2 accepted

ADMISSION REQUIREMENTS:
3.00 GPA (undergraduate), 43 MAT or minimum of 40th percentile on GRE, three strong letters of recommendation

AVAILABLE FOR QUALIFIED STUDENTS:
Research assistantships, teaching assistantships

ASSISTANTSHIPS:
0% fellowships, 50% research assistantships, 50% teaching assistantships, 0% tuition waivers, 0% other forms of financial aid

INTERNSHIP POSSIBILITY:
Yes

INTERNSHIP REQUIRED:
No

NUMBER OF HOURS REQUIRED:
Depends on opportunity; however, we will attempt to amass the 400 hours required for AAASP certification.

CORE GRADUATE CLASSES:

DESCRIPTION OF TYPICAL INTERNSHIP EXPERIENCE:
The student will usually interact with an athlete or a team in a consulting relationship under the guidance of a certified consultant, or will interact with the teams while collecting data for the thesis. The area of emphasis in research is usually intervention/performance enhancement. This is an applied program.

COMMENTS:

Victoria University
School of Human Movement, Recreation, and Performance

Footscray Park Campus
PO Box 14428
Melbourne Mail Centre
Melbourne, VIC
Australia
8001

Contact: Daryl Marchant
Title: HMRP Research & Postgraduate Coordinator
Phone: 03.9919.4035.0403.065358
Fax: 03.9688.4891
Email: daryl.marchant@vu.edu.au
Website: www.vu.edu.au/
Area of Interest: Anxiety, Psychological Skills Training, counseling, applied sport psychology, assessment and psychometrics

Contact: Mark Andersen
Title: Associate Professor
Phone: 61.3.9248.1132
Fax: 61.3.9248.1110
Email: mark.andersen@vu.edu.au
Website: www.vu.edu.au/
Area of Interest: Health psychology, athletic injury, supervision, counseling

Contact: Harriet Speed
Title: Senior Lecturer
Phone: 03.9919.5412
Fax: 03.9919.4891
Email: harriet.speed@vu.edu.au
Website:
Area of Interest: Injury prevention, athlete career education, quantitative methods

Contact: Tony Morris
Title: Professor
Phone: 03.9919.5353
Fax: 03.9919.4891
Email: tony.morris@vu.edu.au
Website:
Area of Interest: Psychological Skills Training, transitions, motivation, counseling, imagery

PROGRAM RATING

1   2   3   4   5   6   7

1 to 3 Applied Orientation, 3 to 6 Equal Emphasis, 6 to 7 Research Orientation: Unrated

DEGREE OFFERED:
MAP by course work, MAS by research, PhD by research, Professional Doctorate

NUMBER OF STUDENTS IN PROGRAM:
12 MAP; 30 MAS/PhD

NUMBER OF STUDENTS IN EACH DEGREE PROGRAM:
28.5% MAP; 71.5% MAS/PhD

NUMBER OF STUDENTS WHO APPLY/ARE ACCEPTED ANNUALLY:
MAP biannually entry in odd years. 25 apply/12 accepted

ADMISSION REQUIREMENTS:
MAP: four years of APS-accredited psychology (national equivalents of the Australian Psychological Society, such as the APA and the BPS, should be accepted); MAS: undergraduate degree in any relevant area (MAS candidates can transfer to PhD subject to satisfactory progress, usually after first study successfully completed); PhD: undergraduate degree and honours year or equivalent

AVAILABLE FOR QUALIFIED STUDENTS:
Research assistantships, teaching assistantships, other forms of financial aid

ASSISTANTSHIPS:
20% fellowships/scholarships, 0% research assistantships, 10% teaching assistantships, 25-40% tuition waivers (approximately 25% of MAS students and 40% of PhD students receive tuition waivers), 0% other forms of financial aid

INTERNSHIP POSSIBILITY:
Yes

INTERNSHIP REQUIRED:
Yes, for MAP only; not required for MAS or PhD

NUMBER OF HOURS REQUIRED:
Approximately 1000 hours total, spread over several practica/internships

CORE GRADUATE CLASSES:

DESCRIPTION OF TYPICAL INTERNSHIP EXPERIENCE:
Students are required to complete one general practicum not in sport psychology (these are quite varied—potentially, at least) and one or more practica in sport psychology. The latter are also potentially varied, including work in our own clinic; work with private practitioners; work at the Australian Institute of Sport, the Victorian Institute of Sport, and other state institutions; work in sports clubs or with teams; and work in exercise settings such as rehabilitation centres and sports medicine clinics. (Note: Practica are only available for PhD and MAS research students and are rather limited, but plans for further opportunities are in development.)

COMMENTS:
The Master of Applied Psychology is offered by Physical Education in conjunction with the Department of Psychology to ensure accreditation within the new Australian system for accrediting sport-psychology-professional training courses. It is one of only four such programs in Australia. The program consists of a core of professional skills in psychology taught with specialists in other areas and including assessment, ethical issues, research methods, counseling practice, and health and organizational psychology. Four specialist subjects in sport psychology cover theory, applications, practice issues, and practice organization. In addition, there are the practicum and a substantial thesis on an applied topic. The thesis topic is largely up to the student to select, provided it has an applied focus. Students are also free to negotiate their own practicum placements, but help is available if needed. Regarding the doctoral/master's research program,

the only required course work for students in Australia (at VUT, at least) is a research design course (exception if equivalent can be demonstrated). Students may choose or be advised to sit subjects relevant to their research/career aims if not experienced in those areas. Students work closely with a principal supervisor backed up by the sport psych team and a range of other specialists. They select and develop their own research areas under guidance. The department has a vast network of local and national connections in all aspects of sport, to offer opportunities for field experiences and research. A sport psychology research group offers opportunities to communicate research plans, results, and conclusions in a friendly atmosphere and to hear and discuss the ideas of staff and other research students on projects and on one another's work. This also offers good practice for conference presentations. There are also area-specific research groups on such issues as imagery, career transitions, motivation, and sports injuries where sufficient staff and student research interest is focused.

Virginia Commonwealth University
Life Skills Center

Virginia Commonwealth University
Department of Psychology
PO Box 2018
Richmond, VA 23284

Contact: Steven J. Danish
Title:
Phone: 804.828.4384
Fax: 804.828.0239
Email: sdanish@vcu.edu
Website: www.has.vcu.edu/psy/counseling/index.html, www.vcu.edu
Area of Interest: Life skills, youth sports, performance enhancement (See Life Skills Center
Website: www.lifeskills.vcu.edu.)

PROGRAM RATING

1 2 3 4 5 **6** 7

1 to 3 Applied Orientation, 3 to 6 Equal Emphasis, 6 to 7 Research Orientation

DEGREE OFFERED:
PhD

NUMBER OF STUDENTS IN PROGRAM:
2 in sport psychology (total of 150 graduate students in psychology, with 35 graduate students in counseling psychology)

NUMBER OF STUDENTS IN EACH DEGREE PROGRAM:

NUMBER OF STUDENTS WHO APPLY/ARE ACCEPTED ANNUALLY:
200 apply/8 accepted (counseling psychology program)

ADMISSION REQUIREMENTS:
There are no minimum GRE or GPA scores. Interested applicants are sent profiles of typical students accepted. Because admission is so competitive, GRE scores, GPA scores, human services and research experiences, the number of psychology courses taken, and references rank as important criteria.

AVAILABLE FOR QUALIFIED STUDENTS:
Fellowships, research assistantships, teaching assistantships, other forms of financial aid

ASSISTANTSHIPS:
During the first three years: 10% fellowships, 30% research assistantships, 60% teaching assistantships, 0% tuition waivers, 0% other forms of financial aid

INTERNSHIP POSSIBILITY:
Yes, paid

INTERNSHIP REQUIRED:
Yes

NUMBER OF HOURS REQUIRED:
2000 hours (APA-approved program)

CORE GRADUATE CLASSES:
See website for sample program.

DESCRIPTION OF TYPICAL INTERNSHIP EXPERIENCE:
Internships in psychology are not done on campus and are a competitive process in themselves. They may have nothing to do with sport psychology. Assistantships may have opportunities associated with one of the life-skills and youth-sport programs, doing research/training.

COMMENTS:
There are no formal courses in sport psychology within the department or within the counseling program. The focus of the training and research opportunities is on children and adolescents through the Life Skills Center, directed by Dr. Danish. Some of the Center programs use sport as a metaphor for teaching life skills; other programs use sport as a vehicle to teach life skills. Sport psychology within the program is defined very broadly: It involves the use of sport to enhance competence and to promote human development throughout the lifespan. Given this definition, sport psychologists are as concerned about life development as they are about athletic development. Students who pursue subspecialties in sport psychology or performance excellence have the opportunity to be supervised. In 1995, The Counseling Psychologist published research by Hanish, Horan, Keen, St. Peter, Ceperich, and Beasley that ranked VCU second in citations among counseling psychology programs nationwide, and fourth in articles listed in PsychLit.

Wayne State University
Division of Health, Physical Education, and Recreation

Wayne State University
Matthaei Building
Detroit, MI 48202

Contact: Jeff Martin
Title:
Phone: 313.577.1381
Fax: 313.577.5999
Email: 993975@wayne.edu
Website: www.wayne.edu/
Area of Interest: Exercise and sport psychology, motivation, self-efficacy, disability sport

PROGRAM RATING

1   2   3   4   5   6   **7**

1 to 3 Applied Orientation, 3 to 6 Equal Emphasis, 6 to 7 Research Orientation

DEGREE OFFERED:
MEd

NUMBER OF STUDENTS IN PROGRAM:
Fewer than 10 (almost all part-time)

NUMBER OF STUDENTS IN EACH DEGREE PROGRAM:

NUMBER OF STUDENTS WHO APPLY/ARE ACCEPTED ANNUALLY:
This is a new program.

ADMISSION REQUIREMENTS:
Minimum 3.00 GPA, degree in related area, and GRE required for regular admission; write for details regarding qualified admission.

AVAILABLE FOR QUALIFIED STUDENTS:
Fellowships, research assistantships, teaching assistantships, other forms of financial aid

ASSISTANTSHIPS:
(All offered on a competitive basis.) 0% fellowships, 5-10% research assistantships, 5-10% teaching assistantships, 5-10% tuition waivers (part of assistantships), 0% other forms of financial aid

INTERNSHIP POSSIBILITY:
Yes

INTERNSHIP REQUIRED:
No

NUMBER OF HOURS REQUIRED:
3 credit hours

CORE GRADUATE CLASSES:

DESCRIPTION OF TYPICAL INTERNSHIP EXPERIENCE:
New program

COMMENTS:

West Virginia University
School of Physical Education, Sport Behavior Program

West Virginia University
268 Coliseum, PO Box 6116
Morgantown, WV 26506-6116

Contact: Sam Zizzi
Title: Program Coordinator & Assistant Professor
Phone: 304.293.3295 x5240
Fax: 304.293.4641
Email: sam.zizzi@mail.wvu.edu
Website:
Area of Interest: Physical activity promotion, exercise psychology, applied sport psychology training and practice

Contact: Dana Brooks
Title: Dean and Professor
Phone: 304.293.3295 x5285
Fax: 304.293.4641
Email: dana.brooks@mail.wvu.edu
Website:
Area of Interest: Leadership, cohesion, African-American athlete

Contact: Jack Watson
Title: Assistant Professor
Phone: 304.293.3295 x5273
Fax: 304.293.4641
Email: Jack.Watson@mail.wvu.edu

Website:
Area of Interest: Social psychology, performance enhancement, counseling psychology, professional issues

Contact: Andrew Ostrow
Title: Professor
Phone: 304.293.3295 x5268
Fax: 304.293.4641
Email: aostrow2@wvu.edu
Website: www.wvu.edu/~physed/sportpsych/spmain.htm
Area of Interest: Sport psychology assessment, developmental sport psychology, performance enhancement

Contact: Edward Etzel
Title: Psychologist/Associate Professor
Phone: 304.293.7062 x4431
Fax: 304.293.4641
Email: Edward.Etzel@mail.wvu.edu
Website:
Area of Interest: Counseling college student-athletes, ethics in sport psychology, career transitions of athletes, sport injury, addictions

PROGRAM RATING

1   2   3   **4**   5   6   7

1 to 3 Applied Orientation, 3 to 6 Equal Emphasis, 6 to 7 Research Orientation: 4

DEGREE OFFERED:
EdD

NUMBER OF STUDENTS IN PROGRAM:
12 to 15

NUMBER OF STUDENTS IN EACH DEGREE PROGRAM:

NUMBER OF STUDENTS WHO APPLY/ARE ACCEPTED ANNUALLY:
40-50 apply/3-5 accepted

ADMISSION REQUIREMENTS:
(January 2 deadline for receipt of all credentials) 3.00 undergraduate GPA (minimum); 1050 GRE or 55 MAT (minimum); three letters of reference; interview (preferably during the program's Interview Weekend, conducted each spring semester on campus); written professional goals statement

AVAILABLE FOR QUALIFIED STUDENTS:
Fellowships, teaching assistantships, other forms of financial aid are available in sport psychology, the CHAMPS/Life Skills program, and with other campus organizations.

ASSISTANTSHIPS:
We offer two graduate teaching assistantships in sport psychology, and teaching assistantships are available in the physical activity Basic Instruction program in the School of Physical Education. We have had a high success rate in placing our graduate students in other funded assistantships (e.g., academic advising, research positions, CHAMPS/ Life Skills program) on the WVU campus. Three of our doctoral applicants have been awarded the prestigious Arlen Swiger fellowship, which pays an annual stipend of $15,000 plus a waiver of tuition and all other fees. For detailed information about financial opportunities, click on www.wvu.edu/~physed/sportpsych/docassistance.htm

INTERNSHIP POSSIBILITY:
Yes

INTERNSHIP REQUIRED:
As part of their doctoral plan of study, students are required to complete 12 credit hours of internship and 4 credit hours of supervision over four semesters. For further details click on www.wvu.edu/~physed/sportpsych/docinternship.htm

NUMBER OF HOURS REQUIRED:
Students are required to complete a minimum of 180 internship hours and 60 hours of supervision. The majority of students complete approximately 300 internship hours and 100 supervision hours.

CORE GRADUATE CLASSES:
See www.wvu.edu/~physed/sportpsych/doccurriculum.htm

DESCRIPTION OF TYPICAL INTERNSHIP EXPERIENCE:
Students complete internships that are arranged by the faculty. The majority of these internships are with university athletic teams, university club teams, a university-based CHAMPS/Life Skills program, and high school teams. Students are also encouraged to complete internship hours in a university-based adult disease prevention program, with chronically ill patients. Other internship opportunities are available off campus.

COMMENTS:

The graduate program in sport psychology has positioned itself as one of the leading programs in applied sport psychology in the country. The program employs four full-time faculty members, two of whom are psychologists with expertise in athlete counseling and performance enhancement interventions. In fact, one licensed psychologist is a former Olympic gold medalist in shooting and is also the psychologist for the WVU Department of Intercollegiate Athletics. The Sport Psychology Graduate Student Club promotes close professional and personal relationships among students enrolled in the program. The graduate program in sport psychology has very close ties with the departments of Counseling, Counseling Psychology, and Rehabilitation Psychology, with several faculty members holding adjunct appointments between departments. There is a strong commitment to interdisciplinary graduate education. The program prides itself on having an excellent balance between research training and opportunities for developing applied skills. What makes the graduate program in sport psychology at West Virginia University unique? First, while there is not a master's degree program track, students can be admitted to the doctoral program with either baccalaureate or master's degrees. Second, students admitted to the doctoral program in sport psychology are also admitted to the master's program in counseling. Thus, graduates of the program can sit for the licensure examination to become professional counselors. For complete details about the program, visit our extensive website at www.wvu.edu/~physed/sportpsych/spmain.htm

Western Illinois University

Department of Kinesiology

Western Illinois University
Brophy Hall
Macomb, IL 61455

Contact: Laura Finch
Title: Professor & CC, AAASP
Phone: 309.298.2350 (office), 309.298.1820 (department)
Fax: 309.298.2981
Email: LM-Finch@wiu.edu
Website: www.wiu.edu/users/mflmf/sportpsych/
Area of Interest: Applied sport psychology, coping strategies, performance enhancement, youth sport, sport sociology

Contact: Steve Radlo
Title: Associate Professor
Phone:
Fax:
Email:
Website:
Area of Interest: EKG, stress management

PROGRAM RATING

1   2   **3.5**   4   5   6   7

1 to 3 Applied Orientation, 3 to 6 Equal Emphasis, 6 to 7 Research Orientation

DEGREE OFFERED:
MS in Kinesiology, MS in Sport Management

NUMBER OF STUDENTS IN PROGRAM:
100 full-time students in the department; about 5 to 6 per year in sport psychology program

NUMBER OF STUDENTS IN EACH DEGREE PROGRAM:
50% MS in Kinesiology/50% MS in Sport Management

NUMBER OF STUDENTS WHO APPLY/ARE ACCEPTED ANNUALLY:
100 apply/50 accepted in department; about 12-16 apply, 8-12 accepted in sport psychology program

ADMISSION REQUIREMENTS:
3.00 undergraduate GPA (cumulative) or 3.20 GPA in last 2 years. Lower GPAs (2.75 – 2.99) may be admitted on probation. No GRE scores are required.

AVAILABLE FOR QUALIFIED STUDENTS:
Fellowships (university based), Research assistantships, Teaching assistantships, Other forms of financial aid (university based, e.g., athletics, University Union, Campus Recreation)

ASSISTANTSHIPS:
00% Fellowships, 33% Research assistantships, 33% Teaching assistantships, 100% Tuition waivers (All students with assistantships receive full tuition waivers.), 33% Other forms of financial aid

INTERNSHIP POSSIBILITY:
Yes

INTERNSHIP REQUIRED:
Recommended for sport psychology specialization, Recommended for coaching/teaching specialization, Required for sport management specialization.

NUMBER OF HOURS REQUIRED:
4-6 semester hours

CORE GRADUATE CLASSES:
KIN 549: Stress Management (2 credits) KIN 556: Motor Learning and Human Performance (3 credits) KIN 559: Sport Psychology (3 credits) KIN 569: Applied Sport Psychology (3 credits) KIN 571: Development of Expert Performance (3 credits) KIN 579: Research & Professional Issues in Sport Psychology (1 credit) KIN 589: Sport Psychology Intervention Techniques (1-3 credits, repeatable)

DESCRIPTION OF TYPICAL INTERNSHIP EXPERIENCE:
Individual and team experiences ranging from youth to college- and master's-level athletes in competitive sport environments as well as exercise and wellness settings. The internship is designed to enrich the student's academic and career goals, so the internship experience varies depending on the student. The student is responsible for demonstrating initiative in securing the internship site. Internships provide individual and team experiences ranging from youth to college- and master's-level athletes in competitive sport environments as well as in exercise and wellness settings. The internship is designed to enrich the student's academic and career goals, so the internship experience varies depending on the student. The student is responsible for demonstrating initiative in securing the internship site.

COMMENTS:
The sport and exercise psychology program at Western Illinois is looking for motivated graduate students who want to adopt a scientist-practitioner framework to structure their study of sport psychology. The goal of the graduate specialization in sport and exercise psychology is twofold: (1) to prepare future professionals in the field of sport and exercise psychology (i.e., doctoral study); or (2) to provide teachers, coaches, and sport, exercise and fitness professionals with specialized study in sport and exercise psychology to compliment their existing knowledge base and careers. You will design your own program around a departmental core. Based on how you choose your electives, your program of study can focus on either sport, physical education, OR exercise. A variety of learning formats are available, including traditional classes, seminars, and workshops, as well as independent studies and research projects. Some summer school is also available. Supporting departmental course work is offered in coaching, pedagogy, sport sociology, fitness and wellness, exercise science, adapted physical education, and sport management. Supervised internship/practica opportunities can be arranged with faculty (AAASP-certified consultant) for additional experiences in sport psychology. Both thesis and non-thesis degree options are available. The sport psychology program recognizes the contributions of both research and practice to sport psychology. The flexibility of the Western Illinois program allows you to pursue either option after your core course work has been successfully completed. Because you are undertaking study in an interdisciplinary

field, it is imperative that you have an understanding of both the "parent" disciplines that comprise the field. Hence, course work is recommended in both Kinesiology and Psychology or Counseling. Suggested options are provided in the outside electives so that the needs of a diverse student body can be met. A dual-degree is available in counseling psychology for those who meet that department's admission requirements. Careful selection of electives will help prepare you for AAASP (Association for the Advancement of Applied Sport Psychology) certification as a sport psychology consultant upon completion of a doctoral degree. WIU is a public university that enrolls about 13,000 students. We are located in a rural community in west central Illinois, approximately 3.5 hours SW of Chicago, and 3 hours N of St. Louis. The program takes 1-2 years to complete, depending on course work choices, thesis option selected, and summer school. Most students begin the program in the fall, but January enrollment is possible. GRE scores are not required. Strong ties exist with the psychology and counseling departments; thus, possibilities for interdisciplinary work are numerous. The program is small enough to allow for one-on-one contact with faculty, yet large enough to allow students to learn from each other in a team approach as well. Students can gain practical experience through teaching opportunities, joint research projects with faculty, and supervised consulting and workshop experiences.

Guide to Appendices

The appendices are designed to facilitate your use of the information in the directory, as well as to provide other resources for you to use to your advantage in learning more about applied sport psychology and in considering the various programs. A brief description of each appendix follows.

Appendix A: Additions and Deletions to Directory Entries indicates the programs that have been added to this current edition of the directory and those that have been deleted from the previous edition. These lists may be particularly useful for those familiar with earlier editions of the directory.

Appendix B: A Word About Internships provides information about internships. Many students are interested in finding internships or learning more about them.

Appendix C: Supervision of Applied Sport Psychology in Graduate School. This new appendix follows on information about internships to provide critical background on supervision of applied sport psychology work in which you will engage in graduate school.

Appendix D: Doctoral Programs in Clinical and Counseling Psychology provides information about doctoral programs in clinical/counseling psychology that are not listed in this directory but may still be of interest to students with a passion for applied sport psychology.

Appendix E: Graduate Training and Career Possibilities provides a copy of the graduate training and career possibilities brochure published jointly by Division 47 (Exercise and Sport Psychology) of the APA (American Psychological Association), the AAASP (Association for the Advancement of Applied Sport Psychology), and the NASPSPA (North American Society for the Psychology of Sport and Physical Activity). This brochure is very valuable background reading for students interested in applied sport psychology.

Appendix F: Ethical Principles and Standards of the Association for the Advancement of Applied Sport Psychology provides a copy of the ethical principles and standards of the AAASP.

Appendix G: Texts in Applied Sport Psychology provides a list of texts in applied sport psychology that readers may wish to consider for valuable background reading in the field.

Appendix H: References in Applied Sport Psychology: Professional and Ethical Issues provides a list of references in applied sport psychology, focusing on professional and ethical issues; readers may wish to consider the list for valuable background reading in the field.

Appendix I: Reading List in Applied Sport Psychology: Psychological Skills Training provides a list of books in applied sport psychology, focusing particularly on psychological skills training; readers may wish to consider for valuable background reading in the field.

Appendix J: Reference List of Mental Training/Sport Psychology Videos provides a list of mental training/sport psychology videos that readers may wish to consider for valuable background information in the field or for current use.

Appendix K: Geographical List of Graduate Programs provides a geographical list, by country, of programs in the directory.

Appendix L: Contact Persons provides an alphabetical list of contact persons, along with emails, telephone numbers, websites, and other information, for programs in the directory.

Appendix M: Surfing the Net: Using the Internet for Success provides information on using the Internet in your work in exercise and sport psychology.

Appendix N: Websites for Programs provides a list of websites for the programs included in the directory.

Appendix O: Location of Graduate Programs: Physical Education and Psychology, Master's and Doctoral Levels provides information on whether programs listed in the directory are in physical education, kinesiology, exercise and sport sciences, or psychology, and whether they offer master's and/or doctoral programs.

Appendix P: Quick Chart of Program Information: Degrees Offered, Program-Emphasis Rating, and Internship Possibility provides an alphabetical list of programs with the information indicated by the title.

Appendix A
Additions and Deletions to Directory Entries

A few programs have been deleted from those listed in the previous edition of the directory, primarily due to programmatic changes, faculty transferring to other universities, or faculty retiring. Deletions may also occur due to a request from the school to be removed or by editorial decision (generally due to no response from school, knowledge of faculty and/or programmatic changes). Programs have also been added to this current edition of the directory. There have been changes to many of the Directory entries—because the Directory is available in an online version through Fitness Information Technology, it is therefore kept relatively current as changes occur. Readers should check all programs in which they might be interested. The specific deletions and additions are as follows:

Deleted:

California State University, Hayward
Deakin University
Mankato State University
University of Memphis (Psychology Dept.)
University of Montana
University of New Orleans
University of Southern Queensland
University of Western Sydney

Added:

California State University, East Bay
East Carolina University
East Tennessee State University
Rutgers University
University of Northern Iowa
University of Windsor

Appendix B
A Word About Internships

Michael L. Sachs, Temple University
Lois A. Butcher, Bucks County Community College
Shelley A. Wiechman, University of Washington
Sam Maniar, West Virginia University

Supervised field experiences are an important component of sport psychology training. A number of institutions in this directory list internships as part of their sport psychology programs. It is imperative that you regard these internship opportunities as vehicles toward practical application of course work and as part of the process for qualification as a certified consultant. Please remember, though, the differences (qualitative and quantitative) between practicum experiences and internships noted in the introduction to this directory and be sure you are informed about what is required of you and what experiences you may gain.

There are some cautions for the prospective student, and once again, as a consumer of the goods and services provided by the institution of your choice, you must make sure you get what you have bargained for. The expectations of a master's student may be quite different from those of a doctoral student or a postdoctoral individual who needs supervised hours to become a certified consultant. Commitment of time is critical! You need to decide if you are able to work independently and if you have enough financial support to get through the entire endeavor. Flexibility is essential. Your ideas about interning may not match the reality of the opportunities offered. For example, if you desire to work with elite athletes only, or to deal with one specific, high-level team, you may not get what you want. It is important to be open to experiences at clubs, schools, YMCAs, etc.

Be aware that if an institution states that it provides internships for its graduate students, only a small number of students in the program may be able to get them. Supervision is another issue. It may be nonexistent, minimal, or not what you expect. Check Appendix C for an excellent section on supervision and a list of references that include some issues regarding supervision.

Some programs have internships already identified for students and simply place students in those "slots." Other programs provide networking opportunities and encourage students to find internships on their own. This has a real-world advantage in that it requires students to make connections, develop relationships, and secure their own opportunities, as many will be required to do after completing their degree work. Clearly, you need to ask questions of faculty and current students, investigate options, and gather additional information to assist you in choosing a school and in avoiding potential problems and disappointments in your program.

Many of the institutions in this directory list internship opportunities for their students. There are internship opportunities that are not listed within the program information. Internships in exercise and sport psychology, as well as APA-approved predoctoral internships, may not be clearly identified within the program listings; a listing of these internships follows this section. This list is provided thanks to Dr. Sam Maniar, of West Virginia University, and developed for the newsletter of Division 47 (Division of Exercise and Sport Psychology), of APA (the American Psychological Association). Check their website at www.psyc.unt.edu/apadiv47. Complete information on one internship opportunity (Washington State University) is provided as well. Another internship opportunity that is not connected with any program listed in this directory is offered by the Lewis-Gale Clinic in Roanoke, VA; information concerning that program follows at the end of this appendix.

It is important to remember, though, the individual nature of each internship experience and of the facilities provided by or connected to each school. It is critical that, as a prospective student, you dig for information, especially if your interests and goals require some practical background experiences. Whether you are in an applied or research area, you must know certain things about what to expect regarding to your time, energy, and resources, and how to best utilize them. A few questions may help you with your search for a fulfilling internship experience:

1. Is the internship a requirement for degree completion?
2. If your interests are research oriented, will you gain practical lab/research experience?
3. If you are a hands-on, applied person, will the internship allow you be able to work with the populations that interest you (e.g., young children, individuals with eating disorders), or will it require you to work only with the teams/athletes at your school?
4. Are internships made available to you through your department or advisor? If so, how many are available for someone with your particular interest or focus? (It helps to know if you must compete for the spot.)
5. Is it up to you to create your own internship or to seek out an experience? Are contact lists provided to aid you in your search?
6. Will you be able to work independently, or would you have to work in tandem with your supervisor and/or another (perhaps more advanced) student-intern as an assistant?
7. If you do work independently, how much supervision will you have? Is supervision available or required for the internship? Who will be your supervisor?
8. Will you receive course credit for your internship work?
9. Are paid internship possible, or is the internship volunteer based? If it is a volunteer position, will you have the financial resources to support yourself during the internship period?
10. How much time are you willing and able to commit to your internship? Don't forget all the details that go into the work of a sport psychologist: Notes must be recorded; records must be kept; meetings with coaches, athletes, and your supervisor need to be arranged; etc. Keeping this information is also important if you decide to apply for certified consultant status (see the appendices for certification requirements of supervised experiences; keep good records!).

To gain especially valuable information on internships, talk to students who have done them. They can tell you what to expect in terms of time and effort, the effects on your personal life, and the impact on your other school- and course-work, as well as what the supervisors are like, etc. The student representatives for Division 47 (Exercise and Sport Psychology) of the American Psychological Association and for the AAASP (Association for the Advancement of Applied Sport Psychology) are also good sources of information.

Remember, internships are a critical means of honing your skills in sport psychology. An internship experience with appropriate supervision will give you important feedback that will allow you to refine your good points, improve your weak areas, and form a solid base for future reference with clients after you've left the cocoon of school and entered the real world.

Sport Psychology Internships

Exercise and Sport Sciences

Many programs provide applied experiences for their own graduate students. These programs are listed in the directory. The following programs provide internships for students separate from their graduate programs:

The Pennsylvania State University—Department of Intercollegiate Athletics (contact Dr. David Yukelson—see PSU entry)

Internship Sites with Sport Psychology Opportunities (rev. 8/14/02 by Sam Maniar, PhD)

Arizona State University Counseling and Consultation
Tempe, AZ 85287-1012
480.965.6147
Julie Savage, PhD
www.asu.edu/counseling_center/index1.html

Ball State University*
Counseling and Psychological Services Center
Muncie, IN 47306-0895
765.285.1267
Lee Van Donselaar, PhD
Jay S. Zimmerman, PhD
www.bsu.edu/students/cpsc

University of California at Davis
Counseling Center
Davis, CA 95616-8568
530.752.0871
Emil Rodolfa, PhD
www.counselingcenter.ucdavis.edu

University of California at Los Angeles
*UCLA Student Psychological Services
Los Angeles, CA 90095-1556
310.794.7950
William Parham, PhD
Tracy Shaw, PhD
Renee Kaplan, PhD
www.saonet.ucla.edu/sps/train/psych.htm

Colorado State University*
University Counseling Center
Fort Collins, CO 80523-8010
970.491.6053
Steve Ross, PsyD
Susan L. MacQuiddy, PhD
www.colostate.edu/Depts/Counseling/intrnltr.html

University of Delaware
Center for Counseling and Student Development
Newark, DE 19716-6501
302.831.8107
Richard S. Sharf, PhD
www.udel.edu/Counseling/

University of Florida*
University Counseling Center
Gainesville, FL 32611-4100
352.392.1575
Wayne D. Griffin, PhD
Michael C. Murphy, PhD
Nancy C. Coleman, PhD
www.counsel.ufl.edu/Internship/intern.html

George Washington University
*University Counseling Center
Washington D.C. 20052
Lori A. Lefcourt, PhD
William G. Pinney, PhD
gwired.gwu.edu/counsel/

University of Iowa
University Counseling Service
Iowa City, IA 52242-1100
319.335.7294
Julie M. Corkery, PhD
www.uiowa.edu/~ucs

Iowa State University*
Student Counseling Service
Ames, IA 50011-2223
515.294.5056
Frank "Marty" I. Martinez, PhD
Jeanne M. Burkhart, PhD
www.public.iastate.edu/~stdt_couns_info/home-page.html

Kansas State University#*
University Counseling Services
Manhattan, KS 66506-3301
785.532.6927
Fred B. Newton, PhD
Sherry A. Benton, PhD
www.ksu.edu/ucs/

University of Massachusetts
Amherst Counseling and Assessment Services
Amherst, MA 01003-0620
413.545.6203
Donald L. Banks, EdD
www.umass.edu/counseling/

University of New Hampshire*
Counseling Center
Durham, NH 03824-3556
603.862.2090
David M. J. Cross, PhD
C. Patricia Hanley, PhD
www.unhcc.unh.edu/

North Shore University Hospital#
Manhasset, NY
516.562.3052

University of Notre Dame*
University Counseling Center
Notre Dame, IN 46556-5693
219.631.7336
Miguel Franco, PhD
Luis G. Manzo, PhD
Susan Steibe-Pasalich, PhD
www.nd.edu/~psyintn/

The Ohio State University*
Counseling and Consultation Service
Columbus, OH 43201-2333
614.292.5766
Neal Newman, PhD
Jerry Stern, PhD
Karen M. Taylor, PhD
ccs-server.ccs.ohio-state.edu

University of Oregon*
Counseling Center
Eugene, OR 97403-1280
541.346.3227
Vivian Barnette, PhD
Shelly Kerr, PhD
darkwing.uoregon.edu/~counsel/broint2.htm

Pennsylvania State University
Counseling and Psychological Services (CAPS)
University Park, PA 16802-4601
814.863.0395
Dennis Heitzmann, PhD
D'Andre Wilson (PhD anticipated)
Joyce Illfelder-Kaye, PhD
www.sa.psu.edu/caps/

Purdue University
Counseling and Psychological Services (CAPS)
West Lafayette, IN 47907-1826
765.494.6995
Barry A. Schreier, PhD
www.purdue.edu/caps

University of Rochester
Counseling & Mental Health Services
Rochester, NY 14627-0356
716.275.2361
Sheila Cummings, PhD
www.rochester.edu/ucc/predoc.htm

University of Southern California
Student Counseling Services
Los Angeles, CA 90089-0051
213.740.7711
Mark A. Stevens, PhD
www.usc.edu/student-affairs/Health_Center/USC_internship

The University of Tennessee
Student Counseling Center
Knoxville, TN 37996-4250
865.974.2196
Philip Johnson, PhD
web.utk.edu/~counsel/intern

Texas A&M University*
Student Counseling Services
College Station, TX 77843-1263
979.845.4427
Brian K. Williams, PhD
W. Andrew Smith, PhD
www.scs.tamu.edu/training

VA Medical Center
Salem, VA#
Salem, VA 24153
540.982.2463
John Heil, DA

M. K. Johnson, PhD
www.avapl.org/training/Salem/application.htm
Virginia Commonwealth University
University Counseling Services
Richmond, VA 23284-1826
804.828.3964
Charles Klink, PhD
Kathleen J. Scott, PhD
www.vcu.edu/safweb/counsel

Virginia Tech#*
Thomas E. Cook Counseling Center
Blacksburg, VA 24061-0108
540.231.6557
Gary T. Bennett, PhD
Robert C. Miller, EdD
Robert C. Miller, EdD
www.ucc.vt.edu

Washington State University
Counseling & Testing Services
Pullman, WA 99164-1065
509.335.4511
Robert H. Ragatz, PhD
www.counsel.wsu.edu

West Virginia University*
Carruth Center for Counseling and Psychological Services
Morgantown, WV, 26506-6422
304.293.4431
Edward F. Etzel, EdD
Lynda Birckhead-Danley, PhD
www.wvu.edu/~cocenter/toc.htm

KEY# = Formal sport psych rotation/concentration
+ = Rotation in academic-athletic counseling
* = In-house staff interest/supervision
Sport psychology contact
Training Director

Psychological Medicine Department
Lewis-Gale Clinic
4910 Valley View Blvd.
Roanoke, VA 24012
Contact Person: John Hell
Phone: 703.265.1605 or 703.772.3485
Fax: 703.366.7353

Faculty
Lola Byrd, PhD
John Heil, DA
Rob Lanahan, PsyD
Samuel Rogers, PhD
Bruce Sellars, PsyD

Comments
Lewis-Gale clinic provides elective training rotations as part of a Veteran's Administration Medical Center, APA-approved, predoctoral psychology internship. The clinic is a multispecialty physician-group practice with approximately 130 physicians representing a wide range of medical specialties. The Psychological Medicine Department has 16 staff members. The department offers a broad range of assessment and treatment approaches to a variety of inpatient and outpatient populations. All interns can elect to serve up to 8 hours per week at the Lewis-Gale Clinic for the training year. Different training experiences are available according to the intern's interests.

Supervision for the sport psychology experience is provided by Dr. John Heil.

Sport Psychology. The sport psychology rotation has two distinct foci: enhancing performance and psychological well-being in athletes (and others who perform in highly demanding environments); and the use of sport, exercise, and performance enhancement techniques in the treatment of medical problems.

Training in the use of sport, exercise, and performance-enhancement methods with general medical populations is centered in the Lewis-Gale Hospital Pain Center. Applications include consultation with rehabilitation staff in the design and monitoring of aerobic and therapeutic exercise programs focusing on goal setting, pacing, motivation, and compliance; resumption of lost recreational activities; use of performance-anxiety treatment protocols; and use of activity-based muscular biofeedback.

Work with athletes and other performers may include participation in educational programs for coaches and parents; consultation with sports teams, sport organizations, and health professionals; and individual consultation and therapy with athletes. Direct work with athletes is contingent on prior training and sport experience. Interns undergo personal mental training for application in performance settings (e.g., sport, music, public speaking).

Washington State University
Dept of Intercollegiate Athletics
Washington State University
Pullman, WA 99164-1610

Contact Person: Mark Summerson (sport psychology and performance-enhancement services)
Phone: 509.335.0267
Fax: 509.335.0328
Email: mtsummer@wsu.edu

Predoctoral Psychology Internship (July 1-June 30)

— Fully approved American Psychological Association Internship Center
— Rotation in sport psychology
— 3 to 5 hours/week—Athletics; approximately 35 hours/week—Counseling Center
— Stipend and benefits provided by WSU Counseling Center
— Intern position, one-year internship

Appication timeframe/requirements

— Application deadline: typically the first week of December Counseling/clinical PhD and PsyD candidates only
— Applications submitted to WSU Counseling and Testing Services
— Application procedures pursuant to internship and postdoctoral programs in professional psychology (Association of Psychology Postdoctoral and Internship Centers)

Predoctoral/master's sport psychology/consultant internship

— 9 month practicum/internship (August-May)
— 15 to 18 hours/week
— Small stipend available (sport psychology funding)

Appendix C
Supervision of Applied Sport Psychology in Graduate School

Renee Newcomer Appaneal, EdD, CC-AAASP, LPC, NCC
Department of Exercise & Sport Science
University of North Carolina at Greensboro, Greensboro, NC

Judy Van Raalte, PhD, CC-AAASP
Psychology Department
Springfield College, Springfield, MA

L. DiAnne Borders, PhD, LPC, NCC, ACS
Department of Counseling Education & Development
University of North Carolina at Greensboro, Greensboro, NC

This Directory is aimed at providing information to assist you in selecting a graduate program that best matches your interests and career goals. If you desire expertise in applied sport psychology (e.g., consulting, counseling), then the availability of supervised applied training will be an important factor in determining when to select a program. Among the over 100 programs listed in this Directory, nearly half (49%) indicate either a primary focus or equal emphasis upon applied sport psychology as compared to research. The quality of these applied experiences, however, may vary greatly, ranging from a single graduate course to multiple courses including practicum or internship opportunities (as described elsewhere in this Directory). Because there are no universal standards for graduate training in sport psychology, applied training and supervision is left up to the program at each institution. The responsibility is fundamentally yours to be honest and clear about your interests in applied training and to choose a program that may provide the best means by which to achieve your career goals. Just as applied training varies, so does the availability and quality of supervision. The purpose of this section is to provide a basic overview of supervision in applied sport psychology so that you will know what to look for when selecting potential graduate programs.

Why is Supervision Important?

Supervision is an integral part of professional development and is required for certification or licensure (in some countries called "registration" or "chartering") in the fields of mental health (e.g., psychology, counseling, social work) and exercise/sport science (e.g., athletic training, strength and conditioning). Students seeking supervision to fulfill degree requirements, or to become eligible for certification/licensure, need to know what requirements are expected by their institutions and the licensing body in that area (e.g., American Counseling Association, American Psychological Association, Association for the Advancement of Applied Sport Psychology [AAASP], British Association of Sport and Exercise Sciences [BASES]). For example, to become a BASES Accredited Sport Psychologist, you must have completed directed studies and consulting under the guidance of a supervisor who is accredited. Similarly, to obtain AAASP certification in sport psychology, you will need to complete coursework and 400 hours of supervised practicum experience. Your supervisor should have the Certified Consultant, AAASP credential. Compared to other related fields, the 400 hour practicum requirement for certification is minimal. For example, to become a Licensed Psychologist or Professional Counselor, one must complete somewhere between 2,000 and 4,000 hours of supervised experience. In Australia, sport psychologists are trained as psychologists, and in order to become a Registered Psychologist, one must complete 1,000 hours of supervised experience in a master's program and 1,500 in an applied doctoral program. Supervision assists students in developing competencies as practitioners in the service delivery of sport psychology knowledge and principles. Supervision may be particularly important in sport psychology in order to maximize your learning within the 400 hours needed to become certified.

What is Supervision?

Based upon current definitions (Bernard & Goodyear, 2004; Borders & Brown, 2005), supervision is a continuous relationship characterized by the following:

- One person of more developed ability and/or higher organizational status and one or more persons of lesser ability and/or lesser organizational status.
- A relationship, understanding, and contract between supervisor and supervisee.
- A process that is aimed at the improvement of the supervisee's clinical performance.
- A responsibility (ethical and, in some instances, legal) on the part of the supervisor for the services delivered to the supervisee's clients.
- An assumption of either formal or informal monitoring of the supervisee's progress, including some form of evaluation.

What Does Supervision Involve?

The quality of supervision varies greatly and depends upon a number of factors, such as the characteristics of the supervisor, characteristics of the supervisee, and the supervisor-supervisee relationship. For example, the supervisor's personality, background and experience providing supervision, and current departmental roles and responsibilities (e.g., research and scholarship, administration) can each influence the supervision process. Supervision generally involves a staff member with expertise in applied sport psychology who mentors and guides a graduate student with no or very little experience in applied work. Although supervision generally occurs during a student's graduate training, it can (and should) continue throughout one's career as a resource for ongoing professional development. One can infer from Principles A and C of the AAASP Code of Ethics (AAASP, 2006a) that members are expected to engage in consultation with their colleagues (e.g., peer supervision) throughout their careers to maintain and promote professional behavior.

Methods of conducting supervision include either direct observation of a supervisee's session with a client or group (live in-person or through a review of audio/videotape) or indirect observation through supervisee self-report or simulation (e.g., role-play). Although there are no specific guidelines for the frequency of contact, the AAASP Certification Committee recommends a 1:10 ratio, or 1 hour of supervision for every 10 hours of client contact (AAASP, 2006b).

Goals of Supervision

Supervision has two primary goals: to (a) protect the well-being of the supervisee's client(s) and (b) facilitate the development of the supervisee into a competent, knowledgeable, and ethical practitioner (Van Raalte & Andersen, 2000). The focus of supervision usually involves some combination of case management (e.g., review of consulting session with the athlete), discussion of service delivery targeted at professional growth (e.g., supervisee's insight, lessons learned), and developing a working relationship between supervisor and supervisee. A recent survey of AAASP members revealed that supervision was predominantly focused on case management for professionals and students (71% and 44%, respectively), and that neither the amount nor type of supervision in sport psychology that students received differed with respect to their academic department (e.g., physical education/exercise sport science versus psychology/counseling; Watson, Zizzi, Etzel, & Lubker, 2004). Although this survey reflects a small portion of the AAASP membership (26%), the ratio of professionals to students was reflective of its members (i.e., 55% and 45%, respectively), suggesting that you can expect the amount of applied sport psychology supervision to be somewhat similar whether you choose a graduate program housed within an exercise/sport science or psychology/counseling department.

To meet basic supervision goals effectively, Van Raalte and Andersen (2000) suggested that supervision should start with an honest assessment of the supervisee (e.g., his or her needs, skills, deficits, orientation, knowledge, anxieties) to determine what may be gained from supervision. Then, the supervisor and supervisee can identify additional mutually agreed-upon goals and plans to evaluate them. This process is typically accomplished through regular conversations between the supervisor and supervisee, which may be done on an individual basis (i.e., supervisor and supervisee), in a group (i.e., supervisor and several supervisees), or a combination of both.

Supervision may focus upon developing rapport, conducting intake interviews, formulating athlete cases, learning cognitive-behavioral techniques, making and learning from mistakes, identifying limits, comprehending one's own needs, understanding oneself in relational contexts with others, record keeping, and ethical considerations (Van Raalte & Andersen, 2000). Because supervision takes place within a relationship, effective communication between supervisor and supervisee is essential. At times students need to communicate with their supervisors about difficult subjects (e.g., mistakes, weaknesses, countertransferential responses). Regular evaluations of one's competency (both skills and deficiencies) mean that some degree of anxiety is inherent in the supervision process. It is important to remember that this anxiety is normal, and perhaps underscores the importance of trust and rapport between the supervisor and supervisee.

Models of Supervision

Only in the past 10-15 years has supervision been examined in applied sport psychology. Not surprisingly, our field has adapted theoretical models from related fields, such as counseling and psychology, which can guide supervision in applied sport psychology. There are a variety of different models used in counseling and psychology supervision, and these models are reflective of psychotherapy and behavior change systems used with clients (Van Raalte & Andersen, 2000). Although it is beyond the scope of this section to conduct an exhaustive review of this literature, a brief overview of five common models, reflective of applied sport psychology supervision, is provided below in an attempt to illustrate the variety of ways supervision may be approached.

Behavioral models are based on learning theories such as operant and classical conditioning, which involve the use of reinforcement of appropriate supervisee behavior and extinction of inappropriate behavior (cf. Strosahl & Jacobson, 1986). The supervisor's role within a behavioral model is primarily as a *teacher*, with supervision focused upon a supervisee's skill development (e.g., teaching mental skills). This model is usually the most appropriate one for beginning students as they first learn how to apply their knowledge through direct service to clients.

Cognitive-behavioral models involve identifying and modifying supervisee's thoughts and behaviors regarding consultation (cf. Schmidt, 1979; Wessler & Ellis, 1980; Morran, Kurpius, & Brack, 1995). This approach is similar to the use of common sport psychology techniques, such as cognitive-restructuring, mental rehearsal, and self-regulation of arousal, thoughts, and attention. For example, new trainees often have needs of *salvation* (e.g., desire to save or rescue a client) or *competence* (e.g., desire to be perceived as an expert), and as a result might ask questions or direct client sessions to meet their own needs as opposed to acting in the best interest of their clients. In these cases, supervision may focus upon increasing awareness and modifying the trainee's irrational beliefs (e.g., I need to be a perfect consultant, I must help the client or I am not competent).

Phenomenological models involve the supervisor providing an environment that fosters the trainee in addressing and resolving challenges (cf. Patterson, 1983; Hackney & Goodyear, 1984). This approach is similar to Rogerian client-centered counseling. A supervisor operating within this framework would provide empathy and unconditional positive regard in order to create a safe environment for the supervisee from which to examine strengths and deficiencies.

Psychodynamic models derive from Freud's work (cf. Dewald, 1987). Two important contributions of this approach to supervision in sport psychology include attention to increased supervisees' awareness of why they chose to pursue this field and issues of transference and countertransference. Considering that the relationship is a central issue, the focus of supervision is to examine how the supervisee relates to the athlete. Often, understanding how the supervisor and supervisee relate to each other is inherently reflective of how the supervisee relates to athletes and coaches. Here, the focus of supervision has moved beyond examining the "*what and how*" of direct service to a more reflective discussion of "*why*." These models may be most effective with more advanced students, helping them explore the inter/intrapersonal dynamics that occur while consulting and the ways in which these dynamics may hinder or facilitate the goals of consultation.

In contrast to the models above, developmental models provide an overall view of consultant growth within supervision, focusing more on how the supervisee develops over time rather than the specific approach(es) used within supervision (Borders & Brown, 2005; Van Raalte & Andersen, 2000). Developmental models suggest that consultants will (one hopes) continually grow and recycle through stages throughout their careers, generally reaching a high level of competency (i.e., master consultant) in no fewer than 20 to 30 years (Borders & Brown, 2005). These models characterize supervisees in the early stages of development as polarized (either black or white) thinkers with generally limited views of their clients. As supervisees develop, they experience fluctuations between autonomy and dependence, although they have clearer understandings of their strengths and limitations as consultants. Supervisees in later stages of their development are able to conceptual-

Table 1. Critical Skills in Supervisee Development

Skill Area	Description
1. Competence	Skills, technique, mastery. Ability to take appropriate action
2. Emotional Awareness	Knowing oneself. Differentiation of feelings. Ability to use own reactions/emotions diagnostically.
3. Autonomy	Sense of one's own choices/decisions. Independence and self-directedness to appropriate degree. Sense of self.
4. Identity	Theoretical consistency. Conceptual integration. Sense of self as a consultant/counselor.
5. Respect for Individual Differences	Deep and basic respect. Active effort to understand. Appreciation of differences.
6. Purpose and Direction	Formulation of treatment plan and appropriate short- and long-term goals. Cognitive map of client progress.
7. Personal Motivation	Personal drives and meaning. Reward satisfaction. Complex and evolving nature of motivation.
8. Professional Ethics	Legal issues, values, professional standards. Integration of these into ongoing practice.

Adapted from Borders, L. D., & Brown, L. L. (2005). *The new handbook of counseling supervision* (p. 16). Mahwah, NJ: Lahaska/Erlbaum.

ize a comprehensive yet specific view of their clients. They have become more comfortable with the inherent difficulties of consultation in sport psychology (e.g., fostering an athlete-client's independence and autonomy within collegiate athletics, where coaches and administrators often exert a significant degree of control over student-athletes' lives).

As previously mentioned, the development of competency in providing sport psychology services is part of an ongoing relationship targeted at the evaluation and development of your proficiencies as a consultant. Hence, supervision involves increasing your own awareness and developing your consultation skills. Borders and Brown (2005) provided a list of *critical skills* addressed in supervision (see Table 1), which may provide you with a clearer understanding of what it means to become proficient in sport psychology consulting.

How Do I Prepare for Supervision?

Supervision is usually a continuing relationship that develops over time, designed to enhance supervisee competence. To ensure that supervision is enjoyable and effective, active participation is necessary. Van Raalte and Andersen (2000) offered a helpful list of responsibilities for both supervisors and supervisees that may be used as a general guide for how to best prepare for supervision.

Supervisor's Responsibilities
- Provide clear delineations of the trainees' and supervisors' roles
- Remain current with trainees' cases and provide adequate amount of direct supervision
- Convey opinions regarding trainees' weaknesses and strengths
- Appropriately discuss nonfulfillment of practicum requirements when necessary
- Display empathy, listen attentively, and encourage trainees' expression of feelings and opinions
- Encourage trainee feedback regarding the supervisory process
- Foster trainee autonomy and independence
- Maintain ethical responsibility to trainees and to athletes (clients) served
- Keep information about trainees' progress confidential
- Provide appropriate models of professional behavior

Supervisee's Responsibilities
- Prepare for supervision sessions
- Keep up-to-date progress notes on individual meetings and group presentations
- Critically examine strengths and weaknesses as sport psychology consultants
- Continually seek clarification of roles and expectations
- Do not conceal any information about the athlete (client) sessions or group meetings from supervisors
- Provide feedback to supervisors on the supervisory process
- Maintain ethical responsibilities to athletes (clients)
- Seek to emulate a model of ethical and professional behavior in interaction with athletes and supervisors

The Realities of Supervised Applied Training

According to surveys of graduate students, many do not complete the 400-hour supervised practicum requirement for AAASP certification before graduation (Andersen, Van Raalte, & Brewer, 1994; Andersen, Williams, Aldridge, & Taylor, 1997). In many programs, applied training is not required, which suggests that students may have to seek applied experience outside of existing coursework and research (e.g., thesis or dissertation) requirements for graduation. It is important to acknowledge that not all graduate students in the field desire to become practitioners, yet the problem of acquiring the necessary supervised experience certainly exists for those who do plan to practice applied sport psychology. This situation may be particularly difficult for those students planning to practice with a terminal master's degree rather than continue their studies for an additional 3-5 years in a doctoral program (with more time to gain additional experience and accumulate hours towards certification). AAASP does provide provisional certification for master's-level practitioners with 400 hours of supervised experience, and provisional Certified Consultants may apply for full certification status with an additional 300 supervised hours (i.e., 700 hours total). As a result, it often becomes necessary to obtain supervision beyond graduate school.

If your goal is to become certified by AAASP, then it will be essential that you find a faculty member or available supervisor who meets the CC, AAASP requirements. This may be done by contacting someone at your current program (or programs to which you are applying for graduate school), or it can be done by searching the database of Certified Consultants available on the AAASP website at http://www.aaasponline.org/cc/ccfinder.php. It would also be helpful to review the specific criteria for certification as well as check out the certification applications so that you are collecting and entering information along the way rather than trying to "recreate" things long after the fact. Information is available at the AAASP website at http://www.aaasponline.org/cc/how.php. If you are pursuing BASES accreditation, then you will need to be familiar with those requirements for supervision which can be found at http://www.bases.org.uk/newsite/supervisedexp.asp.

In summary, it is important to be well informed when applying to graduate programs in this field. We hope this section has provided you with sufficient knowledge to examine the quality of supervision that might be available within a given graduate program. To assist you further in making informed decisions, below is a list of potential questions that you might pose to program faculty and/or students in order to explore supervision in applied sport psychology graduate training.

- What is the availability of supervision (i.e., occurs within practicum or internship, can be done through independent study, must seek on your own outside of degree requirements)?
- What are the credentials of staff teaching and supervising students' applied training? Note: To count towards AAASP certification, the supervisor must be a Certified Consultant (or permission must be granted by the AAASP Certification Committee).
- What is the method of providing supervision (e.g., group vs. individual, direct vs. indirect)?
- How often is supervision provided or required (e.g., weekly, bi-weekly)?
- What are the theoretical approaches used in providing supervision (e.g., models used)?

For more general information regarding supervision in sport psychology, review a recent publication (*Consultation and Supervision in Sport Psychology*) by the APA Division 47 Professional Practice Committee and endorsed by the AAASP Certification Committee. This brochure is available for viewing or downloading from APA Division 47 or AAASP websites at http://www.psyc.unt.edu/apadiv47/brochures.html or http://www.aaasponline.org/publications.php, respectively.

References

Andersen, M. B., Van Raalte, J. L., & Brewer, B. W. (1994). Assessing the skills of sport psychology supervisors. *The Sport Psychologist, 8,* 238-247.

Andersen, M. B., Williams, J. M., Aldridge, T., & Taylor, J. (1997) Tracking graduate students of advanced degree programs in sport psychology, 1989-1994. *The Sport Psychologist, 11,* 326-344.

American Psychological Association Division 47 – Professional Practice Committee. (2006). *Consultation and supervision in sport psychology.* Retrieved February 10, 2006, from http://www.aaasponline.org/publications.php

Association for the Advancement of Applied Sport Psychology. (2006a). *AAASP Governance: Governing documents–Ethics code.* Retrieved February 10, 2006, from http://www.aaasponline.org/governance/committees/ethics/standards.php

Association for the Advancement of Applied Sport Psychology. (2006b). *Become a Certified Consultant: Standard application form.* Retrieved February 28, 2006, from http://www.aaasponline.org/governance/committees/ethics/standards.php

Bernard, J. M., & Goodyear, R. K. (2004). *Fundamentals of clinical supervision* (3rd ed.). Needham Heights, MA: Allyn & Bacon.

Borders, L. D., & Brown, L. L. (2005). *New handbook of counseling supervision*. Mahwah, NJ: Lahaska/Erlbaum.

Dewald, P. A. (1987). *Learning process in psychoanalytic supervision: Complexities and challenges, a case illustration*. Madison, CT: International Universities Press.

Hackney, H., & Goodyear, R. K. (1984). Carl Rogers' client-centered approach to supervision. In R. F. Levant & J. M. Shlein (Eds.), *Client-centered therapy and the person-centered approach: New directions in theory, research, and practice* (pp 278-296). New York: Praeger.

Morran, D. K., Kurpius, D. J., & Brack, C. J. (1995). A cognitive-skills model for counselor training and supervision. *Journal of Counseling & Development, 73*, 384-389.

Patterson, C. H. (1983). A client-centered approach to supervision. *The Counseling Psychologist, 11*, 21-25.

Schmidt, J. P. (1979) Psychotherapy supervision: A cognitive-behavioral model. *Professional Psychology, 10*, 278-284.

Strosahl, K., & Jacobson, N. S. (1986). Training and supervision of behavior therapists. *The Clinical Supervisor, 4*, 183-206.

Van Raalte, J. L., & Andersen, M. B. (2000). Supervision I: From models to doing. In M. B. Andersen (Ed.), *Doing sport psychology* (pp. 153-165). Champaign, IL: Human Kinetics.

Watson, J. C., Zizzi, S., Etzel, E., & Lubker, J. R. (2004). Applied sport psychology supervision: A survey of students and professionals. *The Sport Psychologist, 18*, 415-429.

Wessler, R. L., & Ellis, A. (1980). Supervision in rational-emotive therapy. In A. K. Hess (Ed.), *Psychotherapy supervision: Theory, research, and practice* (pp 181-191). New York: Wiley.

Acknowledgment: The authors would like to thank Dr. Mark B. Andersen for review and comments on this paper.

Appendix D
Doctoral Programs in Clinical and Counseling Psychology

Now that you have examined the offerings of the graduate programs in applied sport psychology that are listed in this directory, you may be feeling a bit overwhelmed. The programs outlined in the directory display a range of interests, applications, and orientations that demonstrate the breadth of the field of applied sport psychology. An additional aspect of your graduate program search to consider is programs in clinical and counseling psychology. While only a few of these programs offer a specialization in sport psychology per se, others offer specialties that relate directly to athletes and exercise/sport/physical activity.

Decisions regarding graduate programs require one vitally important consideration: What do you want at the end of it all? Do you want to work with people? Are your skills strongest in research? Do you enjoy working from a particular theoretical perspective? Will your talents be put to the best possible use through the program you have chosen? Often, the best possible match of a program to a person's goals and talents may be in a clinical/counseling program with sport psychology as a component, rather than as a primary focus. With this in mind, you need to think about where you want to fit in as a professional and where you will best be able to do "your thing" once you have left the cocoon of graduate school. Be sure to read "Taking the Next Step: What to Ask as You Review the Directory," by Patricia Latham Bach.

It is critical that you understand several important points about clinical/counseling programs, including how they are presented in this directory:

1. The programs listed in the specialty categories table are not applied sport psychology programs. They are clinical/counseling psychology programs. Please do not contact these programs for information about their sport psychology specializations; they do not have any! Rather, ask them about their clinical/counseling psychology specializations and follow up with questions about work in exercise and sport. Be sure to talk with the person(s) on the faculty interested in exercise and sport.

2. If the institution you choose offers sport psychology courses, you may be able to take them as electives within your clinical/counseling program of study. Again, be sure to talk with faculty who have an interest in sport and exercise.

3. A number of schools have both a clinical/counseling program and a doctoral program in physical education (or kinesiology, exercise and sport sciences, or a related name). In these cases you might get the best of both worlds. If the two programs have good relations, collaborative work may be more likely than at a school that does not offer both programs. It takes some effort to check out institutions with both programs,

but the end result may be exactly what you want or need.

A resource that will prove to be an important tool in your decision-making process is the *Insider's Guide to Graduate Programs in Clinical and Counseling Psychology* (2004/2005 edition, published 2004) by Michael A. Sayette, Tracy J. Mayne, and John C. Norcross (The Guilford Press, 72 Spring Street, New York, New York 10012; also available in bookstores and on the web through Amazon (www.amazon.com), Barnes and Noble (www.bn.com), etc.).

The *Insider's Guide* provides the prospective student with a wealth of information, from how to choose programs that might make a good match to how to work through the application and interview processes. It offers a visual means of determining the research to application orientations of each program and lists the basic entrance requirements and program prerequisites, the specialty areas of each program, and research/grant funding for those areas.

Sport psychology specialties can be found at the following institutions:
Carlos Albizu University—San Juan
Illinois School of Professional Psychology – Chicago Campus
University of Manitoba
University of Washington
Note that one of these programs (University of Manitoba) is listed in this directory.

The following institutions are listed as having faculty with sport psychology research interests:
University of Albany/State University of New York
Carlos Albizu University—San Juan
Illinois Institute of Technology
University of Manitoba
University of Missouri, Kansas City
University of North Texas
Oklahoma State University
Spalding University
Suffolk University
University of Washington
West Virginia University

Note that four of these programs (University of Manitoba, University of North Texas, Spalding University, West Virginia University) are listed in this directory.

Additional program areas listed related to sport and exercise in the directory include behavioral medicine; biofeedback/relaxation; eating disorders; gender roles/sex differences; health psychology; hypnosis; minority/cross-cultural psychology; pain; and substance abuse/addictive behaviors.

Other resources that may help you decide on a program are available through the American Psychological Association (APA), which offers a helpful booklet titled *Graduate Training and Career Possibilities in Exercise and Sport Psychology* (see Appendix E). The APA also publishes the *Graduate Study in Psychology* volume, which is updated regularly. The 2006 edition (923 pages) was published earlier this year. It should be noted, however, that the *Index of Programs by Area of Study Offered* indicates only three programs under "Sports"—Argosy University @ Phoenix, John F. Kennedy University, and Springfield College (all of which are listed in this directory). The APA guide may be especially helpful if you are interested in programs in kinesiology/physical education/exercise and sport sciences and check whether there are clinical and/or counseling psychology programs on campus (or in close geographical proximity, such as the same city). The APA website may be found at www.apa.org. Contacting the Division 47 (Exercise and Sport Psychology) is another good idea; the address of their website is www.psyc.unt.edu/apadiv47.

Appendix E
Graduate Training and Career Possibilities

Sponsored by:

American Psychological Association Division of Exercise and Sport Psychology (APA Division 47)

Association for the Advancement of Applied Sport Psychology (AAASP)

North American Society for the Psychology of Sport and Physical Activity (NASPSPA)

Table Of Contents

CONSIDERATIONS IN SELECTING
EXERCISE AND SPORT PSYCHOLOGY
CAREERS 1

CAREER TRACK I:
TEACHING/RESEARCH IN SPORT
SCIENCES AND WORK WITH ATHLETES
ON PERFORMANCE ENHANCEMENT 3

CAREER TRACK II:
TEACHING/RESEARCH IN PSYCHOLOGY
AND ALSO INTERESTED IN WORKING
WITH ATHLETES 5

CAREER TRACK III:
PROVIDE CLINICAL/COUNSELING
SERVICES TO VARIOUS POPULATIONS,
INCLUDING ATHLETES 6

CAREER TRACK IV:
HEALTH PROMOTION AND WORKING
WITH ATHLETES BUT NOT NECESSARILY
DIRECTLY IN SPORT PSYCHOLOGY 8

ADDITIONAL SUGGESTIONS 10

SUGGESTED REFERENCES 12

Graduate Training and Career Possibilities In Exercise and Sport Psychology

As interest has grown in exercise and sport psychology, requests from students and prospective students for information about graduate training and career possibilities have increased. This booklet addresses some of the commonly asked questions about careers and academic preparation in the field of exercise and sport psychology. The answers reflect the current state of the field, not necessarily the ideal state.

CONSIDERATIONS IN SELECTING EXERCISE AND SPORT PSYCHOLOGY CAREERS

What roles do exercise and sport psychologists perform?

Exercise and sport psychologists typically perform three primary roles: 1) teaching, 2) research, and 3) practice. Career opportunities in exercise and sport psychology may emphasize various aspects or combinations of these roles. Careful selection of a career track will guide you in determining the type of graduate training needed to qualify for career opportunities available in the field of exercise and sport psychology, hereafter referred to as sport psychology.

What sort of education do I need to become involved in sport psychology?

Sport psychology has traditionally been an interdisciplinary field and, therefore, academic training can come from departments of physical education, psychology, or counseling. Many departments of physical education have changed their emphases and now call themselves Exercise and Sport Sciences, Kinesiology, Movement Sciences, Human Performance, or some similar variation (hereafter referred to as sport sciences). The career track that you select will determine the type of academic preparation needed, and will ultimately influence the career opportunities for which you optimally qualify.

Whatever degree you choose to obtain (masters or doctorate), and whether the degree comes from a department of sport sciences or psychology, you should take supplemental course work from the allied discipline not represented by your home department. For instance, both the U. S. Olympic Committee (USOC) Sport Psychology Registry and the Association for the Advancement of Applied Sport Psychology (AAASP) "Certification Criteria" recommend that psychology majors take sport psychology classes and supplemental course work in sport sciences (e.g., biomechanics, exercise physiology, motor development/learning/ control, and sport sociology). Likewise, sport sciences graduate students specializing in sport psychology should take undergraduate and graduate courses in departments of psychology or counseling psychology (e.g., abnormal psychology, principles of counseling, psychopathology, personality, and social psychology). Further information about the specific coursework requirements for becoming an AAASP certified consultant is available from AAASP.

A well-integrated graduate program would combine traditional psychology, sport sciences, and sport psychology; however, few such formal programs exist. Often students must seek courses as well as research and applied mentoring from professionals in different disciplines/departments.

How much training will I need?

Most of the professional employment opportunities in sport psychology require doctoral degrees from accredited colleges and universities. In addition, students in counseling or clinical psychology doctoral programs usually complete post-graduate internships (normally not in sport psychology) as part of their education. Even if students with a masters degree complete sport psychology internships, these graduates compete at a distinct disadvantage for the limited number of full-time positions available in sport psychology.

Because of the limited number of full-time positions, many individuals work in the sport psychology field on a part-time basis. Whether you want a part- or full-time position in the field is a salient consideration in selecting a graduate program. Depending upon the area you wish to pursue within the field (i.e., teaching, research, and/or practice), there are four possible career tracks that are discussed below. Three of the career tracks (academic sport sciences, academic psychology, clinical/ counseling sport psychology) require doctoral degrees while one rather diverse track (e.g., academic athletic counseling, health promotion, or coaching) requires at least a masters degree.

2

TRACK I

TEACHING/RESEARCH IN SPORT SCIENCES AND WORK WITH ATHLETES ON PERFORMANCE ENHANCEMENT

Educational Requirements for Track I

• Doctoral Degree in Sport Sciences with a Specialization in Sport Psychology and a Significant Proportion of Course Work in Psychology or Counseling.

> Primary Employment for Track I
>
> • Academic Position in College/University
>
> • Researcher in Research Institute or Medical Research Laboratory
>
> • Coaching Educator for College/University or Sport Organization
>
> Opportunities with the above may include part-time consulting with amateur and professional athletes and teams and on *rare* occasions, full-time consulting.

If you decide that you want a job that primarily involves teaching and research in sport psychology as well as the possibility of providing performance enhancement techniques to athletes (e.g., relaxation, imagery, goal setting), a doctoral degree from a graduate program in sport sciences is the safest possibility because, with very few exceptions, the academic positions (mostly tenure track) in sport psychology exist in sport sciences departments. (College or university positions are often tenure-track. A person who receives tenure is assured some job security. Job termination cannot occur without "just cause" [e.g., demonstrated incompetence, substantial neglect of assigned duties, or substantial physical or mental incapacity]).

Individuals trained in sport psychology through sport sciences departments also can provide performance enhancement skills to athletes, but training in recognizing psychopathology is crucial. When athletes experience emotional difficulties such as depression, substance abuse, or eating disorders, individuals consulting with teams/athletes should have the competence to recognize these disorders and refer athletes to licensed clinical/ counseling psychologists.

Because sport sciences departments monopolize the academic job market in sport psychology, applicants for these positions usually need formal academic course work in sport science core areas such as exercise physiology, biomechanics, motor development, motor learning/control, and sport sociology, in addition to specialized training in sport psychology.

Obtaining a job usually depends more on the applicants' research and teaching records in sport psychology than their ability to provide athletes with performance enhancement and consultation. Having a license to provide counseling or clinical services to athletes is not a prerequisite and may even be a liability if it prevents the applicant from developing competence in the research and teaching aspects of the field. Thus, if you want to stress teaching and research in a relatively secure academic environment, a doctoral degree in sport sciences is the most logical route to obtain academic or research positions that deal exclusively with exercise and sport.

On rare occasions (see the last paragraph of Track III), individuals with the preceding training may work full-time primarily consulting with athletes. We cannot emphasize strongly enough, however, how rarely these opportunities occur. When these full-time sport psychology consulting positions do occur, they normally go to individuals with extensive post-doctoral experience working with athletes.

TRACK II

TEACHING/RESEARCH IN PSYCHOLOGY AND ALSO INTERESTED IN WORKING WITH ATHLETES

Educational Requirements for Track II

- Doctoral Degree in Psychological Field with a Significant Proportion of Course Work in Exercise and Sport Science.

Primary Employment for Track II

- Academic Psychology Position in College/University
- Researcher in Research Institute or Medical Research Laboratory

Opportunities with the above may include part-time consulting with amateur and professional athletes and teams and on *rare* occasions, full-time consulting.

This is an appropriate track if your interest lies more in a career in which you teach and conduct psychological research on a variety of topics (including sport psychology) and consult with athletes. Some positions exist each year in research institutes, medical research laboratories, and college or university departments of psychology, counseling psychology, or educational psychology. Applicants usually are hired for their teaching and research competence in traditional subject matter areas of psychology (e.g., counseling psychology, group procedures, learning and motivation, psychotherapy, social psychology) rather than experience in sport psychology. Sometimes, these faculty may offer a sport psychology course, consult with athletes/athletic teams, or conduct research in this area.

To prepare for an academic or research position in psychology, you should attempt to enter a doctoral program in psychology, counseling, or educational psychology. Since these departments typically do not offer training in sport psychology, look for a psychology program that at least permits students to take graduate classes in sport psychology and courses in other relevant areas from a sport sciences department.

TRACK III

PROVIDE CLINICAL/COUNSELING SERVICES TO VARIOUS POPULATIONS, INCLUDING ATHLETES

Educational Requirements for Track III

- Doctoral Degree in an American Psychological Association (APA) Accredited Clinical/Counseling Psychology Program with a Significant Proportion of Course Work in Sport Psychology and Related Sport Sciences.

> **Primary Employment for Track III**
>
> - Private Psychology Practice
> - Clinical/Counseling Psychologist in University Counseling Center
> - University Health Education Psychologist
> - Sports Medicine Clinic Psychological Consultant
> - University Substance Abuse Specialist
> - Career Specialist
>
> Many of the above may include part-time consulting with amateur and professional athletes and teams and on *rare* occasions, full-time consulting.

If you would like a career in which you work with athletes as well as non-athletes (e.g., business people, college students, hospital patients, or the general population) there are several reasons for pursuing a doctoral degree in an APA accredited clinical or counseling psychology program.

First, various career opportunities working with clinical problems *require* a doctoral degree in clinical or counseling psychology from an APA accredited program that includes a 1-year APA approved internship. There are laws that govern the practice of psychology such that, in most states, these positions typically require applicants to have a state license or certificate to practice (see AAASP certified consultant criteria for guidance regarding recommended training for working with athletes). People receiving traditional graduate training from sport sciences departments that are not APA accredited will rarely qualify for these positions. Thus, if you want to provide psychological services for people in general (of whom a percentage may be athletes), this track has the distinct advantage of providing the greatest variety of career opportunities as well as the best chance for you to obtain employment upon completion of a doctoral degree and internship.

Second, very few sport psychologists earn most of their income working full-time with competitive athletes. Those professionals who consult with athletes on a part-time basis usually have other employment, such as academic positions, or more traditional clinical or counseling practices in which they earn most of their income. Over the past 3-5 years, only one or two *full-time* positions occurred each year for people to work with collegiate, Olympic, or professional athletes, or athletes attending private sport academies.

Typically, these positions are filled by people with extensive post-doctoral experience working with athletes. Not only are these positions few in number with no dramatic increase in sight, but they generally offer less job security than other positions. At present, staking your hopes on full-time work with elite athletes appears a risky venture.

TRACK IV

HEALTH PROMOTION AND WORKING WITH ATHLETES BUT NOT NECESSARILY DIRECTLY IN SPORT PSYCHOLOGY

Educational Requirements for Track IV

- Masters Degree in Clinical/Counseling Psychology Program with a Significant Proportion of Course Work in Exercise and Sport Science or Masters Degree in Sport Sciences Department with a Significant Proportion of Course Work in Psychology (some colleges, universities, and health centers look for doctoral degrees)

> Primary Employment for Track IV
>
> - College or University Academic Athletic Advisor
> - Health Promotion Worker
> - Coach

If you would like to provide general support services to and work closely with athletes and/or exercisers, you may decide to pursue a career in academic athletic counseling or coaching. Sport psychology programs that have considerable emphasis in the area of exercise/health psychology may provide opportunities for their graduates to seek careers in health promotion and rehabilitation.

In terms of academic athletic counseling, the vast majority of positions are at Division I colleges and universities. Academic athletic counselors often organize academic tutoring services, monitor academic progress, assist in academic scheduling, and provide other support services for college student-athletes. In larger universities, academic athletic counselors may be assigned to work with a specific team on academic, personal, or sport performance issues, and/or may provide specialized services, such as career development, new student orientation, substance abuse prevention, learning disabilities assessment, or life skills development. In selecting graduate programs that might best prepare you for an academic athletic counseling position, it is imperative to find programs that can offer you fieldwork placements working directly with college student-athletes. Specific course work in counseling, college student development, career development, and sport psychology are particularly relevant. Job opportunities in academic athletic counseling have continued to grow at a slow but steady pace over the last decade.

Health care settings may offer opportunities for people interested in working in health promotion and rehabilitation settings such as employee wellness programs, HMOs, rehabilitation programs, and sports medicine clinics. Although a recent study found that only 2.8% of sports medicine clinics currently have counselors working with injured athletes on psychological factors associated with injury and rehabilitation, it seems likely that employment opportunities in this and other health promotion areas will increase. To maximize your chances in these areas, it is imperative to find a program that permits internships in health promotion. You also may want to seek certification by the American College of Sports Medicine when appropriate to do so.

For individuals interested in coaching, a degree in sport psychology may make you an outstanding candidate for positions at the college or university level. Your degree work should be complemented by coaching experience and knowledge of NCAA guidelines. Certification by the American Coaching Effectiveness Program (ACEP) may increase your marketability if you are considering youth sport jobs.

ADDITIONAL SUGGESTIONS

How can I obtain information about graduate programs in sport psychology?

The Association for the Advancement of Applied Sport Psychology (AAASP) publishes the *Directory of Graduate Programs in Applied Sport Psychology*. The *Directory* describes each graduate program and lists a contact person. The North American Society for the Psychology of Sport and Physical Activity (NASPSPA) publishes a list of graduate programs in sport psychology in its newsletter. The American Psychological Association (APA) also publishes some information about sport psychology graduate programs in its *Graduate Study in Psychology*, but has a focus on programs in psychology departments.

Once you have an idea of what colleges or universities interest you, you can ask them to send you a description of their programs, degrees, and faculty. The types of degrees and specific requirements for a particular degree differ from school to school. Degrees may be available in counseling psychology, clinical psychology, or sport psychology. Departments of education, counseling, psychology, and sports sciences may offer M.A., M.S., M.Ed., Ph.D., Ed.D., or Psy.D. degrees. The Psy.D. is a relatively new degree which is comparable to the Ph.D., and is designed for people who are primarily interested in applied psychology practice with less emphasis on research.

What else should I ask?

Make sure the program offers the career track and degree you desire. Investigate the reputation of the faculty and program in terms of the opportunities and emphasis in sport psychology, the average time taken by students to complete the program, the funding for graduate students, and the success of graduates in obtaining the kind of sport psychology positions you desire.

Next, check to see if appropriate interdisciplinary course work exists and is an accepted part of the program of study. Opportunities for sport psychology research and graduate sport psychology internship/practica experiences also vary across programs. Give careful consideration to the research and/or clinical/practice focus of the program to ensure that the faculty conducts research on topics of interest to you and is qualified to supervise internship/practica experiences.

For the most thorough information, you should talk to both faculty and students at the programs you have selected. Consideration of the preceding factors can lead to better quality training, which ultimately should make you more competitive for part- or full-time sport psychology positions.

SUGGESTED REFERENCES

For further information on graduate training and career possibilities, and the field of sport psychology in general, the following references may be helpful:

Association for the Advancement of Applied Sport Psychology (1990). Certification criteria. *AAASP Newsletter, 5,* (Winter).

Clark, K. S. (1984). The U.S.O.C. sport psychology registry: A clarification. *Journal of Sport Psychology, 6,* 365-366.

Dishman, R. K. (1983). Identity crisis in North American sport psychology: Academics in professional issues. *Journal of Sport Psychology, 5,* 123-134.

Heyman, S. R. (1984). The development of models for sport psychology: Examining the U.S.O.C. guidelines. *Journal of Sport Psychology, 6,* 125-132.

Sachs, M. L. (1991). Reading list in applied sport psychology: Psychological skills training. *The Sport Psychologist, 5,* 88-91.

Sachs, M. L., Burke, K. L., Salitsky, P. B. (1992). *Directory of graduate programs in applied sport psychology* (3rd ed.). Boise, ID: Association for the Advancement of Applied Sport Psychology.

Taylor, J. (1991). Career direction, development, and opportunities in applied sport psychology. *The Sport Psychologist, 5,* 266-280.

Revised June 1994 by:

Judy L. Van Raalte, Ph.D. &
Jean M. Williams, Ph.D.

Appendix F
Ethical Principles and Standards of the Association for the Advancement of Applied Sport Psychology

Considering Ethics

AAASP Ethics Committee

In 1987 AAASP established an ethics committee. After considerable deliberation, this committee recommended that the association temporarily adopt the American Psychological Association's (APA) 1981 Ethics Standards for Psychologists. One reason for this recommendation was the APA tradition for maintaining high standards for practice, research, and teaching. Another reason was that this code addressed many issues that AAASP members appeared to face.

After certification passed, however, the idea of an ethics code for the AAASP membership surfaced. In 1990 the chairman of the Ethics Committee, Al Petitpas, addressed this issue with a study of AAASP members' experiences and attitudes about various ethical problems. The results of this survey revealed the advantages and disadvantages of the continued reliance on the APA Ethics code. Those results were published in the Journal of Applied Sport Psychology in 1994.

With these results in hand, the 1993 Ethics Committee co-chairs, Andy Meyers and Dan Gould, were asked to develop a new code of ethics written specifically for the association. This charge was completed in two steps. The first was the development of a set of ethics principles, or statements of ethical aspirations that should guide members' decision making. These principles were discussed and adopted by the association at the 1994 convention. The second step was to articulate a set of specific ethics guidelines that could be used as rules for specific professional situations. After being approved by the AAASP board, these guidelines, these guidelines were discussed and adopted by the AAASP during the 1996 convention.

Introduction

AAASP is dedicated to the development and professionalization of the field of sport psychology. As we establish ourselves as a profession, we must attend to both the privileges and responsibilities of a profession. Privileges derive from society's agreement to accept our designation as a group of trained individuals possessing specialized knowledge and, therefore, the power implicit in this knowledge. Our responsibilities, in turn, result from the society's trust that the profession will regulate itself to do no harm, and to govern itself to ensure the dignity and welfare of individuals we serve and the public. To maintain this status, professional organizations must develop and enforce guidelines that regulate their members' professional conduct. A code of ethical principles and standards is one such set of self-regulatory guidelines. This code guides professionals to act responsibly as they employ the privileges granted by society. A profession's inability to regulate itself violates the public's trust and undermines the profession's potential to be of service to society.

Ethical codes of conduct that professions adopt are based in the values of the society.

Consequently, these values include the balance between the rights and privacy of the individual and the general welfare of society. Each profession must determine its values and social function. The profession must then develop and adopt an ethics code which guides professional conduct. While no set of guidelines can anticipate all situations, a useful code should provide guidance when problems or dilemmas arise. This code should also proactively direct the actions of its members in work-related settings. If this is accomplished, the code will ensure society's trust in the profession.

The Association for the Advancement of Applied Sport Psychology's (AAASP) Ethical Principles and Standards (hereinafter referred to as the Ethics Code) is presented here and consists of this Introduction, a Preamble, six general Principles, and 25 Standards. The Introduction discusses the intent and organizational considerations of the Ethics Code. The Preamble and General Principles are intended to guide AAASP members toward the highest ideals of the profession. The Standards more precisely specify the boundaries of ethical conduct. Although the Preamble and the General Principles are not themselves enforceable rules, they should be considered by AAASP members in arriving at an ethical course of action. Ethical Standards are enforceable rules that mandate behavioral choices.

Membership in the AAASP commits members to adhere to the AAASP Ethics Code. AAASP members should be aware that, in many situations, additional ethical and legal codes may be applied to them by other professional organizations or public bodies. In the process of making decisions regarding their professional behavior, AAASP members must consider this Ethics Code, in addition to other ethical guidelines or legal codes. If the Ethics Code suggests a higher standard of conduct than is required by legal codes or other ethical guidelines, AAASP members should meet the higher ethical standard. If the Ethics Code standard appears to conflict with the requirements of law, then AAASP members must make known their commitment to the Ethics Code and take steps to resolve the conflict in a responsible manner. If neither law nor the Ethics Code resolves an issue, AAASP members should consider other professional materials (e.g., guidelines and standards that have been adopted or endorsed by other professional physical education, sport science, and social science organizations), the dictates of their own conscience, and consultation with others within the field when this is practical.

Preamble

AAASP members may fulfill many roles based on their professional training and competence. In these roles they may work to develop a valid and reliable body of scientific knowledge based on research; they may apply that knowledge to human behavior in a variety of sport, exercise, physical activity, and health contexts. Their goals are to broaden knowledge of this behavior and, where appropriate, to apply it pragmatically to improve the condition of both the individual and society. AAASP members respect the central importance of freedom of inquiry and expression in research, teaching, and consulting. They also strive to help the public to develop informed judgments and choices concerning sport, exercise, physical activity, and health behavior. This Ethics Code provides a common set of values upon which AAASP members build their professional and scientific work.

This Code is intended to provide the general principles and specific ethical standards for managing many situations encountered by AAASP members. It has as its primary goal the welfare and protection of the individuals and groups with whom AAASP members work. It is the individual responsibility of each AAASP member to aspire to the highest possible standards of conduct. AAASP members respect and protect human and civil rights, and do not knowingly participate in or condone unfair discriminatory practices.

The development of a dynamic ethical code for an AAASP member's work-related conduct requires a personal commitment to a lifelong effort to act ethically; to encourage ethical behavior by students, supervisees, employees, and colleagues, as appropriate; and to consult with others, as needed, concerning ethical problems. Each AAASP member supplements, but does not violate, the Ethics Code's values, on the basis of guidance drawn from personal values, culture, and experience.

General Principles

Principle A: Competence

AAASP members maintain the highest standards of competence in their work. They recognize the boundaries of their professional competencies and the limitations of their expertise. They maintain knowledge related to the services they render, and they recognize the need for ongoing education. AAASP members make appropriate use of scientific, professional, technical, and administrative resources. They provide only those services and use only those techniques for which they are qualified by education, training, or experience. AAASP members are cognizant of the fact that the competencies required in serving, teaching, and/or studying groups of people vary with the distinctive characteristics of those groups. In those areas in which recognized professional standards do not yet exist. AAASP members exercise careful judgment and take appropriate precautions to protect the welfare of those with whom they work.

Principle B: Integrity

AAASP members promote integrity in the science, teaching, and practice of their profession. In these activities AAASP members are honest and fair. When describing or reporting their qualifications, services, products, fees, research, or teaching, they do not make statements that are false, misleading, or deceptive. They clarify for relevant parties the roles they are performing and the obligations they adopt. They function appropriately in accordance with those roles and obligations. AAASP members avoid improper and potentially harmful dual relationships.

Principle C: Professional and Scientific Responsibility

AAASP members are responsible for safeguarding the public and AAASP from members who are deficient in ethical conduct. They uphold professional standards of conduct and accept appropriate responsibility for their behavior. AAASP members consult with, refer to, or cooperate with other professionals and institutions to the extent needed to serve the best interests of the recipients of their services. AAASP members' moral standards and conduct are personal matters to the same degree as is true for any other person, except as their conduct may compromise their professional responsibilities or reduce the public's trust in the profession and the organization. AAASP members are concerned about the ethical compliance of their colleagues' scientific and professional conduct. When appropriate, they consult with colleagues in order to prevent, avoid, or terminate unethical conduct.

Principle D: Respect for People's Rights and Dignity

AAASP members accord appropriate respect to the fundamental rights, dignity, and worth of all people. They respect the rights of individuals to privacy, confidentiality, self-determination, and autonomy, mindful that legal and other obligations may lead to inconsistency and conflict with the exercise of these rights. AAASP members are aware of cultural, individual, and role differences, including those due to age, gender, race, ethnicity, national origin, religion, sexual orientation, disability, language, and socioeconomic status. AAASP members try to eliminate the effect on their work of biases based on those factors, and they do not knowingly participate in or condone unfair discriminatory practices.

Principle E: Concern for Others' Welfare

AAASP members seek to contribute to the welfare of those with whom they interact professionally. When conflicts occur among AAASP members' obligations or concerns, they attempt to resolve those conflicts and to perform those roles in a responsible fashion that avoids or minimizes harm. AAASP members are sensitive to real and ascribed differences in power between themselves and others. They do not exploit or mislead other people during or after professional relationships.

Principle F: Social Responsibility

AAASP members are aware of their professional and scientific responsibilities to the community and the society in which they work and live. They apply and make public their knowledge in order to contribute to human welfare. When undertaking research, AAASP members strive to advance human welfare and their profession while always protecting the rights of the participants. AAASP members try to avoid misuse of their work, and they comply with the law.

General Ethical Standards

These general standards apply to AAASP members across all their professional roles and in all their professional interactions and communications.

1. Professional and Scientific Relationship
   AAASP members provide diagnostic, therapeutic, teaching, research, educational, supervisory, or other consultative services only in the context of a defined professional or scientific relationship or role.
2. Boundaries of Competence
   (a) AAASP members represent diverse academic and professional backgrounds. These different training histories provide different competencies. Those trained in clinical and counseling psychology must be aware of potential limitations in their sport science competencies. AAASP members trained in the sport sciences must be aware of their limitations in clinical and counseling psychology. Individuals from different training backgrounds must deliver services, teach, and conduct research only within the boundaries of their competence.(b) AAASP members provide services, teach, or conduct research in new areas only after taking the necessary actions to guarantee a high level of competence in those areas.(c) AAASP members who engage in assessment, therapy, teaching, research, organizational consulting, or other professional activities maintain a reasonable level of awareness of current scientific and professional information in their fields of activity, and undertake ongoing efforts to maintain competence in the skills they use.(d) AAASP members are aware of the limitations of their scientific work and do not make claims or take actions that exceed these limitations.
3. Human Differences
   (a) AAASP members recognize that differences of age, gender, race, ethnicity, national origin, religion, sexual orientation, disability, language, or socioeconomic status can significantly affect their work. AAASP members working with specific populations have the responsibility to develop the necessary skills to be competent with these populations, or they make appropriate referrals.(b) AAASP members do not engage in unfair discrimination based on age, gender, race, ethnicity, national origin, religion, sexual orientation, disability, socioeconomic status, or any basis proscribed by law.
4. Exploitation and Harassment
   (a) AAASP members do not exploit persons over whom they have supervisory, evaluative, or other authority, such as students, supervisees, employees, research participants, and clients or patients. (b) AAASP members do not engage in behavior that is harassing or demeaning to persons with whom they interact in their work.(c) AAASP members do not solicit testimonials from current psychotherapy clients or patients or other persons who because of their particular circumstances are vulnerable to undue influence.
5. Personal Problems and Conflicts
   (a) AAASP members recognize that personal problems, including addictions, and personal conflicts may interfere with their effectiveness. Accordingly, they refrain from undertaking an activity when their personal problems may harm others to whom they may owe a professional or scientific obligation.(b) AAASP members are aware that the extreme visibility and notoriety of some of the clients and organizations that they work with may compromise their professional objectivity and competence. In such situations, it is the AAASP member's responsibility to take corrective action, including consultation with other professionals and termination and referral if necessary.(c) In their professional roles AAASP members may obtain privileged information about clients or client organiza-

tions. AAASP members do not use this information for personal gain.

6. Avoiding Harm

   AAASP members take reasonable steps to avoid harming their patients or clients, research participants, students, and others with whom they work, and to minimize harm where it is foreseeable and unavoidable.

7. Misuse of AAASP Members' Influence

   Because AAASP members' scientific and professional judgments and actions may affect the lives of others, they are alert to and guard against personal, financial, social, organizational, or political factors that might lead to misuse of their influence.

8. Misuse of AAASP Members' Work

   AAASP members do not participate in activities in which it appears likely that their skills or products will be misused by others. If AAASP members learn of misuse or misrepresentation of their work, they take reasonable steps to correct or minimize the misuse or misrepresentation.

9. Multiple Relationships

   (a) AAASP members must always be sensitive to the potential harmful if unintended effects of social or other nonprofessional contacts on their work and on those persons with whom they deal. Such multiple relationships might impair the AAASP member's objectivity or might harm or exploit the other party.(b) An AAASP member refrains from taking on professional or scientific obligations when preexisting relationships would create a risk of such harm.(c) AAASP members do not engage in sexual relationships with students, supervisees, and clients over whom the AAASP member has evaluative, direct, or indirect authority, because such relationships are so likely to impair judgment or be exploitative.(d) AAASP members avoid personal, scientific, professional, financial, or other relationships with family members of minor clients because such relationships are so likely to impair judgment or be exploitative.(e) If an AAASP member finds that, due to unforeseen factors, a potentially harmful multiple relationship has arisen, the AAASP member attempts to resolve it with due regard for the best interests of the affected person and maximal compliance with the Ethics Code.

10. Barter (with Patients or Clients)

    AAASP members refrain from accepting goods, services, or other nonmonetary remuneration from patients, clients, students, supervisees, or research subjects in return for services, because such arrangements create inherent potential for conflicts, exploitation, and distortion of the professional relationship. In certain circumstances AAASP members may receive tokens of appreciation from clients or client organizations. In these situations it is the AAASP member's responsibility to determine that the gifts are appropriate for the setting, not exploitative, and that the gifts do not serve as payment for services.

11. Consultations and Referrals

    (a) AAASP members arrange for appropriate consultations and referrals based principally on the best interests of their patients or clients, with appropriate consent and subject to other relevant considerations, including applicable law and contractual obligations.(b) AAASP members cooperate with other professionals in order to serve their patients or clients effectively and appropriately.

12. Third-Party Requests for Services

    (a) When an AAASP member agrees to provide services to a person or entity at the request of a third party, the AAASP member clarifies, at the outset of the service, the nature of the relationship with each party. This clarification includes the role of the AAASP member, the probable uses of the services provided or the information obtained, and the fact that there may be limits to confidentiality.(b) If there is a foreseeable risk of the AAASP member's being called upon to perform conflicting roles because of the involvement of a third party, the AAASP member clarifies the nature and direction of his or her responsibilities, keeps all parties appropriately informed as matters develop, and resolves the situation in accordance with the Ethics Code.

13. Delegation to and Supervision of Subordinates
    (a) AAASP members delegate to their employees, supervisees, and research assistants only those responsibilities that such persons can reasonably be expected to perform competently.(b) AAASP members provide proper training and supervision to their employees or supervisees and take reasonable steps to see that such persons perform services responsibly, competently, and ethically.

14. Documentation of Professional and Scientific Work
    AAASP members appropriately document their professional and scientific work in order to facilitate provision of services later by them or by other professionals, to ensure accountability, and to meet other requirements of institutions or the law.

15. Fees and Financial Arrangements
    (a) As early as is feasible in a professional or scientific relationship, the AAASP member and the patient, client, or other appropriate recipient of services reach an agreement clearly specifying the compensation and the billing arrangements.(b) AAASP members do not exploit recipients of services or payers with respect to fees.(c) If limitations to services can be anticipated because of limitations in financing, this is discussed with the patient, client, or other appropriate recipient of services as early as is feasible.(d) AAASP members do not deliver services for future remuneration based on the client's future achievements nor do they accept testimonials in place of fees for services.

16. Definition of Public Statements
    AAASP members are responsible for the clarity and honesty of public statements about their work made to students, clients, colleagues, or the public, by themselves or others representing them. If AAASP members learn of deceptive statements about their work made by others, AAASP members make reasonable efforts to correct such statements.

17. Informed Consent to Practice
    (a) AAASP members obtain appropriate informed consent to educational and counseling procedures, using language that is reasonably understandable to participants. The content of informed consent will vary depending on circumstances. However, informed consent generally implies that the person (1) has the capacity to consent, (2) has been informed of significant information concerning the procedure, (3) has freely and without undue influence expressed consent, and (4) consent has been appropriately documented.(b) When persons are legally incapable of giving informed consent, AAASP members obtain informed permission from a legally authorized person, if such substitute consent is permitted by law.(c) In addition, AAASP members (1) inform those persons who are legally incapable of giving informed consent about the proposed interventions in a manner commensurate with the persons' psychological capacities, (2) seek their assent to those interventions, and (3) consider such persons' preferences and best interests.

18. Maintaining Confidentiality
    (a) AAASP members have a primary obligation to uphold and take reasonable precautions to respect the confidentiality rights of those with whom they work or consult, recognizing that confidentiality may be established by law, institutional rules, and/or professional or scientific relationships.(b) AAASP members discuss with persons and organizations with whom they work (1) the relevant limitations on confidentiality, including limitations where applicable in group, marital, and family counseling or in organizational consulting, and (2) the foreseeable uses of the information generated through their services.(c) AAASP members do not disclose in their writings, lectures, or other public media, confidential, personally

identifiable information concerning their patients, individual or organizational clients, students, research participants, or other recipients of their services that they obtained during the course of their work, unless the person or organization has consented in writing or unless there is other ethical or legal authorization for doing so.

19. Informed Consent to Research

    (a) Prior to conducting research (except research involving only anonymous surveys, naturalistic observations, or similar methods where the risk of harm is minimal), AAASP members enter into an agreement with participants that clarifies the nature of the research and the responsibilities of each party.(b) AAASP members use language that is reasonably understandable to research participants in obtaining their appropriate informed consent. Such informed consent is appropriately documented.(c) Using language that is reasonably understandable to participants, AAASP members inform participants of the nature of the research; they inform participants that they are free to participate or to decline to participate or to withdraw from the research; they explain the foreseeable consequences of declining or withdrawing; they inform participants of significant factors that may be expected to influence their willingness to participate (such as risks, discomfort, adverse effects, or limitations on confidentiality); and they explain other aspects about which the prospective participants inquire.(d) When AAASP members conduct research with individuals such as students or subordinates, AAASP members take special care to protect the prospective participants from adverse consequences of declining or withdrawing from participation. (e) When research participation is a course or team requirement or opportunity for extra course credit, the prospective participant is given the choice of equitable alternative activities.(f) For persons who are legally incapable of giving informed consent, AAASP members nevertheless (1) provide an appropriate explanation, (2) where possible, obtain the participant's assent, and (3) obtain appropriate permission from a legally authorized person, if such substitute consent is permitted by law.

20. Conduct of Research

    (a) AAASP members design, conduct, and report research in accordance with recognized standards of scientific competence and ethical research.(b) AAASP members plan their research so as to minimize the possibility that results will be misleading.(c) AAASP members take reasonable steps to implement appropriate protections for the rights and welfare of human participants, other persons affected by the research, and the welfare of animal subjects.(d) AAASP members obtain from host institutions or organizations appropriate approval prior to conducting research, and they provide accurate information about their research proposals. They conduct the research in accordance with the approved research protocol.(e) AAASP members do not offer excessive or inappropriate financial or other inducements to obtain research participants, particularly when it might tend to coerce participation.

21. Deception in Research

    (a) AAASP members do not conduct a study involving deception unless they have determined that the use of deceptive techniques is justified by the study's prospective scientific, educational, or applied value, will not harm the participant, and that equally effective alternative procedures that do not use deception are not feasible.(b) AAASP members never deceive research participants about significant aspects that would affect their willingness to participate, such as physical risks, discomfort, or unpleasant emotional experiences.(c) Any other deception that is an integral feature of the design and conduct of an experiment must be explained to participants as early as is feasible, preferably at the conclusion of their participation, but no later than at the conclusion of the research. If scientific or humane values justify delaying or withholding this information, AAASP members take reasonable measures to reduce the risk of harm.

22. Minimizing Invasiveness

    In conducting research, AAASP members interfere with the participants or milieu from which data are collected only in a manner that is warranted by an appropriate research design and that is consistent with AAASP members' roles as scientific investigators.

23. Honesty in Research

    (a) AAASP members do not fabricate data or falsify results in their publications.(b) If AAASP members discover errors in their published data, they take reasonable steps to correct such errors in a correction, retraction, erratum, or other appropriate publication means.(c) AAASP members do not present substantial portions or elements of another's work or data as their own, even if the other work or data source is cited occasionally. AAASP members only accept publication and other credit for work that they have created or performed.

24. Conflicts between Ethics and Organizational Demands

    If the demands of an organization with which AAASP members are affiliated conflict with the Ethics Code, members clarify the nature of the conflict, make known their commitment to the Ethics Code, and to the extent feasible, seek to resolve the conflict in a way that permits the fullest adherence to the Ethics Code.

25. Resolution of Ethical Conflicts

    The successful implementation of an ethics code requires a personal commitment to act ethically, encourage ethical behavior by others, and consult with others concerning ethical problems. When applying the code of ethical conduct, AAASP members may encounter problems in identifying unethical conduct or in resolving ethical conflict. When faced with significant ethical concerns, one should consider the following courses of action.

Before any action is taken, one may benefit from advice from uninvolved and objective advisors or peers familiar with ethical issues. When members believes that there may have been an ethical violation by another member, they may attempt to clarify and resolve the issue by bringing the matter to the attention of the other involved parties if such an informal resolution appears appropriate and the intervention does not violate any confidentiality rights that may be involved. Discuss ethical problems with your immediate supervisor except when it appears that the supervisor is involved in the ethical issue, in which case the problem should be presented to the next higher administrative level. If satisfactory resolution cannot be achieved when the problem is initially presented, the issue should be submitted to the next higher administrative level. Contact with levels above the immediate administrator should be initiated only with the administrator's knowledge, assuming that the administrator is not involved. If the ethical problem or conflict still exists after exhausting all levels of internal review, support from appropriate professional organizations should be obtained.

It is important for AAASP members to understand that unethical conduct is a serious matter. However, the primary aims of these ethical principles are to inform and motivate the highest standards of conduct among AAASP members as we serve our clients, our professions, and our community.

(Submitted by Dr. James Whelan, University of Memphis, on behalf of the AAASP Ethics Committee)

This Ethics Code is based in large part on the American Psychological Association's Ethical Principles of Psychologists and Code of Conduct (American Psychologist, 1992, V.47, #12, pp. 1597–1611.). Over 50 other organizational ethics codes, including the code of the American College of Sports Medicine, were also examined and many influenced this document. We wish to thank all of these organizations.

Appendix G
Texts in Applied Exercise and Sport Psychology

There are numerous texts or key reference works in applied exercise and sport psychology that may interest you. Mary Beth Allen's 1994 article in *The Sport Psychologist* (vol. 8, pp. 94–99), entitled "Authorship in Sport Psychology: A Reference List," provides an excellent reference list in this area (although somewhat dated now). You may find the following books to be particularly helpful.

Anshel, M. H. (2000). *Sport psychology: From theory to practice* (4th ed.). Scottsdale, AZ: Gorsuch Scarisbrick.

Cox, R. H. (2007). *Sport psychology: Concepts and applications* (6th ed.). New York: McGraw Hill.

Gill, D. L. (2000). *Psychological dynamics of sport* (2nd ed.). Champaign, IL: Human Kinetics.

Horn, T. S. (Ed.). (2002). *Advances in sport psychology* (2nd ed.). Champaign, IL: Human Kinetics.

Kremer, J. M., & Scully, D. (1994). *Psychology in sport.* Bristol, PA: Taylor & Francis, Inc.

LeUnes, A. D., & Nation, J. R. (2002). *Sport psychology: An introduction* (3rd ed.). Pacific Grove, CA: Wadsworth.

Lidor, R., & Bar-Eli, M. (1999). *Sport psychology: Linking theory and practice.* Morgantown, WV: Fitness Information Technology, Inc.

Morris, T., & Summers, J. (Eds.). *Sport psychology: Theory, applications and issues.* Brisbane, Australia: John Wiley & Sons.

Murphy, S. M. (Ed.). (1995). *Sport psychology interventions.* Champaign, IL: Human Kinetics.

Pargman, D. (1998). *Understanding sport behavior.* Upper Saddle River, NJ: Prentice-Hall.

Rotella, R., Boyce, A. B., Allyson, B., & Savis, J. (1997). *Case studies in sport psychology.* Boston, MA: Jones and Bartlett Publishers.

Silva, J. M., & Stevens, D. E. (2002). *Psychological foundations of sport.* Boston, MA: Allyn & Bacon.

Silva, J. M., & Weinberg, R. S. (1984). *Psychological foundations of sport.* Champaign, IL: Human Kinetics.

Tenenbaum, G. (2001). *The practice of sport psychology.* Morgantown, WV: Fitness Information Technology, Inc.

Wann, D. L. (1997). *Sport psychology.* Upper Saddle River, NJ: Prentice Hall.

Weinberg, R. S., & Gould, D. (2003). *Foundations of sport and exercise psychology* (3rd ed.). Champaign, IL: Human Kinetics.

Williams, J. M. (Ed.). (2006). *Applied sport psychology: Personal growth to peak performance* (5th ed.).New York: McGraw Hill.

Texts in Exercise Psychology

Anhel, M. (2006). *Applied exercise psychology: A practitioner's guide to improving client health and fitness.* New York: Springer Publishing Company.

Berger, B. G., Pargman, D., & Weinberg, R. (2002). *Foundations of exercise psychology.* Morgantown, WV: Fitness Information Technology. (2nd edition coming out soon)

Buckworth, J., & Dishman, R. K. (2002). *Exercise psychology*. Champaign, IL: Human Kinetics.

Carron, A. V., Hausenblas, H. A., & Estabrooks, P. A. (2003). *The psychology of physical activity*. New York: McGraw-Hill.

Duda, J. L. (Ed.) (1998). *Advances in sport and exercise psychology measurement*. Morgantown, WV; Fitness Information Technology.

Hays, K. F. *Working it out: Using exercise in psychotherapy*. Washington, DC: American Psychological Association Press.

Lox, C. L., Martin, K. A., & Petruzzello, S. J. (2003). *The psychology of exercise: Integrating theory and practice*. Scottsdale, AZ: Holcomb Hathaway, Publishers.

Willis, Joe D., & Campbell, L. F. (1992). *Exercise psychology*. Champaign, IL: Human Kinetics.

General/Other References

Begel, D., & Burton, R. W. (Eds.). (2000). *Sport psychiatry: Theory and practice*. New York: W. W. Norton & Company.

Current, definitive edited work in this area.

Carron, A. V., & Hausenblas, H. A. (1998). *Group dynamics in sports* (3rd ed.). Morgantown, WV: Fitness Information Technology.

Overview of work on groups in sport settings.

Dosil, J. (Ed.). (2006). *The sport psychologist's handbook: A guide for sport-specific performance enhancement*. Wet Sussex, England: John Wiley & Sons, Ltd.

Excellent handbook, with 30 chapters on a variety of sport specific and general applied sport psychology areas.

Duda, J. L. (Ed.). (1998). *Advances in sport and exercise psychology measurement*. Morgantown, WV: Fitness Information Technology.

Comprehensive review of measurement issues and information on many instruments used in exercise and sport psychology.

Gardner, F., & Moore, Z. (2006). *Clinical sport psychology*. Champaign, IL: Human Kinetics.

Lidor, R., & Henschen, K. P. (2003). *The psychology of team sports*. Morgantown WV: Fitness Information Technology.

Lidor, R., Morris, T., Bardaxoglou, & Becker, Jr., B. (Eds.). (2001). *The world sport psychology sourcebook*. (3rd ed.). Morgantown, WV: Fitness Information Technology.

Excellent publication with background information and a comprehensive Who's Who in the world of sport psychology.

Murphy, S. (Ed.). (2005). *The sport psych handbook: A complete guide to today's best mental training techniques*. Champaign, IL; Human Kinetics.

Nideffer, R. M., & Sagal, M. (2001). *Assessment in sport psychology*. Morgantown, WV: Fitness Information Technology.

Pargman, D. (1999). *Psychological bases of sport injuries*. (2nd ed.). Morgantown, WV: Fitness Information Technology. (3rd edition coming out soon)

Singer, R. N., Hausenblas, H. A., & Janelle, C. M. (Eds.). (2001). *Handbook of research on sport psychology*. (2nd ed.) New York: John Wiley & Sons, Inc.

This is the definitive reference work in sport psychology, with 33 chapters (876 pages).

Skinner, J. S., Corbin, C. B., Landers, D. M., Martin, P. E., & Wells, C. L. (Eds.). (1989). *Future directions in exercise and sport science research*. Champaign, IL: Human Kinetics.

This volume contains numerous excellent chapters in the exercise and sport sciences in general, with sport psychology chapters written by Deborah Feltz, Daniel Landers, William Morgan, Glyn Roberts, Ronald Smith, and Richard Suinn.

Taylor, J., & Wilson, G. (Eds.) (2005). *Applying sport psychology: Four perspectives*. Champaign, IL: Human Kinetics.

Van Raalte, J. L., & Brewer, B. W. (Eds.). (2002). *Exploring sport and exercise psychology* (2nd ed.). Washington, DC: American Psychological Association.

An excellent resource with 25 chapters in sections on performance enhancement, promoting wellbeing, clinical issues, working with specific populations, and professional issues.

Appendix H
References in Applied Sport Psychology: Professional and Ethical Issues

There are numerous references in applied sport psychology that deal with professional and ethical issues that may interest you. You can find an excellent list in Vincent Granito and Betty Wenz's 1995 article in *The Sport Psychologist* (vol. 9, pp. 96–103) entitled "Reading List for Professional Issues in Applied Sport Psychology." The following list represents an updated version of the list provided in previous editions of this directory. You may wish to review both this list and the Granito and Wenz list.

Allen, M. B. (1994). Authorship in sport psychology: A reference list. *The Sport Psychologist*, 8, 94–99.

American Psychological Association. (1987). *Casebook on ethical principles of psychologists.* Washington, DC: Author.

American Psychological Association. (1990). Ethical principles of psychologists (Amended June 2, 1989). *American Psychologist*, 45, 390–395.

Andersen, M. B. (1994). Ethical considerations in the supervision of applied sport psychology graduate students. *Journal of Applied Sport Psychology*, 6, 152–167.

Andersen, M. B., & Williams-Rice, B. T. (1996). Supervision in the education and training of sport psychology service providers. *Journal of Applied Sport Psychology*, 10, 278–290.

Andersen, M. B., Van Raalte, J. L., & Brewer, B. W. (1994). Assessing the skills of sport psychology supervisors. *The Sport Psychologist*, 8, 238–247.

Anshel, M. H. (1990). Perceptions of black intercollegiate football players: Implications for the sport psychology consultant. *The Sport Psychologist*, 4, 235–248.

Anshel, M. H. (1992). The case against the certification of sport psychologists: In search of the phantom expert. *The Sport Psychologist*, 6, 265–286.

Anshel, M. H. (1993). Against the certification of sport psychology consultants: A response to Zaichkowsky and Perna. *The Sport Psychologist*, 7, 344–353.

Barney, S. T., Andersen, M. B., & Riggs, C. A. (1996). Supervision in sport psychology: Some recommendations for practicum training. *Journal of Applied Sport Psychology*, 8, 200–217.

Brown, J. M. (1982). Are sport psychologists really psychologists? *Journal of Sport Psychology*, 4, 13–18.

Brustad, R. J., & Ritter-Taylor, M. (1997). Applying social psychological perspectives to the sport psychology consulting process. *The Sport Psychologist*, 11, 107–119.

Buceta, J. M. (1993). The sport psychologist/athletic coach dual role: Advantages, difficulties, and ethical considerations. *Journal of Applied Sport Psychology*, 5, 64–77.

Burke, K. L., & Johnson, J. J. (1992). The sport psychologist-coach dual role position: A rebuttal to Ellickson and Brown (1990). *Journal of Applied Sport Psychology*, 4, 51–55.

Butki, B. D., & Andersen, M. B. (1994). Mentoring in sport psychology: Students' perceptions of training in publications and presentation guidelines. *The Sport Psychologist*, 8, 143–148.

Carron, A. V. (1993). The Coleman Roberts Griffith address: Toward the integration of theory, research, and practice in sport psychology. *Journal of Applied Sport Psychology*, 5, 207–221.

Clarke, K. S. (1984). The USOC Sports Psychology Registry: A clarification. *Journal of Sport Psychology*, 6, 365–366.

Danish, S. J., & Hale, B. D. (1981). Toward an understanding of the practice of sport psychology. *Journal of Sport Psychology*, 3, 90–99.

Danish, S. J., & Hale, B. D. (1982). Let the discussions continue: Further considerations on the practice of sport psychology. *Journal of Sport Psychology*, 4, 10–12.

Danish, S. J., Petitpas, A. J., & Hale, B. D. (1990). Sport as a context for developing competence. In T. Gullotta, G. Adams, & R. Monteymar (Eds.), *Developing social competency in adolescence* (vol. 3, pp. 169–194). Newbury Park, CA: Sage.

Danish, S. J., Petitpas, A. J., & Hale, B. D. (in press). Life development intervention for athletes: Life skills through sports. *The Counseling Psychologist* (in special issue on sport psychology—expected date: summer 1993).

Danish, S. J., Petitpas, A. J., & Hale, B. D. (1992). A developmental-educational intervention model of sport psychology. *The Sport Psychologist*, 6, 403–415.

DeFrancesco, C., & Cronin, J. J. (1988). Marketing the sport psychologist. *The Sport Psychologist*, 2, 28–38.

Dishman, R. K. (1983). Identity crises in North American sport psychology: Academics in professional issues. *Journal of Sport Psychology*, 5, 123–134.

Ellickson, K. A., & Brown, D. R. (1990). Ethical considerations in dual relationships: The sport psychologist-coach. *Journal of Applied Sport Psychology*, 2, 186–190.

Gardner, F. L. (1991). Professionalization of sport psychology: A reply to Silva. *The Sport Psychologist*, 5, 55–60.

Gill, D. L. (1994). A feminist perspective on sport psychology practice. *The Sport Psychologist*, 8, 411–426.

Gould, D. (1990). AAASP: A vision for the 1990's. *Journal of Applied Sport Psychology*, 2, 99–116.

Gould, D., Tammen, V., Murphy, S., & May, J. (1989). An examination of U. S. Olympic sport psychology consultants and the services they provide. *The Sport Psychologist*, 3, 300–312.

Granito, Jr., V. J., & Wenz, B. J. (1995). Reading list for professional issues in applied sport psychology. *The Sport Psychologist*, 9, 96–103.

Hale, B. D., & Danish, S. J. (1999). Putting the accreditation cart before the AAASP horse: A reply to Silva, Conroy and Zizzi. *Journal of Applied Sport Psychology*, 11, 321-328.

Halliwell, W. (1989). Applied sport psychology in Canada. *Journal of Applied Sport Psychology*, 1, 35–44.

Hardy, C. J. (1994). Nurturing our future through effective mentoring: Developing roots as well as wings. AAASP 1993 Presidential Address. *Journal of Applied Sport Psychology*, 6, 196–204.

Harrison, R. P., & Feltz, D. L. (1979). The professionalization of sport psychology: Legal considerations. *Journal of Sport Psychology*, 1, 182–190.

Hays, K. F. (1995). Putting sport psychology into (your) practice. *Professional Psychology: Research and Practice*, 26, 33–40.

Heyman, S. R. (1982). A reaction to Danish and Hale: A minority report. *Journal of Sport Psychology*, 4, 7–9.

Heyman, S. R. (1984). The development of models for sport psychology: Examining the USOC guidelines. *Journal of Sport Psychology*, 6, 125–132.

Heyman, S. R. (1987). Counseling and psychotherapy with athletes: Special considerations. In J. R. May & M. J. Asken (Eds.), *Sport psychology: The psychological health of the athlete* (pp. 135–156). New York: PMA Publishing Corp.

Heyman, S. R. (1990). Ethical issues in performance enhancement approaches with amateur boxers. *The Sport Psychologist*, 4, 48–54.

Kirschenbaum, D. S., Parham, W. D., & Murphy, S. M. (1993). Provision of sport psychology services at Olympic events: The 1991 U.S. Olympic Festival and beyond. *The Sport Psychologist*, 7, 419–440.

Krane, V. (1994). A feminist perspective on contemporary sport psychology research. *The Sport Psychologist*, 8, 393–410.

Krane, V., Andersen, M. B., & Strean, W. B. (1997). Issues of qualitative research methods and presentation. *Journal of Sport & Exercise Psychology*, 19, 213–218.

Landers, D. M. (1983). Whatever happened to theory testing in sport psychology? *Journal of Sport Psychology*, 5, 135–151.

Mahoney, M. J., & Suinn, R. M. (1986). History and overview of modern sport psychology. *The Clinical Psychologist*, 10, 64–68.

McCullagh, P. (1998). What is the applied in applied sport psychology? The role of integration. *Journal of Applied Sport Psychology*, 10, S1-S10.

Murphy, S. (Ed.). (1993). *Clinical sport psychology*. Champaign: Human Kinetics.

Nideffer, R. M. (1981). *The ethics and practice of applied sport psychology*. Ithaca, NY: Mouvement Publications.

Nideffer, R. M., Dufresne, P., Nesvig, D., & Selder, D. (1980). The future of applied sport psychology. *Journal of Sport Psychology*, 2, 170–174.

Nideffer, R. M., Feltz, D., & Salmela, J. (1982). A rebuttal to Danish and Hale: A committee report. *Journal of Sport Psychology*, 4, 3–6.

Ogilvie, B. C. (1979). The sport psychologist and his professional credibility. In P. Klavora & J. V. Daniel (Eds.), *Coach, athlete, and the sport psychologist* (pp. 44–55). Toronto, Ontario, Canada: University of Toronto.

Ogilvie, B. C. (1989). Applied sport psychology: Reflections on the future. *Journal of Applied Sport Psychology*, 1, 4–7.

Petitpas, A. J., Brewer, B. W., Rivera, P. M., & Van Raalte, J. L. (1994). Ethical beliefs and behaviors in applied sport psychology: The AAASP Ethics Survey. *Journal of Applied Sport Psychology*, 6, 135–151.

Petitpas, A. J., Giges, B., & Danish, S. J. (1999). The sport psychologist-athlete relationship: Implications for training. *The Sport Psychologist*, 13, 344-357.

Petrie, T. A., & Diehl, N. S. (1995). Sport psychology in the profession of psychology. Professional Psychology: *Research and Practice*, 26, 288–291.

Petrie, T. A., & Watkins, Jr., C. E. (1994a). A survey of counseling psychology programs and exercise/sport science departments: Sport psychology issues and training. *The Sport Psychologist*, 8, 28–36.

Petrie, T. A., & Watkins, Jr., C. E. (1994b). Sport psychology training in counseling psychology programs: Is there room at the inn? *The Counseling Psychologist*, 22, 335–341.

Ravizza, K. (1988). Gaining entry with athletic personnel for season-long consulting. *The Sport Psychologist*, 2, 243–254.

Rejeski, W. J., & Brawley, L. R. (1988). Defining the boundaries of sport psychology. *The Sport Psychologist*, 2, 231–242.

Sachs, M. L. (1991). Reading list in applied sport psychology: Psychological skills training. *The Sport Psychologist*, 5, 88–91.

Sachs, M. L. (1993). Professional ethics in sport psychology. In R. N. Singer, M. Murphey, & K. Tennant, (Eds.), *Handbook on research in sport psychology*. New York: Macmillan Publishing Company.

Sachs, M. L. (1999). Comment on Petitpas, Danish, and Giges, The sport psychologist-athlete relationship: Implications for training. *The Sport Psychologist*, 13, 358-361.

Schell, B., Hunt, J., & Lloyd, C. (1984). An investigation of future market opportunities for sport psychologists. *Journal of Sport Psychology*, 6, 335–350.

Silva, J. M., III (1989). The evolution of AAASP and JASP. *Journal of Applied Sport Psychology*, 1, 1–3.

Silva, J. M., III (1989). Toward the professionalization of sport psychology. *The Sport Psychologist*, 3, 265–273.

Silva, J. M., III (1992). On advancement: An editorial. *Journal of Applied Sport Psychology*, 4, 1–9.

Silva, J. M., III (1996). 1995 Coleman Roberts Griffith address: Profiles of excellence. *Journal of Applied Sport Psychology*, 8, 119–130.

Silva, J. M., III, Conroy, D. E., & Zizzi, S. J. (1999) Critical issues confronting the advancement of applied sport psychology. *Journal of Applied Sport Psychology*, 11, 298-320.

Simons, J. P., & Andersen, M. B. (1995). The development of consulting practice in applied sport psychology: Some personal perspectives. *The Sport Psychologist*, 9, 449–468.

Singer, R. N. (1989). Applied sport psychology in the United States. *Journal of Applied Sport Psychology*, 1, 61–80.

Singer, R. N. (1992). What in the world is happening in sport psychology. *Journal of Applied Sport Psychology*, 4, 63–76.

Smith, D. (1992). The coach as sport psychologist: An alternate view. *Journal of Applied Sport Psychology*, 4, 56–62.

Smith, R. E. (1989). Applied sport psychology in an age of accountability. *Journal of Applied Sport Psychology*, 1, 166–180.

Smith, Y. R. (1991). Issues and strategies for working with multicultural athletes. *Journal of Physical Education, Recreation, and Dance*, 62(3), 39–44.

Straub, W. F., & Hinman, D. A. (1992). Profiles and professional perspectives of 10 leading sport psychologists. *The Sport Psychologist*, 6, 297–312.

Strean, W. B., & Roberts, G. C. (1992). Future directions in applied sport psychology research. *The Sport Psychologist*, 6, 55–65.

Taylor, J. (1991). Career direction, development, and opportunities in applied sport psychology. *The Sport Psychologist*, 5, 266–280.

Taylor, J. (1994). Examining the boundaries of sport science and psychology trained practitioners in applied sport psychology: Title usage and area of competence. *Journal of Applied Sport Psychology*, 6, 185–195.

Taylor, J. (1995). A conceptual model for integrating athletes' needs and sport demands in the development of competitive mental preparation strategies. *The Sport Psychologist*, 9, 339–357.

United States Olympic Committee. (1983). United States Olympic Committee establishes guidelines for sport psychology services. *Journal of Sport Psychology*, 5, 4–7.

Van Raalte, J. L., Brewer, D. D., Brewer, B. W., & Linder, D. E. (1993). Sport psychologists' perceptions of sport and mental health practitioners. *Journal of Applied Sport Psychology*, 5, 222–233.

Vealey, R. S. (1988). Future directions in psychological skills training. *The Sport Psychologist*, 2, 318–336.

Waite, B. T., & Pettit, M. E. (1993). Work experiences of graduates from doctoral programs in sport psychology. *Journal of Applied Sport Psychology*, 5, 234–250.

Weinberg, R. S. (1989). Applied sport psychology: Issues and challenges. *Journal of Applied Sport Psychology*, 1, 181–195.

Weiss, M. R. (1998). "Passionate collaboration": Reflections on the directions of applied sport psychology in the coming millennium. *Journal of Applied Sport Psychology*, 10, S11-S24.

Williams, J. M. (1995). Applied sport psychology: Goals, issues, and challenges. *Journal of Applied Sport Psychology*, 7, 81–91.

Zaichkowsky, L. D., & Perna, F. M. (1992). Certification of consultants in sport psychology: A rebuttal to Anshel. *The Sport Psychologist*, 6, 287–296.

Zeigler, E. F. (1987). Rationale and suggested dimensions for a code of ethics for sport psychologists. *The Sport Psychologist*, 1, 138–150.

Appendix I
Reading List in Applied Sport Psychology: Psychological Skills Training

Michael L. Sachs, Temple University
Alan S. Kornspan, University of Akron

Since the original version of this list first appeared, many applied sport psychology textbooks have been written. The main purpose of the list originally was to provide a resource list of mental training books so that sport psychology consultants could provide resources to individuals seeking information on sport psychology topics (Sachs, 1991). Also, as has been the case since the original list appeared, the authors have continued to list book reviews directly following a books listing if available.

Originally, the list was developed from various library materials, Vealey's (1988) article on future directions in applied sport psychology, and a variety of journals in the field of sport and exercise science (Sachs, 1991). Since the development of the original listing the authors have added many books to the list through the aid of computerized databases that provide listings of books related to applied sport psychology. Computerized databases that have aided the authors in locating books for the present list include databases such as WorldCat, Books in Print, SportDiscus, and Amazon.com.

In analyzing the current list, 356 applied sport psychology books have been listed. A wide variety of sport specific books are covered in the current list. For example, sport specific applied sport psychology texts include books on: archery, auto racing, baseball, basketball, billiards, bodybuilding, bowling, cricket, curling, cycling, equestrian, fencing, football, golf, hockey, rugby, running, shooting, skiing, skating, soccer, softball, surfing, swimming, tennis, track and field, triathlon, volleyball. Thus, 28 sports are represented in the present list. Of the 356 books listed, the sport represented the most is golf - 55 golf specific applied sport psychology books are listed. The second most popular sport listed are books written on the psychology of tennis - 17 books have been included on the psychology of tennis. The third most popular sport specific applied sport psychology books listed are related to the mental game of baseball (n = 12). The other 25 sports represented have 10 or fewer books listed. The following includes the number of books listed for the following sports: archery (n = 1), auto racing (n = 1), basketball (n = 5), billiards (n = 1), bodybuilding (n = 2), bowling (n = 3), cricket (n = 1), curling (n = 1), cycling (n = 2), equestrian (n = 9), fencing (n = 2), fishing (n = 1), football (n = 2), gymnastics (n = 1), hockey (n = 5), rugby (n = 2), running (n = 8), shooting (n = 4), skiing (n = 10), skating (n = 3), soccer (n = 9), softball (n = 2), surfing (n = 1), swimming (n = 10), track and field (n = 1), triathlon (n = 2), and volleyball (n = 1).

Although there are 169 sport specific mental training and applied sport psychology books listed in 28 different sports, there are many sports that do not have sport specific applied sport psychology books listed. For example, there appear to be very few mental training or applied sport psychology books available specifically for the sports of badminton, bobsledding, boxing, canoe, cheerleading, croquet, diving, frisbee, handball, judo, lacrosse, luge, motor cycle racing, modern pentathlon, netball, polo, racquetball, rodeo, rowing, sailing, snowboarding, squash, table tennis, taekwondo, water polo, water skiing, weightlifting, or wrestling. Thus, there appears to be a need for mental training or applied sport psychology books to be developed specifically for these sports in which few, if any, sport specific applied sport psychology books exist.

While there may not be specific mental training books for every sport, there are many general sport psychology books that have been written that may be applicable to sports in which there are not sport specific mental training texts available. For example, the present resource lists 144 books written related to applied sport psychology in general. In addition to general mental training books, the present reading list provides references for 23 books related to youth sport, 6 books on exercise and fitness psychology, 2 books on the topic of the psychology of sport injury, and 4 books related to the topic of team building.

One question that Sachs (1991) asked was what was the effectiveness of applied sport psychology mental training books? Sachs pointed out that studies had not been conducted on how helpful mental skills training books were in helping athletes enhance performance. Since 1991 there do not appear to have been any studies addressing this question in the sport psychology literature. Although studies do not seem to have been conducted, it appears that applied sport psychology and mental skills training have made an impact on the sports world. For example, there have been recent media reports of baseball players reading baseball mental training books written by Harvey Dorfman. For example, Spencer (2006) has reported that Dontrelle Willis, an elite baseball player for the Florida Marlins, was reading Harvey Dorfman's the Mental ABC's of Pitching. Along with reports of athletes reading mental training books, it appears that some coaches are recommending to their athletes that they read mental training books. For example, Salisbury (2006) reported that the Philadelphia Phillies' pitching coach Rich Dubee has recommended that an athlete he coaches read Harvey Dorfman's book the Mental ABC's of pitching.

Readers may be interested in developing separate bibliographies (perhaps annotated!) in selected sports or general areas. One example of a general area bibliography would be one on youth sports. Please see the end of this Appendix for one such bibliography.

In summarizing the updated information, there have been over 350 books published over the last 35 years related to applied sport psychology. However, there are still many sports in which it appears that sport specific mental training texts have not been written. Additionally, it seems that many applied sport psychology texts published since the 1970s have been general applied sport psychology books. Finally, researchers may want to conduct a study to determine the effects of reading applied sport psychology textbooks in enhancing athletic performance.

Adrisani, J. (2002). *Think like Tiger: An analysis of Tiger Woods mental game.* New York: Berkly Publishing.

Aicinena, S. (2002). *Through the eyes of parents, children, and a coach: A fourteen-year participant-observer investigation of youth soccer.* Lanham, MD: University Press of America.

Albinson, J. G., & Bull, S. J. (1988). *The mental game plan.* London, Ontario: Spodym. Book review: TSP, 1990, 4, 76–77.

Alder, H., & Morris, K. (1996). *Masterstroke: Use the power of your mind to improve your golf with NLP neurolinguistic programming.* London: Piatkus.

Alexander, D. (1994). *Think to win.* Cambridge, MA: R. Bentley. (auto racing).

Allen, G. (1983). *The mental game: The inner game of bowling.* Deerfield, IL: Tech Ed Publishing Co.

American Sport Education Program. (1994). *SportParent.* Champaign, IL: Human Kinetics.

Anderson, E. (1994). *Training games: Coaching runners creatively.* Mountain View, CA: TAFNEWS Press.

Andersonn, C., & Andersonn, B. (2000). *Will you still love me if I don't win?* Dallas, TX: Taylor Publishing Co.

Anthony, M. (2001). *Michael Anthony's mental keys to improve your golf.* Danville, CA: T M K Press.

Backley, S., & Stafford, I. (1996). *The winning mind: A guide to achieving success and overcoming failure.* London: Aurum Press.

Baker, J., & Sedwick, W. (2005). *Sport psychology library: Triathlon.* Morgantown, WV: Fitness Information Technology.

Barber, G. (2006). *Sports psychology for runners.* Trafford Publishing.

Barden, R. C., Jackson, B., & Ford, M. E. (1992). *Optimal performance in tennis: Mental skills for maximum achievement in athletics and life.* Plymouth, MN: Optimal Performance Systems Research. Book review: TSP, 1995, 9, 112–113.

Barzdukas, A. (1995). *Gold minds: Gold medal mental strategies for everyday life.* Indianapolis, IN: Masters Press.

Baum, K., & Trubo, R. (1999). *The mental edge: Maximize your sports potential with the mind-body connection.* New York: Berkley Publishing Company.

Bell, B., & Vahle, N. (2005). *Smart baseball: How professionals play the mental game.* New York: St. Martin's Press.

Bell, K. F. (1982). *Winning isn't normal.* Austin, TX: Keel Publications.

Bell, K. F. (1982). *You only feel wet when your out of the water: Thoughts on psychology and competitive swimming.* Austin, TX: Keel Publications.

Bell, K. F. (1983). *Championship thinking: The athlete's guide to winning performance in all sports.* Englewood Cliffs, NJ: Prentice-Hall.

Bell, K. F. (1983). *Target on gold: Goal setting for swimmers and other kinds of people.* Austin, TX: Keel Publications.

Bell, K. F. (1980). *The nuts and bolts of psychology for swimmers.* Austin, TX: Keel Publications.

Bell, K. F. (1985). *Coaching Excellence.* Austin, TX: Keel Publications.

Bell, K. F. (1998). *Swim to win playbook.* Austin, TX: Keel Productions.

Bell, K. F. (2001). *The parent's guide to the proper psychological care and feeding of the competitive swimmer.* Austin, TX: Keel Productions

Bennett, J. G., & Pravitz, J. E. (1982). *The miracle of sports psychology.* Englewood Cliffs, NJ: Prentice-Hall. Book review: JOPERD, 1984, 55(5), 98–99.

Bennett, J. G., & Pravitz, J. E. (1987). *Profile of a winner: Advanced mental training for athletes.* Ithaca, NY: Sport Science International. Book review: TSP, 1987, 1, 361–363.

Bennett, R. (2004). *The surfer's mind: The complete practical guide to surf psychology.* Turquay, Victoria: Surfer's mind.

Benzel, D. (1989). *Psyching for slalom: An illustrated guide to the mind and muscle of the complete skier.* Winter Park, FL: World Publications.

Beswick, B. (2001). *Focused for soccer.* Champaign, IL: Human Kinetics Publishers.

Biller, H. B. (2002). *Creative fitness: Applying health psychology and exercise science to everyday life.* Westport, CT: Auburn House.

Bollettieri, N., & Maher, C. (1996). *Nick Bollettieri's mental efficiency program for playing great tennis.* Chicago: Contemporary: Books.

Braden, V., & Wool, R. (1993). *Vic Braden's mental tennis: How to psych yourself to a winning game.* Boston: Little, Brown and Company.

Brennan, S. J. (1990). *Competitive excellence: The psychology and strategy of successful team building.* Omaha, NE: Peak Performance Publishing. Book review: TSP, 1991, 5, 290–291.

Brennan, S. J. (1993). *The mental edge: Basketball's peak performance workbook* (2nd ed.). Omaha, NE: Peak Performance Publishing. Book review: TSP, 1994, 8, 321–323.

Breslow, D. (2002). *Wired to win: Mental keys to play your best golf.* Bloomington, IN: 1st books library.

Brown, R. A. (1994). *The golfing mind: The psychological principles of good golf.* New York: Lyons & Burford.

Bull, S. J. (1991). *Sport psychology: A self-help guide.* Swindon: Crowood.

Bull, S. J., Albinson, J. G., & Shambrook, C. J. (1996). *The mental game plan: Getting psyched for sport.* Eastbourne: Sports Dynamics.

Bull, S. J., & Shambrook, C. J. (2005). *Soccer: the mind game.* Spring City, PA: Reedswain Publishing.

Bump, L. (1989). *Sport psychology study guide (and accompanying workbook).* Champaign, IL: Human Kinetics. Book review: TSP, 1990, 4, 72–73.

Burbank, P., & Riebe, D. (2002). *Promoting exercise and behavior change in older adults: Interventions with the transtheoretical model.* New York: Springer.

Burke, K. L. & Brown, D. (2003). *Sport psychology library: Basketball.* Morgantown, WV: Fitness Information Technology, Inc. Book Review: TSP, 2003, 17, 290-492.

Burnett, D. J. (1993). *Youth sports & self-esteem: A guide for parents.* Indianapolis, IN: Masters Press.

Busack, M. (2002). Positive mental attitude game plan for winning basketball. Authorhouse.

Butler, R. J. (1996). *Sports psychology in action.* Boston, MA: Butterworth Heinemann.

Cabrini, M. (1999). *The psychology of soccer.* Spring City, PA: Reedswain Books and Videos.

Cahill, B. R., & Pearl, A. J. (1993). *Intensive participation in children's sports.* Champaign, IL: Human Kinetics.

Cale, A. (2004). *The official FA guide to psychology for football.* London: Hodder and Stoughton.

Carlson, R. (2002). *The don't sweat guide to golf: Playing stress-free so you're at the top of your game.* New York: Hyperion.

Clarke, D., & Morris, K. (2005*). Golf: The mind factor.* London: Hodder and Stoughton.

Clarkson, M. (1999). *Competitive fire.* Champaign, IL: Human Kinetics.

Clarkson, M. (2004). *Pressure golf: Overcoming choking and frustration.* Raincoast Books.

Clay, A. (2005). *Riding out of your mind: Equestrian sport psychology.* The writing room.

Clayton, L., & Smith, B. S. (1992). *Coping with sport injuries.* New York: Rosen Publishing Group.

Cluck, B. (2002). *Think better baseball: Secrets from major league coaches and players for mastering the mental game.* Chicago: Contemporary Books.

Cogan, K. D., & Vidmar, P. (2000) *Sport psychology library: Gymnastics.* Morgantown, WV: Fitness Information Technology.

Cohn, P. J. (1994). *The mental game of golf: A guide to peak performance.* South Bend, IN: Diamond Communications. Book review: TSP, 1996, 10, 213–216.

Cohn, P. J. (2000). *Peak performance golf: How good golfers become great ones.* Chicago, IL: Contemporary Books.

Cohn, P. J. (2001). *Going low: How to break your individual golf scoring barrier by thinking like a pro.* Chicago, IL: Contemporary Books.

Cohn, P. J., & Winters, K. (1995). *The mental art of putting: Using your mind to putt your best.* South Bend, IN: Diamond Communications, Inc.

Colby, M. (1996). *Motor learning applied to sports* (2nd ed.). Boston, MA: American Press.

Coles, J. (1999). *Three shot golf.* Springfield, NJ: Burford Books.

Coop, R. H., & Fields, Bill. (1993). *Mind over golf: Play your best by thinking smart.* New York: Macmillan Publishing Company.

Cooper, A. (1998). *Playing in the zone: Exploring the spiritual dimensions of sports.* Boston: Shambhala.

Cratty, B. J. (1984). *Psychological preparation and athletic excellence.* Ithaca, NY: Mouvement Publications. Book review: JSP, 1986, 8, 252–254.

Crossman, J. (2001). *Coping with sports injuries: Psychological strategies for rehabilitation.* Oxford: Oxford University Press.

Cunningham, L. (1981). *Hypnosport: How you can improve your sporting performances.* Glendale, CA: Westwood.

Curtis, J. D. (1989). *The mindset for winning.* La Crosse, WI: Coulee Press. Book review: JSEP, 1990, 12, 439–441.

Dahlkoetter, D. (2002). *Your performing edge: The complete mind-0body guide for excellence in sports.* San Carlos, CA: Pulgas Ridge Press.

Dale, G. (2005). *The fulfilling ride: A parent's guide to helping athletes have a successful sport experience.* Ames, IA: Championship Productions.

Dale, G., & Conant, S. (2004). *101 teambuilding activities: Ideas every coach can use to enhance teamwork, communication and trust.* Durham, NC: Excellence in performance.

Dalloway, M. (1992). *Visualization: The master skill in mental training.* Phoenix, AZ: Optimal Performance Institute Press. Book review: TSP, 1995, 9, 109–111.

Dalloway, M. (1993a). *Concentration: Focus your mind, power your game.* Phoenix, AZ: Optimal Performance Institute Press. Book review: TSP, 1995, 9, 109–111.

Dalloway, M. (1993b). *Drive and determination: Developing your inner motivation.* Phoenix, AZ: Optimal Performance Institute Press. Book review: TSP, 1995, 9, 109–111.

Dalloway, M. (1993c). *Risk taking: Performing your best during critical times.* Phoenix, AZ: Optimal Performance Institute Press. Book review: TSP, 1995, 9, 109–111.

Dalloway, M. (1994). *Reflections on the mental side of sports.* Phoenix, AZ: Optimal Performance Institute Press. Book review: TSP, 1996, 10, 300–301.

Decoursey, D., & Linder, D. E. (1990). *Visual skiing: Essential mental and physical skills for the modern skier.* New York: Doubleday.

Devenzio, D. (1997). *Think like a champion: A guide to championship performance in all sports.* Charlotte, NC: Fool Court Press.

DiCicco, T., Hacker, C., & Salzberg, C. (2002). *Catch them being good.* New York: Viking.

Domey, R. L. (1989). *Mental training for shooting success* (2nd ed.). Pullman, WA: College Hill Communications.

Dorfman, H. A. (1999). *The mental ABC's of pitching: A handbook for performance enhancement.* South Bend, IN: Diamond Communications.

Dorfman, H. A. (2001). *The mental keys to hitting: A handbook of strategies for performance enhancement.* South Bend, IN: Diamond Communications.

Dorfman, H. A., & Kuehl, K. (1995). *The mental game of baseball: A guide to peak performance.* (2nd ed.). South Bend, IN: Diamond Communications, Inc. Book review: TSP, 1991, 5, 92–93.

Dorfman, H. A., & Kuehl, K. (2002). *The mental game of baseball: A guide to peak performance.* (3rd ed.). South Bend, IN: Diamond Communications.

Dosil, J. (2005). *The sport psychologist's handbook: a guide for specific performance enhancement.* Hoboken, NJ: Wiley and Sons.

Douillard, J. (1994). *Body, mind and sport: The mind-body guide to lifelong fitness and your personal best.* London: Bantam Inc.

Edgette, J. H., & Rowan, T. (2003). *Winning the mind game: Using hypnosis in sport psychology.* Camarthen: Crown House.

Edgette, J. S. (1996). *Heads up! Practical sports psychology for riders, their trainers, and their families.* New York: Doubleday.

Elliot, R. (1991). *The competitive edge: Mental preparation for distance running.* Mountain View, CA: TAFNEWS Press.

Engh, F. (2000). *Why Johnny hates sports.* Garden City Park, NY: Avery Publishing Group.

Epstein-Shepherd, B. (1999). *Mental management for great golf: How to control your thoughts and play out of your mind.* Chicago, IL: Contemporary.

Ericksson, S. G., Railo, W., & Matson, H. (2001). *Sven Goran on football, the inner game-improving performance.* London: Carlton.

Evangelista, N. (2000). *The inner game of fencing: Excellence in form, technique, strategy and spirit.* Chicago: Masters press.

Evans, E. (1990). *Mental toughness training for cross-country skiing.* New York: The Stephen Greene Press/Pelham Books.

Fancher, B. (2002). *Pleasures of small motions: Mastering the mental game of pocket billiards.* Lyons Press: Guilford, CT.

Farley, K. L., & Curry, S. M. (1994). *Get motivated: Daily psych-ups.* New York: Fireside/Simon & Schuster.

Fasciana. G. S. (2000). *Golf's mental magic: Four strategies for mental toughness.* Greenville, SC: Health and Performance Associates.

Figone, A. (1991). *Teaching the mental aspects of baseball: A coach's handbook.* Madison, WI: Brown & Benchmark.

Fine, A. H., & Sachs, M. L. (1997). *The total sports experience for kids: A parent's guide to success in youth sports.* South Bend, IN: Diamond Communications, Inc.

Fortanasce, V. M. (1995). *Life lessons from Little League: A guide for parents and coaches.* New York: Image/Doubleday.

Foster, S., & Prussack, T. (1999). *Skate your personal best: A guide to mastering intermediate and advanced technique, achieving optimal performance skills and skating excellence.* San Francisco, CA: Rudi Publishing.

Fox, A. (1993). *Think to win: The strategic dimension of tennis.* New York: Harper.

Fox, A. (2005). *The winner's mind: A competitor's guide to sports and business success.* Vista, CA: RacquetTECH Publishing.

Gallwey, W. T. (1998). *The inner game of golf* (rev. ed.). New York: Random House.

Garfield, C. A., & Bennett, H. Z. (1984). *Peak performance: Mental training techniques of the world's greatest athletes.* Los Angeles: Jeremy P. Tarcher, Inc. Book review: JOPERD, 1985, 56(9), 77–78.

Garrat, T. (2001). *Sporting excellence: Optimising sport performance using NLP.* Norwalk Connecticut: Crown House Publishing.

Gauron, E. F. (1984). *Mental training for peak performance.* Lansing, NY: Sport Science Associates. Book review: JSP, 1987, 9, 83–84.

Gibson, M. (1994). *Going for it! A gym bag companion for living our dreams.* Perkasie, PA: Wind Dancer Publications.

Ginsburg, R. D., Durant, S., & Baltzell, A. (2006). *Who's game is it anyways: A guide to helping your child get the most from sports.* Boston: Houghton Mifflin.

Glad, W., & Beck, C. (1999). *Focused for golf.* Champaign, IL: Human Kinetics.

Goldberg, A. S. (1998). *Sports slump busting.* Champaign, IL: Human Kinetics.

Goldberg, A. (1988). *The sports mind: A workbook of mental skills for athletes.* Northampton, MA: Competitive Advantage.

Graham, D., & Stabler, J. (1999). *The 8 traits of champion golfers.* New York: Simon & Schuster.

Graham, D., & Yocum, G. (1990). *Mental toughness training for golf.* New York: Stephen Greene Press/Pelham Books.

Grant, R. W. (1988). *The psychology of sport: Facing one's true opponent.* Jefferson, NC: McFarland.

Greenlees, I., & Moran, A. (Eds.) (2003). *Concentration skills training in Sport.* Leicester: British Psychological Society.

Gourley, M. (2003). *The psychological edge in rugby: Leadership and motivation in coaching team sports.* Auckland, New Zealand: Human Synergistics.

Hackfort, D. (1994). *Psycho-social issues and interventions in elite sport.* New York: P. Lang.

Halden-Brown, S. (2003). *Mistakes worth making: How to turn sports errors into athletic excellence.* Champaign, IL: Human Kinetics Publishers.

Hale, B. D., & Collins, D. J. (2002). *Rugby tough.* Champaign, IL: Human Kinetics.

Hardy, L., Jones, J. G., & Gould, D. (1996). *Understanding psychological preparation for sport: Theory and practice of elite performers.* New York: J. Wiley.

Harley, N. R. (1994). *Let's go skiing with a psychiatrist: The mental game of sensational skiing.* Vail, CO: Vail Press.

Harris, D. V., & Harris, B. L. (1984). *The athlete's guide to sports psychology: Mental skills for physical people.* New York: Leisure Press.

Hassler, J. K., & Jahiel, J. (1993). *In search of your image: A practical guide to the mental and spiritual aspects of horsemanship.* Colora, MD: Goals Unlimited Press.

Henderson, A. & Helgeland, G. (2003). *On target for understanding winning archery.* Mequon, WI: Target Communications.

Henderson, J. (1991). *Think fast: Mental toughness training for runners.* New York: Pengiun Books.

Henderson, J. (Ed.) (1972). *Practical running psychology.* Mountain View, CA: Runner's World Magazine.

Hendricks, G., & Carlson, J. (1982). *The centered athlete: A conditioning program for your mind.* Englewood Cliffs, NJ: Prentice-Hall.

Hennessey, D. (2006). *Improving your home run state of mind. 25 valuable success nourishing tips for baseball players.* North Vancouver, Canada: Terrain Vague 2.

Herbison, W. (2000). *Head games: The mental advantage for baseball excellence.* Cleveland, MS: Head Games Press.

Hinitz, D. (2002). *Focused for bowling.* Champaign, IL: Human Kinetics.

Hogg, J. M. (1995a). *Mental skills for competitive swimmers.* Edmonton, Alberta, Canada: Sport Excel Publishing.

Hogg, J. M. (1995b). *Mental skills for competitive swimmers: A workbook to improve mental performance.* Edmonton, Alberta, Canada: Sport Excel Publishing.

Hogg, J. M. (1995c). *Mental skills for swim coaches: A coaching text on the psychological aspects of competitive swimming.* Edmonton, Alberta, Canada: Sport Excel Publishing.

Hogg, J. M. (1997). *Mental skills for young athletes: A mental skills workbook for athletes 12 and under.* Edmonton, Alberta, Canada: Sport Excel Publishing. Book review: TSP, 1998, 12, 358-360.

Holzel, P., & Holzel, W. (1996). *Learn to ride using sports psychology: A training aid for riders and instructors.* North Pomfret, VT: Trafalgar Square.

Huang, C. A., & Lynch, J. (1992). *Thinking body, dancing mind: Taosports for extraordinary performance in athletics, business, and life.* New York: Bantam Books.

Humphrey, J. H., Dow, D. A., & Bowden, W. W. (2000). *Stress in college athletics: Causes, consequences, coping.* Binghamton, NY: Haworth Press.

Jackson, A. (1995). *Eye on the ball, mind on the game.* New York: Barnes & Noble.

Jackson, S. A., & Csikszentmihalyi, M. (1999). *Flow in sports.* Champaign, IL: Human Kinetics.

Jaeger, A. J. (1994). *Getting focused, staying focused: A Far Eastern approach to sports and life.* Glendale, CA: Griffith Printing.

Janssen, J. (1998). *Perform to your potential: 20 peak performance articles on the mental game, credible coaching & championship team building.* Tucson, AZ: Winning the Mental Game.

Janssen, J. (2002). *Championship team building: What every coach needs to know to build a motivated, committed, and cohesive team.* Tucson, AZ: Winning the Mental Game.

Janssen, J., & Candrea, M. (1994). *Mental toughness training for softball: A guide and workbook for athletes and coaches.* Casa Grande, AZ: Southwest Camps Publications.

Janssen, J., & Dale, G. (2002). *The seven secrets of successful coaches: How to unlock and unleash your teams full potential.* Tucson, AZ: Winning the Mental Game.

Jennings, K. (2002). *Mind in sport: Directing energy flow into success.* Cape Town, South Africa: Juta and Company.

Jones, C. (1999). *What makes winners win: Thoughts and reflections from successful athletes.* New York: Broadway Books.

Jones, C., & Doren, K. (2000). *Be the ball: A golf instruction book for the mind.* New York: MJF Books.

Jordan, J. H. (1995). *Total mind-body training: A guide to peak athletic performance.* Hartford: Turtle Press.

Jordan, T. J., & De Michele, P. E. (1997). *Overcoming the fear in riding.* Sharon Hill, PA: Breakthrough Publications.

Kappas, J. G. (1984). *Self-hypnosis: The key to athletic success.* Englewood Cliffs, NJ: Prentice-Hall.

Kauss, D. R. (1980). *Peak performance: Mental game plans for maximizing your athletic potential.* Englewood Cliffs, NJ: Prentice-Hall. Book review: JSP, 1982, 4, 410–413.

Kauss, D. (2001). *Mastering your inner game: A self-guided approach to finding your unique sports performance keys.* Champaign, IL: Human Kinetics.

Keefe, R. S. (2003). *On the sweet spot: Stalking the effortless present.* New York: Simon & Schuster.

Kellmann, M., & Kallus, W. (2001). *The recovery-stress-questionnaire for athletes.* Champaign, IL: Human Kinetics.

Keogh, B. K., & Smith, C. E. (1985). *Personal par: A psychological system of golf for women.* Champaign, IL: Human Kinetics. Book review: JOPERD, 1986, 57(8), 83.

Kerr, J. (2001). *Counseling athletes: Applying reversal theory.* New York: Routledge.

Keyes, M. J. (1996). *Mental training for shotgun sports.* Auburn, CA: Shotgun Sports, Inc.

Kimiecik, J. C. (2002). *The intrinsic exerciser: Discovering the joy of exercise.* Boston: Houghton Mifflin.

Kirschenbaum, D. S. (1997). *Mind matters: Seven sport psych steps to maximize performance.* Carmel, IN: Cooper Publishing Group.

Klavora, P., & Chambers, D. (2001). *The great book of inspiring quotations: Motivational sayings for all occasions.* Toronto: Sport Books Publisher.

Knight, S. (2004). *Winning state football: Program your mind win the confidence battle.* Portland, OR: Let's Win Publishing.

Knight, S. (2005). *Winning state basketball: Program your mind be the complete athlete.* Portland, OR: Let's Win Publishing.

Kogler, A. (1993). *Preparing the mind: Improving fencing performance through psychological preparation.* Lansdowne, PA: ConterParry Press.

Kress, J. (1999). Mental training for competitive cycling. Boulder, CO: Velo Press.

Kubistant, T. (1986). *Performing your best: A guide to psychological skills for high achievers.* Champaign, IL: Human Kinetics.

Kubistant, T. (1988). *Mind pump: The psychology of bodybuilding.* Champaign, IL: Leisure Press.

Kubistant, T. (1994). *Mind links: The psychology of golf.* Reno, NV: Performance and Productivity Specialists.

Kuehl, K., Kuehl, J., & Tefertiller, C. (2005). *Mental toughness: A champion's state of mind.* Chicago, IL: Ivan R. Dee

Lasser, E. S., Borden, F., & Edwards, J. (2006). *Sport psychology library: Bowling—The handbook of bowling psychology.* Morgantown, WV: Fitness Information Technology.

Leith, L. (1998). *Exercising your way to better mental health.* Morgantown, WV: Fitness Information Technology.

Leith, L. (2003). *The psychology of coaching team sports: A self-help guide.* Toronto: Sport Books Publisher.

Liggett, D. (2000). *Sport hypnosis.* Champaign, IL: Human Kinetics.

Lilliefors, J. (1978). *The running mind.* Mountain View, CA: World Publications, Inc.

Llewellyn, J. H. (2001). *Let 'em play: What parents, coaches and kids need to know about youth baseball.* Marietta, GA: Longstreet Press.

Llewellyn, J. H. (2000). *Coming in first: Twelve keys to being a winner every day.* Marietta, GA: Longstreet Press.

Loebs, T. W. (2004). *Magical Golf a magical transformation: How to achieve mental and emotional control over your golf game.* Bloomington, IN: Authorhouse.

Loehr, J. E. (1982). *Mental toughness training for sports: Achieving athletic excellence training.* Lexington, MA: Stephen Greene.

Loehr, J. E. (1990). *The mental game.* New York: The Stephen Greene Press/Pelham Books.

Loehr, J. E. (1994). *The new toughness training for sports: Achieving athletic excellence.* New York: Dutton.

Loudis, L. A., Lobitz, W. C., & Singer, K. M. (1986). *Skiing out of your mind.* Champaign, IL: Leisure Press.

Loundagin, C. (2004). *The inner champion: a mental toughness training manual for figure skaters* (2nd ed.). Santa Rosa, CA: InnerChamp Books.

Lucas, G. (1987). *Images for golf: Visualizing your way to a better game.* Calgary: Arizona Academic Sport Resources.

Lynberg, M. (1993). *Winning: Great coaches and athletes share their secrets of success.* New York: Doubleday.

Lynch, J. (1987). *The total runner: A complete mind-body guide to optimal performance.* Englewood Cliffs, NJ: Prentice-Hall. Book review: TSP, 1987, 1, 265–266.

Lynch, J. (2001). *Creative coaching.* Champaign, IL: Human Kinetics. Book Review: TSP, 2003, 17, 120-121.

Lynch, J., & Scott, W. (1999). *Running within: A guide to mastering the body-mind-spirit connection for ultimate training and racing.* Champaign, IL: Human Kinetics.

Mack, G., & Casstevens, D. (2001). *Mind gym: An athlete's guide to inner excellence.* Chicago: Contemporary Books.

Mackenzie, M. M., & Denlinger, Ken. (1990). *Golf: The mind game.* New York: Dell. Book review: TSP, 1992, 6, 314.

Mackenzie, M. M., & Denlinger, K. (1991). *Skiing: The mind game.* New York: Dell.

Mackenzie, M. M., & Denlinger, K. (1991). *Tennis: The mind game.* New York: Dell.

Marcus, B., & Forsyth, L. (2003). *Motivating people to be physically active.* Champaign, IL: Human Kinetics.

Margenau, E. (1990). *Sports without pressure: A guide for parents & coaches of young athletes.* New York: Gardner Press.

Martens, R. (1987). *Coaches' guide to sport psychology.* Champaign, IL: Human Kinetics. Book review: TSP, 1990, 4, 78.

Martin, G. L. (1997). *Sport psychology consulting: Guidelines from behavioral analysis.* Winnipeg, Manitoba, Canada: Sport Sciences Press. Book review: TSP, 1998, 12, 104-105.

Martin, G. L., & Ingraham, D. (1993). *New mental skills for better golf: Test your self-talk.* Winnipeg, Manitoba, Canada: Sport Sciences Press.

Martin, G. L., & Ingram, D. (2001). *Play golf in the zone: The psychology of golf made easy.* San Francisco: Van der Plas.

Martin, G. L., Toogood, A., & Tkachuk, G. (1997). *Behavioral assessment forms for sport psychology consulting.* Winnipeg, Manitoba, Canada: Sport Sciences Press. Book review: TSP, 1998, 12, 104-105.

May, J. R., & Asken, M. J. (Eds.). (1987). *Sport psychology: The psychological health of the athlete.* New York: PMA Publishing Corp. Book review: TSP, 1989, 3, 274–277.

Mays, R. (2001). *Power of the mind: Mental training for goaltenders.* Burlington, Ontario: On-ice Publications.

Mazzoni, W. (2006). *You vs. you: Sport psychology for life.* Bridgeport, CT: Mazz Marketing.

Meyer, J. E., & Plodzien, C. A. (1988). *Excelling in sports through thinking straight.* Springfield, IL: Charles C. Thomas. Book review: JSEP, 1990, 12, 437–438.

Micheli, L. J. (1990). *Sportswise: An essential guide for young athletes, parents, and coaches.* Boston: Houghton Mifflin Company.

Michels, R. (2002). *Teambuilding: The road to success.* Spring City, PA: Reedswain Books and Videos.

Mikes, J. (1987). *Basketball fundamentals: A complete mental training guide.* Champaign, IL: Leisure Press. Book review: JOPERD, 1987, 58(9), 141–142.

Miller, B. (1998). *Gold minds: The psychology of winning in sport.* North Pomfret, VT: Trafalgar Square Trafalgar Square Publishing.

Miller, L. (1996). *Golfing in the zone: Merging mind, body, and spirit through golf.* New York: MJF Books.

Miller, S. (2003). *Hockey tough.* Champaign, IL: Human Kinetics.

Miller, S., & Hill, P. M. (1999). *Sport psychology for cyclists.* Boulder, CO: Velo Press.

Miller, S. E. (2001). *The complete player: The psychology of winning hockey.* Toronto: Stodart Press.

Millman, D. (1999). *Body mind mastery: Creating success in sport and life.* Novato, CA: New World Library.

Mills, B. D. (1994). *Mental training and performance enhancement: A guide for volleyball coaches and players.* Dubuque, IA: Eddie Bowers Publishing, Inc. Book review: TSP, 1996, 10, 415–416.

Miner, M. J., Shelley, G. A., & Henschen, K. P. (1995). *Moving toward your potential: The athlete's guide to peak performance.* Farmington, UT: Performance Publications.

Missoum, G. (1991). *Guide du training mental.* Paris: RETZ. Book review: TSP, 1992, 6, 315–316.

Moran, A. P. (Ed.). (1996). *The psychology of concentration in sport performers: A cognitive analysis.* Hove: Psychology Press.

Morrison, L. (2002). *Simple steps to riding success: Feel the power of positive riding with NLP sports psychology techniques.* England: David and Charles Publishers.

Murphy, S. (1996). *The achievement zone: Eight skills for winning all the time from the playing field to the boardroom.* New York: G. P. Putnam's Sons.

Murphy, S. (1999). *The cheers and the tears: A healthy alternative to the dark side of youth sports today.* San Francisco: Jossey-Bass Publishers.

Murray, J., & Frey, R. (1998). *Smart tennis: How to play and win the mental game.* San Francisco: Jossey Bass.

Mycoe, S. (2001). *Unlimited sport success: The power of hypnosis.* San Jose: Writers Club Press.

Nakamura, R. M. (1996). *The power of positive coaching.* Sudbury, MA: Jones and Bartlett Publishers, Inc.

Nideffer, R. (1976). *The inner athlete: Mind plus muscle for winning.* New York: Crowell.

Nideffer, R. M. (1981). *The ethics and practice of applied sport psychology.* Ithaca, NY: Mouvement Publications. Book review: JOPERD, 1982, 53(4), 100.

Nideffer, R. M. (1985). *Athletes' guide to mental training.* Champaign, IL: Human Kinetics.

Nideffer, R. M. (1992). *Psyched to win.* Champaign, IL: Leisure Press: Book reviews: JSEP, 1993, 15, 355–356. TSP, 1993, 7, 204–206.

Nilsson, P., Marriott, L., & Sirak, R. (2005). *Every shot must have a purpose.* New York: Gotham Books.

Nowicki, D. (1993). *Gold medal mental workout: A step-by-step program of mental exercises to make you a winner every time.* Island Pond, VT: Stadion Publishing Co., Inc.

O'Connor, J. (2001). *NLP & sports: How to win the mind game.* London: Thorsons.

Orlick, T. (1986). *Coaches training manual to psyching for sport.* Champaign, IL: Leisure Press. Book review: TSP, 1987, 1, 82.

Orlick, T. (1986). *Psyching for sport: Mental training for athletes.* Champaign, IL: Leisure Press. Book review: TSP, 1987, 1, 82.

Orlick, T. (1990). *In pursuit of excellence: How to win in sport and life through mental training.* (2nd ed.). Champaign, IL: Human Kinetics. Book review: TSP, 1992, 6, 99–100.

Orlick, T. (1992). *Nice on my feelings.* Sacramento, CA: ITA Publications.

Orlick, T. (1993). *Free to feel great: Teaching children to excel at living.* Carp, Ontario, Canada: Creative Bound, Inc.

Orlick, T. (1995). *Nice on my feelings: Nurturing the best in children and parents.* Carp, Ontario, Canada: Creative Bound, Inc.

Orlick, T. (1998). *Embracing your potential.* Champaign, IL: Human Kinetics.

Orlick, T., & Partington, J. (1986). *Psyched: Inner views of winning.* Ottawa, Canada: The Coaching Association of Canada. Book review: TSP, 1987, 1, 166–167.

Owens, D., & Kirschenbaum, D. (1997). *Smart golf: How to simplify and score your mental game.* San Francisco: Jossey-Bass Publishers.

Parent, J. (2002). *Zen golf: Mastering the mental game.* New York: Random House.

Pargman, D. (1986). *Stress and motor performance: Understanding and coping.* Ithaca, NY: Mouvement Publications. Book review: TSP, 1988, 2, 266–267.

Phillips, L., & Stahl, B. (2000). *Parenting, sportsmom style: Real-life solutions for surviving the youth sports scene.* Maumee, OH: 307 Books.

Pierro, P. S. (2002). *The coach's tool box - Using sports psychology with your kids.* Oklahoma City, OK: Peregrine Press of Oklahoma.

Pirozzolo, F. J., & Pate, R. (1996). *The mental game pocket companion for golf.* New York: Harper Collins Publishers.

Pitcher, B. L. (1996). *The Mental Proficiency System: A proven, step-by-step guide to thinking and planning your way to lower golf scores.* Safety Harbor, FL: Pitcher Golf Group.

Porter, C. W. (1993). *Top golf: Peak performance through brain body integration.* Sparks, NV: Life Enhancement Services.

Porter, K. (2003). *The mental athlete.* Champaign, IL: Human Kinetics Publishers. Book Review: *Athletic Insight: The online Journal of Sport Psychology*, 3, 1-2

Porter, K., & Foster, J. (1986). *The mental athlete.* Dubuque, IA: Wm. C. Brown Co. Book review: TSP, 1988, 2, 173–174.

Porter, K., & Foster, J. (1990). *Visual athletics.* Dubuque, IA: Wm. C. Brown Co.

Quinnett, P. (1998). *Pavlov's trout: The incomplete psychology of everyday fishing.* Andrew McMeel Publishing.

Railo, W. (1986). *Willing to win.* West Yorkshire, England: Springfield Books Limited. Book review: JSP, 1987, 9, 186–189.

Ravizza, K., & Hanson, T. (1995). *Heads-up baseball: Playing the game one pitch at a time.* Indianapolis: Masters Press.

Reilly, A. S. (2000). *A sport psychology book for riders.* London: J. A. Allen.

Richard, J. (1991). *Not too high, not too low: Stress management strategies for professional baseball players and their fans.* Dubuque, IA: Kendall/Hunt.

Rodionow, A. W. (Ed.). (1982). *Psychology for training and competition.* L. Pickenhain, Trans. Berlin: Sportverlag Berlin. Book review: TSP, 1989, 3, 278–280.

Roland, D. (1997). *The confident performer.* Paddington, NSW. Australia: Currency Press Ltd. Book review: TSP, 1998, 12, 228-229.

Rotella, R. J., & Bunker, L. K. (1981). *Mind mastery for winning golf.* Englewood Cliffs, NJ: Prentice-Hall.

Rotella, R. J., & Bunker, L. K. (1982). *Mind, set and match.* Charlottesville, VA: LINKS, Inc.

Rotella, R. J., & Bunker, L. K. (1987). *Parenting your superstar.* Champaign, IL: Human Kinetics. Book review: TSP, 1989, 3, 281–282.

Rotella, R., & Cullen, B. (1995). *Golf is not a game of perfect.* New York: Simon & Schuster.

Rotella, R., & Cullen, B. (1996). *Golf is a game of confidence.* New York: Simon & Schuster.

Rotella, R., & Cullen, B. (1997). *The golf of your dreams.* New York: Simon & Schuster.

Rotella, B., & Cullen, B. (2001). *Putting out of your mind.* New York: Simon & Schuster.

Rotella, R. J., & Cullen, B. (2005). *The golfer's mind: Play to play great.* New York: Free press.

Rushall, B. S. (1979). *Psyching in sports.* London: Pelham Books.

Rushall, B. S. (1986). *The psychology of successful cross-country ski racing.* Ottawa, Ontario, Canada: Cross Country Canada.

Rushall, B. S. (1991). *Imagery training in sports: A handbook for athletes, coaches, and sport psychologists.* Spring Valley, CA: Sport Science Associates.

Rushall, B. S. (1992). *Mental skills training for sports: A manual for athletes, coaches, and sport psychologists.* Spring Valley, CA: Sport Science Associates.

Rushall, B. S. (1995). *Think and act like a champion.* Spring Valley, CA: Sport Science Associates.

Rushall, B. S., & Potgieter, J. (1987). *The psychology of successful competing in endurance events.* Pretoria: South African Association for Sport Science, Physical Education, and Recreation.

Sailes, Gary A. (1995). *Mental training for tennis.* Dubuque, IA: Kendall/Hunt Publishers.

Saunders, T. (2005). *Golf: Lower your score with mental training.* Norwalk, CT: Crown House Publishing.

Savoie, J. (1992). *That winning feeling: A new approach to riding using psychocybernetics.* London: Allen.

Schultheis, R. (1996). *Bone games: Extreme sports, shamanism, zen and the search for transcendence.* New York: Breakaway Sports.

Scott, M. D., & Pellicioni, L., Jr. (1982). *Don't choke: How athletes can become winners.* Englewood Cliffs, NJ: Prentice-Hall. Book review: JOPERD, 1984, 55(2), 73.

Scott, N. S. (1999). *Smart soccer: How to use your mind to play your best.* Brookfield, CT: Milbrook Press.

Scott, N. S., & Green A. C. (1999). *The thinking kid's guide to successful soccer.* Brookfield, CT: Milbrook Press.

Selder, D. J. (1998). *Smart skiing: Mental training for all ages and all skill levels.* San Francisco: Jossey Bass.

Selleck, G. A. (1995). *How to play the game of your life: A guide to success in sports and life.* South Bend, IN: Diamond Communications, Inc.

Selleck, G. A. (2002). *Raising a good sport in an in-your-face world: Seven steps to building character on the field and off.* Lincolnwood, IL: Contemporary Books.

Shapiro, A. (1996). *Golf's mental hazards: Overcome them and put an end to the self-destructive round.* New York: Fireside/Simon & Schuster.

Shaw, D., Gorley, T., & Corban, R. (2005). *Sport and exercise psychology.* New York: Bios Scientific Publishers.

Sheikh, A. A., & Korn, E. R. (Eds.). (1994). *Imagery in sports and physical performance.* Amityville, NY: Baywood.

Shoemaker, F., & Shoemaker, P. (1996). *Extraordinary golf: The art of the possible.* New York: Berkley Publishing Group.

Sholz, G. H., & Bernard, C. L. (2005). *Between the sheets: Creating curling champions.* Franklin, TN: Hillsboro Press.

Simek, T. C., & O'Brien, R. M. (1981). *Total golf: A behavioral approach to lowering your score and getting more out of your game.* New York: Doubleday & Company. Book review: JOPERD, 1982, 53(4), 102, 104.

Singer, R. N. (1986). *Peak performance . . . and more.* Ithaca, NY: Mouvement Publications. Book review: JOPERD, 1987, 58(9), 141.

Skinner, C. (2002). *The shooter's personal coach – always on call. The mental art of world class competitive pistol shooting.* Wilmington, DE: Entity International.

Slaikeu, K., & Trogolo, R. (1999). *Focused for tennis.* Champaign, IL: Human Kinetics.

Smith, A. M. (1991). *Power play: Mental toughness for hockey and beyond.* Rochester, MN: Power Play.

Smith, A. M. (2000). *Power play: Mental toughness for hockey and beyond* (3rd edition). Flagler Beach, FL: Athletic guide publishing.

Smith, E. W. L. (1989). *Not just pumping iron: On the psychology of lifting weights.* Springfield, IL: Charles C. Thomas.

Smith, M. (1998). *Developing mental skills for artistic sports.* Calgary, Canada: Johnson Gorman Publishers.

Smith, N. J., Smith, R. E., & Smoll, F. L. (1983). *Kidsports: A survival guide for parents.* Reading, MA: Addison-Wesley Publishing Company.

Smith, R. E., & Smoll, F. L. (1996). *Way to go, coach: A scientifically proven approach to coaching effectiveness.* Portola Valley, CA: Warde.

Smith, R. E., & Smoll, F. L. (2002). *Way to go coach: A scientifically-proven approach to youth sports coaching effectiveness.* (2nd ed.). Portoloa Valley, CA: Warde Publishers.

Smoll, F. L., & Smith, R. E. (1987). *Sport psychology for youth coaches: Personal growth to athlete excellence.* Washington, DC: National Federation for Catholic Youth Ministry. Book review: TSP, 1988, 2, 175–177.

Smoll, F. L., & Smith, R. E. (1995). *Children and youth in sport: A biopsychosocial perspective.* Dubuque, IA: Brown and Benchmark.

Solomon, G., & Becker, A. (2004). *Focused for fastpitch.* 80 drills to play and stay sharp. Champaign, IL: Human Kinetics.

Srebo, R. (2002). *Winning with your head: A complete mental training guide to soccer.* Spring City, PA: Reedswain Books and Videos.

Stankovich, C. E., & Kays, T. M. (2002). *The parent's playbook: Developing a gameplan for maximizing your child's athletic experience.* Columbus, OH: Champion Athletic Consulting.

Stein, M., & Hollowitz, J. (1994). *Psyche and sports: Baseball, hockey, martial arts, running, tennis, and others.* Wilmette, IL: Chiron.

Steinberg, G. M. (2003). *Mental rules for golf: 61 innovative strategies for unleashing your golf potential.* Lanham, Md: Towlehouse Publishing.

Straub, W. F., & Williams, J. M. (Eds.). (1984). *Cognitive sport psychology.* Lansing, NH: Sport Science Associates.

Strossen, R. J. (1994). *IronMind: Stronger minds, stronger bodies.* Nevada City, CA: IronMind Enterprises, Inc.

Sugarman, K. (1999). *Winning the mental way: A practical guide to team building and mental training.* Burlingame, CA: Step Up Publishing.

Suinn, R. M. (1986). *Seven steps to peak performance: The mental training manual for athletes.* Lewiston, NY: Hans Huber Publishers. Book reviews: TSP, 1987, 1, 359–360. JSEP, 1989, 11, 343–345.

Swindley, D. (1996). *Decide to win: A total approach to winning in sport and life.* London: Ward Lock.

Syer, J., & Connolly, C. (1984). *Sporting mind, sporting body: An athlete's guide to mental training.* New York: Cambridge University Press.

Taylor, D. (1989). *Challenge yourself: Goal-setting workbook for athletes.* Coquitlam, British Columbia, Canada: Challenge Yourself Press.

Taylor, J. (1993). *The mental edge for competitive sports* (3rd ed.). Aspen, CO: Alpine* Taylor Consulting. Book review: TSP, 1996, 10, 298–299.

Taylor, J. (1994a). *The mental edge for alpine ski racing.* Aspen, CO: Alpine*Taylor Consulting.

Taylor, J. (1994b). *The mental edge for golf.* Aspen, CO: Alpine*Taylor Consulting.

Taylor, J. (1994c). *The mental edge for tennis.* Aspen, CO: Alpine*Taylor Consulting.

Taylor, J. (1994d). *The mental edge for skiing.* Aspen, CO: Alpine*Taylor Consulting.

Taylor, J. (2000). *Prime sport: Triumph of the athlete mind.* New York: Writers club press. Book Review; TSP, 2002, 16, 457-458.

Taylor, J. (2000). *Prime skiing: Triumph of the racer's mind.* San Jose: Writers club press.

Taylor, J. (2000). *Prime tennis: Triumph of the mental game.* San Jose: Writers club press.

Taylor, J., & Schneider, T. (2005). *The triathlete's guide to mental training.* Boulder, Colorado: Velopress.

Taylor, M. H. (1997). *Clay target shooting: The mental game.* Arvada, CO: MMC Enterprises.

Taylor, M. H. (1999). *Rifle and pistol shooting: Winning with the mental edge.* Arvada, CO: MMC Enterprises.

Terry, P. (1989). *The winning mind.* Wellingborough, Northamptonshire, England: Thorsons Publishing Group. Book reviews: JSEP, 1990, 12, 434–436; TSP, 1990, 4, 437–439.

Thomas, J. R. (Ed.) (1977). *Youth sports guide for coaches and parents.* Washington, DC: AAHPERD Publications.

Tomasi, T. J., & Maloney, K. (2001). *The 30-second golf swing: How to train your brain to improve your game.* New York: Harper Resource.

Tutko, T., & Tosi, U. (1976). *Sports psyching: Playing your best game all of the time.* New York: J. P. Tarcher.

Underwood, T. (1998). *Christian golf psychology.* Grand Island, NE: Cross Training Publishing.

Ungerleider, S. (1996). *Mental training for peak performance: Top athletes reveal the mind exercises they use to excel.* Emmaus, PA: Rodale Press, Inc.

Ungerleider, S. (2005). *Mental training for peak performance: Top athletes reveal the mind exercises they use to excel.* Emmaus, PA: Rodale.

Valiante, G., & Stachura, M. (2005). *Fearless golf: Conquering the mental game.* New York: Doubleday.

Van Raalte, J. L., & Silver-Bernstein, C. (1999). *Sport psychology library: Tennis.* Morgantown, WV: Fitness Information Technology, Inc. Book Review: TSP, 2001, 15, 453-454.

Vanthuyne, C. E. (1999). *Mind works: Psychology of a golf learning program.* Victoria, B.C: Trafford.

Vardy, D. (1996). *The mental game of golf.* Thrumpton: Castle.

Vernacchia, R. (2003). *Inner strength: the mental dynamics of athletic performance.* Palo, Alto, CA: Warde Publishers.

Vernacchia, R. A., McGuire, R. T., & Cook, D. L. (1992). *Coaching mental excellence: "It does matter whether you win or lose…"* Dubuque, IA: Brown & Benchmark. Book review: TSP, 1993, 7, 210–212.

Vernacchia, R., & Statler, T. (eds.) (2005). *The psychology of high-performance track and field.* Mountainview, CA: Tafnews.

Vicory, J. (1996). *Mind golf: It's brain over ball.* Aurora, IL: Kelmscott Press.

Villepigue, J. C. (2006). *Mind over muscle: Using the power of the mind to manifest the body of your dreams.* Long Island City, NY: Healthy Living Books.

Voight, M. (2005). *Mental toughness training for football.* Monterey, CA: Coaches Choice.

Voight, M. (2005). *Mental toughness training for volleyball.* Monterey, CA: Coaches Choice

Waitley, D. (1994). *The new dynamics of winning: Gain the mind-set of a champion.* London: Brealey. (Originally published 1993 by Nightingale-Conant.)

Wallach, J. (1995). *Beyond the fairway: Zen lessons, insights, and inner attitudes of golf.* New York: Bantam Books.

Wanless, M. (1991). *Ride with your mind: An illustrated master class in right brain riding.* North Pomfrey, VT: Trafalgar Square Publishing.

Weinberg, R. S. (1988). *The mental advantage: Developing your psychological skills in tennis.* Champaign, IL: Leisure Press. Book reviews: TSP, 1988, 2, 357–358.JSEP, 1990, 12, 98–99.

Weinberg, R. S. (2002). *Tennis: Winning the mental game.* H. O. Zimman. Book review: *ITF coaching and Sport Science Review*, 2003, 30, 14.

Whitmarsh, B. (2001). *Mind and muscle.* Champaign, IL: Human Kinetics.

Whitmore, J, & Whitmore, J., Sr. (1998). *Mind games: Mental fitness for tennis.* Shaftesbury: Elementary Children's books.

Whittam, P. (1995). *Tennis talk, psych yourself in to win!!! Affirmations for mental fitness in tennis.* Bahamas: Sapphire Publishing Corporation.

Williams, J. M. (Ed.). (2001). *Applied sport psychology: Personal growth to peak performance* (4th ed.). Palo Alto, CA: Mayfield.

Wilt, F., & Bosen, K. (1971). *Motivation and coaching psychology.* Los Altos, CA: TAFNEWS Press.

Winter, B. (1981). *Relax and win: Championship performance in whatever you do.* La Jolla, CA: A. S. Barnes and Company. Book reviews: JOPERD, 1982, 53(7), 86. JSP, 1983, 5, 466–467.

Winter, G. (1992). *The psychology of cricket: How to play the inner game of cricket.* Melbourne, Australia: Sun.

Winter, G., & Martin, C. (1988). *A practical guide to sport psychology.* Underdale, Australia: SA Sports Institute.

Winters. R. K. (2004). *The ten commandments of mindpower golf: no-nonsense strategies for mastering your mental game.* New York: McGraw Hill.

Wiren, G. (2002). *The Golf Magazine mental golf handbook.* Guilford, CT: Lyons Press.

Wiren, G., Coop, R., & Sheehan, L. (1985). *The new golf mind.* New York: Simon & Schuster.

Wolff, R. (1993). *Good sports.* New York: Dell.

Yandell, J. (1999). *Visual tennis.* Champaign, IL: Human Kinetics.

Young, B., & Bunker, L. K. (1995). *The courtside coach.* Charlottesville, VA: LINKS, Inc.

Zaichkowsky, L., D., & Sime, W. E. (Eds.). (1982). *Stress management for sport.* Reston, VA: American Association for Health, Physical Education, Recreation, and Dance.

Zinsser, N. (1991). *Dear Dr. Psych.* Little Brown: Boston.

Zulewski, R. (1994). *The parent's guide to coaching physically challenged children.* Cincinnati, OH: Betterway Books.

References

Sachs, M. L. (1991). Reading list in applied sport psychology: Psychological skills training. *The Sport Psychologist, 5,* 88-91.

Salisbury, J. (2006). *Phillies Notes: Looking Beyond Pitching Motion.* Retrieved May 24 from http://www.philly.com/mld/inquirer/sports/14437203.htm

Scogin, F., Bynum, J., Stephens, G., & Calhoon, S. (1990). Efficacy of self-administered treatment programs: Meta-analytic review. *Professional Psychology: Research and Practice, 21(1)*, 42–47.

Spencer, C. (2006). *Willis, Pierre trying to help each other cure slumps.* Retrieved May 24 from http://www.miami.com/mld/miamiherald/sports/14586989.htm

Vealey, R. S. (1988). Future directions in psychological skills training. *The Sport Psychologist, 2*, 318–336.

There are specific areas in which bibliographies may be developed that would be especially helpful. As noted earlier, there are many books on golf and tennis, and separate bibliographies (perhaps annotated!) would be helpful in these areas. The following list deals with a more general topic—that of youth sport, with special emphasis on youth sports parenting. It was compiled by Steve McWilliams, of Villanova University (and a doctoral student in exercise and sport psychology at Temple University) with assistance from Michael Sachs. Please note that some, but not all, of these books are also listed earlier in this Appendix.

Bibliography

"Youth Sports Parenting"

Andersonn, B., & Andersonn, C. (2000). *Will you still love me if I don't win: A guide for parents of young athletes.* Lanham, MD: Taylor Trade Publishing.

Bigelow, B., Moroney, T., & Hall, L. (2001). *Just let the kids play: How to stop other adults from ruining your child's fun and success in youth sports.* Deerfield Beach, FL: Health Communications, Inc.

Brady, V. (2003). *The score is love all: Timely tips for strong parent-child relations in youth sports.* Lincoln, NE: I-Universe Books.

Burnett, D. (2001). *It's just a game! Youth sports and self-esteem: A guide for parents.* I-Universe.com.

Burnett, D. (1993). *Youth sports and self-esteem: A guide for parents.* Springfield, MA: Masters Press & Spalding.

De Knop, P. (1994). *Youth in sports clubs: Toward a youth friendly approach.* Brussels, Belgium: VUB Brussels University Press.

Devine, J., Gilles, C. (1997). *Victory beyond scoreboard: Building winners in life through sport.* Wilsonville, OR: Bookpartners.

DiCicco, A., & Hacker, C. (2002). *Catch them being good: Everything you need to know to successfully coach girls.* New York: Viking Press.

Engh, F. (2002). *Why Johnny hates sports: Why organized sports are failing our children and what can be done about it.* Garden City Park, NY: Square One Publishers.

Epperson, D., & Selleck, G. (1999). *From the bleachers with love: Advice to parents with kids in sports.* Washington, DC: Alliance.

Epperson, D., & Selleck, G. (2000). *Beyond the bleachers: The art of parenting today's athletes.* Washington, DC: Alliance.

Erickson, D. (2004). *Molding young athletes: How parents and coaches can positively influence kids in sports.* Oregon, WI: Purington Press.

Fine, A., & Sachs, M. (1997) *The total sports experience for kids: A parents guide to success in youth sports.* South Bend, IN: Diamond Communications, Inc.

Fish, J. (2003). *101 ways to be a terrific sports parent: Making athletics a positive experience for your child.* New York: Simon & Schuster.

Fortanasce, V. (2001). *Life lessons from soccer: What your child can learn on and off the field – A guide for parents and coaches.* New York: Simon & Schuster.

Goodman, G. (2000). *101 things parents should know before volunteering to coach their kids sports teams.* Chicago: Contemporary Books.

Hochevar, G. (1989). *Who's coaching your kids?* Washington, DC: Safesports Publishing Company.

Humphrey, J. (2003). *Child development through sports.* Binghampton, NY: Harworth Press.

Koehler, M. (2004). *Your kids and sports: Everything you need to know from grade school to college.* Notre Dame, IN: Sorin Books.

Kuchenbecker, S. (2000). *Raising winners: A parent's guide to helping kids succeed.* New York: Times Books.

Lancaster, S. (2002). *Fair play: Making organized sport a great experience for your kids.* Saddle River, NJ: Prentice Hall Publishers.

LeBlanc, J., & Dickson, L. (1997). *Straight talk about children and sports: Advice for parents, coaches, and teachers.* Cincinnati, OH: Mosaic Press.

Malina, R., & Clark, M. (2003). *Youth sports: Perspective for a new century.* Monterey, CA: Coaches Choice.

Margenau, E. (1990). *Sports without pressure: A guide for parents and coaches of young athletes.* Palm Beach Gardens, FL: Gardner Press.

Marra, R. (1991). *The quality of effort: Integrity in sport and life for student athletes, parents, and coaches.* Aptos, CA: Heart Press.

Mastrich, J. (2002). *Really Winning: Using sports to develop character and integrity in our boys.* New York: St. Martins Press.

McCoglin, C. (2003). *Surviving youth sports.* Victoria, BC: Trafford Publishing.

McInnally, P. (1988). *Moms and dads: Kids and sports.* New York: Scribner Press.

Micheli, L., & Jenkins, M. (1990). *Sportswise: An essential guide for young athletes, parents, and coaches.* Boston: Houghton-Mifflin.

Murphy, S. (1999). *The cheers and tears: A healthy alternative to the dark side of youth sports today.* San Francisco: Jossey-Bass.

Odback, A. (1997). *Pocket coach to parenthood: Good sports make winning parents.* Santa Barbara, CA: Light Beams Press.

Orlick, T., & Botterill, C. (1975). *Every kid can win.* Chicago, IL: Nelson-Hall.

Perkins, W., & Cooper, R. (1989). *Kids in sports: Shaping a child's character from the sidelines.* Sister, OR: Multnomah Publishing.

Phillips, L., Stahl, B., & Meyer, B., Ewing, K. (1999). *Parenting, sportsmom style: Real life solutions for surviving the youth sports scene.* Maumee, OH: Three Hundred Seven Books.

Poretta, V. (1997). *Mom's guide to sports.* New York: Macmillan.

Ripken, C., Jr., & Wolff, R. (2006). *Parenting young athletes the Ripken way.* New York: Gotham Books.

Rotella, R., & Bunker, L. (1998). *Parenting our superstar: How to help your child balance achievement and happiness.* Chicago, IL: Triumph Books.

Rotella, R., & Bunker, L. (1987). *Parenting your superstar: How to help your child get the most out of sports.* Champaign, IL: Human Kinetics.

Ruettinger, D., Leddy, P., & Phillips, D. (2005). *Rudy in you: A youth sports guide for players, parents, and coaches.* Santa Monica, CA: Bonus Books, Inc.

Sanders, S. (2000). *Champions are raised, not born: How my parents made me a success.* New York: Dell Books.

Schock, B. (1987). *Parents, kids, and sports: Making the experience positive.* London, UK: Moody Press.

Selleck, G. (2002). *Raising a good sport in an in-your face world.* New York: McGraw-Hill.

Selleck, G. (2000). *Beyond the bleachers: The art of parenting today's athletes.* Washington, DC: Alliance Publications.

Sheehy, H. (2002). *Raising a team player.* North Adams, MA: Storey Books.

Sibley, C. (2000). *Games girls play.* New York: St. Martins Press.

Small, E. (2002). *Kids and Sports: Everything you and your child need to know about sports, physical activity, and good health – A doctor's guide for parents and coaches.* New York: Newmarket Press.

Smith, D., & Schulman, L. (2000). *From prom to pros: The athlete's, parent's, and coach's guide.* Santa Ana, CA: Seven Locks Press.

Smith, R., Smoll, F., & Smith, N. (1983). *Kidsports: A survival guide for parents.* Boston: Addison-Wesley.

Smoll, F., & Smith, R. (1995). *Children and youth in sport.* New York: Brown and Benchmark.

Stankovich, C. E., & Kays, T. M. (2002). *The parent's playbook: Developing a game plan for maximizing your child's athletic experience.* Columbus, OH: Champion Athletic Consulting.

Storm, H. (2002). *Go girl: Raising healthy, confident, and successful girls through sport.* Naperville, IL: Sourcebooks.

Taylor, J. (2005). *Your children under attack: How popular culture is destroying your kids values and how you can protect them.* Naperville, IL: Sourcebooks.

Taylor, J. (2002). *Positive Pushing: How to raise a successful happy child.* New York: Hyperion Press.

Thompson, J. (2003). *The double goal coach: Positive coaching tools for honoring the game and developing winners in sport and life.* New York: Harper Resource.

Tofler, I., & DiGeronimo, T. (2000). *Keeping your kids out front without kicking them from behind: How to nurture high achieving athletes, scholars and performing artists.* Hoboken, NJ: John Wiley & Sons.

Votano, P. (2000). *Trouble with youth sports: What the problems are and how to solve them.* Philadelphia: XLibris Corporation.

Wilson, S. (2000). *Motivating girls to start and stay with sports.* New York: Simon & Schuster.

Wolff, R. (1998). *The training camp guide to sports parenting: Encouraging your child on and off the field.* Lincoln, NE: I-Books Incorporated.

Wolff, R. (1996). *Good sports: The concerned parent's guide to competitive youth sports.* Champaign, IL: Sports Publishing, LLC.

Wolff, R., & Vrato, E. (2003). *The sports parenting edge: The winning game plan for every athlete from t-ball to college recruiting.* Philadelphia: Running Press Book Publishers.

Zimmerman, J. (1999). *Raising our athletic daughters: How sports can build self-esteem and save girls lives.* New York: Main Street Books.

Zinsser, N. (1991). *Dear Dr. Psych.* New York: Little, Brown.

Appendix J
Reference List of Mental Training/Sport Psychology Videos

Alan S. Kornspan, University of Akron
Christopher Lantz, Truman State University
Bart S. Lerner, Arizona School of Professional Psychology
Scott R. Johnson, West Virginia University
Cassandra P. Smisson, Georgia Southern University

Author Notes

Alan S. Kornspan, Department of Physical and Health Education; Christopher Lantz, Department of Health and Exercise Science; Bart S. Lerner, Counseling Center; Scott R. Johnson, School of Physical Education; Cassandra P. Smisson, Department of Public Health

Reprinted from A. S. Kornspan, C. Lantz, B. S. Lerner, and S. R. Johnson. (1998). "A Reference List of Mental Training/Sport Psychology Videos." In W. K. Simpson, A. LeUnes, & J. S. Picou (Eds.), Applied Research in Coaching and Athletics Annual. Boston: American Press. Additional information added.

Abstract

The continued growth of sport psychology has resulted in an influx of mental training techniques. These techniques are presented in a variety of books, journals, and audio/visual materials. While reference lists exist for sport psychology texts (Allen, 1994; Sachs & Kornspan, 1995) and journal articles (Granito & Wenz, 1995), there remained no such resource for locating and obtaining sport psychology videos. This article presents an extensive list of mental training and sport psychology videos that can be used by sport psychologists, coaches, and athletes. In addition, this list provides purchasing information such as addresses, telephone numbers, and price of the video.

Reference List of Mental Training/Sport

Psychology Videos

As the field of sport psychology experiences increasing popularity, members of the athletic community are recognizing the benefits of psychological skills training. As a result, coaches and athletes are obtaining sport psychology information from books and videos. As technology continues to advance in the classroom and on the field, many coaches and sport psychologists are beginning to use videos to introduce athletes to psychological skills training.

Often, the coach or sport psychologist will introduce athletes to mental skills training through the use of videotapes. Murphy (1991) explains how he has used the video "Visualization: What You See Is What You Get" to lead into group discussions. For example, Murphy explained, "I might have one group identify ways visualization can be used in practice and may tell another group to watch for ways visualization can be used at competition" (p. 95). Gould (1987) suggests that videos introducing mental training can be useful, but the teacher, coach, or sport psychologist should provide guidance to athletes on the use of the video. Further, Weinberg (1990) suggests that some videos may be limited in that they do not give specific demonstrations of how to use the psychological techniques. However, Weinberg suggests that videos can be useful in introducing basic information for those who are unfamiliar with applied sport psychology.

Although sport psychology videos may be useful (Gould, 1987; Murphy, 1988; Weinberg, 1990), a problem exists in that only a very limited number of videos have been reviewed in the literature. Also, the phone numbers and prices that are listed in the video review are often outdated. Thus coaches and sport psychology consultants may have great difficulty in locating and purchasing sport psychology videos. While reference lists exist for sport psychology texts (Allen, 1994; Sachs & Kornspan, 1995) and journal articles (Granito & Wenz, 1995), there remained no such resource for locating and obtaining sport psychology videos.

An effort to provide the coaching community with information on sport psychology videos began with a comprehensive list generated via various computerized searches. It should be noted that these videos address a wide range of sport psychology and coaching topics. It is not the purpose of this article to review the videos presented but to provide the information necessary to help individuals in locating videos of interest.

References

Allen, M. B. (1994). Authorship in sport psychology: A reference list. *The Sport Psychologist, 8,* 94–99.

Gould, D. (1987). Mental training for peak athletic performance [Review of the video program Mental training for peak athletic performance]. *The Sport Psychologist, 1,* 364–365.

Granito, V., & Wenz, B. (1995). Reading list for professional issues in applied sport psychology. *The Sport Psychologist, 9,* 96–103.

Murphy, S. M. (1991). Visualization: What you see is what you get [Review of the video program Visualization: What you see is what you get]. *The Sport Psychologist, 5,* 94–95.

Sachs, M. L., & Kornspan, A. (1995). Reading list in applied sport psychology: Psychological skills training. In M. Sachs, K. Burke, & L. Butcher (Eds.), *Directory of graduate programs in applied sport psychology* (4th ed.; pp. 216–227). Morgantown, WV: Fitness Information Technology.

Weinberg, R. (1990). Sports psychology: The winning edge in sports [Review of the video program Sports psychology: What winning edge in sports]. *The Sport Psychologist, 4,* 192–194.

Video List

Bassham, L. (1989). *Mental management seminar, part 1. The principles of mental management* [Videotape]. (Available from Mental Management Systems, P.O. Box 225, Seguin, TX, 78155).

Bassham, L. (1989). *Mental management seminar, part 2. Mental tools and techniques* [Videotape]. (Available from Mental Management Systems, P.O. Box 225, Seguin, TX, 78155).

Bassham, L. (1989). *Mental management seminar part 3. Mental tools and techniques* [Videotape]. (Available from Mental Management Systems, P.O. Box 225, Seguin, TX, 78155.

Blanchard, K. (1994). *The golf university swing school videos: Mastering the mental game of golf* [Videotape]. (Available from The Golf University, 17550 Bernardo Oaks Drive, San Diego, CA 92128, 1-800-426-0966, $24.95).

Botterill, C., & Orlick, T. (1988). *Visualization: What you see is what you get* [Videotape]. (Available from Coaching Association of Canada, 1600 James Naismith Drive, Gloucester, ON K1B 5N4 Canada, 613-748-5624, $19.95 Canadian). Video Review: Murphy, S. M. (1991). Visualization: What you see is what you get [Review of the video program *Visualization: What you see is what you get*]. *The Sport Psychologist, 5,* 94–95.

Braden, V. (1994). *Mental tennis: Hidden secrets to why you win and lose!* [Videotape]. (Available from Vic Braden Tennis College, 23335 Avenida La Caza, Coto de Caza, CA 92769; 1-800-42COURT, $39.95).

Cairns, K. (1989). *Our inner selves, (Program 2)* [Videotape]. (Available from Human Kinetics Publishers, P.O. Box 5076,

Champaign, IL 61825-5076; 1-800-747-4457, $15.95).

Cohn, P., & Waite, G. (1996). *Make your most confident stroke: A guide to a one putt mindset* [Videotape]. (Available from Peak Performance Sports, 7380 Sand Lake Rd., Suite 500, Orlando, FL 32819; 1-888-742-7225, $22.95).

Cox, B. (1982). *Sports psychology for youth coaches* [Videotape]. (Available from Distinctive Home Videos, 391 El Portal Road, San Mateo, CA 94402; 415-344-7756, $59.95).

Cox, B. (1982). *Tom Tutko's coaching clinic* [Videotape]. (Available from Distinctive Home Videos, 391 El Portal Road, San Mateo, CA 94402; 415-344-7756, $39.95).

Curtis, J. (1988). *The mindset for winning* [Videotape]. (Available from Cambridge Career Products, Cambridge Physical Education & Health, P.O. Box 2153, Department PE15, Charleston, WV 25328-2153; 1-800-468-4227, $39.95).

Duda, J., & Retton, M. L. (1994). *Mental readiness* [Videotape]. (Available from USA Gymnastics, 1036 N. Capital Ave., Suite E. 235, Indianapolis, IN, 46204; 1-800-4USAGYM, $4.95).

Ellis, R. (1990). *Mental mechanics and hitting simplification* [Videotape]. (Available from Championship Books and Video Productions, 2730 Graham St., Ames, IA 50010; 1-800-873-2730, $29.95).

Giges, B., Ravizza, K., Van Raalt, J., & Zaichowsky, L. (2002). *Brief contact interventions in sport psychology* [Videotape]. (Available from Fitness Information Technology, WVU-PE, PO Box 6116, Morgantown, WV 26506; 1-800-477-4348, $39.95).

Goshen, B. (1987). *The mental game* (Videotape]. (Available from Professional Image, 9422 E. 55th Place, Tulsa, OK, 74145-8154, 918-622-8899, $39.95). Video Review: Sime, W.E. (1992). The mental game [Review of the video program *The mental game*]. *The Sport Psychologist, 6,* 204–205.

Gould, D. (2001). *Five essential mental skills for sport* [Videotape]. (Available from Fitness Information Technology, WVU-PE, PO Box 6116, Morgantown, WV 26506; 1-800-477-4348, $14.95).

Gould, D. (1987). *Sport psychology* [Videotape]. Champaign, IL: Human Kinetics Publishers. (Available from Human Kinetics Publishers, P.O. Box 5076, Champaign, IL 61825-5076; 1-800-747-4457, $70.00).

Gould, D. (2001). *Teaching mental skills for sport* [Videotape]. (Available from Fitness Information Technology, WVU-PE, PO Box 6116, Morgantown, WV 26506; 1-800-477-4348, $29.95).

Hamshire, R., Iveson, I., & Catell, R. (1994). *Winning with sports psychology* [Videotape]. Available from I.C.C. Entertainment P/L, The Marina 13/1 Bradley Ave., Kirribill, NSW, 2061, Australia, 6129955-2297; US $29.95). Video Review: Sargent, G. (1995). Winning with sports psychology [Review of the video program *Winning with sports psychology*]. *The Sport Psychologist, 4,* 433–434.

Hogan, C. (1988). *Nice shot* [Videotape]. (Available from Cambridge Career Products, Cambridge Physical Education & Health, P.O. Box 2153, Department PE15, Charleston, WV 25328-2153; 1-800-468-4227, $29.95). Video Review: Armstrong, H.E. (1990) Nice Shot [Review of the video program *Nice shot*]. *The Sport Psychologist, 4,* 433–434.

Jacobs, A., Hill, C., & Allen, L. (1987). *Sports psychology: The winning edge in sports* [Videotape]. (Available from Cambridge Career Products, Cambridge Physical Education & Health P.O. Box 2153, Department PE15, Charleston, WV 25328-2153; 1-800-468-4227, $89.95). Video Review: Weinberg, R. (1990). Sports psychology: The winning edge in sports [Review of the video program *Sports psychology: The winning edge in sports*]. *The Sport Psychologist, 4,* 192–194.

LaTreill, D., & Theilen, A. (1994). *Mental golf* [Videotape]. (Availability, Vestron Video, 15400 Sherman Way, P.O. Box 10124, Van Nuys, CA 91410-0124; $19.95).

Loehr, J. (1989). *Mental toughness training for tennis: "The 16 Second Cure"* [Videotape]. (Available from LGE/Sport Science, 9757 Lake Nona, Orlando, FL 32827-7017; 1-800-543-7764, $30.00).

Loehr, J. (1989). *Tips to mental toughness* [Videotape]. (Available from LGE/Sport Science, 9757 Lake Nona, Orlando, FL 32827-7017; 1-800-543-7764, $40.00).

Martin, C., & Winter, G. (1990). *What is sport psychology?* [Videotape]. (Available from South Australian Sports Institute, P.O. Box 219, Brooklyn Park, SA 5032).

Martin, G. (1989). *Sport psychology for figure skaters* [Videotape]. (Available from Canadian Figure Skating Association, 200 Main St., Winnipeg, Manitoba R3C 4MZ; 204-985-4064, $28.00 Canadian). Video Review: Jackson, S. (1991). Sport psyching for figure skaters. [Review of the video program *Sport psyching for figure skaters*]. *The Sport Psychologist, 5,* 194–195.

Mudra, D. (1986). *The creative edge in sports psychology* [Videotape]. (Available from Championship Books and Video Productions, 2730 Graham St., Ames, IA 50010; 1-800-873-2730, $29.95).

Murphy, S., & McCann, S. (1994). *Sports mental training* [Videotape]. (Available from USOC, Judine Anseimo, Sports Science & Technology Division, USOC, One Olympic Plaza, Colorado Springs, CO 80909; $4.99).

National Collegiate Athletic Association. (1988). *Athletes at risk* [Videotape]. (Available from Karol Media, 350 N. Pennsylvania Ave., Wilkesbarre, PA 18773, 1-800-526-4773, $17.95).

National Collegiate Athletic Association. (1988). *Drugs and the collegiate athlete* [Videotape]. (Available from Karol Media, 350 N. Pennsylvania Ave., Wilkesbarre, PA 18773, 1-800-526-4773, $17.95).

National Collegiate Athletic Association. (1989). *Afraid to eat: Eating disorders and student-athletes* [Videotape]. (Available from Karol Media, 350 N. Pennsylvania Ave., Wilkesbarre, PA 18773, 1-800-526-4773, $17.95).

National Collegiate Athletic Association. (1989). *Eating disorders: What can you do?* [Videotape]. (Available from Karol Media, 350 N. Pennsylvania Ave., Wilkesbarre, PA 18773, 1-800-526-4773, $14.95).

Nideffer, R., & Coffey, R. (1989). *Psychological preparation of the elite athlete* [Videotape]. (Availabe from Australian Coaching Council, P.O. Box 176, Belconnen, ACT 2616).

Orlick, T. (1995). *Coaching the spirit of sport: Building self-esteem* [Videotape]. Ontario, Canada: Canadian Sport Association. (Available from The Spirit of Sport Foundation, 1600 J. Naismith Drive, Gloucester, Ontario, K1B 5N4; 1-800-672-7775, $17.95).

Porter, K., & Foster, J. (1985). Mental training for peak athletic performance [Videotape]. Eugene, OR: Westcom Productions, Inc. (Available from Cambridge Career Products, Cambridge Physical Education & Health, P.O. Box 2153, Department PE15, Charleston, WV 25328-2153, 1-800-468-4227, $59.95). Video Review: Gould, D. (1987). Mental training for peak athletic performance [Review of the video program *Mental training for peak athletic performance*]. *The Sport Psychologist, 1,* 364–365.

Ravizza, K. (1989). *Stress management for baseball: 3-2 count bases loaded, "no sweat"* [Videotape]. (Available from Australian Baseball Federation, P.O. Box 58, Malvern, Victoria, Australia, 3144).

Scolinos, J. (1983). *Mental approach to baseball* [Videotape]. (Available from Australian Baseball Federation, P.O. Box 58, Malvern, Victoria, Australia, 3144).

Stewart, A., & Heading, R. (1990). *Psychology and motivation in Australian football* [Videotape]. (Available from National Football Council, 120 Jolimont Road, Jolimont, Victoria, Australia).

Stockton, B. A. (1985). *Coaching psychology* [Videotape]. (Available from Championship

Books and Video Productions, 2730 Graham St., Ames, IA 50010; 1-800-873-2730, $39.95).

Sutphen, R. (1989). *Golf: Mindprogramming to increase your skill* [Videotape]. (Available from Valley of the Sun Publishing, P.O. Box 683, Ashland, OR 97520-0023; 1-800-225-4717, $19.95).

Tharrett, S. (1999). *Psychology of exercise adherence* [Videotape]. (Available from Fitness Information Technology, WVU-PE, PO Box 6116, Morgantown, WV 26506; 1-800-477-4348, $39.95).

Virtual Sport Psychology: Three approaches to sport psychology consulting. (2000). [Videotape]. (Available from Virtual Brands, www.vbvideo.com; 1-800-215-2275)

Voderman, C. (1988). *Mind over matter* [Videotape]. (Available from National Coaching Foundation, 4 College Close, Beckett Park, Leeds, England LS6 3QHUK).

Whitaker, J. (1991). *Brainwaves golf* [Videotape]. (Available from Televisual Communications, 300 S. Duncan Ave., Suite 112, Clearwater, FL 34615; 813-442-6480, $19.95).

Note: The video list has been updated since it appeared in the sixth edition of the directory. It now includes videos and reviews since the list was first published in 1998. Also, to aid the reader in locating and purchasing videos of interest, website addresses have been provided for the 53 videos added to the list. When available the updated list provides websites and current prices for locating and ordering videos listed on the previous list.

Additional Videos (7th edition of the Directory)

Appleseed Productions. (1994). *Motivation (Lifting your game series)* [Videotape]. (Available from Insight Media Inc., 2162 Broadway, New York, NY, 10024 http://www.insight-media.com; 1-800-233-9910, $179).

Appleseed Productions. (1995). *Teamwork (Lifting your game series)* [Videotape]. (Available from Insight Media Inc., 2162 Broadway, New York, NY, 10024, http://www.insight-media.com; 1-800-233-9910, $179).

Bartholomew, J. (2000). *Performing under stress: What every coach should know* [Videotape]. (Available from Champonline Sports Videos and Books 2730 Graham Street Ames, IA 50010, http://www.champonline.com; 1-800-873-2730, $39.95).

Bartholomew, J. (2000). *Attaining peak performance under pressure* [Videotape]. (Available from Champonline Sports Videos and Books 2730 Graham Street Ames, IA 50010, http://www.champonline.com; 1-800-873-2730, $39.95).

Bassham, L. (no date listed). V1 - Winning the mental game [Videotape]. (Available from Lenny Bassham Mental Management Systems, 2509 Dartmouth drive, Flower Mound, TX 75022, http://www.lannybassham.com; 1-800-879-5079, $39.99).

Bassham, L. (no date listed). *V2 - Performing under pressure* [Videotape]. (Available from Lenny Bassham Mental Management Systems, 2509 Dartmouth drive, Flower Mound, TX 75022, http://www.lannybassham.com; 1-800-879-5079, $39.99).

Bassham, L. (no date listed). *V3 - Goal setting* [Videotape]. (Available from Lenny Bassham Mental Management Systems, 2509 Dartmouth drive, Flower Mound, TX 75022, http://www.lannybassham.com; 1-800-879-5079, $39.99).

Bassham, L. (no date listed). *V4 - Mastering self-image* [Videotape]. (Available from Lenny Bassham Mental Management Systems, 2509 Dartmouth drive, Flower Mound, TX 75022, http://www.lannybassham.com; 1-800-879-5079, $39.99).

Bassham, L. (no date listed). *V5 - Mastering the mental game* [Videotape]. (Available from Lenny Bassham Mental Management Systems, 2509 Dartmouth drive, Flower Mound, TX 75022, http://www.lannybassham.com; 1-800-879-5079, $39.99).

Bassham, L. (no date listed). *V6 - Mental Management for parents and coaches*

[Videotape]. (Available from Lenny Bassham Mental Management Systems, 2509 Dartmouth drive, Flower Mound, TX 75022, http://www.lannybassham.com; 1-800-879-5079, $39.99).

Bassham, L. (no date listed). *V10 - Mental applications for rifle shooting* [Videotape]. (Available from Lenny Bassham Mental Management Systems, 2509 Dartmouth drive, Flower Mound, TX 75022, http://www.lannybassham.com; 1-800-879-5079, $39.99).

Bassham, L. (no date listed). *Mental Applications for pistol shooting* [Videotape]. (Available from Lenny Bassham Mental Management Systems, 2509 Dartmouth drive, Flower Mound, TX 75022, http://www.lannybassham.com; 1-800-879-5079, $39.99).

Bennett, B. (1998). *Championship plays: The mental game* [Videotape]. (Available from onlinesports.com, $29.95).

Blevins, G. (1997). *Mental conditioning for softball* [Videotape]. (Available from onlinesports.com, $29.95).

Brechtelsbauer, K. (1998). *Mental aspects for the game* [Videotape]. (Available from onlinesports.com, $29.95).

Brouse, D., & Penley, L. (2000). *Golf psychology* [Videotape]. (Available from Champonline Sports Videos and Books 2730 Graham Street Ames, IA 50010, http://www.champonline.com; 1-800-873-2730, $29.95).

Callazo, L. (2002). *The mental side of pitching* [Videotape]. (Available from Champonline Sports Videos and Books 2730 Graham Street Ames, IA 50010, http://www.champonline.com; 1-800-873-2730, $39.95).

Carnahan, S. (1993). *Mental game and player evaluation* [Videotape]. (Available from onlinesports.com, $29.95).

Conviser, J. (1999). *Decreasing the risk of eating disorders among athletes* [Videotape]. (Available from Healthy Learning Videos, P. O. Box 1828, Monterey, CA, 93942, http://www.healthylearning.com; 1-888-229-5745, $40.00).

Curry, G. (1997). *The coaches' ten commandments to positive athletic parenting* [Videotape]. (Available from Karol Media P.O. Box 7600, Wilkes-Barre, PA 18773-7600, http://www.karolmedia.com; 1-800-884-0555, $12.95)

Dalloway, M. (1999). *Visualization training exercises: Training video for athletes* [Videotape]. (Available from Peak Performance Media, 5501 N 7th ave. #921, Phoenix, AZ, 85013-1755, http://www.performance-media.com; 602-274-1889, $29.95

Dalloway, M. (2001). *Stress control: Training video for athletes* [Videotape]. (Available from Peak Performance Media, 5501 N 7th ave. #921, Phoenix, AZ, 85013-1755, http://www.performance-media.com; 602-274-1889, $29.95).

Doyle, M. W. (1999). *Kid's sports* [Videotape]. (Available from Films for the Humanities and Sciences, P.O. Box 2053, Princeton, NJ, 08543-2053, http://www.films.com; 1-800-257-5126, $89.95).

Finke, B. (1998). *A mental approach to softball* [Videotape]. (Available from onlinesports.com, $29.95).

Finke, B. (1998). *Mental approach to hitting* [Videotape]. (Available from onlinesports.com, $29.95).

Giges, B., Ravizza, K., Van Raalte, J., & Zaichkowsky, L. (2000). *Brief contact interventions in sport psychology* [Videotape]. (Available from Virtual Brands, 10 Echo Hill Road, Wilbraham, MA 01095, http://www.vbvideo.com; 1-877-633-4656, $29.95). Video Review: Lesyk, J. J. (2003). Brief contact interventions in sport psychology [review of the video program *Brief contact interventions in sport psychology*]. *The Sport Psychologist, 17*, 246-247.

Giges, B., Ravizza, K., & Murphy, S. (2001). *Three approaches to sport psychology consulting* [Videotape]. (Available from Virtual Brands, 10 Echo Hill Road, Wilbraham, MA 01095, http://www.vbvideo.com; 1-877-633-4656, $39.95).

Gleason, T. (2002). *The mental game of golf: Pres-shot routine and post-shot analysis* [Videotape]. (Available from Champonline Sports Videos and Books 2730 Graham

Gould, D. (2001). *Teaching mental skills for sport* [Videotape]. (Available from Virtual Brands, 10 Echo Hill Road, Wilbraham, MA 01095, http://www.vbvideo.com ; 1-877-633-4656, $29.95). Video Review: Salitsky, P. (2002). Teaching mental skills for sport. [Review of the video program *Teaching mental skills for sport*]. *The Sport Psychologist, 16*, 337-338.

Gould, D. (2001). *5 essential mental skills for sport* [Videotape]. (Available from Virtual Brands, 10 Echo Hill Road, Wilbraham, MA 01095; http://www.vbvideo.com/; 1-877-633-4656, $14.95). Video Review: Getty, D. (2002). 5 essential mental skills for sport. [Review of the video program *5 essential mental skills for sport*]. *The Sport Psychologist, 16*, 339.

Goldberg, D. (2000). *Investigative reports: playing to extremes* [Videotape]. (Available from A & E Television Networks http://store.aetv.com/; 1-888-423-1212, $24.95).

Harris, G. (2000). *Peak performance: Sports and the mind* [Videotape]. (Available from Beacon Productions at http://www.bodyansoultv.com; 617-924-7711, $29.95).

Hays, K. (2003). *Exercise* [Videotape]. (Available from American Psychological Association, American Psychological Association, 750 First St, NE, Washington, DC 20002-4242; http://www.apa.org; 1-800-374-2721, $69.95 member or affiliates of APA, $99.95 nonmembers).

House, T. (1993). *Preparation to pitch: Mental Conditioning* [Videotape]. (Available from onlinesports.com, $29.95).

House, T. (1995). *Mental and emotional aspects of pitching* [Videotape]. (Available from onlinesports.com, $29.95).

Janssen, J. (1996). *Winning the mental game: How you can develop the motivation, confidence, and focus of champions* [Videotape]. (Available from Janssen Peak Performance, Inc. 285 S. NightFall Ave, Tuscon AZ 85748, http://www.jeffjanssen.com; 1-888-721-8326, $29.95.

Janssen, J. (1997). *Psychology of sensational hitting* [Videotape]. (Available from Janssen Peak Performance, Inc. 285 S. NightFall Ave, Tuscon, AZ, 85748; http://www.jeffjanssen.com; 1-888-721-8326, $39.95.

Jaure, P. (2002). *Golf psychology "The pre-shot routine"* [Videotape]. (Available from amazon.com; $19.90).

Johnson, K. (1993). *Mental approach to baseball* [Videotape]. (Available from onlinesports.com, $29.95).

Joseph, J. (1996). *Developing the mental game* [Videotape]. (Available from onlinesports.com, $29.95).

Kimiecik, J. (1999). *Exercise behavior change programs for the physically inactive* [Videotape]. (Available from Healthy Learning Videos, P. O. Box 1828, Monterey, CA, 93942, http://www.healthylearning.com; 1-888-229-5745, $40.00).

Kimiecik, J. (1999). *Exercise behavior change from the inside out* [Videotape]. (Available from Healthy Learning Videos, P. O. Box 1828, Monterey, CA, 93942, http://www.healthylearning.com; 1-888-229-5745, $40.00).

Kundrat, S. M. (1999). *Preventing eating disorders in teen athletes* [Videotape]. (Available from Healthy Learning Videos, P. O. Box 1828, Monterey, CA, 93942, http://www.healthylearning.com; 1-888-229-5745, $40.00).

Loehr, J. (1996). *Pro secrets video clinic: Pro secrets of mental toughness* [Videotape]. Available from Dunham's sports, Dunham's Sports, Customer Service 5000 Dixie Highway Waterford, MI 48329, www.dunhamsports.com; 1-888-801-9158, $39.99).

Officer, J. (2002). *"Warrior Ethos" the making of a warrior: Mental toughness on the tennis court* [Videotape]. (Available from Champonline Sports Videos and Books, 2730 Graham Street Ames, IA 50010, http://www.champonline.com; 1-800-873-2730, $29.95).

Rotella, B., & Faxon. B. (1998). *Putt to win* [Videotape]. (Available from OnlineSports.com; 1-800-856-2638, $39.95).

Scott, J. (1998). *The mental game (golf)* [Videotape]. (Available from amazon.com, $29.95).

Somerlot, R. (1995). *Mental preparation for track and field* [Videotape]. (Available from onlinesports.com, $29.95).

Tharrett, S. (1998). *Psychology of exercise adherence* [Videotape]. (Available from Healthy Learning Videos, P. O. Box 1828, Monterey, CA, 93942, http://www.healthylearning.com; 1-888-229-5745, $40.00).

Thompson, W. R. (1999). *Predictors of exercise compliance: Strategies to improve adherence to exercise programs* [Videotape]. (Available from Healthy Learning Videos, P. O. Box 1828, Monterey, CA, 93942, http://www.healthylearning.com;1-888-229-5745, $40.00).

Trikojus, T. (2000). *Sport and psychology* [Videotape]. (Available from Video Education Australasia, ABN 50 007 156 318, 111A Mitchell Street, Bendigo VIC 3550 Australia, 03 54422433, $99.95 Australian).

Trikojus, T. (2001). *Sport and competition* [Videotape]. (Available from Video Education Australasia, ABN 50 007 156 318, 111A Mitchell Street, Bendigo VIC 3550 Australia, http://www.vea.com.au; 03 54422433, $99.95 Australian).

United States Tennis Association. (1997). *Playing better tennis under pressure* [Videotape]. (Available from Human Kinetics Publishers, P. O. Box 5076, Champaign, IL, http://www.hkusa.com; 1-800-747-4457, $24.95

Information and Updates for Previously Listed Videos

The following information provides updated prices and websites for videos from the previous list. The information below was retrieved from the following websites on July 19, 2003. Updated information for websites and prices was found for 11 videos. Also according to the Coaching Association of Canada website (www.coach.ca/e/products/clearout.htmthe videos) *Coaching the spirit sport: Building self-esteem and Visualization:*

What you see is what you get are no longer available from the Canadian Coaches Association.

Make your most confident stroke: A guide to a one putt mindset. Available at www.peaksports.com/, $19.95.

Mental mechanics and hitting simplification. Available at prohitter.home.mindspring.com/; $29.95.

Mental readiness. Available at usagym.sportgraphics.biz, $4.95.

Mental tennis: Hidden Secrets why you win or loose. Available at www.vicbraden.com/pros.html, $39.95.

Mental training for peak athletic performance. Available at www.videolearning.com/, $39.95.

Mental toughness training for tennis: The 16 second cure. Available at onlinesports.com. $34.95.

Nice shot. Available at amazon.com.

Sport psyching for figure skaters. Available at www.skatetape.com/, $24.95

Sport psychology for youth coaches. Available at www.distinctivehomevideo.com, $39.00).

Tom Tutko's coaching clinic. Available at www.distinctivehomevideo.com, $24.94).

An Update of DVDs and Videos in Applied Sport Psychology

Note: The video list has been updated since it appeared in the seventh edition of the directory. Videos and reviews since the list was last published have been added. Many of the videos in the current list were also cited in Kornspan (in press, a), Kornspan (in press, b), and Kornspan (2005).

References

Kornspan, A. S. (in press, a). Audiovisual aids in applied sport psychology. In J. Williams (ed.), *Instructor's Manual in Applied Sport Psychology*. Boston: McGraw Hill.

Kornspan, A. S. (in press, b). New books, DVDs and videos. *AAASP Newsletter, 21(1)*.

Kornspan, A. S. (2005). AAASP Newsletter, 20(3), New books, DVDs and videos. *AAASP Newsletter, 20(3)*, 33.

Address correspondence to: Alan S. Kornspan, Department of Sport Science and Wellness Education, University of Akron, 140 Memorial Hall, Akron, OH 44325-5103;
330-972-8145 (work)
330-972-5293 (fax)
alan3@uakron.edu

Aberman, R., & Anderson, J. (2005). *Managing yourself while leading others* [Videotape]. (Available from Coaches Choice, PO Box 1828, Monterey, CA, 93942; 1-888-229-5745; www.coacheschoice.com; $40.00).

Aberman, R., & Anderson, J. (2005). *Emotional intelligence and optimal performance* [Videotape]. (Available from Coaches Choice, PO Box 1828, Monterey, CA, 93942; 1-888-229-5745; www.coacheschoice.com; $40.00).

Aberman, R., & Anderson, J. (2005). *The performance sweet spot* [Videotape]. (Available from Coaches Choice, PO Box 1828, Monterey, CA, 93942; 1-888-229-5745; www.coacheschoice.com; $40.00).

Arnold, A. (n.d.). The *five rings of mental toughness training* [DVD]. (Available from Allisson Arnold, Ph.D., Head Games, 812 N. 2nd Ave. Phoenix Ave., 85003; 602-462- 1608; www.headgames.ws; $75.00).

Carlstedt, R. (2005). *Carlstedt Protocol: Evidence based sport psychology* [DVD]. (Available from American Board of Sport Psychology; www.americanboardofsportpsychology.org).

Dale, G. (2003). *The coach's guide to team building* [Videotape]. (Available from Champonline Sports Videos and Books 2730 Graham Street Ames, IA 50010, 1-800-873-2730, www.championshipproductions.com; $39.95).

Dale, G. (2004). *Becoming a champion athlete: Goal setting for success!* [DVD]. (Available from Champonline Sports Videos and Books 2730 Graham Street Ames, IA 50010, 1-800-873-2730, www.championshipproductions.com; $29.95).

Dale, G. (2004). *Becoming a champion athlete: Making every practice count!* [Videotape]. (Available from Champonline Sports Videos and Books 2730 Graham Street Ames, IA 50010, 1-800-873-2730, www.championshipproductions.com; $29.95).

Dale, G. (2004). *Becoming a champion athlete: Mastering pressure situations!* (Available from Champonline Sports Videos and Books 2730 Graham Street Ames, IA 50010, 1-800-873-2730, www.championshipproductions.com; $29.95).

Video Review: Madeson, M. (2004). Becoming a champion athlete: Mastering pressure situations. [Review of the video program Becoming a champion athlete: Mastering pressure situations]. *The Sport Psychologist, 18*, 355.

Dale, G. (2004). *Goal setting for success: The coach's guide* [DVD]. (Available from Champonline Sports Videos and Books 2730 Graham Street Ames, IA 50010, 1-800-873-2730, www.championshipproductions.com; $39.95).

Video Review: Arceo, A. (2004). Goal setting for success: The coach's guide. [Review of the video program *Goal setting for success*]. *The Sport Psychologist, 18*, 473-474.

Dale, G. (2005). *Becoming a champion athlete: An athletes guide to building self-Confidence* [DVD]. (Available from Champonline Sports Videos and Books 2730 Graham Street Ames, IA 50010, 1-800-873-2730, www.championshipproductions.com; $39.95).

Dale, G. (2005). *Coach's guide to team building: Volume II* [DVD]. (Available from Champonline Sports Videos and Books 2730

Graham Street Ames, IA 50010, 1-800-873-2730, www.championshipproductions.com; $39.95).

Dale, G. (2005). *Coaching the perfectionist athlete* [DVD]. (Available from Champonline Sports Videos and Books 2730 Graham Street Ames, IA 50010, 1-800-873-2730, www.championshipproductions.com; $39.95).

Dale, G. (2005). *Developing confident athletes: A coach's guide* [DVD]. (Available from Champonline Sports Videos and Books 2730 Graham Street Ames, IA 50010, 1-800-873-2730, www.championshipproductions.com; $39.95).

Dale, G. (2005). *Promoting a positive athletic experience: The parent's guide* [DVD]. (Available from Champonline Sports Videos and Books 2730 Graham Street Ames, IA 50010, 1-800-873-2730, www.championshipproductions.com; $39.95).

Dunagan, D., & Lodden, J. (2003). *Using your offense, not your defense: Strategies for coaches in dealing with parents* [Videotape]. (Available from Champonline Sports Videos and Books 2730 Graham Street Ames, IA 50010, 1-800-873-2730, www.championshipproductions.com; $29.95).

Dunagan, D. B., & Lodden, J. (2003). *Team training for the mental game* [Videotape]. (Available from Champonline Sports Videos and Books, 2730 Graham Street, Ames, IA 50010, 1-800-873-2730, www.championshipproductions.com; $29.95).

Dunagan, D. B., & Lodden, J. (2003). *Mental imagery for performance enhancement: The athlete's guide.* (Available from Champonline Sports Videos and Books, 2730 Graham Street Ames, IA 50010, 1-800-873-2730, www.championshipproductions.com; $29.95).

Eustachy, L. (2002). How to coach mental toughness [Videotape]. Available from Champonline Sports Videos and Books 2730 Graham Street Ames, IA 50010, 1-800-873-2730, www.championshipproductions.com; $39.95).

Evans, N. (2005). *The softball pitching factory: Mentally tough on the mound!* [DVD]. (Available from Champonline Sports Videos and Books 2730 Graham Street Ames, IA 50010, 1-800-873-2730, www.championshipproductions.com; $39.95).

Gable, D. (2004). Dan Gable: *Coaching mental toughness on the mat* [DVD]. (Available from Champonline Sports Videos and Books 2730 Graham Street Ames, IA 50010, 1-800-873-2730, www.championshipproductions.com; $39.95).

Gould, D. (2005). *Mental skills for young athletes* [DVD]. (Available from Virtual Brands, 10 Echo Hill Road, Wilbraham, MA 01095, www.vbvideo.com; 1-877-633-4656, $24.95).

Gould, D., & Kernodle, M. (2004). *Sport Psychology/Motor Learning* [DVD]. (Available from United States Professional Tennis Association, 3535 Briarpark Drive, Suite One, Houston, TX 77042; www.usprotennisshop.com; 713-978-7782; $44.95.

Haley, M., & Voight, M. (2006). *Mick Haley's winning strategies: Positive self-talk and mental conditioning.* [DVD]. (Available from Champonline Sports Videos and Books 2730 Graham Street Ames, IA 50010, 1-800-873-2730, www.championshipproductions.com; $39.95).

Marriott, L., & Nilson, P. (2004). *Coach54: Golf Fundamentals for the future* [DVD]. (Available from Virtual Brands, 10 Echo Hill Road, Wilbraham, MA 01095, www.vbvideo.com ; 1-877-633-4656, $24.95). Video Review: Albaugh, G., & Sverduk, K. (2005). Coach54: Golf fundamentals for the future. [Review of the video program *Coac54: Golf Fundamentals for the Future*]. *The Sport Psychologist, 19*, 221-223.

Morris, K. (n. d.). *Train your golf brain – Live in Dublin* [DVD]. (Available from Train Your Golf Brain, 95 Common Lane, Culcheth, Warrington, WA3 4HF; 0 1925764053; www.golf-brain.com).

Musselman, E. (2004). *Motivating your team* [Videotape]. (Available from Champonline

Sports Videos and Books 2730 Graham Street Ames, IA 50010, 1-800-873-2730, www.championshipproductions.com; $39.95).

Parker, D. (2004). *Developing an attitude of excellence* [Videotape]. (Available from Coaches Choice, PO Box 1828, Monterey, CA, 93942; 1-888-229-5745; www.coacheschoice.com; $40.00).

Parker, D. (2004). *Developing a positive self-image* [Videotape]. (Available from Coaches Choice, PO Box 1828, Monterey, CA, 93942; 1-888-229-5745; www.coacheschoice.com; $40.00).

Parker, D. (2004). *Implementing a mental training program* [Videotape]. (Available from Coaches Choice, PO Box 1828, Monterey, CA, 93942; 1-888-229-5745; www.coacheschoice.com; $40.00).

Peak Performance for the 21st Century. [DVD]. (Available from Championship Performance, 10151 University Blvd., Suite 103, Orlando, FL, 32817; 866-242-6711; www.championshipperform.com; $49.00).

Robertson, J. E., & Sime, W. (2004). *The mind side of serving: Developing a successful mental routine* [Videotape]. (Available from Champonline Sports Videos and Books, 2730 Graham Street Ames, IA 50010, 1-800-873-2730, www.championshipproductions.com; $39.95).

Silby, C. (2000). *Sports Psychology: Stress* [Videotape]. (Available from Professional Skater's Association, 3006 Allegro Park SW, Rochester, MN 55902; 507-281 5891; www.skatepsa.com).

Yukelson, D., & Reina, R. (n.d.). *Sports psychology and motivation* [Videotape]. (Available from Ken Chertow's Wear and Gear.com; 814-466-3466; www.wearandgear.com; $25.00).

Welch, M. (2004). *The volleyball coach's guide to team-building for high performance* [videotape]. (Available from Coaches Choice, PO Box 1828, Monterey, CA, 93942; 1-888-229-5745; www.coacheschoice.com; $40.00).

Weiskamp, K. (2005). *Student-athlete stress management* [Videotape]. (Available from Coaches Choice, PO Box 1828, Monterey, CA, 93942; 1-888-229-5745; www.coacheschoice.com; $40.00)

Appendix K
Geographical List of Graduate Programs

There are six countries represented in this directory. The total number of programs represented is as follows:
Australia: 4 programs
Canada: 13 programs
Great Britain: 7 programs
Singapore: 1 program
South Africa: 1 program
United States: 77 programs (in 34 states)

Australia
University of Canberra
University of Queensland
Victoria University
University of Western Australia

Canada
University of Alberta
Lakehead University
University of Manitoba
University of Manitoba (Psychology Department)
McGill University
Université de Montréal
University of Ottawa
Université du Québec à Trois-Rivières
Queen's University
Université de Sherbrooke
University of Waterloo
University of Western Ontario
University of Windsor

Great Britain
University College Chichester
DeMontfort University Bedford
University of Edinburgh
University of Exeter
Leeds Metropolitan University
Manchester Metropolitan University
Staffordshire University

Singapore
Nanyang Technological University

South Africa
Stellenbosch University

United States

Arizona
Argosy University
Arizona State University
University of Arizona

California
California State University, East Ba;y
California State University, Fresno
California State University, Fullerton
California State University, Long Beach
California State University, Sacramento
University of California, Los Angeles
Humboldt State University
John F. Kennedy University

Optimal Performance Institute and University
San Diego State University
San Diego University For Integrative Studies
San Jose State University

Colorado
University of Northern Colorado

Connecticut
Southern Connecticut State University

Florida
Barry University
Florida State University
University of Florida

Georgia
Georgia Southern University
University of Georgia

Idaho
Boise State University
University of Idaho

Illinois
Illinois State University
University of Illinois
Northern Illinois University
Southern Illinois University, Carbondale
Southern Illinois University Edwardsville
Western Illinois University

Indiana
Ball State University
Indiana University
Purdue University

Iowa
Iowa State University
University of Iowa
University of Northern Iowa

Kansas
Kansas State University
University of Kansas

Kentucky
Spalding University

Louisiana
Southeastern Louisiana University

Maryland
University of Maryland, College Park

Massachusetts
Boston University
Springfield College (Graduate Studies)
Springfield College (Psychology Department)

Michigan
Michigan State University
Wayne State University

Minnesota
University of Minnesota

Missouri
University of Missouri, Columbia

New Hampshire
University of New Hampshire

New Jersey
Rutgers University

New Mexico
The University of New Mexico

New York
Ithaca College

North Carolina
East Carolina University
University of North Carolina, Greensboro

North Dakota
University of North Dakota

Ohio
Bowling Green State University
Cleveland State University
Miami University

Oregon
Oregon State University

Pennsylvania
La Salle University
Pennsylvania State University
Temple University

Tennessee
East Tennessee State University
University of Memphis (Human Movement Sciences and Education)
University of Tennessee, Knoxville

Texas
University of Houston
University of North Texas (Psychology)
University of North Texas (Kinesiology)
University of Texas, Austin
Texas Christian University (Kinesiology and Physical Education)
Texas Tech University

Utah
Utah State University
University of Utah

Virginia
University of Virginia
Virginia Commonwealth University

Washington
Western Washington University

West Virginia
West Virginia University

Wisconsin
University of Wisconsin, Milwaukee

Appendix L
Contact Persons

School	Contact
Argosy University/Phoenix	Robert Harmison
Arizona State University	Daniel M. Landers
Ball State University	Jeffrey S. Pauline
Barry University	Artur Poczwardowski
Boise State University	Linda M. Petlichkoff
Boston University	Leonard D. Zaichkowsky
Bowling Green State University	Bonnie Berger
California State University, East Bay	Penny McCullagh
California State University, Fresno	Wade Gilbert
California State University, Fullerton	Debra Rose
	Lenny Wiersma
California State University, Long Beach	T. Michelle Magyar
	Sharon Guthrie
California State University, Sacramento	Gloria B. Solomon
Cleveland State University	Susan Ziegler
DeMontfort University, Bedford	Howard K. Hall
East Carolina University	Thomas Raedeke
East Tennessee State University	Kevin L. Burke
Florida State University	Gershon Tenenbaum
Georgia Southern University	Daniel R. Czech
Humboldt State University	Al Figone
Illinois State University	Anthony J. Amorose
Indiana University	John S. Raglin
Iowa State University	Rick Sharp
Ithaca College	Greg A. Shelley
John F. Kennedy University	Gail Solt

Kansas State University	David Dzewaltowski
La Salle University	Frank Gardner
Lakehead University	Jane Crossman
Leeds Metropolitan University	Mark Nesti
Manchester Metropolitan University	Nick Smith
McGill University	Gordon Bloom
Miami University	Robert Weinberg
Michigan State University	Martha Ewing
Nanyang Technological University	Daniel Smith
Northern Illinois University	Laurice Zittel
Optimal Performance Institute and University	John J. Farley
Oregon State University	Vicki Ebbeck
Pennsylvania State University	David E. Conroy
Purdue University	Alan Smith
Queen's University	Janice Deakin
Rutgers University	Dr. Charlie Maher
San Diego State University	Simon Marshall
San Diego University for Integrative Studies	Cristina Bortoni Versari
San Jose State University	David M. Furst
Southeastern Louisiana University	Dan Hollander
Southern Connecticut State University	David S. Kemler
Southern Illinois University, Carbondale	Julie Partridge
Southern Illinois University, Edwardsville	Curt L. Lox
Spalding University	Thomas Titus
Springfield College Psychology Department	Judy L. Van Raalte
Springfield College School of Graduate Studies	Betty L. Mann
Staffordshire University	Paul McCarthy
Stellenbosch University	Justus R. Potgieter
Temple University	Michael L. Sachs
Texas Christian University	Matt Johnson
Texas Tech University	Lanie Dornier
Universite de Montreal	Wayne R. Halliwell
Universite de Sherbrooke	Paul Deshaies
Universite du Quebec à Trois-Rivieres	Pierre Lacoste
University College, Chichester	Jan Graydon
University of Alberta	Anne Jordan
University of Arizona	Jean M. Williams
University of California, Los Angeles	Bernie Weiner
University of Canberra	John B. Gross
University of Edinburgh	Dave Collins

University of Exeter	Tim Rees
University of Florida	Christopher M. Janelle
University of Georgia	Rod K. Dishman
University of Houston	Dale G. Pease
University of Idaho	Damon Burton
University of Illinois	Edward McAuley
University of Iowa	Dawn E. Stephens
University of Kansas	Mark Thompson
University of Manitoba Department of Physical Education	Dennis Hrycaiko
University of Manitoba Department of Psychology	Garry Martin
University of Maryland, College Park	Donald H. Steel
University of Memphis	Mary Fry
University of Minnesota	Diane Wiese-Bjornstal
University of Missouri, Columbia	Richard H. Cox
University of New Hampshire	Heather Barber
University of New Mexico	Joy Griffin
University of North Carolina, Greensboro	Diane L. Gill
University of North Dakota	Sandra Short
University of North Texas Department of Kinesiology, Health Promotion, and Recreation	Christy Greenleaf
University of North Texas Department of Psychology	Trent Petrie
University of Northern Colorado	Robert Brustad
University of Northern Iowa	Jennifer Waldron
University of Ottawa	Lise O'Reilly
University of Queensland	Stephanie Hanrahan
University of Tennessee, Knoxville	Craig A. Wrisberg
University of Texas at Austin	John B. Bartholomew
University of Utah	Keith Henschen
University of Virginia	Maureen R. Weiss
University of Waterloo	Nancy Theberge
University of Western Australia	J. Robert Grove
University of Western Ontario	Craig R. Hall
University of Windsor	Todd Loughead
University of Wisconsin, Milwaukee	Barbara B. Meyer
Utah State University	Richard Gordin
Victoria University	Daryl Marchant
Virginia Commonwealth University	Steven J. Danish
Wayne State University	Jeff Martin
West Virginia University	Sam Zizzi
Western Illinois University	Laura Finch

Appendix M:
Surfing the Net: Using the Internet for Success

Kevin L. Burke, East Tennessee State University
David Dillard, Temple University
Vince J. Granito, John Carroll University
Lindsey C. Blom, University of Southern Mississippi
Michael L. Sachs, Temple University

This appendix includes three sections. The first section is written by David Dillard and provides a background primer for effective use of computer and Internet-information skills in sport psychology. The second section, written by Kevin L. Burke, Vince Granito, Lindsey C. Blom, and Michael Sachs, offers some detailed information on surfing the web within exercise and sport psychology, along with an extensive list of websites for that area. Two new subheadings of websites have been added in this second section: career information sites and journals. The third section, written by Kevin L. Burke and Lindsey C. Blom, presents information about online sport psychology courses and programs, a growing option in the field.

Database and Internet Search Tools of Use to Scholars and Students in Sport Psychology
David Dillard
Temple University

Beginning around 1970, computers and databases have had a growing—and now tremendous—impact on channeling and meeting the information needs of professionals and learners in all fields, including those of sport psychologists. By facilitating information searching to meet research needs, the Internet has served to geometrically increase computer growth as an information resource for professionals.

The Internet, in the last decade of the twentieth century, featured a limited amount of quality resources and information. At that time, search engines provided huge results to terms that many Internet surfers found to have little bearing on the searched topic. Nevertheless, CD-ROM versions of databases faded from use. The Internet became a highway of electronic telecommunication as the servers of commercial, fee-based databases were leased for a subscription period by institutions, schools, colleges and library systems. By this time, many databases existed that have quality content in a wide range of subject fields with each database covering a specific subject discipline, group of disciplines, or type of content. Since the change of the century, in addition to the content of fee-based databases, there is a rapidly growing, diverse collection of information that is freely available to all Internet users at no cost. Also, there are exciting new tools that facilitate the finding of these sources, often with the links to access these documents and resources online (in some cases for a fee and in other cases at no cost to the user).

Despite the tremendous growth in free web-based content in all subject disciplines, databases still hold the upper hand; databases are storehouses for the important sources, in both content quality and quantity, for the disciplines they cover. This is not just because these databases have controlled content, but also because their use is facilitated by a much more powerful and complex searching logic than is provided by Internet search engines. These powerful search interfaces can handle a complex statement of the information needed, a statement which much more accurately describes the various facets of a complicated topic. Thus, with the complex research questions that are asked in this era, the user will get much more precise and source-controlled results in an infinitely shorter time than is possible using web search engines, through the well planned and thought-out use of the enhanced searching capabilities of these database search-software features.

Nevertheless, there are search tools and resources on the Internet that the user must use to get a more complete result for a research topic. Furthermore, since sport psychology is a very interdisciplinary topic, there are quite a few databases that provide important article, book, and other resource listings that are pertinent to this field. This is a list of some important databases useful to sports psychology and an indication of the quantity of pertinent information that is found in these databases. They are the result of a search of the phrases "sport psychology" and "sports psychology." This will serve as just one indicator of the importance of these databases for research in sport psychology. Numbers under the database name indicate the number of documents that were found from a search of these two phrases—or a variant thereof—to meet the requirements of the database search software.

Medline
70

Journals@Ovid Full Text
227

CINAHL - Cumulative Index to Nursing & Allied Health Literature
157

SPORTDiscus OVID
4479

SPORTDiscus EBSCO
7901

PsychInfo
1460

Digital Dissertations
278

Academic Search Premier
1985

Education Abstracts
714

ERIC
211

Social Sciences Abstracts
197

Health Source - Consumer Edition
44

Health Source: Nursing/Academic Edition
48

Newspaper Source
63

America: History & Life
10

ABI/Inform
13

CWI* Contemporary Women's Issues (health and human rights)
63

Periodical Abstracts
1607

Physical Education Index
14096

WorldCat
954

Blackwell-Synergy (FT)
3876

CiteSeer
128

Compendex and Inspec
28

Criminal Justice Abstracts
15

Emerald
139

Ethnic NewsWatch (ENW), Ethnic NewsWatch: A History (ENWH)
256

RLG's Eureka
FRANCIS
(Humanities & Social Sciences)
92

JSTOR
10733

LexisNexis Academic
Substantial but numerically undetermined

Papers First
1,381

Professional Development Collection
339

PubMed Central
251

PubMed
4541

RedLightGreen
399

RILM Abstracts of Music Literature
41

ScienceDirect
86

The Philosopher's Index
6

Web of Science
821

The found sources from databases with few hits resulting from the search of the phrases "sport psychology" or "sports psychology" can still represent an important result. It can be important to know that a small amount of literature exists in which sport psychology plays a role in fields that are remotely related to sport psychology. It is significant that some literature exists which mentions sport or sports and psychology in the databases for disciplines like engineering, history and philosophy. It is certainly of interest to learn what types of documents have such content. Even an off the wall database selection can produce something significant and useful in its holdings. Consider this one citation found in the Essay & General Literature Index:

Athletic performance and spectator behavior: the humanistic concerns of sports psychology.
Goldstein, Jeffrey H.;
In: American sport culture.
Bucknell Univ. Press 1985. Bucknell Univ. Press, 1985.
[Book Chapter]

Also, in the Regional Business News database from EBSCO, one finds only six citations, but these include a few probative article titles like these two:

• Coach helps jocks win mind games
• Golf and the Asian work ethic

It has been noted that databases are more precise tools for finding content pertinent to complex search topics that are beyond the search capabilities of Internet search engines like Google and Yahoo. This is because of their more sophisticated searching software. Many databanks (that provide access to databases) facilitate finding a word, anywhere in the text, within so many words of another term. It also allows the user to find words only in the subject heading, title, or another specified part of the article citation record. These databanks also enable combining search steps that require the statements of two or more steps to occur within the restrictions created by the Boolean operators used to combine these search steps.

There is another important factor that empowers databases to provide much more precision in the content they find. Databases cover a delimited and restricted group of resources, such as indexing only the articles in a specific (although sometimes large) group of journals. No matter how excellent of an article one may find about the history of medicine in the Canadian Journal of History, this article will not be indexed in Medline or SportsDiscus, that is, if this title is simply not amongst the journal titles covered by these databases. The key to selecting which database to use is knowing the types of journals and other publications that are indexed and abstracted in that database. Also, if any of those journals are carried as full text content of the database. Hence, it is crucial to learn which databases have journal coverage that is core to the search topic that the user is researching. A specific research topic, moreover, may lead to the use of databases not thought of as core to the field in which the user is conducting research. Hence, if the user is searching for ethical issues in the interactions between the sport psychologist and the athlete, and expanding this interaction to include psychologist and psychiatrist interaction with athletes, the user may well consider trying the Philosopher's Index and the ATLA Religion Database with ATLASerials as sources (due to their strong content in the area of ethics).

Learning how to use the search techniques and tools provided in the software of the databank is a vital part of effectively using these databases, as well. The help menus found as a part of the websites of most databanks provide an excellent place to start this learning process. Library reference desks and "Ask a Librarian" sites on the Internet are among the best places to seek answers to specific searching questions. If the user is uncertain how to find an "Ask a Librarian" site on the Internet, Google might be able to help with this need.

Searching the phrase "Ask a Librarian" in Google leads to this result:

Web Results of about 15,100,000 for "Ask a Librarian"

As noted, going to database vendor websites is an excellent way to learn about searching technique. In addition, visit the website of the databank that provides the database and view the help pages and search instruction documents that teach the use of the system—this is another excellent way to learn searching technique. You can often use the website of the database itself provided by the producers of that specific database for additional information and technique tips. Thus, if you have access to the PsychInfo database through the OVID searching service, you may find useful information about searching PsychInfo from the search guides for OVID and for PsychInfo on the OVID website. You can also gain useful guidance for searching the OVID version of PsychInfo from the American Psychological Association's website area that pertains to discussing how to search PsychInfo and, in particular, PsychInfo searching using the OVID interface.

Some of the databanks that provide databases include Dialog, Datastar, OVID, SilverPlatter, Cambridge Scientific Abstracts, FirstSearch, Infotrac, Institute for Scientific Information (ISI), H.W. Wilson, EbscoHost, ABC-CLIO, Proquest Direct, and others. You cannot effectively use such an array of complex and divergent tools as databanks without search documentation. This is provided, both by the databank vendors, and on some of the database-related instruction pages of colleges and universities that provide access to these databanks. Searching in Internet search engines for the name of a database will help find library pages that provide some guidance in the use of these databases. However, make certain that the library is using the same databank as your home institution; otherwise, search results may be quite bazaar, error-message laden, or empty.

Sometimes you may learn that one or several periodicals are important to the topic being researched. You may use one of several versions of JAKE available on the Internet to find out what databases index, abstract, and provide the full text of specific journal titles content to the extent that this free service is kept up to date.

Jointly Administered Knowledge Environment (JAKE)
<http://jake.med.yale.edu/record/819>
<http://jake.lib.sfu.ca/>
<http://jake.openly.com/>

Sample Entry in JAKE: Sports Coach

Sports Coach (serial)
jake id 23145 issn 0314-5468
7 relationships
resource links abstracts fulltext
Australia New Zealand Reference Centre
jake relid 219078 - 1994-10-01 - -
EBSCO MasterFILE Online
jake relid 203376 - + -
MasterFILE Elite
jake relid 203377 - 1994-10-01 - -
MasterFILE Premier
jake relid 203375 - 1994-10-01 - -
MasterFILE Select
jake relid 206166 - 1994-10-01 - -
Professional Development Collection
jake relid 207688 - 1994-10-01 - -
World Magazine Bank
jake relid 210343 - + -

<http://jake.med.yale.edu/record/23145>

Many libraries subscribe to one of a number of services that provide indications of which databases index, abstract, or provide full text content from the journal. Links in the record, which result from the search in this database finding tool, take the user to the journal content sought inside that database.

The Internet is also growing extensively in the quantity of high quality resources to be found in its jungle of content. Important Internet search tools that scan the content of a research topic are so prolific they are now being ignored at the cost of weakening the research projects that fail to use them. In addition, Internet search results have added to the overall quality of sources found in searching. These are just some of the useful tools to be found on the Internet that are available at no cost to researchers. Some of these search engines and other tools provide links to full text copies of at least some of the articles and documents that they index.

Wikipedia
<http://www.wikipedia.org/>
English Wikipedia
<http://en.wikipedia.org/wiki/Main_Page>

This is a controversial and huge resource with coverage of a tremendous range of topics. Content may be provided by anyone, but there are some developing controls. Many Wikipedia articles are excellent in quality, but because anyone can contribute, article quality can vary substantially. A critical eye and mind is important for the effective use of this tool, but it is an excellent starting point for learning about a new subject or term.

There is also a Wiktionary for learning definitions of terms.

Wiktionary
<http://en.wikipedia.org/wiki/Wiktionary>

For finding definitions of terms the YourDictionary.com website leads to a large collection of general, language, and subject specific dictionaries.

YourDictionary.com
<http://www.yourdictionary.com/>

Fields for which there are specialty dictionaries, which include the subject specific dictionaries, are to be found here.

Specialty Dictionaries in English
<http://www.yourdictionary.com/specialty.html>

Some search engines that help with finding sources of information from the Internet include these examples.

Google
<http://www.google.com/>

This is a general search engine of the Internet that has a standing reputation for providing quality search results.

- Web Results of about 32,700,000 for sports psychology
- Web Results of about 8,670,000 for sport psychology

You can often find articles in full text by searching for the article title in quotation marks in Google.

Yahoo
<http://www.yahoo.com/>

This is another quality general search engine of Internet resources.

- About 617,000 for "sports psychology"
- About 974,000 for "sport psychology"

Can picture images about sports psychology be found?

Google Images
<http://images.google.com/>

- About 3,260 for "sports psychology"
- About 3,090 for "sport psychology"

Yahoo Images
<http://www.yahoo.com>

- About 965 for "sports psychology"
- About 848 for "sport psychology"

This is a very different use of information tools. You can find pictorial content that ties in with other matters being presented in a publication or presentation to enhance understanding. In publications, bearing in mind copyright issues, you may want to use links rather than reproduction in their published content. The web pages on which the images are found often lead to a useful Internet resource as well, as the photograph is usually found in a context.

Google Scholar
<http://scholar.google.com/>

"In November 2004, Google released Google Scholar, a search engine that indexes the full text of scholarly literature across an array of publishing formats and scholarly fields. Today, the index includes virtually all peer-reviewed journals available online, except those published by Elsevier Science, the world's largest scientific publisher. Comparable in function to Elsevier's Scopus and Thomson ISI's subscription-based Web of Science service, through more inclusive in sources and languages, Google Scholar is the world's largest index of the "Deep Web" or content that is only available to entitled users."

Source: The Wikipedia
<http://en.wikipedia.org/wiki/Google_Scholar>

Google Scholar Search Results
• About 1,590 for "sports psychology"
• About 5,670 for "sport psychology"

Here are a few sample titles from this result.

- Coaches guide to sport psychology
- Sport psychology: concepts and applications
- Advances in exercise adherence
- Validity in qualitative inquiry and the problem of criteria:
- Implications for sport psychology
- Cross-cultural analysis in exercise and sport psychology: A void in the field
- Sports participation and emotional wellbeing in adolescents
- A global strategy for prevention and detection of blood doping with erythropoietin and related drugs

Google Books
<http://books.google.com>

Book Search
Formerly Google Print

"At the Frankfurt Book Fair in October 2004, Google introduced its Google Print service, now known as Google Book Search. This tool searches the full text of books that Google scans and stores in its digital database. When relevant to a user's keyword search, up to three results from the Google Book Search index are displayed above search results in the Google Web Search service (google.com). Or, a user may search just for books at the dedicated Google Book Search service. [1] Clicking a result from Google Book Search opens an interface in which the user may view pages from the book as well as content-related advertisements and links to the publisher's website and booksellers. Through a variety access limitations and security measures, some based on user-tracking, Google limits the number of viewable pages and prohibits page printing and text copying.

As of December 2005, the Google Book Search service remains in a beta stage but the underlying database continues to grow, with more than a hundred thousand titles added by publishers and authors and some 10,000 works in the public domain now indexed and included in search results. A similar service, known as Search Inside the Book, is offered by Amazon.com's A9.com."

Source: Wikipedia
<http://en.wikipedia.org/wiki/Google_books>

- Books with 1420 pages on "sports psychology"
- Books with 4670 pages on "sport psychology"

This is the listing in the Google Book search results for one of this group of books found with this search.

Emotions in Sport
by Yuri L Hanin - Sports & Recreation - 1999 - 395 pages
Page 394 - He has been a member of the editorial board of the International Society of Sport Psychology and an Expert at the National Swedish Board of Universities and . . . [More results from this book]

Gmail email accounts are free from Google by invitation and are required for the more complete use of Google Books. You must log in with their Gmail account to see full pages from book citations resulting from Google Book searches at least some of the time. You can find a route to getting a Gmail invitation and more about Gmail discussed at the website cited in this Net-Gold discussion group posting.

EMAIL: SERVICES:
GMAIL Invitations and GMAIL Services
<http://snipurl.com/lpw7>

This is some of what you may find out about the book cited from the search result example noted above, all by clicking on the link to the complete record in the Google Books database and checking the various parts of the record. Gmail login was required for this title to see actual pages of the book.

Synopsis

Related information

Web search for reviews of Emotions in Sport

Other web pages related to Emotions in Sport

Bibliographic information

Title Emotions in Sport
Author(s) Yuri L Hanin
Publisher Human Kinetics
Publication Date Oct 1, 1999
Subject Sports & Recreation
Format Paperback
Pages 395
Dimensions 6.20 x 9.29 x 1.23 in
ISBN 0880118792

Pages 1 - 10 of 87 in book for "sport psychology"

Page ix
For instance, most sport psychology research during the last two decades has been negatively biased, focusing on anxiety-performance relationships and using . . .

Page 27
Although new theories (in both psychology and sport psychology) are emerging, this work has typically been a theoretical. While this review is merely . . .

Page 65
. . . performance in mainstream and sport psychology, and also presented basic concepts, terminology, and a description of emotion as an unfolding process . . .

Page 66

Recently this emphasis on the individual athlete has been gaining ground in sport psychology (Gould & Krane, 1992; Weinberg, 1990; Vanden Auweele, Cuyper . . .

Page 69
self-regulation strategies can be developed for sport psychology practice . . . principles developed in general, social, educational, and sport psychology . . .

Page 70
For instance, nomothetic anxiety models used in sport psychology usually stress anxiety-performance relationships at the intergroup, intragroup . . .

Page 71
This is a quite common but relatively narrow approach in both mainstream and sport psychology. individual Zones of Optimal Functioning . . .

Page 73
. . . in sport psychology, and present one approach to describing emotions as components of performance-related states. Issues of Multidimensionality in . . .

Page 76
Most existing sport psychology research examines either cognitive or Affective and somatic components using standardized scales . . .

Page 77
. . . in sport psychology (Bejek & Hagtvet, 1996; Hanin, 1992,1993). One reason may be the predominance of the nomothetic approach to the study of emotions. . .

Google Uncle Sam
<http://www.google.com/unclesam>

This is a search tool that covers government and government related publications and documents.

The Wikipedia provides a link list of government search tools that includes the Google Uncle Sam tool and quite a few others.

Government document search tools
From Wikipedia, the free encyclopedia.
<http://en.wikipedia.org/wiki/Government_document_search_tools>

A shorter URL for the above link:
< http://snipurl.com/lpww>

This article in LLRX provides some views about Google Uncle Sam.

The Government Domain
Why Google Uncle Sam?
By Peggy Garvin

Peggy Garvin of Garvin Information Consulting is author of The United States Government Internet Manual (Bernan Press) and contributing author for The Congressional Deskbook (TheCapitol.Net). Published February 13, 2005

<http://www.llrx.com/columns/govdomain2.htm>

Quoting:

"Not so long ago, a variety of free niche search engines for U.S. government information marketed themselves to web researchers. Remember GovBot, SearchGov.com, and SearchMil.com? GovBot is gone. SearchGov and SearchMil live on, but only as facades: type a search in the box and you'll be ushered into Google. Google's Uncle Sam - released in 1999, the same year as Google itself - is one niche search engine that is still around today. Despite little promotion from Google, its Uncle Sam search has become popular with researchers, librarians, and others who train novices, create search guides, and recommend resources. Given some of its limitations, which I describe in this column, I have always wondered why."

Search results from Google Uncle Sam for Sports Psychology:

- About 752 for "sports psychology"
- About 214 for "sport psychology"

Here are a few search results from the above search of Google Uncle Sam for Sports Psychology:

[PPT] SPORTS PSYCHOLOGY File Format: Microsoft Powerpoint 97 - View as HTML
SPORTS PSYCHOLOGY. Click to add sub-title. Strengthen the mind to improve Physical Performance. "I always felt my greatest asset was not my physical ability . . .
https://www.cnet.navy.mil/nascweb/protected/powerpoints/pp1.3%20sports%20psychology.ppt

The Learning Page—Getting Started: Directory of Internet Resources Applied Sports Psychology - Students may take interest in this introduction from the Association for the Advancement of Applied Sports Psychology . . .
memory.loc.gov/learn/start/inres/ss/psych.html - 18k - Jan 17, 2006

Cannabis use to enhance sportive and non-sportive performances . . . Adolescent; Adult; Competitive Behavior; Doping in Sports/psychology; Doping in Sports/statistics & numerical data*; Female; France/epidemiology; Humans . . .
www.ncbi.nlm.nih.gov/entrez/query.fcgi?cmd=Retrieve&db=PubMed&list_uids=16022934&dopt=Citation

Creatine use among young athletes.... Doping in Sports/psychology; Doping in Sports/statistics & numerical data* ... Sports/psychology; Sports/statistics & numerical data; Sports Medicine* . . .
www.ncbi.nlm.nih.gov/entrez/query.fcgi?cmd=Retrieve&db=PubMed&list_uids=11483809&dopt=Citation

[PDF] Youth Sports in America: An Overview *File Format: PDF/Adobe Acrobat - View as HTML
Tennant (Eds.), Handbook of research on sports psychology (pp. 695-717). New York: Macmillan. ... Sports psychology: An introduction. Chicago: Nelson-Hall . . .
www.fitness.gov/youthsports.pdf

In my experience, Google Uncle Sam has been a very useful tool.

Scirus
<http://www.scirus.com/srsapp/>

"Scirus is a comprehensive science-specific search engine. Like Citeseer and Google Scholar it is focused on scientific information."

Source: Wikipedia
Scirus
From Wikipedia, the free encyclopedia.
< http://en.wikipedia.org/wiki/Scirus>

Scirus search results for sports psychology

All of the words: "sports psychology"

Found:: :17,248 total | 91 journal results | 81 preferred web results | 17,076 other web results

All of the words: "sport psychology"

Found:: :30,740 total | 378 journal results | 280 preferred web results |
30,082 other web results

Google News provides a tool for those interested in sport psychology to find out what is being discussed in a wide range of news sources regarding—or relevant to—sport psychology.

Google News
<http://news.google.com/>

These are the number of hits found in Google News.

- About 104 for sports-psychology
- About 14 for sport-psychology

These results include these article titles.

- New program brings sports into the classroom
- Cycling: Using Pain to your advantage
- Bhagwad Gita as sports psychology

- Sports psychology: Mental training- "New Years resolutions"
- Steelers fans love their rituals
- As our bodies age and change so should our workouts

One form of discussion group is the Newsgroup that, at one time, was the purview of Deja-News. Subsequently, it was purchased by Google and now is the Google service called Google Groups. All Deja-News historical content is now held in the Google Groups archives, as well as active or current Google Groups posting records. This includes currently active Google Groups discussion groups. Those looking for opinion and discussion of issues can find a variety of sources here to complement the discussion group based on the Temple Listserv, SportsPsy that is moderated by Temple University sports psychology professor Michael Sachs.

SportPsy
<http://listserv.temple.edu/archives/sportpsy.html>

Google Groups
<http://groups.google.com/>

For the sport psychology searches, Google Groups found this result:

- 2,810 for "sports psychology"
- 2,210 for "sport psychology"

With this sampling of post titles found by this search engine on this topic.

- II International Congress of the Sport Psychology (CUBA 1999)
- Sport Psychology Online Course
- African Sport Psychology Association (Yahoo! Group)
- Sport Psychology by Sport Resource Page
- Hypnosis and sports improvement

Now to this tool may add to Google Groups a newer Google search tool that searches weblogs.

Google Blog Search
http://blogsearch.google.com/

Which holds this quantity of results for a search of sport psychology.

- About 3,927 for "sports-psychology"
- About 1,318 for "sport-psychology"

Another useful search tool that has content pertinent to sports psychology is the search tool OMNI.

OMNI
<http://omni.ac.uk/>

Here this search (sport or sports) and psychology finds eight websites in its results for this search, including these website titles:

- Drugs in sport news
- Journal of sport and exercise psychology
- Oxford handbook of sports medicine

Finally, for those doing searching for topics in sport psychology—or any other field for that matter—it is important to spend the time that it takes to prepare for a search. This is done by writing down the vocabulary for their search topic prior to even going into a database or Internet search engine. Searching that utilizes incomplete vocabulary is likely to be searching that finds incomplete and less productive results (as contrasted with searching that has a rich vocabulary for the topical components of a research project).

This is an example of such search term preparation.

Topic

Impact of Sports on Urban Youth

Phrases or words wanted in proximity to each other are enclosed in parentheses.

Concept One: sports program

(sport program) or (sport programs) or (sports program) or (sports programs) or (recreation programs) or (recreation program) or (recreational activities) or (athletic programs) or (athletic program) or afterschool or (after school) or (play activities) or (leisure education) or (social skills)

Concept Two: Urban

urban or city or cities or urbanized or metropolitan or metropolis or innercity or innercities

Concept Three: Adolescents

youth or youths or teenager or teen or teens or teenage or teenagers or adolescent or adolescents or juveniles or preteen or preteenagers or preadolescent or preadolescents or children or (school age) or (school aged)

Concept Four: Results or Impact

results or impact or effect or effects or outcome or outcomes or longitudinal or (long term) or effectiveness or assessment or evaluation or evaluations or growth or improvement

Databases and Internet search tools provide an important team of information-finding tools that are vital for research (regarding the many topics of studies taken in sports psychology and beyond). Without using these important tools, research can be much less effective and far more time consuming.

These Net-Gold posts will add to the discussion provided above.

SPORTS: RESEARCH: RESOURCES: SPORTS: RESEARCH:
Gary Price Provides a Group of Excellent Sports Research Resource Websites on His Resource Shelf
< http://snipurl.com/lv06>

BIOMECHANICS: RESOURCES: DATABASES: MEDICAL HEALTH BIOSCIENCES BIOLOGY PSYCHOLOGY:
Databases and Research Guides for the Field of Biomechanics
< http://snipurl.com/lv0j>

SPORTS: PSYCHOLOGY: The Roles of Anxiety and of Confidence in Sports Performance: A Selective and Brief Literature Review of Books, Articles and Web Based Sources
< http://snipurl.com/lv0m>

TOURISM AND TRAVEL: RESOURCES:
RECREATION: RESOURCES:
SPORTS MANAGEMENT: RESOURCES:
Subject Guides in Progress for Tourism, Hospitality, Leisure, Sports Management, Recreation, Outdoor Recreation, Outdoor Recreation and General Internet Sources in Progress with Tourism Country Guide Incomplete [The country segment of the tourism section of this guide is incomplete]
< http://snipurl.com/lv0w>

David Dillard
Temple University
(215) 204 - 4584
jwne@temple.edu
<http://groups.yahoo.com/group/net-gold>
<http://www.edu-cyberpg.com/ringleaders/davidd.html>
<http://listserv.temple.edu/archives/net-gold.html>
<http://www.LIFEofFlorida.org>
Digital Divide Network
<http://www.digitaldivide.net/profile/jwne>
<http://groups.yahoo.com/group/K12Admin/>

Surfing the Net

Kevin L. Burke, East Tennessee State University
Vince J. Granito, John Carroll University
Lindsey C. Blom, University of Southern Mississippi
Michael L. Sachs, Temple University
Elizabeth A. Loughren, Temple University

Attaining information about the field of sport psychology in general—or about graduate programs specifically—is in many cases, as easy as typing on a computer keyboard. Thanks to the convenience of the Internet, a wealth of sport psychology information lies at your fingertips. Many colleges and universities make, through their World Wide Web sites, much of the same graduate program information available as published in graduate catalogues. You may be able to find graduate program applications, assistantship information and applications, graduate course offerings and requirements, and information about (perhaps even photos of) the graduate faculty involved in the programs that interest you.

The Internet, specifically email, can allow you to contact faculty at programs of interest (see email addresses of contact persons for the graduate programs in this directory). Other sources (e.g., AAASP Membership Directory) provide email addresses for colleagues in the field with whom you can discuss the hot sport-psychology topics of the day and/or where to eat at the site of the next sport psychology conference. Email is certainly a viable (and in some ways preferable) option for communication, as compared to letters, faxes, or telephone calls.

Numerous sites on the Internet address exercise- and sport-related issues. The most established site in sport psychology is SPORTPSY, originally established in 1987 at the University of Maryland at Baltimore and still coordinated by Michael Sachs at Temple University. SPORTPSY deals with a wide variety of areas in exercise and sport psychology from discussions on issues, such as certification and confidentiality to conference information, job announcements, and requests for information on topics within the field. You can join by sending the following message to

LISTSERV@LISTMAIL.TEMPLE.EDU
SUB SPORTPSY your name
SPORTPSY is at LISTSERV.TEMPLE.EDU.

If the above commands don't work, just write to Michael Sachs directly at msachs@temple.edu and he can add you himself (given his "vast" powers as list coordinator).

The Internet has grown exponentially, and a dizzying number of sites have been developed from a diverse population ranging from individual faculty members to international organizations. Search engines are available to help users search for information on various topics (see David Dillard's article in this directory or your local Internet guru for suggestions on the latest/best resources). The list that follows was compiled by the four authors (with some helpful additions from Dr. Jack Lesyk of the Ohio Center for Sport Psychology. Check out his website under Sport Psychology Related Sites), and addresses are hopefully still correct. No attempt has been made to screen these sites for the quality of their information. Most of the information should be of good quality and derived from reputable sources; however, especially for "personal" websites, there is no screening regarding information posted on a website. Therefore, the cardinal rule is always "User Beware."

Enjoy your surfing (always physical activity involved!) through the Internet.

Websites for Sport and Exercise Psychology

Associations and Organizations

American College of Sports Medicine
www.acsm.org

American Counseling Association
www.counseling.org

American Medical Society for Sports Medicine
www.newamssm.org

American Psychological Association
www.apa.org/

American Sport Education Program
www.asep.com/

Association for the Advancement of Applied Sport Psychology
www.aaasponline.org/

The Center for Sport Psychology & Performance Excellence
www.sportpsych.unt.edu

Coaching Association of Canada
coach.ca/

Division 47 (Exercise and Sport Psychology) of the American Psychological Association
www.psyc.unt.edu/apadiv47

Fitness Information Technology
www.fitinfotech.com

German Association of Sport Psychology
www.uni-potsdam.de/u/asp/english

Human Kinetics Publishers
www.humankinetics.com/

International Institute for Sport & Human Performance
darkwing.uoregon.edu/~iishp/index.html

International Society of Sport Psychology
www.issponline.org/

Michigan State University's Youth Sports Institute
ed-web3.educ.msu.edu/ysi/

National Alliance for Health, Physical Education, Recreation, and Dance
www.aahperd.org/

National Alliance for Youth Sports
www.nays.org

National Strength and Conditioning Association
www.nsca-lift.org

North American Society for Psychology of Sport and Physical Activity
www.naspspa.org

Women's Sports Foundation
www.womenssportsfoundation.org

Sport Psychology-Related Sites

Art, Writing, and Sport Services
www.awss.com/index.htm

Australian College of Applied Psychology
www.acap.edu.au

Enhanced Performance Systems
www.enhanced-performance.com/

Focused Training
www.focusedtraining.com/

Golf Psych: The Leading Golf Psychology System
www.golfpsych.com/

John Murray (articles on the mental side of tennis)
www.tennisserver.com/

Journal of Psychology and the Behavioral Sciences
view.fdu.edu/default.aspx?id=784

The Mental Edge Article
users.rcn.com/dupcak/mntledge.html

Mind Tools column on Sport Psychology
www.mindtools.com/

Ohio Center for Sport Psychology (Jack Lesyk)
www.sportpsych.org

Peak Performance Online
www.pponline.co.uk/

Peak Performance Sports
www.peaksports.com/

The Physician & Sports Medicine (using the mind power for healing)
www.physsportsmed.com/

Positive Coaching Alliance
www.positivecoach.org

Potentium: The Coaching Network
www.potentium.ca/

Psychology in Spain
www.cop.es/
(English version available at the bottom of the page.)

Sport Psychology with Dr. Kevin L. Burke
www.sport-psychology.com

Sport Psychology and Golf
www.golfweb.com/instruction/cohn

Sport Psychology with Karlene Sugarman
www.psywww.com/sports/

Sport Psychology in Spain
www.ucm.es/OTROS/Psyap/hispania/cruz.htm

Sport Science

www.sportsci.org

Sporting Excellence
ds.dial.pipex.com/town/avenue/xhi48/target-resources/index.htm

Sports Coach
www.brianmac.demon.co.uk

Sports Psychology
www.sportspsychology.com/

Cristina Versari (self-help and psychology magazine)
www.selfhelpmagazine.com/about/staff/biocv.html

Sport Psychology Products

American Psychological Association Books
www.apa.org/books/homepage.html

Brent Rushall (sport psychology workshops offered for coaches)
www-rohan.sdsu.edu/dept/coachsci/index.htm

Sport Psychology for Athletes
www.drrelax.com

Sport Psychology Oversite
www-personal.umich.edu/~bing/oversite/sportpsych.html

Sport Psychology Services (Apex)
www.ux1.eiu.edu/~cfglc/Apexmain.htm

University of Washington's Husky Sport Psychology Services
depts.washington.edu/hsps/

Winners Unlimited Inc.
www.winnersunlimited.com/

Resource List

Psychwatch-Sport Psychology
www.psychwatch.com/sport_psychology.htm

Sport Psychology-research sources
server.bmod.athabascau.ca/html/aupr/sport.htm

Strength Online
www.deepsquatter.com

Supertraining (book about training)
www.sportsci.com/SPORTSCI/JANUARY/textbooks_by_m_c_siff.htm

Specific Sport Information Sites

Amateur Softball Association
www.softball.org/

American Youth Soccer Association
www.soccer.org/

CNN Sports
www.cnnsi.com/index.html

Coaching Youth Sports
www.youth-sports.com

Complete Soccer Academy
www.socceracademy.com/

Cool Running
www.coolrunning.com

The Cooper Institute for Aerobic Research
www.cooperinst.org/

The Cyclotherapist (cycling and sport psychology)
www.thecyclotherapist.com/

ESPN's Sport Zone
www.espn.go.com/

Golf
www.igolf.com/

The Golf Psychology Training Center
www.drsport.com/

Golf Web
www.golfweb.com/

Major League Baseball
www.majorleaguebaseball.com/

Mind Games: Sport Psychology for Every Sport
drrelax.com/run.htm
drrelax.com/pwrlift.htm
drrelax.com/soccer.htm
drrelax.com/baseball.htm
drrelax.com/volley.htm
drrelax.com/bskball.htm

Multi-sport (running)
www.multisport.com/

National Basketball Association
www.nba.com/

NCAA
www.ncaa.org

NCAA Championships
www.ncaasports.com

National Hockey League
www.nhl.com/

The National Strength and Conditioning Association
www.nsca-lift.org/menu.htm

Peak Running Performance
www.peakrun.com

Sport Information
www.sirc.com

Sport Information Resource Center (SIRC)
www.sirc.ca

Stadiums and Arenas
beta.collectingchannel.com/?page=welcome/stadiums

Swimming Science Journal
www-rohan.sdsu.edu/dept/coachsci/swimming/index.htm

Title IX Information
bailiwick.lib.uiowa.edu/ge/

Olympic Games
Beijing 2008: www.beijng2008.com
Vancouver 2010 : www.vancouver2010.com/en
London 2012 : www.london2012.org

U.S. Olympic Committee
www.usoc.org/

U.S. Youth Soccer Association
www.usyouthsoccer.org

USA Hockey
www.usahockey.com/

USA Today Sports Section
www.usatoday.com/sports/sfront.htm

USA Wrestling
www.usawrestling.org/

United States Golf Association
www.usga.org

United States Swimming
www.usswim.org/

United States Tennis Association
www.usta.com/

The Virtual Resource Centre for Sports Information
www.sirc.ca
www.sportdiscus.com/

Career Information Sites (Job Postings)

APA Division 47: Job Postings
www.psyc.unt.edu/apadiv47/jobs.html

Careers in Sport Psychology
www.wcupa.edu/_Academics/sch_cas.psy/Career_Paths/Sports/Career07.htm

Jobs in the United Kingdom
www.jobs.ac.uk/

NCAA
www1.ncaa.org/eprise/main/Public/hr/careers.html

Opportunities in Physical Education and Related Areas
www.csufresno.edu/kines/programs/opera/

Updated Job Openings in Sport and Exercise Psychology
www.wvu.edu/~physed/sportpsych/jobs.htm

The Chronicle of Higher Education
chronicle.com/jobs/100/

Journals

Athletic Insight: The Online Journal of Sport Psychology
www.athleticinsight.com/

British Journal of Sports Medicine
bjsm.bmjjournals.com/

Canadian Journal for Women in Coaching
www.coach.ca/women/e/journal/

Coach and Athletic Director
newfirstsearch.oclc.org/route=ALTIP;dbname=WilsonSelectPlus;done=referer;FSIP

Coaching Science Abstracts
www-rohan.sdsu.edu/dept/coachsci/index.htm

Exercise and Sport Sciences Reviews
www.acsm-essr.com

International Journal of Sport and Exercise Psychology
www.fitinfotech.com/IJSEP/IJSEP.tpl

Journal of Applied Sport Psychology
journalsonline.tandf.co.uk/link.asp?id=108048

Journal of Psychology and the Behavioral Sciences
alpha.fdu.edu/psychweb/JPBS.htm

Journal of Sport Behavior
search.epnet.com/direct.asp?db=aph&jn=%22SRB%22&scope=site

Journal of Sport and Exercise Psychology
www.humankinetics.com/JSEP/journalAbout.cfm

Journal of Sport Sciences
www.tandf.co.uk/journals/titles/02640414.html

Journal of Sport Science and Medicine
www.jssm.org/

Journal of Strength and Conditioning Research
www.nsca-lift.org/Publications/#JSCR

Medicine & Science in Sports and Exercise
www.acsm-msse.org/

Psychology of Sport and Exercise
www.elsevier.com/wps/find/journaldescription.cws_home/620792/description#description

Sociology of Sport Journal
www.humankinetics.com/products/journals/journal.cfm?id=SSJ

Sport Journal
www.thesportjournal.org/siteIndex.asp

SportPsych Unpublished
www.geocities.com/CollegePark/5686/journal.html

Swimming Science Journal
www-rohan.sdsu.edu/dept/coachsci/swimming/index.htm

The Coach
www.thecoach-online.co.uk/

The Sport Psychologist
www.humankinetics.com/TSP/journalAbout.cfm

Online Sport Psychology Courses

Kevin L. Burke, East Tennessee State University
Lindsey C. Blom, University of Southern Mississippi

A fast-growing and exciting dimension of the field of exercise and sport psychology is the availability of online courses (and even complete degree programs). The following list is most likely incomplete due to the exponential development of such offerings. However, it provides a starting point for possibilities. Networking with colleagues, belonging to SPORTPSY, and using available search engines may help you to uncover other possibilities. Please note that the following information was provided by the programs indicated and should be checked with the programs for accuracy. No endorsement of any particular program(s) is implied.

California State University, Dominguez Hills

This is a non-degree, Sport and Fitness Psychology certificate program that is offered entirely online. This certificate consists of 5 courses of 3 units each. At least one course is offered a semester and all courses are transferable for graduate credit. To enroll, contact the Extended and International Education Unit at the California State University, Dominguez Hills. Contact Lynn Hutcheson at lhutcheson@csudh.edu.

PSY 480: Sport Psychology
An in-depth analysis and application of psychological principles and research in motivation, psychophysiology, personality, cognition, and emotion in sport settings.

PSY 481: Applied Sport and Fitness Psychology
Scientific research results in the field of psychology are used to illustrate how participation in sports and physical activity can facilitate psychological development and physical well-being.

PSY 482: Psychology of Coaching and Team-Building
Group processes, team-building techniques, leadership skills, and interpersonal communication skills will be applied to the enhancement of team sports performance and individual well-being.

PSY 483: Contemporary Issues in Sport and Fitness Psychology
Psychological theories will be applied to the identification and treatment of those problems that people who participate in sports may have, as well as, applied to the promotion of mental health.

PSY 486: Internship in Sport and Fitness Psychology
Supervised application of psychological principles applied to sports and fitness to promote performance and optimal well-being. A special feature of this program is the opportunity to work with professional teams at the Home Depot Center or Staples Center in Los Angeles through a cooperative arrangement with the Anschultz Entertainment Group.

Contact Information:
California State University, Dominguez Hills
1000 E. Victoria Street
Carson, California 90747
Extended and International Education Unit
Phone: 310.243.3741
Website: www.csudh.edu/extendeded/sportpsychology.htm

California University of Pennsylvania, Global Online

Cal U Global Online is a worldwide learning community providing convenient and state-of-the-art classroom delivery of quality academic programs. Programs are delivered completely over the Internet so that students can log on and complete their school work when it's convenient for them. Cal U offers an online Bachelor of Science in Sport Management: Wellness and Fitness Concentration degree that includes a sport psychology course as well as other health and wellness related courses. Additionally, there are graduate level courses that are sport and wellness related.

Contact Information:
California University of Pennsylvania
Office of Web-Based Programs
250 University Ave.,
California, PA 15419
Phone: 724.938.5958, toll free 866.595.6348
Fax: 724.938.4270
Email: calugo@cup.edu
Website: www.cup.edu/go/index.jsp

Capella University

All courses in the School of Psychology are offered in an online-course format. Courses are accessed through the Capella University website and start at the beginning of a quarter. Each course is divided into ten learning units, and learners complete one unit each week. Approximately two weeks will be left at the end of the course before the quarter is officially over, allowing learners plenty of time to complete the final course paper before the next quarter begins. Each course is assigned five quarter credits, enrolls fifteen to twenty learners, and has an instructor. The instructor for each course posts assignments and discussion questions each week. At the beginning of each week, learners log into their courses to get the assignments and read the questions. Later, they log in and post their in-depth responses to the discussion questions, as well as read and respond to their fellow learners' responses. It is advised that learners will spend a minimum of ten hours per course, each week. About half of this time will actually be spent online. At Capella University, you can obtain a Master's of Science in Psychology with a Sport Psychology Specialization entirely online.

PSY8840: Principles of Sport Psychology
This course is an overview of the field of sport psychology. It covers a broad range of topics that will be investigated in greater detail in additional courses. Topics include personality, attention, anxiety and arousal, arousal adjustment strategies, cognitive-behavioral intervention, causal attribution, motivation, self-confidence, psychobiology, and social issues of sport. The learner will leave this

course with an eclectic understanding of sport psychology.

PSY8841: Performance Enhancement in Sports
Performance enhancement is the most common issue dealt with by sport psychologists. Knowing how to improve performance through mental strategies in the arena of sport is a critical factor in an athletic success. This course examines the mechanisms by which athletes can exceed their perceived physical limitations, and explores strategies, such as visualization, meditation, hypnosis, autogenic training, biofeedback, and progressive relaxation.

PSY8842: Applied Sport Psychology
This course focuses on how the sport psychologist interacts with individuals within a sport context. Methods of providing effective professional guidance in the areas of learning, motivation, and social interaction are examined, as is mental training for performance enhancement. The course also explores such issues as referrals, drug abuse, burnout, injury, and termination from athletics.

PSY8843: Exercise Psychology
This class covers all the psychological aspects of exercise, including the theoretical foundations of motives for exercise, exercise adherence, personality factors in exercise, and psychological effects of exercise. The course also addresses applied issues such as motivation, cognitive- and behavioral-change strategies, leadership, and counseling in exercise.

PSY8844: Psychology of Injury
This course examines the effects of the injured athlete. It investigates the psychological factors of injury from the points of view of the athlete, the coach, the physician, and the sport psychologist. The behavioral risk factors, injury prevention, and overstraining will be studied as a means of prevention. Injury assessment and the management of injury treatment from assessment to recovery is a central focus and will also include the biomedical issues of injury. Additionally, the course covers the interaction of the sport psychologist and the sports medicine team.

PSY8845: Current Issues in Sport Psychology
This class involves in-depth reading and critical analysis of current issues in sport psychology. The content of this course closely examines current research and theoretical directions in the field.
Contact Information:
Capella University
225 South 6th Street, 9th floor
Minneapolis, MN 55402
Phone: 612.339.8650
Toll-free: 888.227.2736
Website: www.capella.edu/default.aspx

Desert Southwest Fitness, Inc.

Desert Southwest Fitness, Inc. provides continuing education for health and fitness professionals and offers a number of courses relevant to exercise and sport psychology. Courses include the highest quality professional development materials for the health, fitness, wellness and clinical professional.
Contact Information:
Desert Southwest Fitness Inc.
602 East Roger Road
Tucson, AZ 85705
Phone:520.292.0011, toll free 800.873.6759
Fax: 520.292.0066 (fax)
Email: info@dswfitness.com
Website: www.dswfitness.com

East Tennessee State University

SALM 5235: Sport Psychology
Instructor: Dr. Kevin L. Burke
This course examines the psychological factors that may lead to quality performances in sport. Students will be introduced to the physical, mental and emotional variables related to the readiness states of performance. Research and interventions associated with the common qualities of performance will be discussed.

SALM 5215: Sport in Society
Instructor: Dr. Kevin L. Burke

This course provides an introduction to the study of sport and its relationship to society and other social institutions.
Contact Information:
East Tennessee State University
Deptartment of PEXS
P.O. Box 70654
Johnson City, TN 37601
Phone: 423.439.4362
E-mail = burkek@etsu.edu
Website = www.etsu.edu

Empire State College

HDV 282364 Sport Psychology
This course allows students to explore the specific theories, concepts and interventions related to today's sport experience. Additionally students will examine how motivation is used as a tool, and examine how athletes manage and incorporate anxiety, arousal and mood into a performance instrument. Students will discover how group dynamics make a team triumphant, and how the use of interventions, such as imagery, hypnosis and other psychological trainings, help combat a variety of sport behaviors. This course will discuss drug abuse, eating disorders and athlete injury that lead to ineffectual personal leadership or deficient character growth.
Contact Information:
111 West Ave.
Saratoga Springs, NY 12866-6048
Phone: 518.587.2100 ext. 2300, toll free 800.847.3000 ext. 2300
Fax: 518.587.2660
E-mail: cdl@esc.edu
Website: www.esc.edu/cdl

Fairleigh Dickinson University

PSYC 6901: Interventions in Sport Psychology
Instructor: Mitch Abrams, PsyD
This graduate course examines the application and effectiveness of psychological interventions for enhancing performance in sports. Major topics include historical and contemporary foundations of sport psychology, psychological factors and peak performance, establishing commitment and self-control, mental imagery and performance, improving confidence and performance, building concentration, development and implementation of a psychological training program, effective communication, dealing with staleness and burnout, and the use of non-psychological ergogenic aids.
Contact Information:
University College: Arts, Sciences, and Professional Studies
Teaneck-Hackensack Campus
School of Psychology
201.692.2300
Graduate Division*
Spring 2000 (January 24 to May 13)
Website: www.fdu/academic/uc/psych/sportpsych/
Mitch Abrams: MAbrams589@aol.com
* Please note that admission to the Graduate Division of Fairleigh Dickinson University as a nonmatriculating student requires proof of an undergraduate degree from a four-year, baccalaureate-granting institution. Advanced undergraduate students may also enroll in this course, as long as they have permission from their home institutions. Students must also have access to a personal computer and the Internet in order to enroll in this course.

Human Kinetics

HF-FT 105 Exercise and Sport Psychology Course
This course is being offered through the Human Kinetics Online Education Center and is part of the FitPro series for fitness professionals. The FitPro series is designed for fitness professionals who wish to expand and update their understanding of essential psychological principles. Courses can be used for pre- or post-certification of continuing education or for university credit.
Website: www.hkeducationcenter.com/index.cfm

Kilroy's College

Kilroy's College is Ireland's largest provider of study at home opportunities. They offer courses in the Health and Sport area, which include several sport psychology related courses.
Fitness, Health & Nutrition
This distance learning course is for the person who wants to look and feel better. Losing weight, taking regular exercise, acquiring proper eating habits

must have the genuine commitment of the participant in the programme.

Sport Psychology
This course will help students understand the 'mental factor' in sporting success and in how to improve performance in competition.

Golf Psychology
Golf Psychology helps students train their mind and discover what happens when they learn how to let their swing play the game and free themselves from over-thinking results.
Contact Information:
Kilroy's College,
Wentworth House,
Grand Canal Street,
Dublin 2, Ireland
Ireland Local 1 850 700 700
International Phone + 353 1 662 0538
Fax: + 353 1 662 0539
Email: homestudy@kilroyscollege.ie
Website: www.kilroyscollege.ie/

Open Learning Centre International
The OLCI offers about 1000 online courses with an introduction to sport psychology course, as well as others in the sport and leisure and counseling areas. Because these courses are offered in the open learning format, students may begin the courses at any time throughout the year.
Contact Information:
Open Learning Centre International
24 King Street
Carmarthen
SA31 1BS
UK Phone: 0800 393 743
UK Fax: +44 1267 238 179
Int'l Phone: +44 1267 235 268
Email: infor@olci.info

Parkland Community College
Parkland does not offer complete degrees online, but they do offer an undergraduate introduction to sport psychology course through the Kinesiology department.
Contact Information:
Parkland College
2400 West Bradley Avenue
Champaign, Illinois 61821
Phone: 217.351.2200, toll free 800.346.8089
Website: online.parkland.edu/

Prince George's Community College
Prince George's Community College in Maryland offers a master's level Introduction to Sport Psychology course online.
Contact Information:
Prince George's Community College
301 Largo Road
Largo, MD 20774
Phone: 301.583.5219
Email: FairleLK@pgcc.edu
Website: www.marylandonline.org/Jump?to= http://www.pgcconline.com/

Professional Career Development Institute
PCDI offers an online sport psychology course taught by Nicole Detling.
Contact Information:
430 Technology Parkway
Norcross, Georgia 30092-3406
Phone: 770.729.8400, toll free 800.223.4542
Email: infor@pcdi.com
Website: www.pcdi.com/about/

Rusland College, UK
Rusland College offers an introduction to sport psychology course, as well as other sport and/or psychology related courses. Students can take individual courses or work toward a diploma.
Contact Information:
Rusland College Ltd
P.O. Box 183
BATH BA1 2WH ENGLAND
Local Phone: 0800 195 8507
International: +44 (0) 1225 849175
Email: support@ruslandcollege.co.uk
Website: www.ruslandcollege.co.uk/index.html

San Diego University for Integrative Studies
Established April 3, 2000 (This University also has an entry in the main body of the directory). Online students can earn master's and doctoral degrees in

sport psychology, sport counseling, and transpersonal psychology. Each class presents essential information for counselors and professional therapists. The courses chosen reflect our commitment to offering our students access to the very best in current information and to giving them the unique opportunity to experience education through modern technology.

SPO 600 Sport Psychology Business Principles
Students will learn how to set up their Sport Psychology practice, start a business, and network for success. The course will cover marketing techniques to professional sport organizations, office and self management, and record and bookkeeping.

SPO 651: Introduction to Sport Counseling
This overview of Sport Psychology will focus on the history, current status, and future perspectives in the field of psychology as applied to sports. Students will have an opportunity to become familiar with different approaches in sport counseling from an international perspective. Special emphasis will be placed on philosophical and scientific systems of thought, which influence current psychological practice in sports.

SPO 652 Assessment and Evaluation in Sport Counseling
This course will focus on the utilization of assessment instruments and interviewing techniques in Sport Counseling. It will include the application, scoring, and evaluation of the Test of Attentional and Interpersonal Style (TAIS), Myers-Briggs Type Indicator (MBTI), among other commonly used instruments.

SPO 653 Adult Fitness and Performance
This course focuses on the study of various theories and techniques utilized to enhance performance in sports and other areas of physical and mental development. Students will have the opportunity to experience techniques and develop their individual approaches to performance enhancement. Additional topics include identification of primary factors in health risks, optimum training methods and psychological issues confronted in personal physical challenges.

SPO 668 Career Transition and Athletic Retirement
This course will focus on the career cycle of professional and elite athletes and teams, with special focus on the career transition process. Students will learn to assess, evaluate, and make proper recommendations to athletes in the areas of academic and career development and planning. Topics covered in this course include reasons for career transition among athletes, career-transition needs, elements and models for successful career transition, and career transition problem areas: psychological, physical, social, and economic.

SPO 751 Seminar in Sport Psychology
Review and analysis of current research, trends, and issues related to Sport Psychology.

SPO 754 Nutrition and Lifestyle Management
This class will explore the role of athletic training, diet, and life-style issues in peak athletic performance. Principles of exercise physiology, optimal nutrition management, and counseling for optimal physical and mental health will be emphasized. Skill development with assessment tools and with development of preventive and rehabilitation programs is also included.

SPO 766 Psychology of Coaching
This course provides students with theoretical and practical knowledge of this process. Students will learn coaching strategies and techniques that will help them to work with this unique population.

SPO 767 Advanced Sport Psychology Intervention Techniques
This course will provide students with theoretical and practical knowledge in intervention techniques in Sport Psychology. Students will learn different working models they can use to assess and evaluate athletes and to develop programs to serve this unique population. Counseling practice and feedback will be provided through case presentation and analysis to enhance students'

therapeutic effectiveness and ability to create strategies for successful intervention.

Additional course descriptions are available at www.sduis.edu

For more information and to register contact SDUIS at admissions@sduis.edu
San Diego University for Integrative Studies
3900 Harney Street, Suite # 210
San Diego, CA 92110
Phone: 619.297.1999, toll free 800.234.7041
Fax: 619.542.1999
Website: www.sduis.edu
Email: admissions@sduis.edu

United States Sports Academy

The United States Sports Academy offers distance-learning options in a number of its graduate programs. Course offerings include sport psychology and related topics.

Contact information:
The United States Sports Academy
One Academy Drive
Daphne, AL 36526-7055
Phone: 334.626.3303
Website: www.ussa.edu

University of Southern Mississippi

Through the School of Human Performance and Recreation at USM, students are able to obtain a Master's degree in Sport Coaching Education and Sport Management completely online. This program offers sport psychology courses, as well as courses in sport injuries, sport skill analysis, motor development, sport law and others.

Contact Information:
Rosalie Ward, Online Programs Graduate Advisor
School of Human Performance and Recreation
118 College Drive #5142
Hattiesburg, MS 39406-001
Phone: (601 266-6957
Email: rosalie.ward@ums.edu
Website: www.usm.edu/hpr/html/gi_graduate_programs.html

University of Texas System

The University of Texas System offers a choice of four degree plans and the flexibility of online, web-based instruction through the UT TeleCampus. Through the UT, one can earn a Master's Degree in Kinesiology Online. Several sport psychology courses are offered online through this program.

Contact Information:
UT TeleCampus
The University of Texas System
702 Colorado
CLB - Suite 4.100
Austin, Texas 78701
Phone: 512.499.4323, toll free 888.TEXAS.16
Email: TeleCampus@utsystem.edu
Email: Hale_L@utpb.edu
Website: www.telecampus.utsystem.edu

University of Waikato

The University of Waikato has an established reputation and record of achievement for innovation in e-education. It has a strong focus on the development of teaching and learning opportunities through learning environments that meet the diverse needs of students at all levels. It offers a range of programs and qualifications available as fully online, or partially online. A variety of sport psychology related courses are offered through the Sport and Leisure Studies Department.

Contact Information:
The University of Waikato
Gate 1 Knighton Road
Private Bag 3105
Hamilton, New Zealand
Phone: +64 7 856 2889
Fax: +64 7 8383 4300
Email: info@waikato.ac.nz
Website: online.waikato.ac.nz/

Walden University

Walden University's Psychology Division offers doctoral and master's degrees in psychology, as well as a post-doctoral certificate. Study includes reading, observation, and research, and affords students a comprehensive exploration into the emotional and behavioral characteristics of individuals, groups, and activities.

PSYC 8560: Sport Psychology

This course explores the history and the emergence of sport psychology as a field within the psychology discipline. Early developments, major figures, and practical applications in work with individual athletes, teams, coaches, and observers are discussed.

Contact Information:
Walden University
155 Fifth Avenue South
Minneapolis, MN 55401
Phone: 612.338.7224, toll free 800.WALDEN-U
Fax: 612.338.5092
Website: www.waldenu.edu/

Appendix N
Websites for Programs

The following listing provides website addresses for the programs listed in this directory. The listing is provided alphabetically by program. Only those programs that submitted website addresses are included in this list. Because web addresses frequently change and some programs have no website listed, you are encouraged to surf the web to locate or verify the current address of a program.

University of Alberta
www.uofaweb.ualberta.ca/per/

Argosy University
www.aspp.edu

Arizona State University
www.asu.edu/clas/espe/

University of Arizona
www.arizona.edu

Ball State University
www.bsu.edu/physicaleducation

Barry University
www.barry.edu

Boise State University
www.boisestate.edu

Boston University
www.bu.edu/education

Bowling Green State University
www.bgsu.edu

California State University, East Bay
www.csueastbay.edu

California State University, Fresno
www.csufresno.edu/

California State University, Fullerton
www.fullerton.edu

California State University, Long Beach
www.csulb.edu/depts/kpe/

California State University, Sacramento
www.hhs.csus.edu

University of California, Los Angeles
www.ucla.edu

University of Canberra
www.canberra.edu.au

Cleveland State University
www.csuohio.edu

University College Chichester
www.ucc.ac.uk/

DeMontfort University Bedford
www.dmu.ac.uk/

East Carolina University
www.ecu.edu

East Tennessee State University
http://faculty.etsu.edu/burkek/

University of Edinburgh
www.ed.ac.uk/

University of Exeter
www.exeter.ac.uk/education

Florida State University
www.epls.fsu.edu/edpsych/sportPsych.htm

University of Florida
www.hhp.ufl.edu/ess

Georgia Southern University
chhs.georgiasouthern.edu/health/m_sport_psych.html (Sport Psychology Program Information)
chhs.georgiasouthern.edu/health/sport_psych_lab.htm/ (Sport Psychology Laboratory)
www.applyweb.com/apply/gasgrad/menu.html (Online Application)
cogs.georgiasouthern.edu/ (College of Graduate Studies)
chhs.georgiasouthern.edu/health/index.htm (Department of Public Health)
chhs.georgiasouthern.edu/ (College of Health & Human Sciences)
www.georgiasouthern.edu (Georgia Southern University)

University of Georgia
www.coe.uga.edu/kinesiology

University of Houston
www.coe.uh.edu

Humboldt State University
www.humboldt.edu/

University of Idaho
coe.ed.uidaho.edu/index.cfm?SiteID=8

Illinois State University
www.ilstu.edu

University of Illinois
www.als.uiuc.edu/kines/default.htm
www.grad.uiuc.edu

Indiana University
www.indiana.edu/~kines/

Iowa State University
www.iastate.edu

University of Iowa
www.uiowa.edu/~shlps/grad.htm

Ithaca College
www.ithaca.edu/grad/grad1

John F. Kennedy University
www.jfku.edu/

Kansas State University
www.ksu.edu/

University of Kansas
www.kansas.edu/

La Salle University
www.lasalle.edu

Lakehead University
www.lakeheadu.ca (Go to Admissions, then Arts and Sciences.)

Leeds Metropolitan University
www.lmu.ac.uk/

Manchester Metropolitan University
www.mmu.ac.uk

University of Manitoba (Physical Education)
www.umanitoba.ca/faculties/physed

University of Maryland
www.umd.edu

McGill University

www.education.Mcgill.ca/phys_ed

University of Memphis (Human Movement Sciences)
hmse.memphis.edu/

Miami University
www.units.muohio.edu/eap/departments/phe/phe.htm

Michigan State University
www.educ.msu.edu/

University of Minnesota
www.education.umn.edu/KLS/default.htm

University of Missouri, Columbia
www.missouri.edu/index.cfm/

University of Montreal
www.umontreal.ca/english/index.htm

Nanyang Technological University
www.ntu.edu.sg/publicportal

University of New Hampshire
www.unh.edu

University of New Mexico
www.unm.edu/~sportad /

University of North Carolina, Greensboro
www.uncg.edu

University of North Dakota
www.und.ed

University of North Texas
www.coe.unt.edu

University of Northern Colorado
www.unco.edu

Northern Illinois University
www3.niu.edu/knpe/

University of Northern Iowa
www.uni.edu

Optimal Performance Institute and University
www.opi.edu

Oregon State University
www.hhs.oregonstate.edu/nes/index.html

University of Ottawa
www.health.uottawa.ca/hkgrad

Pennsylvania State University
www.hhdev.psu.edu/kines/ (Department of Kinesiology)
www.psu.edu (PSU)
www.hhdev.psu.edu / (College of Human Development)
www.psu.edu/ur/prospective.html (Information for Prospective Students)
www.gradsch.psu.edu / (Graduate School)
www.personal.psu.edu/dec9/ (Dr. David Conroy's web page)
www.personal.psu.edu/sms18 (Dr. Sam Slobounov's web page)

Purdue University
www.cla.purdue.edu/hk

University of Quebec
www.uqtr.ca/InfoGen/Anglais/

Queens University
www.queensu.ca/

University of Queensland
www.hms.uq.edu.au/
www.uq.edu.au/study/program.html?acad_prog=5214&page_number=1&year=2003&PHPSESSID=1a98cc11e9d5251a4d4911dc289a15e2

Rutgers University
gsappweb.rutgers.edu/SportPsychology/SportPsych.htm

San Diego State University
www.rohan.sdsu.edu/~psyched

San Diego University For Integrative Studies
www.sduis.edu

San Jose State University
www.sjsu.edu/sportpsych

Université de Sherbrooke
www.usherbrooke.ca/

Southeastern Louisiana University
www.selu.edu

Southern Connecticut State University
www.southernct.edu

Southern Illinois University, Carbondale
www.siuc.edu

Southern Illinois University Edwardsville
www.siue.edu

Spalding University
www.spalding.edu

Springfield College (Graduate Studies)
www.springfieldcollege.edu

Springfield College (Psychology)
www.spfldcol.edu

Staffordshire University
www.staffs.ac.uk/schools/health/she/shehole.htm

University of Stellenbosch
www.sun.ac.za/index.asp

Temple University
www.temple.edu

University of Tennessee, Knoxville
www.tennessee.edu

University of Texas
www.utexas.edu

Texas Christian University (Kinesiology)
www.tcu.edu

Texas Tech University
www.hess.ttu.edu/

Utah State University
www.usu.edu

University of Utah
www.health.utah.edu/ess/

Victoria University
www.vu.edu.au/

Virginia Commonwealth University
www.vcu.edu/

University of Virginia
curry.edschool.virginia.edu/kinesiology/sprtpsy/

University of Waterloo
healthy.uwaterloo.ca/kin/

Wayne State University
www.wayne.edu/

West Virginia University
www.wvu.edu/~physed/sportpsych/spmain.htm

University of Western Australia
www.general.uwa.edu.au/~hmweb/

Western Illinois University
www.wiu.edu/users/mflmf/sportpsych/

Western Washington University
www.wwu.edu/

University of Western Ontario
www.uwo.ca/fhs/

University of Windsor
www.uwindsor.ca/

University of Wisconsin, Milwaukee
www.uwm.edu/CHS/ugp/kin/index.html

Appendix O
Location of Graduate Programs: Physical Education and Psychology, Master's and Doctoral Level Physical Education Programs*

Master's Programs (87 programs)

University of Alberta
Arizona State University
Ball State University
Barry University
Boise State University
Bowling Green State University
California State University, East Bay
California State University, Fresno
California State University, Fullerton
California State University, Long Beach
California State University, Sacramento
University of Canberra
University College Chichester
Cleveland State University
DeMontfort University Bedford
East Carolina University
East Tennessee State University
University of Edinburgh
University of Exeter
University of Florida
Georgia Southern University
University of Georgia
University of Houston
Humboldt State University
University of Idaho
Illinois State University
University of Illinois
Indiana University
Iowa State University
University of Iowa
Ithaca College
Kansas State University
Lakehead University
Leeds Metropolitan University
Manchester Metropolitan University
University of Manitoba
University of Maryland, College Park
McGill University
University of Memphis
Miami University
Michigan State University
University of Minnesota
Université de Montréal
Nanyang Technological University
University of New Hampshire
University of New Mexico
University of North Carolina, Greensboro
University of North Dakota
University of North Texas
University of Northern Colorado
University of Northern Iowa
Northern Illinois University
Oregon State University
University of Ottawa
Pennsylvania State University
Purdue University
Université du Québec à Trois-Rivières
Queen's University
University of Queensland
San Diego State University
San Jose State University
Universite de Sherbrooke
Southeastern Louisiana University

Southern Connecticut State University
Southern Illinois University, Carbondale
Southern Illinois University, Edwardsville
Springfield College (Health, Physical Education, and Recreation)
Staffordshire University
University of Stellenbosch
Temple University
University of Tennessee, Knoxville
University of Texas, Austin
Texas Christian University
Texas Tech University
Utah State University
University of Utah
Victoria University
University of Virginia
University of Waterloo
Wayne State University
West Virginia University
Western Illinois University
Western Washington University
University of Western Australia
University of Western Ontario
University of Windsor
University of Wisconsin, Milwaukee

Doctoral Programs (43 programs)

University of Alberta
Arizona State University
University College Chichester
DeMontfort University Bedford
University of Edinburgh
University of Exeter
University of Florida
University of Georgia
University of Houston
University of Idaho
University of Illinois
University of Iowa
University of Kansas
Leeds Metropolitan University
Manchester Metropolitan University
University of Maryland, College Park
Michigan State University
University of Minnesota
Université de Montréal
Nanyang Technological University

University of New Mexico
University of North Carolina, Greensboro
University of Northern Colorado
Optimal Performance Institute and University
Oregon State University
University of Ottawa
Pennsylvania State University
Purdue University
Queen's University
University of Queensland
Springfield College (Health, Physical Education, and Recreation)
Staffordshire University
University of Stellenbosch
Temple University
University of Tennessee, Knoxville
Texas Tech University
University of Utah
Victoria University
University of Virginia
University of Waterloo
West Virginia University
University of Western Australia
University of Western Ontario

Psychology Programs

Master's Programs (11 programs)
Argosy University
Boston University**
Florida State University***
John F. Kennedy University
University of Manitoba
University of Missouri, Columbia
Optimal Performance Institute and University
University of Queensland
San Diego University for Integrative Studies
Spalding University
Springfield College (Psychology)

Doctoral Programs (18 programs)
Argosy University
University of Arizona
Boston University**
University of California, Los Angeles
Florida State University***

John F. Kennedy University
LaSalle University
University of Manitoba
University of Missouri, Columbia
University of North Texas
Optimal Performance Institute and University
University of Queensland
Rutgers University
San Diego University for Integrative Studies
University of Southern Queensland
Spalding University
Texas Christian University
Virginia Commonwealth University

*   Primarily found in Departments of Physical Education, but also found under many other names, including Kinesiology, Exercise and Sport Sciences, etc.
**   Department of Developmental Studies and Counseling
***   Department of Educational Research, Program in Educational Psychology

Appendix P
Quick Chart of Program Information: Degrees Offered, Program-Emphasis Rating, and Internship Possibility

School	Contact	Phone	Email
Argosy University/Phoenix	Robert Harmison	602.216.2600	rharmison@argosyu.edu
Arizona State University	Daniel M. Landers	480.965.7664	landers@asu.edu
Ball State University	Jeffrey S. Pauline	765.285.3286	jpauline@bsu.edu
Barry University	Artur Poczwardowski	305.899.3490	sportsciences@mail.barry.edu
Boise State University	Linda M. Petlichkoff	208.426.1231	lpetlic@boisestate.edu
Boston University	Leonard D. Zaichkowsky	617.353.3378	sport@acs.bu.edu
Bowling Green State University	Bonnie Berger	419.372.2334	bberger@bgnet.bgsu.edu
California State University, East Bay	Penny McCullagh	510.885.3050	penny.mc@csueastbay.edu
California State University, Fresno	Wade Gilbert	559.278.5170	wgilbert@csufresno.edu
California State University, Fullerton	Debra Rose	714.278.3432	
	Lenny Wiersma	714.278.3432	
California State University, Long Beach	T. Michelle Magyar	562.985.4116	mmagyar@csulb.edu
	Sharon Guthrie	562.985.7487	casteln@aol.com
California State University, Sacramento	Gloria B. Solomon	916.278.7309	solomong@csus.edu
Cleveland State University	Susan Ziegler	216.687.4876	
DeMontfort University, Bedford	Howard K. Hall	(01234) 793316	HKHall@DMU.AC.UK
East Carolina University	Thomas Raedeke	252.328.0005	raedeket@mail.edu.edu
East Tennessee State University	Dr. Kevin L. Burke	423-439-4362	Burkek@etsu.edu
Florida State University	Gershon Tenenbaum	850.644.8780	
Georgia Southern University	Daniel R. Czech	912-486-7424	drczech@georgiasouthern.edu
Humboldt State University	Al Figone	707.826.3557	
Illinois State University	Anthony J. Amorose	309.438.8590	ajamoro@ilstu.edu
Indiana University	John S. Raglin	812.855.1844	raglinj@indiana.edu
Iowa State University	Rick Sharp	515.294.8650	rlsharp@iastate.edu
Ithaca College	Greg A. Shelley	607.274.1275	gshelley@ithaca.edu
John F. Kennedy University	Gail Solt	925.969.3413	gsolt@jfku.edu
Kansas State University	David Dzewaltowski	785.532.7750	DADX@KSU.EDU
La Salle University	Frank Gardner	215.951.1350	gardner@lasalle.edu
Lakehead University	Jane Crossman	807.343.8642	Jane.Crossman@lakeheadu.ca
Leeds Metropolitan University	Mark Nesti	0113 2837566	M.Nesti@lmu.ac.uk
Manchester Metropolitan University	Nick Smith	(44) 161-247-5455	N.C.SMITH@MMU.AC.UK

GRADUATE PROGRAMS IN APPLIED SPORT PSYCHOLOGY

Website	Rating	Degrees Offered	Internship
http://www.argosyu.edu/	2	PsyD	Yes
http://www.public.asu.edu/~atdml/	5	MS,PHD	Yes
http://www.bsu.edu/physicaleducation/sportpsychology/	2,3	MA,MS	Yes
http://www.barry.edu/	4	MS	Yes
http://www.boisestate.edu/	4	MS	Yes
http://www.bumc.bu.edu/Dept/Content.aspx?DepartmentID=391&PageID=9645			
http://www.bgsu.edu/	5	MEd	No
http://www.csueastbay.edu	4	MS	Yes
http://www.fresnostatesportpsych.org/	5	MA	Yes
http://www.fullerton.edu/	3	MS	Yes
http://www.csulb.edu/depts/kpe/	4	MA,MS	Yes
http://www.hhs.csus.edu/	4	MS	Yes
http://www.csuohio.edu/	3	MEd	No
www.dmu.ac.uk	6	MS, MPhil, PhD	No
www.ecu.edu	4	MA	Yes
http://faculty.etsu.edu/burkek/	3	MA	Yes
http://www.epls.fsu.edu/edpsych/sportPsych.htm	4	MS, PhD	Yes
http://www.georgiasouthern.edu/~drczech/	2	MS	Yes
http://www.humboldt.edu/	N/R	MS	Yes
http://www.ilstu.edu/	6	MS	Yes
http://www.indiana.edu/~kines/	7	MS	No
http://www.iastate.edu/	4	MS	Yes
http://www.ithaca.edu/grad/grad1/	2	MS	Yes
http://http://www.jfku.edu	2	MA,PsyD	Yes
http://www.kstatechi.org/	N/R	MS	Yes
http://www.lasalle.edu/academ/grad/doc_psych/docpsych.htm	3,4	PsyD	Yes
http://bolt.lakeheadu.ca/~kinesiology/wp/?pg=47	4	MS	Yes
http://www.lmu.ac.uk/	4	MS, MPhil, PhD	No
http://www.mmu.ac.uk/	4	MS, MPhil, PhD	No

School	Contact	Phone	Email
McGill University	Gordon Bloom	514-398-4184, ext. 0516	gordon.bloom@mcgill.ca
Miami University	Robert Weinberg	513.529.2728	WEINBER@MUOHIO.EDU
Michigan State University	Martha Ewing	517.353.4652	
Nanyang Technological University	Daniel Smith	65-460-5368	desmith@nie.edu.sg
Northern Illinois University	Laurice Zittel	815.753.1425	lzape@niu.edu
Optimal Performance Institute and University	John J. Farley	408-200-7426	johnfarley@opi.edu
Oregon State University	Vicki Ebbeck	541.737.6800	vicki.ebbeck@oregonstate.edu
Pennsylvania State University	David E. Conroy	814.863.3451	David-Conroy@psu.edu
Purdue University	Alan Smith	765.494.3178	alsmith@cla.purdue.edu
Queen's University	Janice Deakin	613.533.6601	deakinj@post.queensu.ca
Rutgers University	Dr. Charlie Maher	732.445.2000 x103	camaher@rci.rutgers.edu
San Diego State University	Simon Marshall	619.594.7272	slevy@mail.sdsu.edu
San Diego University for Integrative Studies	Cristina Bortoni Versari	858.638.1999	cversari@sduis.edu
San Jose State University	David M. Furst	408.924.3039	furstd@kin.sjsu.edu
Southeastern Louisiana University	Dan Hollander	504.549.3870	dhollander@selu.edu
Southern Connecticut State University	David S. Kemler	203.392.6040	Kemlerd1@southernct.edu
Southern Illinois University, Carbondale	Julie Partridge	618.453.3324	jpartrid@siu.edu
Southern Illinois University, Edwardsville	Curt L. Lox	618.650.5961	clox@siue.edu
Spalding University	Thomas Titus	502.585.9911	
Springfield College Psychology Department	Judy L. Van Raalte	413.748.3388	jvanraal@spfldcol.edu
Springfield College School of Graduate Studies	Betty L. Mann	413.748.3125	
Staffordshire University	Paul McCarthy		P.McCarthy@staffs.ac.uk
Stellenbosch University	Justus R. Potgieter	(27) 21-8084915	JRP@MATIES.SUN.AC.ZA

Website	Rating	Degrees Offered	Internship
http://www.education.mcgill.ca/phys_ed/default.htm	5	MA	Yes
http://www.units.muohio.edu/eap/phs/index.html	4	MS	Yes
http://www.educ.msu.edu/	5	MS, PhD	Yes
http://www.ntu.edu.sg/publicportal/	4	MA, PhD	Yes
http://www3.niu.edu/knpe/	4	MSEd	No
http://www.opi.edu/	3	MA	Yes
http://www.hhs.oregonstate.edu/exss/graduate/index.html	6	MS, PhD	No
http://www.personal.psu.edu/dec9	6	MS, PhD	Yes
http://www.cla.purdue.edu/sportpsych	6	MS, PhD	Yes
http://www.phe.queensu.ca/employees/faculty/faculty_detail.php?show=deakin	6	MA, PhD	Yes
http://gsappweb.rutgers.edu/SportPsychology/SportPsych.htm	5	PsyD, PhD	Yes
http://www-rohan.sdsu.edu/dept/ens/ens_web/faculty/levy.htm	5	MA	Yes
http://www.sduis.edu/	1	PhD	Yes
http://www.sjsu.edu/sportpsych	6	MA	Yes
http://www.selu.edu/	6	MA	Yes
http://www.southernct.edu/	4	MS	Yes
http://www.siu.edu/departments/coe/physed	4	MS	Yes
http://www.siue.edu/EDUCATION/kinesiology/index.html	5	MSEd	Yes
http://www.spalding.edu/	1	MA, PsyD	Yes
http://www.spfldcol.edu/homepage/dept.nsf/	4	MEd, MS, CAS	Yes
http://www.springfieldcollege.edu/	4	MS, DPE	Yes
http://www.staffs.ac.uk/	5	MPhil, MS, PhD	Yes
http://www.sun.ac.za/index.asp	4	MHS, PhD	No

School	Contact	Phone	Email
Temple University	Michael L. Sachs	215.204.8718	msachs@temple.edu
Texas Christian University	Matt Johnson	817.257.6866	m.johnson@tcu.edu
Texas Tech University	Lanie Dornier	806.742.3371	Lanie.Dornier@ttu.edu
Universite de Montreal	Wayne R. Halliwell	514.343.7008	
Universite de Sherbrooke	Paul Deshaies	819.821.8000 (x3721)	PDESHAIES@FEPS.USHERB.
Universite du Quebec à Trois-Rivieres	Pierre Lacoste	819.376.5128, poste 3780	
University College, Chichester	Jan Graydon	01243 816320	100443.2067@compuserve.com
University of Alberta	Anne Jordan	780.492.3198	anne.jordan@ualberta.ca
University of Arizona	Jean M. Williams	520.621.6984	williams@u.arizona.edu
University of California, Los Angeles	Bernie Weiner	310.825.2750	Weiner@psych.ucla.edu
University of Canberra	John B. Gross	(06) 2012009	gross@science.canberra.edu.au
University of Edinburgh	Dave Collins	44-131-312-6001	d.collins@ed.ac.uk
University of Exeter	Tim Rees	44 1392 262892	E.M.Davies@exeter.ac.uk
University of Florida	Christopher M. Janelle	352.392.0584 (x 1270)	cjanelle@hhp.ufl.edu
University of Georgia	Rod K. Dishman	706.542.9840	rdishman@uga.edu
University of Houston	Dale G. Pease	713.743.9838	DPEASE@UH.EDU
University of Idaho	Damon Burton	208.885.2186	dburton@uidaho.edu
University of Illinois	Edward McAuley	217.333.6487	emcauley@uiuc.edu
University of Iowa	Dawn E. Stephens	319.335.9348	dawn-e-stephens@uiowa.edu
University of Kansas	Mark Thompson	913.864.0778	drt@ku.edu
University of Manitoba Department of Physical Education	Dennis Hrycaiko	204.474.8764	hrycaik@Ms.UManitoba.ca
University of Manitoba Department of Psychology	Garry Martin	204.474.8589	
University of Maryland, College Park	Donald H. Steel	301.405.2490	
University of Memphis	Mary Fry	901.678.4986	maryfry@memphis.edu
University of Minnesota	Diane Wiese-Bjornstal	612.625.6580	dwiese@umn.edu
University of Missouri, Columbia	Richard H. Cox	573.882.7602	coxrh@missouri.edu
University of New Hampshire	Heather Barber	603.862.2058	HB@CISUNIX.UNH.EDU

Website	Rating	Degrees Offered	Internship
http://www.temple.edu/chp/kinesiology/human_mov.htm	5	MEd, PhD	Yes
http://www.kinesiology.tcu.edu	6	MS	Yes
http://www.hess.ttu.edu/	6	MS, EdD	Yes
http://www.umontreal.ca/english/index.htm	N/R	MS, PhD	No
http://www.usherbrooke.ca/	5	MS	No
http://www.uqtr.ca/InfoGen/Anglais/	N/R	MS	Yes
http://www.ucc.ac.uk/	N/R	MPhil, MS, PhD	Yes
http://www.physedandrec.ualberta.ca/	6.5	MA, PhD	No
http://www.arizona.edu/	5.5	PhD	Yes
http://www.ucla.edu/	6	PhD	No
http://www.canberra.edu.au/	2	Grad Diploma	Yes
http://www.ed.ac.uk/	N/R	MS, MPhil, PhD	Yes
http://www.ex.ac.uk/sshs	6	MS, MPhil, PhD	No
http://www.hhp.ufl.edu/ess/FACULTY/cjanelle/cjanelle.htm	6	MS, PhD	Yes
http://www.coe.uga.edu/kinesiology	7	MS, PhD	No
http://www.hhp.uh.edu/	6	MEd, MS, PhD	Yes
http://www.uidaho.edu/ed/hperd/	4	MS, PhD	Yes
http://www.kines.uiuc.edu/expsych/	7	MS, PhD	No
http://www.uiowa.edu/~hss/faculty/Stephens.htm	7	MA, PhD	No
http://www.ku.edu	1	MS, EdD, PhD	Yes
http://www.umanitoba.ca/Faculties/Physed/	4	MA, MS, PhD	Yes
http://www.umanitoba.ca/Faculties/Physed/	4	MA, MS, PhD	Yes
http://www.umd.edu/	6	MA, PhD	No
http://hmse.memphis.edu/	4	MS	Yes
http://www.education.umn.edu/kin/faculty/dwiese.htm	5	MA, PhD	Yes
http://www.missouri.edu/index.cfm	5	MA, MEd, PhD	Yes
http://www.unh.edu/	4	MS	Yes

School	Contact	Phone	Email
University of New Mexico	Joy Griffin	505.277.3534	jgriffin@unm.edu
University of North Carolina, Greensboro	Diane L. Gill	336.334.4683	dlgill@uncg.edu
University of North Dakota	Sandra Short	701.777.4325	Sandra_short@und.nodak.edu
University of North Texas Department of Kinesiology, Health Promotion, and Recreation	Christy Greenleaf	940.565.3415	cgreenleaf@coefs.coe.unt.edu
University of North Texas Department of Psychology	Trent Petrie	940.565.4718	PETRIET@UNT.EDU
University of Northern Colorado	Robert Brustad	970-351-1737	bob.brustad@unco.edu
University of Northern Iowa	Jennifer Waldron	319.273.2730	jennifer.waldron@uni.edu
University of Ottawa	Lise O'Reilly	613.562.5800 (x5752)	lcosa@uottawa.ca
University of Queensland	Stephanie Hanrahan	(61) 7-3365-6453	Steph@hms.uq.edu.au
University of Tennessee, Knoxville	Craig A. Wrisberg	865.974.1283	mwirtz@utk.edu
University of Texas at Austin	John B. Bartholomew	512.471.4407	john.bart@mail.utexas.edu
University of Utah	Keith Henschen	801.581.7558	khensche@hsc.utah.edu
University of Virginia	Maureen R. Weiss	434.924.7860	mrw5d@virginia.edu
University of Waterloo	Nancy Theberge	519.888.4567 x 3534	theberge@healthy.uwaterloo.c
University of Western Australia	J. Robert Grove	(61-8) 9380-2361	Bob.Grove@uwa.edu.au
University of Western Ontario	Craig R. Hall	519.661.2111 (x88388)	chall@uwo.ca
University of Windsor	Todd Loughead	519.253.3000 x 2450	loughead@uwindsor.ca
University of Wisconsin, Milwaukee	Barbara B. Meyer	414.229.4591	bbmeyer@uwm.edu
Utah State University	Richard Gordin	435.797.1506	gordin@cc.usu.edu
Victoria University	Daryl Marchant	03 9919 4035 0403 065358	daryl.marchant@vu.edu.au
Virginia Commonwealth University	Steven J. Danish	804.828.4384	sdanish@vcu.edu
Wayne State University	Jeff Martin	313.577.1381	993975@wayne.edu
West Virginia University	Sam Zizzi	304.293.3295 (x5240)	sam.zizzi@mail.wvu.edu
Western Illinois University	Laura Finch	309.298.2350	LM-Finch@wiu.edu
Western Washington University	Ralph A. Vernacchia	360.650.3514	Ralph.Vernacchia@wwu.edu

Website	Rating	Degrees Offered	Internship
http://www.unm.edu/~sportad/	4	MS, PhD	Yes
http://www.uncg.edu/ess/faculty/dianegill.html	5	MS, PhD	Yes
http://www.und.edu/	4	MS, PhD	Yes
http://www.unt.edu/	N/R	MS	No
http://www.sportpsych.unt.edu/	4	PhD	Yes
http://www.unco.edu/	6	MA, PhD	Yes
http://www.uni.edu	5	MA	Yes
http://www.health.uottawa.ca/hkgrad	1,6	MA, PhD	Yes
http://www.hms.uq.edu.au/	4	MA, MS, MSEP, PhD	Yes
http://web.utk.edu/7/Esals	4	MS, PhD	Yes
http://www.utexas.edu/	6	MA, MEd, PhD	Yes
http://www.health.utah.edu/ess/	5	MS, PhD	Yes
http://www.curry.edschool.virginia.edu/kinesiology/sprtpsy/	6	MEd, PhD	Yes
http://www.uwaterloo.ca/	4	MS, PhD	Yes
http://www.general.uwa.edu.au/~hmweb/	4	MS, PhD	Yes
http://www.uwo.ca/kinesiology/	6	MA, PhD	Yes
http://www.uwindsor.ca/	N/R	MHK	Yes
http://www3.uwm.edu/chs/faculty/faculty.asp?facultyID=51	5	MS, PhD	Yes
http://www.usu.edu/	3	MS	Yes
http://www.vu.edu.au/	N/R	MAP, MAS, PhD	Yes
http://www.has.vcu.edu/psy/counseling/index.html	6	PhD	Yes
http://www.wayne.edu/	7	MEd	Yes
http://www.wvu.edu/~physed/sportpsych/spmain.htm	4	EdD	Yes
http://www.wiu.edu/users/mflmf/sportpsych/	3.5	MS	Yes
http://www.wwu.edu/pehr	5	MS	Yes

Editor Biographies

Michael L. Sachs, PhD

Michael L. Sachs is a professor in the Department of Kinesiology, College of Health Professions, at Temple University, Philadelphia, PA. He received his PhD in sport psychology in 1980 from Florida State University. In addition to a master's in general-experimental psychology from Hollins College (Virginia) in 1975, he received a second master's in counseling psychology from Loyola College (Maryland) in 1989. He received his bachelor's degree in psychology from Union College (NY) in 1973. Prior to coming to Temple University in 1989, Sachs taught at the University of Quebec at Trois-Rivieres (1980-1983) and was a researcher at the University of Maryland at Baltimore (1983-1989). He is a licensed psychologist in the state of Maryland.

Sachs is associate editor of *Psychology of Running* (Michael H. Sacks & Michael L. Sachs) and co-editor (with Gary Buffone) of *Running as Therapy: An Integrated Approach*. He also co-wrote *The Total Sports Experience for Kids: A Parents' Guide to Success in Youth Sports* with Aubrey Fine. He has written or co-authored numerous book chapters, academic articles on various topics within exercise and sport psychology, and articles on the psychology of running in popular publications. He is a co-editor of *The Running Psychologist*, newsletter of Running Psychologists (part of Division 47, the Division of Exercise and Sport Psychology, of APA). His research interests focus upon exercise psychology, particularly motivation and adherence, excusercise, exercise addiction, and the psychology of running.

Sachs is a Charter Member and Fellow of the Association for the Advancement of Applied Sport Psychology (AAASP) and served as the first Health Psychology Chairperson of AAASP (1985-1988) as well as AAASP's President (1991-92). He is also a Certified Consultant, Association for the Advancement of Applied Sport Psychology. He is a member of numerous other professional organizations, including AAHPERD, APA, and Pennsylvania AHPERD.

Sachs enjoys exercising, particularly running, and reading. He has run two marathons: the Joe Steele Rocket City Marathon (Huntsville, Alabama) in 1978 and the New York City Marathon in 1979. He lives in Elkins Park, PA, with his wife and two daughters.

Kevin L. Burke, PhD

Kevin L. Burke is Professor and Chair of the Department of Kinesiology, Leisure and Sport Sciences at East Tennessee State University. He received the Bachelor of Arts degree in psychology and recreational studies (double major), with a minor in sociology, from Belmont Abbey College. Burke was a member of the Pi Gamma Mu National Social Science Honor Society, played on the men's tennis team, and was a National Association of Intercollegiate Athletics Academic All-American Tennis Team nominee, making the N.A.I.A. All-District 26 Tennis Team in both singles and doubles play. Burke received the Master of Arts degree in social/organizational psychology from East Carolina University, where he was a member of Psi Chi, The National Honor Society in Psychology. He earned the Doctor of Philosophy degree in sport psychology from Florida State University. Burke also earned the Education Specialist degree in counseling from Georgia Southern University and has been a Licensed Professional Counselor with a private practice.

A Fellow, charter member, current member of the Performance Enhancement/Intervention committee, and past Secretary-Treasurer of the Association for the Advancement of Applied Sport Psychology (AAASP), Burke also served on AAASP's original Executive Board as the first Student Representative. He has presented and published through local, state, regional, national, and international channels. He has co-authored two books entitled, *Sport Psychology Library Series: Basketball* and *Tennis*. He also has served as co-editor of eight editions of the "Directory of Graduate Programs in Applied Sport Psychology." Burke is a past Associate Editor for the *Journal of Applied Sport Psychology* and on the Editorial Boards for the *Journal of Sport Behavior*, *Strategies*, and a past Associate Editor for the *Journal of Interdisciplinary Research in Physical Education*. He has served as a guest reviewer for *The Sport Psychologist*, *Journal of Sport & Exercise Psychology*, *Journal of Experimental Social Psychology*, *Research Quarterly for Exercise and Sport*, and *Perceptual and Motor Skills*. He also has served as a Sport Psychologist Digest compiler for the *Journal of Sport & Exercise Psychology*, and as Associate Editor for the AAASP Newsletter. Burke has served as a Research Dissemination Committee member of the Research Consortium of the American Alliance of Health, Physical Education, Recreation and Dance, and as a Research Works Contributing Editor for the *Journal of Physical Education, Recreation, and Dance*.

Burke operates Kevin L. Burke Enterprises, LLC, a private business, and has assisted professional, college, high school, and recreational athletes from various sports as a sport psychology consultant and is a "Certified Consultant, AAASP." His current research interests are in optimism/pessimism, momentum, humor, concentration, personal control, and the effectiveness of intervention techniques in sport and exercise. Burke has been nominated for university awards for Excellence in Scholarship and Teaching. He received college awards for Excellence in Teaching and Scholarship. Burke has been nominated for the prestigious "Dorothy V. Harris Young Scholar/Practitioner" award, selected for leadership training, and previously won an award for teaching while in graduate school. Burke was an intercollegiate basketball official and is a past member of the International Association of Approved Basketball Officials. He completed 23 seasons as an interscholastic basketball official in which he was certified at the state's highest level, served as a state evaluator, and as the Vice-President of the Southern Basketball Officials Association, International Association of Approved Basketball Officials Board 323. He officiated the Georgia High School Association and Georgia Independent School Association state tournaments, Georgia High School Association boys' all-star game, and was selected by the Georgia Athletic Coaches Association as an all-star official. He has also served as the Head Coach of three National Collegiate Athletic Association Division I tennis teams. Burke has driven a stock car at Lowe's (Charlotte) Motor Speedway and Atlanta Motor Speedway, and is a member of the United States Tennis Association. Burke has also performed in the Johnson City Community Theatre.

Elizabeth A. Loughren, MS

Elizabeth A. Loughren is a doctoral student in the Department of Kinesiology, College of Health Professions, with an emphasis in exercise and sport psychology, at Temple University, Philadelphia, PA. A native of Winthrop, Iowa, she received her Bachelor of Science degree in sport, health, leisure, and physical studies from the University of Iowa in 1999, and her Master of Science degree in physical education with an emphasis in sport and exercise psychology from Ball State University in 2003. Her research interests include exercise adherence, behavior change, and exercise enjoyment. In her spare time she enjoys traveling, running, and playing tennis. In 2005, she completed her first marathon, the LaSalle Bank Chicago Marathon, and has been an annual participant in the Indianapolis Mini-Marathon since 2003.